CHARLES IVES
AND HIS WORLD

OTHER PRINCETON UNIVERSITY PRESS VOLUMES
PUBLISHED IN CONJUNCTION WITH
THE BARD MUSIC FESTIVAL

Brahms and His World
edited by Walter Frisch (1990)

Mendelssohn and His World
edited by R. Larry Todd (1991)

Richard Strauss and His World
edited by Bryan Gilliam (1992)

Dvořák and His World
edited by Michael Beckerman (1993)

Schumann and His World
edited by R. Larry Todd (1994)

Bartók and His World
edited by Peter Laki (1995)

Charles
Ives
and His World
Edited by J. Peter Burkholder

PRINCETON UNIVERSITY PRESS
PRINCETON, NEW JERSEY

Published by Princeton University Press, 41 William Street,
Princeton, New Jersey 08540
In the United Kingdom: Princeton University Press,
Chichester, West Sussex

Library of Congress Cataloging-in-Publication Data

Charles Ives and his world / edited by J. Peter Burkholder.
p. cm.—(The Bard Music Festival series)
Includes bibliographical references and index.
Contents: Essays—Letters—Reviews—Contemporary views of
Ives and his music: profiles 1932–1955.
ISBN 0-691-01164-8 (cloth : alk. paper).—ISBN 0-691-01163-X (pbk. : alk. paper)
1. Ives, Charles, 1874–1954—Criticism and interpretation.
2. Ives, Charles, 1874–1954—Correspondence. I. Burkholder,
J. Peter (James Peter) II. Series.
ML410.I94C33 1996
780.92—dc20   96-21393

This book has been composed in Baskerville
by Juliet Meyers

This publication has been produced by the Bard College Publications Office:
Ginger Shore, Director
Juliet Meyers, Assistant Director

Music typeset by Don Giller

Princeton University Press books are printed on acid-free paper and meet the
guidelines for permanence and durability of the Committee on Production
Guidelines for Book Longevity of the Council on Library Resources

Printed in the United States of America
by Princeton Academic Press

1 3 5 7 9 10 8 6 4 2

(Pbk.) 1 3 5 7 9 10 8 6 4 2

Designed by Juliet Meyers

Contents

CONTENTS

PART IV
CONTEMPORARY VIEWS OF IVES
AND HIS MUSIC: PROFILES 1932–1955

Preface and Acknowledgments

Charles Ives had one of the most unusual careers of any of the great composers. After a thorough training in composition and fourteen years as a professional church organist, he "gave up music" to work in life insurance. He founded one of the most successful insurance agencies in the United States and developed new concepts that are now universal in the industry, such as training for agents and estate planning. He continued to compose, and in the early 1920s introduced himself to the musical world with his Second Piano Sonata (the *Concord Sonata*) and a book of songs, both of which met with more incomprehension than sympathy. Although he soon stopped composing, over the next three decades he gained a number of devoted advocates who praised, performed, or published his music. His major works were premiered in roughly reverse chronological order, culminating in the premieres of his romantic Second and First Symphonies shortly before his death in 1954. The first book on Ives, a biography and study of his music by his friends Henry and Sidney Cowell, appeared the next year, along with Gilbert Chase's *America's Music*, which devoted an entire chapter to Ives.[1] The number of performances, recordings, and scholarly considerations of his music has continued to rise over the last four decades. Yet his name and his music have remained less familiar to the musical public than Copland's or Stravinsky's.

That may be about to change. Ives has attracted more interest in recent years than ever before, even eclipsing the flurry of attention around his 1974 centennial. There are more recordings available of his major orchestral works than ever, from such major orchestras as Chicago, Cleveland, St. Louis, Detroit, and the New York Philharmonic, along with several competing recordings of his string quartets, violin sonatas, piano sonatas, and songs. The years since 1985 have seen the publication of more than twenty new books on Ives—more than half the total number ever published—including two biographies, two guides to research, several analytical surveys of his music, and multiple studies of his piano music, of his musical borrowings, of his aesthetics, and of his place in the American musical tradition. The same years have seen four music festivals focused on Ives: a year-long concert series in 1987–88, "Charles Ives and American

Music," sponsored by the Westdeutschen Rundfunk and the city of Duisburg, Germany, and an associated symposium at the University of Cologne; an Ives and Copland festival at the University of Northern Colorado in Greeley in October 1993; the BBC Music Festival in London in January 1996; and the Bard Music Festival, for which this book was commissioned, at Bard College in August and at Lincoln Center, New York, in November 1996.

A faithful follower of the Bard Music Festivals and of the book series that began with *Brahms and His World* in 1990 and has continued with Mendelssohn, Strauss, Dvořák, Schumann, and Bartók might wonder what Charles Ives has in common with this august company. Much of Ives's early support came from the ultramodernist wing of American music in the 1920s and 1930s, and his iconoclastic attitudes, daring experiments, and use of American tunes have nurtured his image as a musical radical, totally American, who owed nothing to the European tradition. But to characterize Ives in this way is to miss his deep debt to European art music and his close ties to the late-Romantic and early-twentieth-century composers whose music was featured at earlier festivals. Dvořák's *New World* Symphony was the principal model for Ives's First Symphony, whose scherzo recalls the elfin grace of Mendelssohn's scherzos. Ives modeled his early art songs on songs by Schumann and Brahms, and his Second Symphony borrows several passages and the formal plan for its last two movements from Brahms's First Symphony.[2] Strauss was the most prominent exponent of the symphonic poem in Ives's lifetime, and Ives absorbed his techniques in his own symphonic poems, while rejecting Strauss's choice of subject matter.[3] Bartók was younger than Ives and not well known in the United States while Ives was still composing, but the two show strong parallels in the way they combine national traditions with the German-Austrian tradition of Bach, Beethoven, and Brahms. Ives is in many senses America's Bartók, and his music is just as deeply indebted to the German Romantics and—like all of them—to Beethoven. So it is exactly right and long overdue for Ives to be grouped with Brahms, Mendelssohn, Strauss, Dvořák, Schumann, and Bartók. The subtitle of the Bard Music Festivals is "Rediscoveries"; in that spirit, placing Ives in this company allows us to rediscover in him a modernist, nationalist composer firmly rooted in the central European Romantic tradition. Once his affinity for their music is clear, his uniqueness comes into even sharper focus.

The concert programs, pre-concert lectures, and panels of the Bard Music Festival place Ives in the context of music he knew and music that paralleled his own efforts, including his American predecessors and contemporaries. This book places Ives in his context through a series of critical essays, a sampling of his correspondence, a compilation of reviews of his music published in his lifetime, and a selection from the longer critical essays on Ives and his music that began to appear in the last two decades of his life.

The essays in Part I explore Ives's connections to the musical traditions he knew, especially the European Romantic tradition, and to aspects of the culture and landscape of America that exercised a strong but little-noticed influence on his ideas and his music.

My essay shows that Ives was a composer equally at home in four distinctive musical traditions: American popular music, Protestant church music, European art music, and experimental music. His mature art music uses elements drawn from the other three traditions, exploiting the familiarity of popular and church music and the unfamiliarity of his experimental techniques to convey specific extramusical meanings. Far from ignoring his audience, as some have argued, Ives sought to please a variety of different audiences at different times and in different works, creating in the process an oeuvre of unparalleled diversity.

Leon Botstein explores the apparent paradox that Ives used modernist sounds and innovative procedures to celebrate a past remembered from pre-modern, nineteenth-century America. A comparison with Mahler shows that both composers believed that music had a moral role to play in society. Seeking to uphold the virtues of the past as a force to counteract the negative consequences of modern urban life, yet rejecting the routine conservativism of their musical contemporaries as lacking in moral force, they wrote music that used radical means to reclaim past values. Thus, in the works of both composers, musical modernism emerged from profoundly antimodern sensibilities.

David Michael Hertz reveals unsuspected parallels between one of Ives's most famous pieces, the Second Piano Sonata, *"Concord, Mass., 1840–1860,"* and piano works of his predecessors and contemporaries. Motives, textures, and procedures in Ives's sonata resemble and reinterpret passages from Beethoven's "Hammerklavier" Sonata, Liszt's Sonata in B Minor, works by Chopin and Debussy, and Scriabin's sonatas. These references show Ives's close relation to the European pianistic tradition, at the same time that his reworking of his models and his innovative approach to form demonstrate his originality.

Michael Broyles reexamines Ives's political and social ideas, which inspired many of his compositions, and places them in the context of his times. Ives was neither a populist nor a progressive, as he has been characterized. Rather, he drew on myths about the American pre-industrial past that were current in his time, notably the republican concept of personal responsibility and the belief that the New England town meeting was the cradle of American democracy, and absorbed as his own the ideals articulated by insurance industry leaders in the wake of a 1905 scandal that might have threatened Ives's career and reputation.

Mark Tucker shows the importance for Ives of the Adirondack mountains of upstate New York. This was the favorite vacation area for the Twichell family, and Ives's visits there at the invitation of his college friend David Twichell led to Ives's falling in love both with the landscape and, eventually, with David's sister Harmony, whom he married in 1908. Ives frequently composed on these vacations, and images of hiking up a mountain, sound heard over water, and rugged scenery found their way into the Second String Quartet, the *Robert Browning Overture*, *Mists*, and the *Universe Symphony*, among other works.

The letters in Part II show Ives in the contexts of his family, his courtship with his future wife Harmony, the search for performance and publication of his music, and his professional friendships. Among the most interesting letters are those that reflect on his music and its effect on the writer, such as the comments from Ives's brother-in-law Joseph H. Twichell about a concert in 1940 of Ives piano music and songs played by John Kirkpatrick:

> I don't know a single thing about music—not a single thing, except that I like it or don't like it; except how it makes me *feel*. Well, and I'm trying to speak as thoughtfully and carefully as I know how, I enjoyed that afternoon's music more than any other music I remember ever hearing. It seemed to me the most *honest* music I ever listened to. I don't know what that means; maybe you do. And it was so clean and wholesome. I came out of that place a better man than I went in.[4]

It is hard to imagine a response to his music that could have pleased Ives more.

Through the reviews in Part III and the longer profiles and evaluations in Part IV, we can trace the way Ives's music was received during his lifetime. When his mature music began to appear in the 1920s, some reviewers were uncomprehending, mocking, or hostile. But from the start there were those who supported him, and major critics such as Paul Rosenfeld, Olin Downes of the *New York Times*, and Lawrence

Gilman of the *New York Herald Tribune* praised his music. The reviews of John Kirkpatrick's premiere of the *Concord Sonata* in 1939 established Ives as a major figure, and reviews and several extended profiles from then until the end of his life often retell the story of his emergence from obscurity to become a candidate for the best composer in the classical tradition the United States has produced.

The collection closes with a retrospective consideration of Ives published in the year after he died by the distinguished musicologist Leo Schrade, who finds in Ives America's Debussy, committed to the constant renewal of musical form in response to each new artistic intention. Earlier I compared him to Bartók and noted that Leon Botstein's essay compares him to Mahler and David Hertz's essay links him to Debussy and Scriabin; another recent collection contains essays comparing him to Mahler, Schoenberg, Berg, and Stravinsky.[5] The strong parallels between Ives and his European contemporaries, argued in these essays and audible in the programs of the Bard Music Festival, should lay to rest at last the once common idea that Ives was an American original, totally isolated from currents in the musical mainstream. He was a composer of his time as well as of his place, as much at home in the European musical tradition as in the American. Rediscovering his music in this context will shed new light not only on Ives but on the wider musical world of which he was a part.

Many people played vital roles in the creation of this book. Thanks are due first of all to Charles Ives himself, for leaving us with such rich music and so many fascinating questions. Special thanks to Leon Botstein, founder of the Bard Music Festival, for devoting the 1996 festival to Ives, asking me to edit a book to join the distinguished series, contributing an essay, and giving me a free hand in shaping the volume. I am grateful to David Hertz, Michael Broyles, and Mark Tucker for their pathbreaking essays, to Tom C. Owens for his cheerful editing of the letters section, and to Geoffrey Block for helping to gather and select the profiles as well as the reviews. Joyce Li and Michael LaBaugh typed the reviews and profiles, and Joyce Li, David Hertz, and Fabienne Meadows helped with the translations of the French reviews. Ginger Shore organized and supervised the production of the book on an astonishingly compact schedule. Paul De Angelis copyedited with elegance and restraint, clarifying many passages and preventing potentially embarrassing errors while preserving the flavor of each writer's style. Juliet Meyers designed the book beautifully and helped with many final details. Mark Loftin guided and aided this project from start to finish. David Ezer helped obtain permissions to reprint the reviews and profiles, for which thanks are given to *The New York Times* and *Time* magazine. I am also grateful to Yale University for granting permission to reprint Charles Ives's letters. For Princeton University Press, Elizabeth Powers and Lauren Oppenheim provided guidance and encouragement in the early stages, and Malcolm Litchfield and Heidi Sheehan saw the project through to completion. As always, my deepest personal thanks to my husband, Doug McKinney, for his support and seemingly endless patience.

—J. Peter Burkholder

The following copyright holders have graciously given permission to reprint musical excerpts from copyrighted works by Charles Ives. Acknowledgments and copyright notices for some additional works appear under some of the figures.

Crossing the Bar. © 1974 by Associated Music Publishers, Inc. (BMI). International Copyright Secured. All Rights Reserved. Reprinted by Permission.

Symphony No. 1. © Copyright 1971 by Peer International Corporation. International Copyright Secured. All Rights Reserved. Used by Permission.

Scherzo (Over the Pavements). © Copyright 1971 by Peer International Corporation. International Copyright Secured. All Rights Reserved. Used by Permission.

Second Piano Sonata (Concord Sonata). Copyright © 1947, 1976 by Associated Music Publishers, Inc. (BMI). International Copyright Secured. All Rights Reserved. Reprinted by Permission.

Symphony No. 2. © Copyright 1951 by Southern Publishing Co., Inc. Copyright Renewed by Peer International Corporation. International Copyright Secured. All Rights Reserved. Used by Permission.

In the Alley. © Copyright 1958 by Peer International Corporation. International Copyright Secured. All Rights Reserved. Used by Permission.

Down East. © Copyright 1958 by Peer International Corporation. International Copyright Secured. All Rights Reserved. Used by Permission.

Third Symphony. Copyright © 1947 (Renewed) by Associated Music Publishers, Inc. (BMI). International Copyright Secured. All Rights Reserved. Reprinted by Permission.

Fourth Symphony. Copyright © 1965 (Renewed) by Associated Music Publishers, Inc. (BMI). International Copyright Secured. All Rights Reserved. Reprinted by Permission.

Permission is gratefully acknowledged to reprint letters and photographs from the Charles Ives Papers, Yale University Music Library, copyright © 1996 by the American Academy of Arts and Letters.

Thanks also to the Yale University Music Library for allowing us to quote from a letter from Carl and Charlotte Ruggles; to Bess Lomax Hawes, to quote from a letter from John A. Lomax; to Frances Mullen Yates, to reprint letters from Peter Yates; and to Nicolas Slonimsky, to quote from a letter of his.

The copyright holders listed below have graciously given permission to reprint the following copyrighted material:

Excerpt from Stephen Somervel, "Music: Chamber Orchestra of Boston." Copyright © 1931 by *The Boston Herald*. Reprinted by permission.

Excerpt from Winthrop Tyron, "'Freischütz' at the Metropolitan—Other Music of a New York Week." Copyright © 1924 by *The Christian Science Monitor*. Reprinted by permission.

Henry Cowell, "Charles E. Ives." Copyright © 1932 by *Disques*.

Henry Bellamann, "Reviews: 'Concord, Mass., 1840–1860' (A Piano Sonata by Charles E. Ives)." Copyright © 1921 by *The Double Dealer*.

Paul Moor, "On Horseback to Heaven: Charles Ives." Copyright © 1948 by *Harper's* magazine. Reprinted by permission.

Aaron Copland, "One Hundred and Fourteen Songs," copyright © 1934; Paul Rosenfeld, "Ives's Concord Sonata," copyright © 1939; Elliott Carter, "The Case of Mr. Ives," copyright © 1939; Elliott Carter, "Ives Today: His Vision and Challenge," copyright © 1944; and Bernard Herrmann, "Four Symphonies by Charles Ives," copyright © 1945—by *Modern Music*.

Ernest Walker, Review of *Second Pianoforte Sonata, "Concord, Mass., 1840–1860"* and *Essays Before a Sonata*, by Charles E. Ives. Copyright © 1921 by *Music & Letters*. Reprinted by permission.

A. Walter Kramer, "A Pseudo-Literary Sonata!!!" copyright © 1921; Goddard Lieberson, "An American Innovator, Charles Ives," copyright © 1939; excerpt from Robert Sabin, "Bernstein Conducts Ives Symphony No. 2," copyright © 1951; and the excerpt from Nicolas Slonimsky, "Charles Ives—America's Musical Prophet," copyright © 1954—by *Musical America*.

"Concord Unconquered," copyright © 1921; "Ives," copyright © 1922; and "Recent Publications: New Music, January 1929," copyright © 1929—by *The Musical Courier*.

T. Carl Whitmer, "New Music." Copyright © 1929 by *The Musical Forecast*.

Excerpt from Henry Bellamann, "Charles Ives: The Man and His Music," copyright © 1933; and Henry Cowell, excerpt from "Current Chronicle," copyright 1951—by *The Musical Quarterly*. Reprinted by permission of Oxford University Press.

John Sebastian [Goddard Lieberson], "Charles Ives at Last." Copyright © 1939 by *The New Masses*.

Paul Rosenfeld, "Charles E. Ives." Copyright © 1932 by *The New Republic*. Reprinted by permission.

"Goldstein Completes 'Modernist' Recital at Aeolian Hall," copyright © 1924; an excerpt from Lawrence Gilman, "Music," copyright © 1927, and the same author's "Music: A Masterpiece of American Music Heard Here for the First Time," copyright © 1939; Francis D. Perkins, "Kirkpatrick Plays Program of Ives' Work," copyright © 1939, and an excerpt from the same author's "Music," copyright © 1940; excerpt from Lou Harrison, "Yaddo Festival," copyright © 1946; excerpts from two articles by Virgil Thomson, "Music: Crude but Careful," copyright © 1948, and "Music: From the Heart," copyright © 1951; excerpt from Peggy Glanville-Hicks, "William Masselos: Pianist Presents Ives Sonata at Y.M.H.A. Hall," copyright © 1949—by *The New York Herald Tribune*.

NOTES

1. Henry Cowell and Sidney Cowell, *Charles Ives and His Music* (New York: Oxford University Press, 1955); Gilbert Chase, *America's Music: From the Pilgrims to the Present* (New York: McGraw-Hill, 1955).

2. See J. Peter Burkholder, *All Made of Tunes: Charles Ives and the Uses of Musical Borrowing* (New Haven: Yale University Press, 1995), 89–95 on the First Symphony, 27–34 on the art songs, and 126–33 on the Second Symphony.

3. See his critique of Strauss in Charles E. Ives, *Essays Before a Sonata, The Majority, and Other Writings*, ed. Howard Boatwright (New York: W. W. Norton, 1970), 83.

4. Letter of 26 January 1940 from Joseph H. Twichell to the Ives family, in the Ives Collection, Yale University Music Library, Mss. 14, box 32, folder 10, reprinted in part III below.

5. *Charles Ives and the Classical Tradition*, ed. Geoffrey Block and J. Peter Burkholder (New Haven: Yale University Press, 1996).

·

Part I
ESSAYS

·

Ives and the Four Musical Traditions

J. PETER BURKHOLDER

One of the most salient facts about Ives's music is its diversity. There are marches for band and symphonies for orchestra, popular songs and art songs, sincere sentimental songs and wickedly satirical ones, serious sonatas and musical jokes, programmatic tone poems and purely abstract compositions, winningly attractive melodies and shocking dissonances, pieces that use common-practice harmony and pieces that invent new harmonic systems, pieces that use the same style throughout and pieces that mix widely disparate styles, passages of astonishing complexity and moments of utter simplicity, effects borrowed from Tchaikovsky or Wagner and passages that echo ragtime or Tin Pan Alley, works with musical quotations in almost every measure and works that sound like nothing ever heard before. Behind this great diversity lie Ives's training and experience as a composer working in four different traditions of music, joined with his desire to communicate concrete ideas to a given audience in the most direct and effective manner. His background gave him the capacity to speak many native languages as a composer. Rather than renounce any of them, he developed the flexibility to use the idiom or combination of idioms that was appropriate to the particular audience and purpose for each piece.

During his career as a performer and composer, Ives worked in four separate and distinct musical traditions and eventually synthesized them all. He grew up in the first of these, American popular music, learning from a young age the repertoire of his father's band and the popular songs of several generations, from Stephen Foster and Civil War songs to the sentimental parlor songs, ragtime, and Tin Pan Alley styles of his own time. His first compositions were in this tradition, and this was also the first tradition whose forms and genres he abandoned as a composer, yet its tunes and sounds permeate his mature music. The second tradition, American Protestant church music, he absorbed as a boy attending church and studied professionally as an organist and young composer. He left this tradition too when still a young man, resigning his last position as a church organist when he was twenty-seven and ceasing to write music for church services, yet hymn tunes and organists' habits are present throughout his later music. The tradition of European classical music is one he began to encounter in his teens but fully assimilated only in his early to middle twenties through his studies with Horatio Parker at Yale and subsequent work on his own. Here too he wrote successful music in the current style and then moved on. Yet his relationship to this tradition is different. Although he moved beyond traditional styles and procedures to develop his own idiom, he continued to write in the genres and with the aesthetic presumptions of the art music tradition; this was where the synthesis of his many musical identities could take place. The final tradition is that of experimental music, works—usually small—that try out a new musical resource or change the rules of composition in an orderly way, in order to test both the new devices and, by implication, the standard conventions of music. Ives is almost certainly the first composer to do this repeatedly and systematically, and he stands at the beginning of a century-long tradition.

Ives's mature music draws elements from all four of these traditions and synthesizes them in a new modernist idiom within the genres and expectations of European concert music. Individual works continue to vary in style and intention. In about 1923, for example, near the end of his compositional career, Ives wrote *Peaks* and *Yellow Leaves,* two songs in a modernist, post-impressionist style; *The Celestial Railroad,* a programmatic piano fantasy in his mature idiom that mixes fragments of three hymns, two patriotic songs, two Civil War songs, two Stephen Foster songs, ragtime, and a band march with complex dissonances, virtuosic passagework, and Lisztian developmental techniques; *Three Quarter-tone Pieces* for two pianos tuned a quarter tone apart, an avowedly experimental work intended to test the possibilities for using quarter tones that borrows parts of three patriotic tunes and four of Ives's own works; *Psalm 90* for chorus and organ, a sacred work in mature style which incorporates some experimental ideas and refers to several traditional types of church music; and *The One Way,* a song in a purely tonal, sentimental, retrogressive Romantic style satirizing popular song composers who still used that style.[1] In this group of works, each of the four traditions is still a strong presence, although the mix of influences in each piece is unique.

This is an extraordinary career. We are unaccustomed to composers who exhibit this kind of diversity. Composers who straddle two traditions, such as Arthur Sullivan, George Gershwin, or Frank

Zappa, or who write in a variety of styles during their career, such as Schoenberg or Stravinsky, already challenge our assumption that a composer's body of work will be consistent and coherent. Ives's music is so varied that we do not know what to expect of a piece we have not heard before: it may be composed along conventional lines in any of three different musical traditions; it may be experimental, consistent within itself but operating according to wholly individual rules; or it may draw elements from two, three, or all four of these traditions in an entirely novel synthesis. This lack of consistency between works, and the juxtapositions of diverse styles within most of the works that draw on more than one tradition, have made Ives's music seem incoherent to many listeners and critics.[2]

Yet Ives's career and his music are coherent, once one abandons the expectation that coherence requires consistency, sameness, and a single line of development. Other composers have assimilated into their music elements of diverse musical traditions. Bach blended the north German contrapuntal style of his upbringing with the forms, textures, and figurations of Vivaldi's concertos to create fugues and concertos of unparalleled richness. Beethoven infused the conventions and genres of French Revolutionary music into works based in the Viennese idiom of Haydn and Mozart. Bartók imitated composers from Mozart through Brahms in his early compositions, absorbed the influences of Richard Strauss and Debussy in his early twenties, and then changed the style of his works in classical genres through his study of Hungarian, Romanian, and other peasant music. Ives is like these composers in creating a unique synthesis of very disparate traditions. But two things differentiate Ives from these composers. First, they continued to work in the tradition in which they received their early training, blending into it aspects of the traditions they encountered in their twenties. For Ives, it was the reverse: the traditions he grew up in, popular music and church music, were unable to absorb such diversity, and he abandoned them; it was in the tradition he learned in his twenties, European concert music, that his synthesis was achieved. Second, Bach, Beethoven, and Bartók never wrote music in the traditions they absorbed, while Ives wrote marches, parlor songs, and service music that partake fully of those traditions. If we imagine a Bartók who grew up singing and dancing to the peasant music of his region, put in several years as a pianist in a café playing urban popular music, created new music in both traditions, then learned the classical tradition as a young adult studying at the Budapest Conservatory, and ultimately composed music that absorbed the peasant and popular traditions into the classical, we come close to a career like that of Ives.

Such a career is not incoherent, nor is it entirely unique. William Grant Still, Virgil Thomson, Aaron Copland, Leonard Bernstein, and many younger American composers have blended the popular and religious traditions that surrounded them in their youth with the classical tradition they learned in private music lessons or in college. Nor is Ives's music incoherent, particularly for those who have shared his experience of multiple musical traditions, for Ives's principal subject in his mature works in classical genres is the way popular music and church music are experienced by Americans like himself. Ives is important precisely because he shows a way to bridge the gulfs between the utilitarian music of the church service, the music of popular entertainment, speculative experimental music, and the experience of music as art.

Ives's reconciliation of these distinctive traditions depended, first, on his command of each of them individually and, second, on his ability to use each as a source for rhetorical effects within pieces whose genre and function place them squarely in the classical tradition. While working in each tradition, he was capable of writing within a single style, and he tailored each piece to its expected audience.[3] His later pieces typically combine styles, some borrowed from these traditions and some newly invented, in order to convey his thought most effectively.

American Popular Music

Ives's first teacher was his father George, who played the violin and cornet and led the town band in Danbury, Connecticut, where Ives grew up. While George Ives had been trained in classical music, even writing a series of fugues, his main activities were in providing music for popular entertainment.[4] Thus Charles Ives's first attempts at composition were primarily in the genres of popular music. His first publicly performed piece was apparently the march *Holiday Quickstep*, scored for piccolo, cornets, violins, and piano and premiered in January 1888, when he was thirteen. It was singled out for praise in an article about the evening in *The Danbury Evening News*, which said that "Master Ives is certainly a musical genius," and the march "is worthy a place with productions of much older heads."[5] The musical style is eminently that of the mid-to-late-19th-century march, as shown in Figure 1.1.

Figure 1.1: *Holiday Quickstep*, mm. 60–63

Indeed, this passage was modeled on the trio of a well-known march that was apparently a favorite of George and Charles Ives's, the *Second Regiment Connecticut National Guard March* by David Wallis Reeves, one of the leading march composers of the day. Ives's other very early music includes a *New Year's Dance* in fiddle-tune style, parlor songs, and a Polonaise for two cornets and piano that, like much cornet music of the time, was modeled on the Italian operatic style popular in transcriptions for band or orchestra.[6] In every piece, Ives conformed to the expected style for a work of its type. It can be assumed that his primary intended audience in these pieces was his father, who was instructing him in composition and whom he would have been anxious to please. But they are also clearly intended to please the Danbury public.

Ives continued to write music in popular genres throughout his teens and his college years at Yale in 1894–98, achieving a high enough level of polish and professionalism to have some pieces published. He wrote about a dozen marches, including the *March "Intercollegiate,"* which was published in Philadelphia in 1896 and performed at the 1897 inauguration of President William McKinley.[7] In 1896 Ives had also written a campaign song for McKinley, published by a firm in New York.[8] In December of that year, the *Yale Courant* published *A Scotch Lullaby*, an earnest parlor song in an up-to-date style, one of several such songs from Ives's late teens and twenties.[9] While in college, he wrote several works for male chorus, some of which were sung by the Yale Glee Club. Three were published: *For You and Me!* in 1896 by the New York publisher George Molineux, *A Song of Mory's* in a February 1897 issue of the *Yale Courant,* and *The Bells of Yale* in a 1903 collection titled *Yale Melodies.*[10] He also wrote music for several fraternity shows while at Yale. Most of this music is lost; what survives are high-spirited or satirical songs in a popular style.[11] In all of these pieces, Ives sought to entertain his listeners without challenging their assumptions, and the performances and publications are a sign of his success. That he stopped writing music in popular genres after graduating from Yale and moving to New York in 1898 is less a sign of discontent with the styles he had learned than of a shift of his aspirations from music intended merely for entertainment to church music and music in the classical tradition.

Protestant Church Music

Ives attended the Methodist church regularly with his parents, studied the organ with several teachers, and occasionally substituted at services even before his fourteenth birthday. In February 1889, only fourteen years of age, he became the regular organist at the Second Congregational Church in Danbury. Later that year he moved to the Baptist Church, and he continued to serve as organist at churches in New Haven, Bloomfield (New Jersey), and New York until resigning from his last position in June 1902 after thirteen years as a professional organist.[12] Throughout this period, Ives was writing music for use in the services. If entertainment music served one social need, church music served another, seeking not merely to divert its listeners but to elevate their thoughts in worship. As Ives once commented, he was careful to suit his music to the appropriate state of mind for worship and thus felt constrained to use only those styles and idioms to which the congregation was accustomed.[13]

Gayle Sherwood has recently discerned three overlapping stages of development in the choral music Ives wrote for use in religious services during his years as an organist.[14] Her insight extends to his other church music as well. The first genre Ives mastered as a child in church and as an organist was the hymn, and he recalled his father leading the hymn singing at the camp-meeting revivals outside Danbury with his voice and arms or playing the cornet, French horn, or violin.[15] Accordingly, Ives's early church music is hymn-based, as in the choral works *Psalm 42* (ca. 1892) and *Search Me, O Lord* (ca. 1892–93), whose texts are taken from hymns and whose music follows in many respects the style, phrasing, and form of hymns.[16] The same can be said of his religious songs of this period, *Abide With Me* (ca. 1890–92) and *Rock of Ages* (ca. 1891 or 1892).[17] The influence of hymns at this early stage is also evident in Ives's two sets of variations, both of which are on hymn tunes: the *Fantasia on "Jerusalem the Golden"* (1888 or 1889) and the *Variations on "America"* (1891–92).

The second stage in Ives's church music, from about 1893, is marked by the influence of Dudley Buck, a prominent organist and composer of service music and anthems, and of Buck's student Harry Rowe Shelley.[18] Their organ works, organ transcriptions, and choral anthems were part of Ives's performing repertoire and library from about 1890 on, and Ives studied organ with both in the spring of 1894. Buck's choral music was particularly suited to the quartet choir then standard in Protestant churches, an amateur choir led by a paid quartet of soloists and section leaders. His music was rewarding for amateurs to sing, lyrical, of only moderate difficulty, and of sufficient quality to interest the congregation, in a style that was colored by the close voicings and chromatic harmony of the contemporary secular style now associated with barbershop quartet singing. Ives's *Benedictus* (ca. 1893–94) and *Crossing the Bar* (ca. 1894) for chorus and organ show the strong influence of this style, with more varied rhythm, flexible phrasing, chromaticism, and changes of texture than in the earlier hymn-based works, including a cappella passages suited to the solo quartet. A passage from *Crossing the Bar* in Figure 1.2 illustrates these characteristics.

As with Ives's music in popular genres, these works show a determined effort to please his listeners. He also sought to please his employers. From May 1893 through April 1894, while studying at Hopkins Grammar School in New Haven to prepare for the Yale entrance examinations, Ives was organist at St. Thomas Episcopal church in New Haven. Here Ives encountered the practice of pointing chant, in which the congregation chants a psalm, canticle, or liturgical formula in free rhythm while the organist supplies an accompaniment in sustained chords. His *Nine Experimental Canticle Phrases* from this period show his attempts to assimilate this practice, and his *Communion Service* sets the main texts of the Episcopal liturgy.

The third main influence on Ives's choral music was Horatio Parker, his teacher at Yale.[19] Ives apparently audited Parker's courses in music history and harmony during his first two years in college, and then took counterpoint, composition, and two years of instrumentation from Parker as a junior and senior.[20] Parker's influence enters gradually into the music of Ives's Yale years but is most strongly felt after September 1897, when he enrolled in Parker's composition course. In his ideals for church choral music Parker disdained both

Figure 1.2: *Crossing the Bar,* mm. 44–60

the gospel hymns Ives learned in his youth and the chromatic, popular style of Buck. Accordingly, the music Ives wrote for the choir at
Centre Church in New Haven, where he served as organist from fall
1894 through spring 1898, gradually changed from settings of hymn
texts in a style derived from that of Buck and Shelley to settings of
religious poetry in a more restrained and elevated style, as in *The Light
That is Felt* and *The All-Forgiving* (both ca. 1898).

The capstone of Ives's choral music was his cantata *The Celestial
Country* (1898–99), in a style that blended aspects of Buck's and
Parker's approaches. Ives's efforts to make this work appeal to its
intended audience and his success in most respects are made clear by
the kind of praise it received from reviewers on the occasion of its premiere in April 1902. The *New York Times* reviewer called it "scholarly
and well made" but "also spirited and melodious," and the *Musical
Courier,* after introducing Ives as "a Yale graduate and pupil in music
of Professor Parker" and noting that "the work shows undoubted
earnestness in study and talent for composition," praised "the interweaving of appropriate themes" that are anticipated and recalled
throughout the cantata, the lyric grace of the solo movements, the
intermezzo for strings ("full of unusual harmonies and pleasing
throughout"), and the finale, which "shows some original ideas, many
complex rhythms and effective part writing."[21] The aspects of the
piece that won the attention of both reviewers are its conformity to the
accepted rules and conventions for works of this sort, its pleasing lyricism, and its introduction of novelties that interest the listener without leaving the bounds of good taste and decorum.

Soon after the premiere of his cantata in April 1902, Ives left his
last position as an organist and ceased writing music for religious services, making this the second musical tradition he had learned, practiced, and abandoned. His career as a composer of church music, like
his composing in popular genres, shows Ives eager to assimilate the
prevailing styles and forms as he encountered them and to give his listeners what they wanted to hear. This is hardly surprising for a composer working in traditions where music served a specific social function and audience response was immediate and crucial to his success.

European Classical Music

European art music served a different sort of purpose. This was not
music in the service of entertainment or social conviviality, as was the
popular music of Ives's youth. Nor did it serve religious devotion.
Rather, art music asked to be listened to for its own sake, with focused

attention, and its purpose was to convey an artistic experience from the composer to the individual listener. In this tradition, audience reaction was less important than the intrinsic value of a piece as judged by its authenticity, depth, integrity, and durability. Ives encountered European art music in Danbury, in his lessons and recital pieces and in occasional concerts, but his first real compositions in the European tradition stem from his Yale years and his classes with Parker.[22] After leaving Yale, Ives continued for the next four years to work independently in the same genres and styles he had studied with Parker until he completed his first major, multi-movement works, the First Symphony and the First String Quartet.

In a favorite assignment of Parker's, Ives wrote a number of art songs to German texts previously set by Schubert, Schumann, Franz, Brahms, and other composers, using the original setting as a model but seeking a completely different musical interpretation of the same text. For example, Peter Cornelius's *Ein Ton* represents its text's central image, the tone the poet hears sounding in his heart, through a vocal line that repeats a single tone throughout. Ives's setting of the same poem from about 1898 uses the Cornelius as a model for its style and structure but places the repeated tones in the piano and the melody in the voice, reversing their respective roles. Schumann's *Ich grolle nicht* is relatively fast and loud, with a pounding piano accompaniment that conveys the defiance and wounded pride of a jilted lover; Ives's setting, again modeled on its predecessor in structure and details, is slower, softer, more lyrical, and more varied in figuration, creating an entirely different mood.[23] These and other settings from ca. 1898–1902 fully adopt the ethos of the Romantic art song, in which the music's purpose is to deepen the emotions in the poem and to capture its imagery, conveying what words cannot. But they also show Ives attempting to assimilate the methods of European composers and to create something of his own in the classical tradition.

Parker also introduced Ives to some of the major genres of classical instrumental music. In his instrumentation class, Ives transcribed a Beethoven sonata movement for string quartet, and piano works by Schubert and Schumann for orchestra, apparently his first experience with such ensembles.[24] His first works for orchestra, a Postlude in F and an unfinished Overture in G, date from his last year at Yale and were probably exercises for his classes with Parker. His First Symphony and First String Quartet were both apparently begun while at Yale, perhaps under Parker's supervision, and were completed by 1902.[25] The First Symphony is modeled closely on Dvořák's "New World" Symphony, most noticeably in the slow second movement with an English horn theme paraphrased from Dvořák's. Figure 1.3 shows the opening of Ives's scherzo movement, which by key, imitative texture, and melodic contour evokes the scherzo of Beethoven's Ninth Symphony and by grace and lightness recalls Mendelssohn's scherzos. Other movements include strong echoes of the first movement of Schubert's "Unfinished" Symphony and the march in Tchaikovsky's *Pathétique* Symphony, showing Ives's determination to place his work next to some of the most popular symphonies of the nineteenth century.[26] At the same time, Ives's fondness for orchestration that juxtaposes and combines choirs of like instruments and reserves the full orchestra for endings and climaxes betrays his experience as an organist with alternating and mixing stops.

Figure 1.3: First Symphony, third movement, mm. 1–20

Ives's art songs and orchestral works throughout this period from his last years at Yale to 1902 show that he quickly became fluent in the late Romantic style and in the genres of European art music, making this the third distinctive musical tradition he assimilated. While he would ultimately develop a highly individual musical idiom, he never abandoned the genres and ethos of art music, as he had abandoned first American popular music and then Protestant church music. His mature works are in the standard concert genres of the symphony, overture, symphonic poem, string quartet, piano trio, violin sonata, piano sonata, art song, and choral work with orchestral accompaniment. Like the Romantic composers he had taken as models, Ives adopted a conception of music as an art practiced for its own sake, in which the experience of the individual listener was paramount, rather than a communal experience of entertainment or worship. A composition was expected to reflect authentically the composer's nationality and personality, rather than conform to the conventions of a universally accepted style. It was in the tradition of art music that Ives found both his highest aspiration and the means to weave together the diverse strands of his own musical life.[27]

Experimental Music

The fourth tradition Ives practiced, experimental music, is one he seems to have invented. All of the pieces discussed so far were intended for public performance and designed to please listeners familiar with the sounds and procedures of a particular musical tradition. But Ives was also accustomed to writing compositional exercises designed to practice a certain technique, from early exercises in part-writing to the three-part invention and fugues he wrote for Parker's classes at Yale. These were private, intended only to develop procedures that then might be used less strictly in concert works. Apparently as a spin-off from these compositional exercises, Ives began while still a teenager to write sketches and short pieces whose main or only purpose was to try out, not a conventional procedure, but a new means of organizing pitch or rhythm. After his studies with Parker, these experimental works became more finished and polished, producing a series of astonishing compositions that anticipated the experimental music of Henry Cowell, John Cage, Conlon Nancarrow, and many later composers.[28] While those of his teen years and early twenties are mostly short sketches for keyboard, the experiments of ca. 1898–1902 are mostly for chorus or chorus and organ, reflecting his position as an organist with potential access to a choir and soloists for reading through his music. Those after 1902 are mostly for chamber ensembles, and some may have been tried out by musicians he knew. Ives made no effort to have his experimental works performed in public or published until late in his life, when Cowell and other ultramodern composers became interested in them; for Ives, these pieces seem to have been laboratories for trying out new effects, as private as his compositional exercises in traditional procedures, or perhaps intended only to be shared privately with friends such as his flatmates in his apartment in New York.[29] Most of the devices he first tried in these small experiments were later used in a less strict manner in his concert music, in almost exact parallel to the more conventional procedures he had learned in his other compositional exercises.[30]

In Ives's early experiments, he typically preserves most rules of traditional music theory but changes one or more to see what happens. In this way, the music serves not only as a test of new procedures, but as a critique of traditional ones.[31] Several early works from ca. 1890–1902 are polytonal, with the melody in one key and the accompaniment in another, as in the setting of "London Bridge Is Falling Down" (between 1892 and 1898) with the melody in F and the accompaniment in G♭, or in the *Fugue in Four Keys on "The Shining Shore"* (ca. 1902), which has fugal entrances in the keys of C, G, D, and A. As Ives comments in his *Memos,* "if you can play a tune in one key, why can't a feller, if he feels like [it], play one in two keys?"[32] That is, what happens if one preserves the way that music is traditionally composed but changes the rule that all parts have to be in the same key at any one time? This is an experimental approach, akin to the biologist who seeks to find out the role of a particular gene in a fruit-fly by changing that gene and seeing what happens. Later in the *Memos,* Ives asks, "if you can have two 3rds, major or minor, in a chord, why can't you have another one or two on top of it, etc."[33] Four little organ interludes from ca. 1898–1902 harmonize phrases of hymn tunes with parallel eight-note chords of stacked thirds, such as D–F♯–A–C–E♭–G–B♭–D♭.[34] The opening of *Psalm 67* for unaccompanied chorus (ca. 1898–1902) appears to be polytonal, but is actually based on transpositions of a five-note sonority of stacked thirds. *Processional* for chorus and organ (first sketched ca. 1902) presents over a C pedal point a series of chords, each a stack of one or two harmonic intervals in a gradually expanding sequence: from a unison to major and minor seconds, then thirds, then fourths, fourths mixed with tritones, fifths, minor sixths, mixed minor and major sixths, major sixths, minor sevenths, mixed minor and major sevenths, and major sevenths, increasing in size and dissonance level until it resolves in octaves at the end of the phrase.[35] There are a dozen other experimental choral works, most of them settings of psalms first sketched in ca. 1898–1902 and revised or completed later.

As the experimental works before 1902 often explore issues of pitch organization and tonality, those after 1902 often focus on rhythmic combinations and superimposed independent musical layers. *From the Steeples and the Mountains* (ca. 1902–7) includes four sets of bells in three different keys (high bells in C and B and low bells in D♭ and C) that play descending scales in canon, each successive scale in shorter note values from half notes to sixteenth notes, and then reverse the process, producing a wave of gradually increasing and decreasing rhythmic density.[36] *All the Way Around and Back* (ca. 1906) for chamber ensemble is an almost perfect palindrome, gradually building up layers until at the climax units of one, two, three, five, seven, and eleven equal divisions of the measure are sounding simultaneously, then proceeding in retrograde. *Scherzo (Over the Pavements)* for piano, winds, brass, and percussion (ca. 1906–13) was inspired by the sound of people and horses in the street, each moving in his or her own rhythm.[37] To reflect this, the piece layers incommensurate pulses and meters on top of each other. At one point near the climax, shown in Figure 1.4, the basic beat—the dotted quarter note—is divided into two, three, or four smaller units in the various parts. This is made more complex by grouping these subdivisions in ways that do not match up with the beat or with each other: the half-beats in the piccolo and piano left hand are grouped in threes, then twos; the third-beats in the brass, percussion, and piano right hand are grouped in twos, then threes; the third-beats in the bassoon are in groups of four; and the quarter-beats in the clarinet are in groups of five.

The experience of these experiments changed Ives in two significant ways. It made him aware of new possibilities beyond those certified by custom and convention, and he later found these new resources useful in a wide range of compositions. But it also led him naturally and logically to produce musical works that were likely to startle, displease, and even offend listeners accustomed to music in the other three traditions he had assimilated. These experimental works by definition broke the rules and substituted new ones, which was enough to rattle most listeners; in doing so, they introduced unprecedented levels of dissonance and rhythmic complexity.

Figure 1.4: *Scherzo (Over the Pavements)*, mm. 61–62

Yet even these pieces were carefully tailored to their intended audience. The primary audience was of course Ives himself, as he tested new ideas in his compositional workshop. But he also shared several of them with friends and tried them out with fellow musicians, usually in private. Ives was aware of the resistance his experiments were likely to provoke, and so he couched many of them as "jokes" or "stunts."[38] This made them more palatable, while at the same time allowing listeners—himself chief among them—to come gradually to accept the new sounds as interesting in their own right and as potentially valuable additions to the musical palette. His recollections of experiments in his youth, at college, and during his first decade in New York, when he shared a series of apartments with friends from Yale, are peppered with references to having fun and then learning to tolerate or even appreciate the new textures or sonorities. Recalling his youthful experiments with reproducing drum patterns through dissonant chords on the piano, Ives wrote that "what started as boy's play and in fun, gradually worked into something that had a serious side to it that opened up possibilities—and in ways sometimes valuable, as the ears got used to and acquainted with these various and many dissonant sound combinations."[39] At Yale, some of Ives's fellow students were interested in his experiments (which he remembered doing "half in fun, half serious"), such as introducing familiar tunes as counterpoints or playing off-beats on a chord a half-step away, "and often men would ask to have those 'stunts' put in. Some said—one was Sid Kennedy—that it made the music stronger and better, after he had got used to it." In New York his flatmates good-naturedly tolerated his trying out new sounds at the keyboard, calling them "resident disturbances," and Ives noted their approval of some of his experiments in memos on the manuscripts. While working with a string quartet in 1903, Ives wrote "a little practice piece called *Holding your own* as a joke (partly serious)," in which "one man plays the chromatic scale and another a diatonic [scale] in different time etc.—we played it over and had a laugh. But the last time I found it, it seemed quite (or partially) musical, and worth playing—and [I] put it, as a slow bit, into a fast Scherzo."[40] In all of these experiences, Ives's personal relationship with his audience made possible a friendly reception for his novel ideas; his friends liked him, so they were willing to give his music a try, and his light approach allowed them to accept sounds they might otherwise never have approved.

Ives considered the encounter with new sounds and procedures to be good for his listeners, a kind of aural exercise. From his own experience, he concluded that "the human ear (not one but all) will learn to digest and handle sounds, the more they are heard and then understood." About his experiments at Yale, he argued that "if more of this and other kinds of ear stretching had gone on, if the ears and minds had been used more and harder, there might have been less 'arrested development' among nice Yale graduates—less soft-headed ears running the opera and symphony societies in this country. . . . There may be an analogy between (or at least similar results from similar processes of) the ear, mind, and arm muscles. They don't get stronger with disuse."[41] Just as his exercises in conventional musical procedures and his experiments with new resources had furthered his own musical education, Ives saw the exercise of coming to terms with new sounds and textures as good for the listener, improving the ability to comprehend unfamiliar music and to think for oneself. Humor sweetened the medicine, but the medicine was the point.

Ives's later, more finished experimental pieces also make an appeal on the basis of the meaning the music can convey. Several, shared mostly with his Yale friends, evoke memories of college, such as *Yale–Princeton Football Game* (ca. 1899, revised ca. 1914–19), a favorite of Huntington Mason (Yale 1899), and *Calcium Light Night* (late 1910s), marked on the manuscript "approved by Yale Club of 34 Gramercy Park [the last apartment Ives shared with his Yale friends]."[42] In the former, dissonant ostinatos represent the noise of

the crowd, over which appear college cheers and songs; the traditional wedge play is depicted by musical wedges, chords that contract
into a cluster of tightly spaced notes; and a fast, meandering trumpet
melody stands for the quarterback's broken-field run. The latter
suggests the torchlight parades on the night of student society elections through an arch structure: as the marchers approach, the sound
of the band gets louder and the cacophony of different tunes more
prominent; then the parade passes by, the sounds recede, and the
same music is heard with the sections arranged in the opposite order.
Others capture life in and around New York, as does *Scherzo (Over the
Pavements)*, discussed above. *The General Slocum* (early 1910s), on a
disaster in the summer of 1904, depicts the pleasure boat *General
Slocum* through popular tunes in various keys, representing orchestras
on different decks, and the explosion that sank the boat through a
rapid crescendo of density and intensity. *Central Park in the Dark*
pictures the sounds of nature one might hear from a bench at night in
Central Park through a soft, dissonant series of experimental chords in
the strings, over which the tunes and noises of the city are heard.[43]

So Ives cared about the audience for his experimental music, small
though that audience was. He saw the experience of unfamiliar sounds
and procedures as good in itself, and he made the unfamiliar as palatable as possible by placing it in a humorous context or using it as a special effect to convey a textual or programmatic meaning. There is perhaps no greater evidence for Ives's solicitude for his audience even in
his experimental music than his most famous piece, *The Unanswered
Question* (ca. 1907, later revised), an experimental work that has
enjoyed wide audience appeal. Strings, representing the "Silences of
the Druids," play a soft, serene passage in G major. Above this, a solo
trumpet poses seven times "The Perennial Question of Existence," a
five-note melody that suggests no key, and four flutes answer each
question but the last with dissonant, atonal figures that become faster,
louder, and more frenetic each time. This is a radical experiment: a
combination of tonal and atonal music in simultaneous independent
streams, something which had never before been accomplished and
which this piece was designed to prove could be done. But it is an
experiment that is easy to follow and to like. The unfamiliar sounds in
it are explained by the program, the ear gradually grows accustomed
to increasing dissonance over the course of the work, the form of the
piece is very clear, and the whole is pleasing and enormously popular.
While Ives began his research program in music with a series of private exercises, it is clear that the question of how to share these new
sounds with others was one to which he gave a good deal of attention.

Here, as in his music in the other three traditions, he knew his audience and calculated his music to attain the effects he desired.

Synthesizing the Four Traditions

While working in these different traditions, Ives was capable of writing within a single style, and he tailored each piece to its expected audience: entertainment music for his father, the Danbury public, publishers, or his fraternity brothers; devotional music in the prevailing styles of hymn tunes, liturgical chant, Buck, and Parker for congregations familiar with those idioms; late-Romantic art music for his teacher Parker and the audience for classical concert music; experimental music for himself, his friends, and the rare listener sympathetic to radically new ideas. This ability to write in numerous different styles, changing his idiom in order to have a certain effect on a particular audience, persisted past his apprenticeship. Ives had become so skilled at speaking in different tongues to different listeners that he was something of a musical chameleon. During his courtship with Harmony Twichell, he composed songs to poems she suggested (*Pictures*, ca. 1906) or wrote (*The World's Highway*, 1906) or adapted music he had written previously to her poetry (*Spring Song* and *Autumn*, both 1907). These were written to please her and perhaps her family, so their style is Romantic and tonal, drawing most strongly on the art song tradition, with some tinges of parlor song style or harmony. They entirely avoid the new sounds and textures of his experiments written around the same time, such as *From the Steeples and the Mountains*, *All the Way Around and Back*, *Scherzo (Over the Pavements)*, or *The Unanswered Question*. When Henry Bellamann, who had written the first sympathetic review of Ives's *Concord Sonata* in 1921, gave Ives some of his own imagist poetry in about 1923, Ives set two of the poems in a Debussy-influenced style that he anticipated Bellamann would like.[44] Around the same time, Ives was writing a completely different kind of music for another friend, E. Robert Schmitz, whose Franco-American Musical Society sponsored the premiere in early 1925 of Ives's experimental *Three Quarter-tone Pieces* for two pianos tuned a quarter-tone apart, which were apparently composed for this performance.[45] And the piano parts Ives wrote to accompany a *Christmas Carol* (1925) with melody and words by his young daughter and the black spiritual *In the Mornin' (Give Me Jesus)* (1929) as sung by a family friend are entirely tonal and largely diatonic, with rhythmic irregularities in the latter to catch the free style of singing typical of unaccompanied spirituals. These and other works show that Ives maintained throughout his career the ability to write in any one of the many idioms he had mastered and to maintain a consistent style throughout a piece—when he wanted to do so.

His ability to suit himself to his audience was manifest not just in his music, but in his life as well. Besides being a musical chameleon, he was a social chameleon, willing to play a role to fit in with his surroundings. At home he played the dutiful son and willing student, in church the talented organist and budding composer, but at the same time he made sure to fit in with other boys his age in school and on the ball field; an early story about him is that when someone learned he was a musician and asked what he played, he answered "shortstop."[46] His fellow students at Yale found him a good classmate and loyal fraternity brother, active in college social life, and he was prominent enough to be elected to Wolf's Head, one of three prestigious secret societies at Yale.[47] He was a convivial companion to his New York roommates, but once he married Harmony he settled down into a quiet home life surrounded more by books and music than by friends and activities.[48] He was an innovative businessman, originating the ideas of estate planning and training for insurance agents that eventually became standard across the industry.[49] In all of these environments, Ives proved himself able to play the role expected of him. He was such an accomplished actor that he could use role-playing to his own ends. In the *Essays Before a Sonata*, published in 1920, he cast himself as a Beethoven disciple; once he attracted the interest of the ultramodernists around Henry Cowell and Nicolas Slonimsky, he recast himself in his *Memos* of the early 1930s as a radical experimentalist.[50] In some measure he was both, as he was in part all the roles he had played, when he chose to play them.

In tailoring himself to his audience, in person or through music, Ives appealed to the experiences he shared with them. His mature music makes its appeal through shared experience as well. Within the frame of art songs, sonatas, chamber music, and symphonic works stemming from the Classic-Romantic tradition, Ives introduces elements drawn from the three other traditions. As foreign elements in a concert piece, they immediately suggest extramusical meanings, whether focused in a program or more diffuse in a piece that merely suggests a certain character. When Ives uses tunes, textures, and sounds from the traditions of American popular music and Protestant church music, they convey meanings by invoking associations with certain activities, events, people, or places. When he uses novel techniques drawn from his experimental music, they convey meanings through their very novelty or through the same kind of musical metaphors he used to represent certain kinds of motions or sounds in his experimental pieces.

At first Ives drew into his music in European genres only the other performance traditions, not experimental music. His First String Quartet (ca. 1898–1902) uses themes paraphrased from Protestant hymns and gospel songs, suffusing the music with the sound of American religious tunes while remaining true to European models in form, style, and technique. His Second Symphony (ca. 1902–7) paraphrases American popular songs and hymns in its themes and countermelodies, borrows transitional and episodic passages from Bach, Brahms, and Wagner in its transitions, and combines them into a coherent whole in European forms and late-Romantic style. Through both of these works, Ives proclaims the unity of his own experience as an American familiar with all three of these traditions and claims a place for distinctively American music in the quartet and symphonic repertoires.[51] The Third Symphony, subtitled "The Camp Meeting" (ca. 1907–11), is again based on hymn tunes and uses procedures of motivic fragmentation and development from European symphonic music. It differs from the First Quartet in using a new form, called "cumulative form," in which the hymn tune theme appears in its entirety only at the end, after it is developed. Although the symphony is not programmatic, it suggests the coming together of individual voices and the fervent spirit of hymn singing at the camp-meeting revivals of Ives's youth through the form itself, in which the theme comes together gradually from individual motives and fragments after a long and dramatic development, finally achieving wholeness in a quiet, fervent statement.[52] Ives frequently also makes reference to popular or church music, not through direct borrowing or paraphrase, but through stylistic allusion, as in the ragtime rhythms of the *Ragtime Dances,* the brief fife-and-drum episode in the Second Symphony finale, or the organ-like texture of its opening.

But Ives also began to draw on his musical experiments for techniques whose very unfamiliarity made them useful as signs that an extramusical interpretation was being called for and whose working out of musical processes suggested movement. In *The Housatonic at Stockbridge* (ca. 1908–19), the third movement of *Three Places in New England,* Ives captured the scene on a Sunday morning walk he took with his wife Harmony shortly after they were married. The sound of "the distant singing from the church across the river" is conveyed by a hymn-like melody shared between horn and English horn, while the movement of "the mists . . . , the colors, the running water, [and the] elm trees" is suggested by four distinctive layers of repeating figures in the muted violin and violas, each layer using a different set of pitches, a different subdivision of the beat as a basic pulse, and a different grouping of pulses.[53] In *Scherzo (Over the Pavements),* this kind of rhythmic complexity (as shown in Figure 1.4) was an experiment; here in *The Housatonic at Stockbridge* it is a wonderful metaphor in sound for the simultaneous but mutually independent motions of the lapping and curling water, the mist over the river, and the leaves waving gently in the breeze. In *Washington's Birthday* (ca. 1913–19), the first movement of the *Holidays Symphony,* dissonant mostly whole-tone chords rise and fall in parallel motion to suggest the snowdrifts and hills; fiddle tunes depict a barndance, while multiple overlapping dissonant ostinatos evoke the hubbub of the crowd; and in the final section a parody of a sentimental song in G major is joined by a quiet, muted solo violin playing reminiscences of the fiddle tunes in the distant keys of A♭ and B♭, representing memories of the dance that echo in the minds of the young folk as they head home from the dance singing sentimental songs.[54] In *The Fourth of July* (ca. 1913–19), the third movement of the *Holidays Symphony,* Ives recalls the sounds of patriotic tunes, a fife and drum corps, and the fireworks exploding, the last using loud string glissandos, multiple chromatic figuration in the winds and brass, irregular rhythms in the percussion, and huge clusters played by the forearms on the piano. In the song *Paracelsus* (1921), a chromatic uprush and parallel dissonant chords depict the words "I gazed on power till I grew blind"; the bitonal combination of C minor and D minor triads suggests the dignity and omnipresence of God at the words "the power I sought seemed God's"; and the style of a Protestant hymn with a harmonization in traditional style captures the submission and repentance of the following line, "I learned my own deep error," more powerfully and efficiently than any other setting could do. In these and many other works, the techniques Ives cultivated in his experimental music are as important as the references to popular music or hymnody in conveying the experience Ives meant his audience to have.

Band music, hymn tunes, popular songs, and musical experimentation all are interwoven in *General William Booth Enters Into Heaven* (1914).[55] This is a setting of Vachel Lindsay's famous poem on the death of the founder of the Salvation Army, whom Lindsay imagines entering Heaven beating a bass drum at the head of an army of the souls he had saved. At the opening, shown in Figure 1.5, Ives evokes Booth's bass drum through his technique of reproducing drumbeats as dissonant chords on the piano, one of his experiments from his teens, and

General William Booth Enters into Heaven. © 1935 by Merion Music, Inc. Used by Permission.

Figure 1.5: *General William Booth Enters Into Heaven,* mm. 1–8

through the rhythmic pattern of the "street beat," the cadence drummers use to keep marchers moving in step and one of the first things Ives would have learned as a drummer in his father's band. Meanwhile, the vocal melody is derived from the hymn "There Is a Fountain Filled with Blood," just as Lindsay's meter and refrain are taken from "Are You Washed in the Blood?," a hymn full of similar imagery.

Lindsay's poem describes Booth's followers, and each group receives a different musical characterization from Ives. In the second stanza of the poem, the parade has arrived at the center of Heaven, which Lindsay imagines as a grand courthouse square. Ives suggests the milling about of the crowd, constantly moving without going any-where, through a rising and falling whole-tone scale in the voice and two repeating figures in the piano, the first (mm. 40–47) mixing the notes of F major and D major and the second (mm. 47–51) featuring parallel sevenths, as shown in Figure 1.6. At the line "Big-voiced lassies made their banjos bang," Ives paraphrases in the piano the

General William Booth Enters into Heaven. © 1935 by Merion Music, Inc. Used by Permission.

Figure 1.6: *General William Booth Enters Into Heaven,* mm. 40–54

Figure 1.6, continued

nineteenth-century minstrel-show song "Oh, Dem Golden Slippers" by James A. Bland, a song about going to Heaven whose second verse begins "Oh my ole banjo."

At the climax of the poem, Jesus comes out of the courthouse and blesses the marchers, and all are immediately transformed. Having hinted at it repeatedly, Ives presents the entire verse of "There Is a Fountain Filled with Blood" for this moment of transformation, over the drum patterns in the piano, as shown in Figure 1.7. The action stops, and the closing refrain is set twice, at first over soft, arpeggiated chords, then in four-part harmony reminiscent of the hymn har-monizations in Protestant hymnals. The sudden turn to such simple, familiar harmony in the context of a song full of novel sounds is star-tling. By suggesting the humble devotion of a hymn, it brings the

General William Booth Enters into Heaven. © 1935 by Merion Music, Inc. Used by Permission.

Figure 1.7: *General William Booth Enters Into Heaven*, mm. 97–113

Figure 1.7, continued

message of the song home to us. While we have been watching Booth and his followers all along, here the composer turns to us and asks us to consider our own faith in the light of their example. The moment is soon over, and the parade fades away in the distance, the clusters in the piano breaking up and becoming faint.

This is an art song; like all Romantic art songs, it attempts to capture the images and feelings of the text and convey to the listener a vicarious experience of the events of the poem. But here the majority of the images are drawn, not from the tradition of art music, but from the other traditions Ives had assimilated as a young man: American popular music in the bass drum patterns and minstrel tune, Protestant church music in the hymn and the hymn-like harmony near the end, and experimental music in the drumming on the piano, bitonal chordal clashes, and clusters. Not every Ives work is this diverse, nor this overt in referring to each of the musical traditions, for the idiom or idioms he used depended entirely on what he was trying to achieve in the piece at hand. Ives used the diverse languages available to him as vehicles for the content he wanted to convey.[56] He refused to choose only one tradition, to speak only one language, to stick to one style at a time, or even to follow a predictable pattern in the way he mixed his influences. In this way, he was true to the diversity of his experience as an American familiar with more than one musical culture; this is part of his appeal to us today, as citizens of a world whose cultures increasingly interact and intermingle. Perhaps more importantly, he made use of all the idioms he had learned because that was the best way to say what he had to say. In his mature music, the art music tradition offers a framework within which he could write music that speaks of individual experience and expects its audience to listen with complete attention; the tradition of experimental music offers techniques whose novelty and embodiment of musical motion create useful metaphors for extramusical events; and the traditions of popular music and church music call up for listeners familiar with this music the situations and surroundings in which they are heard and other associations they may carry. Ives mixes all of these elements in order to realize in a modern context the aesthetic ethos he had learned from his European models: to put into music as authentically as possible a reflection of his own experience and to inspire an emotionally powerful aesthetic experience in the individual listener.

It has long been said of Ives that he did not care about his audience, that he was writing only for himself. This goes back at least to Aaron Copland's review of Ives's collection of *114 Songs*, in which Copland interpreted the astonishing diversity of the songs in style, subject, and quality and Ives's self-deprecating remarks in his postface about having included "plenty of songs which have not been and will not be asked for" as implying that "Ives apparently not only had no public in mind when printing this book, but he hardly had even the 'few friends' of whom he speaks in mind. The truth is he had only *himself* in mind."[57] This cannot be true. A composer who so carefully calculates music in so many different traditions to appeal to its intended audience, and then constructs music whose references to diverse traditions are intended to invoke associations shared with his audience and thus convey serious and specific meanings, would be acting completely out of character to go to the expense of publishing over a hundred songs with no intention of reaching an audience. Quite the opposite: the collection is so diverse because Ives intended it as a sampler or portfolio of his art, a way to reach all his potential audiences at once. One can imagine that, after the uncomprehending reception for his *Concord Sonata*, which he had self-published and distributed the year before, Ives wanted to provide something in his next book for each potential reviewer and recipient to like. Given the rifts in the musical world of his time, Ives no doubt miscalculated badly if he was seeking to attract a wide range of performers and listeners, for he included in his volume of songs something to offend everybody; those who approved of his art songs in the traditional nineteenth-century idiom would dislike his modernist experiments and vice versa, and both camps would likely reject his songs in popular styles, his church anthems, and his songs based on hymns. There are few musicians in any age whose tastes are as catholic as Ives's, and he seems not to have realized that discovering what they do not like in this volume would prevent so many from discovering the songs they would like, although his defensive comments in his postface seem designed to prevent just such a reaction, just as his comments about the merits of not being a professional composer are a transparent defense against those who would accuse him of amateurism.

The variety of his music is a sign, not of a lack of discipline, nor of the absence of a unified vision, but of a rare versatility that has made it possible for his music to appeal to a wide range of listeners for a wide range of reasons and has opened it to a great many interpretations. The diversity of Ives's music allows him to have many different audiences, depending on the piece. The *Variations on America* has become a school band favorite in transcription, the Second and Third Symphonies and the symphonic poems are frequently played in orchestral concerts, music theorists often teach the finale of the Second Violin Sonata because of its interesting mixture of whole-tone effects, polytonality, and tonality, music appreciation courses often include *The Unanswered Question* because of its simple structure and striking program, and new music groups are more likely to program the experimental works like *Tone Roads*.[58] This also means that Ives has been constructed in different ways: as a radical pioneer, as an American original, and as an heir to the European tradition. The best way to encounter Ives is to view him as the diverse composer he is, to recognize that he is after different things in different pieces, and to engage each piece on its own terms. Each of us will almost certainly like some of his pieces better than others, because tastes differ. But there is an Ives for almost every taste. Let us admit this, and enjoy it.

NOTES

1. See J. Peter Burkholder, *All Made of Tunes: Charles Ives and the Uses of Musical Borrowing* (New Haven: Yale University Press, 1995), 358–60 and 392–401 on *The Celestial Railroad*, 276 on the *Three Quarter-tone Pieces*, 274–75 on *Psalm 90*, and 279–80 on *The One Way*.

2. See for example the reviews reprinted in Part III of this volume of Ives's *Concord Sonata* by Ernest Walker and Irving Kolodin, *114 Songs* by Aaron Copland, and *Washington's Birthday* by Israel Citkowitz, and Gerald Abraham's recent dismissal of Ives's music as a "bizarre unintegrated mixture of daring sophistication and homespun crudity" in *The Concise Oxford History of Music* (London: Oxford University Press, 1979), 824. Lawrence Starr points out the critical reaction to the stylistic diversity of Ives's music and suggests an analytical approach in "Charles Ives: The Next Hundred Years—Towards a Method of Analyzing the Music," *The Music Review* 38 (May 1977): 101–11. Starr has further developed this approach in *A Union of Diversities: Style in the Music of Charles Ives* (New York: Schirmer Books, 1992).

3. Lawrence Starr was apparently the first to point out that Ives's music before about 1902 is marked both by a wide variety of styles between pieces and by stylistic uniformity within each piece. See "The Early Styles of Charles Ives," *19th-Century Music* 7 (Summer 1983): 71–80, especially p. 79.

4. The most thorough discussions of George Ives's training and activities as a musician are in Laurence Wallach, "The New England Education of Charles Ives" (Ph.D. diss., Columbia University, 1973), 1–69, and Stuart Feder, *Charles Ives, "My Father's Song": A Psychoanalytic Biography* (New Haven: Yale University Press, 1992), 19–61.

5. "Amusements: The German Dramatic Association," *The Danbury Evening News*, 17 January 1888, p. 3, reprinted in Part III of this volume.

6. On these pieces, see Burkholder, *All Made of Tunes*, 14–20. The Polonaise was specifically modeled on the opening of the sextet from Donizetti's *Lucia di Lammermoor*.

7. Charles E. Ives, *Memos*, ed. John Kirkpatrick (New York: W. W. Norton, 1972), 148, 149, and 154.

8. Ibid., 176, and John Kirkpatrick, *A Temporary Mimeographed Catalogue of the Music Manuscripts and Related Materials of Charles Edward Ives 1874–1954* (New Haven: Library of the Yale School of Music, 1960; reprint, 1973), 172. The song, *William Will*, appears in Charles E. Ives, *Forty Earlier Songs*, ed. John Kirkpatrick (New York: Associated Music Publishers, Peer International, and Theodore Presser, 1993), 47–49.

9. Charles Ives, *Eleven Songs and Two Harmonizations*, ed. John Kirkpatrick (New York: Associated Music Publishers, 1968), 13 and 16–17. See also *There Is a Certain Garden* (1893), *God Bless and Keep Thee* (1897?), and *No More* (1897) from this volume and several songs in other collections.

10. Ibid., 145–46. See also the program for an 1899 performance of *The Bells of Yale* by the Yale Glee Club, reprinted in Vivian Perlis, *Charles Ives Remembered: An Oral History* (New Haven: Yale University Press, 1974; repr. New York: W. W. Norton, 1976), 26. On the style of the secular part songs, see Gayle Sherwood, "The Choral Works of Charles Ives: Chronology, Style, Reception" (Ph.D. diss., Yale University, 1995), 126–28.

11. See Kirkpatrick, *Temporary Mimeographed Catalogue,* 112–13. Perlis, *Charles Ives Remembered,* 22–23 reprints the program of one fraternity show.

12. See the "Chronological Index of Dates" in Ives, *Memos,* 325–28. The best treatment of Ives's career as an organist is William Osborne, "Charles Ives the Organist," *The American Organist* 24/7 (July 1990): 58–64.

13. Ives, *Memos,* 128–29.

14. Sherwood, "Choral Works," 84–153, summarized on pp. 85, 91–92, 110–112, and 153. The following summary is indebted to Sherwood's study. One of Sherwood's greatest contributions in this dissertation has been to put the chronology of Ives's works on a much firmer footing by combining dating of the music paper he used with dating of his handwriting. See her discussion of the problem, her methods, and her conclusions on pp. 2–82, 306–63, and 366–70. The dates used in this essay for Ives's choral works are those from Sherwood's dissertation. Dates for most of his other works are those in Burkholder, *All Made of Tunes,* which are based on information supplied by Sherwood; details of Sherwood's dating are provided in the notes, generally in the first note listed in the index for each Ives composition.

15. Ives, *Memos,* 133.

16. For editions of these works, see Wendell Clarke Kumlien, "The Sacred Choral Music of Charles Ives: A Study in Style Development" (D.M.A. thesis, University of Illinois, 1969), 393–402 and 435–36. Sherwood, "Choral Works," 88–90, suggests that the early, textless *Hymn* and *Chant* of ca. 1887, also based on hymn style, appear to have been exercises in part-writing.

17. See the discussion of these songs in Burkholder, *All Made of Tunes,* 23 and 21 respectively.

18. Sherwood, "Choral Works," 92–110, on which the following paragraph is based.

19. Ibid., 112–53.

20. For Ives's classes with Parker, see Ives, *Memos,* 180–84, and Sherwood, "Choral Music," 503–8.

21. "A New Cantata," *The New York Times,* 20 April 1902, p. 12, and "Charles E. Ives' Concert and New Cantata, 'The Celestial Country,'" *Musical Courier* 44, no. 17 (23 April 1902): 34. Both reviews are reprinted in Part III of this volume. It should be noted that the brief introductions and interludes between numbers, featuring dissonant eight-note chords of stacked thirds (e.g., E–G♯–B–D–F–A–C–E♭) that move in parallel motion, were composed later, about 1909, and were not performed at the premiere.

22. On Parker's role in introducing Ives to the ideals and ethos of European art music, see J. Peter Burkholder, *Charles Ives: The Ideas Behind the Music* (New Haven: Yale University Press, 1985), 58–66.

23. On these songs and their relation to their models, see Burkholder, *All Made of Tunes,* 24–34.

24. On the Beethoven transcription, see ibid., 46–48, and Geoffrey Block, "Ives and the 'Sounds That Beethoven Didn't Have,'" in *Charles Ives and the Classical Tradition,* ed. Geoffrey Block and J. Peter Burkholder (New Haven: Yale University Press, 1996), 34–37.

25. Ives stated in a memo on the full score that the second and fourth movements of the symphony were part of his thesis for Parker in June 1898; see Kirkpatrick, *Temporary Mimeographed Catalogue,* 1. Sherwood, "Choral Music," 504–8, suggests that the fugal first movement of the quartet may have been written for Parker's strict composition course and the first movement of the symphony for Parker's free composition course, both during Ives's senior year. The surviving sketches and drafts for the second, third, and fourth movements of both works all postdate Ives's Yale years.

26. For the relation of Ives's First Symphony to the Dvořák, Beethoven, Schubert, and Tchaikovsky symphonies, see Burkholder, *All Made of Tunes*, 88–102. David Eiseman, "Charles Ives and the European Symphonic Tradition: A Historical Reappraisal" (Ph.D. diss., University of Illinois at Urbana-Champaign, 1972), was the first to demonstrate the strength of Ives's connection to the European symphonic tradition.

27. Burkholder, *Charles Ives*, 83–84.

28. On Ives's experimental works, see especially Thomas Dyer Winters, "Additive and Repetitive Techniques in the Experimental Works of Charles Ives" (Ph.D. diss., University of Pennsylvania, 1986); J. Philip Lambert, "Compositional Procedures in the Experimental Works of Charles E. Ives" (Ph.D. diss., Eastman School of Music, 1987); and J. Peter Burkholder, "The Critique of Tonality in the Early Experimental Music of Charles Ives," *Music Theory Spectrum* 12 (Fall 1990): 203–23. David Nicholls, *American Experimental Music, 1890–1940* (Cambridge: Cambridge University Press, 1990) places Ives at the head of the American experimental tradition that developed in the first half of the twentieth century, including Cowell, Cage, and several others.

29. Burkholder, *Charles Ives*, 48–49 and 89–91.

30. John McLain Rinehart, "Ives' Compositional Idioms: An Investigation of Selected Short Compositions as Microcosms of His Musical Language" (Ph.D. diss., The Ohio State University, 1970), points out that most of the novel devices Ives used in his mature works were first tried out in these small experimental pieces.

31. Burkholder, "Critique of Tonality."

32. Ives, *Memos*, 47; John Kirkpatrick's editorial brackets.

33. Ibid., 120.

34. On the hymn interludes and "London Bridge" settings, see Burkholder, *All Made of Tunes*, 218.

35. See Burkholder, "Critique of Tonality," 209–15 on *Psalm 67* and 218–20 on *Processional*, and Lambert, "Compositional Procedures," 25–28 on *Psalm 67* and 366–70 on *Processional*. On the experimental choral works in general, see Sherwood, "Choral Works," 154–201.

36. Lambert, "Compositional Procedures," 182–87.

37. Ives, *Memos*, 62–63.

38. See the discussion of humor in Burkholder, *Charles Ives*, 89–91.

39. Ives, *Memos*, 43. On Ives's drumming at the piano, see J. Philip Lambert, "Ives's 'Piano-Drum' Chords," *Intégral* 3 (1989): 1–36.

40. Ives, *Memos*, 41, 61, 266, and 34.

41. Ibid., 43 and 41–42 respectively.

42. Ibid., 61 and 266.

43. See Burkholder, *All Made of Tunes*, 342–45 for brief discussions of these pieces. On *Calcium Light Night*, see also Lambert, "Compositional Procedures," 160–64, and Feder, *Charles Ives*, 161–64. On *Central Park in the Dark*, see J. Peter Burkholder, "The Evolution of Charles Ives's Music: Aesthetics, Quotation, Technique" (Ph.D. diss., University of Chicago, 1983), 494–520.

44. Bellamann's review is printed below in Part III of this volume.

45. A review of this concert by Olin Downes appears in Part III, below.

46. Henry Cowell and Sidney Cowell, *Charles Ives and His Music*, 2nd ed. (New York: Oxford University Press, 1969), 27.

47. See the recollections of Ives by fellow students in Perlis, *Charles Ives Remembered*, 21 and 24, and the account of Yale social life in Frank R. Rossiter, *Charles Ives and His America* (New York: Liveright, 1975), 68–78.

48. See John Kirkpatrick's description of Ives's flatmates in New York in Ives, *Memos*, 262–67, and Rossiter, *Charles Ives and His America*, 172–74 on life at home with Harmony.

49. Perlis, *Charles Ives Remembered*, 46, and Julian Myrick's recollections on pp. 34–36.

50. As described in J. Peter Burkholder, "Charles Ives and His Fathers: A Response to Maynard Solomon," *Institute for Studies in American Music Newsletter* 18, no. 1 (November 1988): 8–11. See also Burkholder, "Ives and the Nineteenth-Century European Tradition," in *Charles Ives and the Classical Tradition*, ed. Block and Burkholder, 11–33.

51. See Burkholder, *All Made of Tunes*, 49–75 on the First Quartet and 102–36 on the Second Symphony.

52. See ibid., 137–54, 238–40, and 244–53, especially 252.

53. See Ives's description of this movement in *Memos*, 87–88.

54. See Burkholder, *All Made of Tunes*, 383–85.

55. See ibid., 253–62, on which the following is based.

56. The article by Leo Schrade at the end of this volume makes a similar point.

57. Aaron Copland, "One Hundred and Fourteen Songs," *Modern Music* 11 (January–February 1934), 61; the entire review is reprinted below in Part III.

58. For example, the finale of the Second Violin Sonata is included in Mary Wennerstrom, *Anthology of Twentieth-Century Music* (New York: Appleton-Century-Crofts, 1969; 2nd. ed, Englewood Cliff, N.J.: Prentice-Hall, 1988).

Innovation and Nostalgia: Ives, Mahler, and the Origins of Twentieth-Century Modernism

LEON BOTSTEIN

I. Understanding the Career of Charles Ives

Charles Ives—despite significant recent contributions to the analytic and biographical literature—has lost little of his aura as an anomalous, enigmatic, and paradoxical figure in the history of music. He remains hard to place in a larger historical narrative and explanatory framework. His music has been judged to be ahead of its time and uniquely innovative, rebellious, and modernist. At the same time, Ives's personal history, writings, and use of vernacular materials in his music—the sources and strategy of quotation and borrowing—reveal an allegiance to a past remembered, a pre-modern, nineteenth-century America. Cultural nostalgia and aesthetic innovation seem inextricably but counterintuitively linked in Ives's music.[1]

Ives's music and aesthetics stand apart uncomfortably in characterizations of turn-of-the-century American society and culture because Ives, apart from his career as a businessman, was hidden from view. Beethoven may have been an eccentric iconoclast and innovator, but from the start of his career, his music was written in the context of a visible engagement with his contemporaries—colleagues, listeners, publishers, and patrons.[2] He became a legend in his own time well beyond the confines of Vienna. Ives was unknown as a composer until after he stopped writing music. This has lent continued plausibility to the idea that his work is incomparable, without precedent, and disengaged from the world in which he lived. If Ives had wished to puzzle, if not defy, the writers of history, he succeeded.

Consider, for the sake of contrast, the case of the composer Arthur Foote (1853–1937). Like Ives, Foote was a Protestant New Englander born to a respected family in a small city, Salem, near a metropolis, Boston.[3] Also like Ives, after instruction from locals he studied in the nearest Ivy League university with a German-trained composer (with John Knowles Paine at Harvard), graduated in music, and worked as a church organist. Foote thought about the law but embarked instead on a long, successful career as a professional musician. His career contradicts many of the prevalent hypotheses about Ives.[4]

For example, Frank Rossiter argued in his biography of Ives that Ives resisted a musical career and spiked his music with dissonance in order to avoid being identified with a feminized musical culture. The so-called genteel tradition of music-making in late-nineteenth-century New England turns out, however, to be perfectly "masculine" as a profession and as a socially acceptable pastime.[5] Foote was married, had a child, and was a convivial college classmate, country club chum, avid sportsman, and golfing buddy. From childhood on, Foote seems to have embraced the Europeanized world of music-making in America without any of the culturally determined, psychosexual conflicts that commentators, from Rossiter to Stuart Feder, have adduced to explain Ives's self-image, career choice, and aesthetic stance. Ives was indeed rabid in his characterization of certain types of concert and church music in his own day as "soft" and feminine in the most conventionally contemptuous sense. And he did reserve the epithets of masculine, muscular, and strong for what he regarded as the "right" kind of music. But precisely because Ives isolated himself from the professional community for much of his career, his idiosyncratic vocabulary of judgment (no matter how revealing it is about his personality) should not be confused with a reasonable description of turn-of-the-century musical culture. Foote and Daniel Gregory Mason shared with Ives an admiration for Brahms.[6] Unlike Ives, however, they believed that America, beginning with Paine, Chadwick, and Parker, was well on the way to taking its place alongside Europe in the creation of serious music of an acceptably masculine sort.

One can argue that when Ives went to Yale in 1894, he could easily have concluded, as Foote did, that music as a profession was a promising and respected possibility, even for a Yale man of his social class. Through his contact with John Cornelius Griggs (Yale '89), Ives certainly would have encountered the view that America had changed sufficiently since the Civil War to insure that George Ives's fate in Danbury—the failure to make a living as a musician and maintain a high social status despite his talent—would not be his own fate if he chose music as a career. Griggs was the only other musician outside of his father for whom the young Ives had both professional regard and personal affection. One can only assume that in the years they worked together at Center Church in New Haven, Ives must have been exposed to the opinions Griggs expressed in his dissertation on music in America, published right around the time Ives met Griggs in 1894. In Griggs's views, we can see outlined a path that Ives did not elect to take.

Griggs was a patriot. America was indisputably "the greatest historical phenomenon" of the nineteenth century. It was using all its economic and industrial power to bring itself rapidly up on a par with the "cultivation and heritage" of older nations.[7] Griggs bemoaned the fact that because of the legacy of the hostility to music within the Puritan tradition and weak American choral traditions, the explosion of interest in music after the Civil War had become too centered on the piano. The superiority of the American piano and the marketing genius of its manufacturers made it possible for Americans (to an extent far greater than other nationalities) to gain the bulk of their musical experiences from keyboard instruments. The piano had its negative side in that it was not ideally suited to develop "musical thinking" or an ear the way training on string instruments or the voice was.[8]

Nonetheless, Griggs praised the growth of music teaching in public schools and universities and the rapid evolution of concert and opera organizations. Even though the Anglo-Saxon race, for Griggs, showed little capacity to generate creative new music, the massive immigration, particularly of Germans, did bode well for the future. So too did the drift away from rote singing in church to the tradition, bolstered by singing schools, of part singing. Griggs expressed concern about the future of church music and church musicians. Nevertheless, he was convinced that America was poised for a great musical future. He too cited the example of Paine, Chadwick, and Parker (as well as Dudley Buck) as early signs of this.[9]

"The future of music lies in America," not in Europe, wrote Griggs, even though he remained least confident, in the short run, about the arena of composition. Griggs took the position that a characteristically American school of composition would emerge over time naturally if composers resisted the temptation to be obviously American. It was dangerous to display prematurely a superficially American voice. If Americans systematically and patiently absorbed the accumulated wisdom of all nations—which America was ideally suited to do, owing to its wealth—a genuine American school of music ultimately would emerge.[10] Ives might well have been encouraged by Griggs to absorb European habits and pursue a path similar to the career on which Foote embarked. Griggs's own concerts, from the available records of his years at Vassar before World War I, show a strong interest not only in the history of music, but in American composers. He programmed Farwell, Beach, Chadwick, and Parker along with Grieg, Schubert, Massenet, Beethoven, and Mozart.[11]

Ives did not take this route. After stepping down in 1902 as a church organist in New York, he composed in private and without an official career or any recognition. But Ives's well-known hostility to the way in which Dvořák and others sought to inject an American dimension echoed Griggs's views.[12] Ives, perhaps inspired by Griggs's critique of efforts at an Americanism that used African-American and Native American materials, began to experiment after 1902 with elaborate formal strategies as complex and subtle as those used in European tradition (as J. Peter Burkholder has elegantly demonstrated).[13]

In Ives's case, American materials from his New England experience and older popular music would play a novel and integral role. This strong, new American music would not merely blend American tunes into standard, pre-existing European patterns and render them, in sound, pseudo-European. It is revealing that some of Ives's early works—particularly the Second Symphony—did fit into this imitative mold. Later on, particularly after 1902, Ives worked systematically to do something different.[14]

In the years between the World Wars, after he had ceased writing music, Ives was discovered by a new generation of American musicians.[15] From World War II to the early 1970s, Ives for the first time played a public role in American culture, the one his biographers Henry and Sidney Cowell helped assign him: that of the unrecognized prophet and precursor of a burgeoning but embattled (vis-à-vis the audience) twentieth-century musical modernism.[16] They celebrated the extent to which Ives was not really a man of his era—the sort of professional Griggs envisaged and Foote turned out to be. Rather, Ives fit in perfectly with subsequent generations. His achievement vindicated the historical teleology that sanctioned the modernist direction of contemporary music in America.

Ives's place in the modernist pantheon as an early unrecognized prophet working in a vacuum was fortuitous, since it filled an uncomfortable gap. From the perspective of post-World War I America, American music needed a distinctly American hero who came out of the nineteenth century. An authentic American precursor would legitimate America's arrival in the twentieth century as a cultural equal to Europe. In this narrative, the trajectory of American culture ran nearly parallel with the country's economic, military, and political preeminence in world affairs. Ives had not been trained in Europe. His work was unmistakably modern and tied to American life. As the Cowells argued, Ives fashioned himself and his sensibilities as an American along lines articulated by America's finest original, Ralph Waldo Emerson. Ives's innovations were home-grown, so to speak, and seemed to parallel, if not predate, the pathbreaking models of Stravinsky and Schoenberg.[17]

Ives provided the contemporaries of Henry Cowell, John Cage, and Lou Harrison an unexpected and welcome independent American lineage, something quite useful in the wake of the European emigration after 1933. A new wave of European influence on music in America developed out of the arrival of Arnold Schoenberg, Paul Hindemith, Hanns Eisler, Ernst Toch, and their emigre contemporaries in universities, conservatories, and concert halls—and on Broadway and in Hollywood (such as Kurt Weill and Erich Wolfgang Korngold). Their impact exceeded that of the nineteenth-century emigration of musicians to America and the turn-of-the-century habits of sending American musicians to Europe for training and recruiting famous Europeans with large sums of money to direct American orchestras and conservatories (such as Gericke, Muck, Dvořák, Toscanini, and Mahler).

The political and cultural crises of the late 1960s and the subsequent retreat from modernism in contemporary music during the 1970s coincided with the beginning of a fundamental revisionism with respect to Ives. Rossiter challenged the idea that Ives had been out of step with his times. He sought to recast Ives's self-image as a radical and place him alongside members of his social class.[18] Furthermore, a different Ives began to emerge in the 1970s, as new contemporary music derived from the traditions of Cowell and Cage on the one hand and Schoenberg on the other lost its short-lived monopoly as the legitimate consequence of the logic of history. Concurrently an under-valued conservative tradition of American concert music (including the work of Samuel Barber, Howard Hanson, and Roy Harris) began to make a slow comeback.

II. Ives and Mahler: Parallel Careers and Twin Revivals

The new post-modernist Ives benefited from the explosion of interest in the music of Gustav Mahler that occurred in the mid-1960s. (No doubt this was in part the result of Leonard Bernstein's advocacy of both composers.) In tandem with Mahler, Ives emerged as a witty narrative composer, whose formal framework and ambitions now seemed more old-fashioned and sentimental. Ives appeared less radical and more naive and quaint—an "authentic primitive," as Bernstein put it.[19] Superficially Ives and Mahler fit together because they both drew on local vernacular materials.[20] Ives's Danbury, Yale College, and New York were Mahler's Iglau and Vienna.[21] Their use of the "harsh" elements of musical modernism—dissonance, asymmetry, and rhythmic complexity—seemed entirely framed by the familiar and old-fashioned.

Mahler and Ives communicated to the audiences of the 1970s and 1980s a Proustian sensibility. Bittersweet nostalgia for a bygone time was heard—a yearning for lost virtues and values. The politics of nostalgia of the 1980s in America and the success of postmodernism helped reinvent Ives's achievement as marking (despite his isolation) the end of one tradition rather than the beginning of another. Ives now became the lonely nineteenth-century seer, in whose works the impending disasters of the twentieth century were audible in the form of ominous and ironic distortions of and departures from nineteenth-century musical expectations and practices. In concert performance the music of Ives and Mahler became less brittle and harsh and tended to the saccharine, lush, and smooth. It seemed to carry with it—with good reason—extramusical ideas that were easier to grasp than the music itself.[22]

Not surprisingly, in this revisionist phase Ives's claims to priority in terms of originality were challenged.[23] In addition, largely through Burkholder's work, Ives's debt to European models was exposed.[24] It turned out that Ives learned much more from Horatio Parker than he and his earlier defenders were willing to admit.[25]

This period of revision included psychohistory, pursued most effectively by Stuart Feder. With the publication of Feder's biography in 1992, a crucial step was taken in the reinterpretation of the Ives that Cowell's generation had fashioned. Ives's career and achievement were entirely dehistoricized and depoliticized through the virtuosic application of psychobiography.

In the picture drawn by Feder, Ives's father, George Ives, turned out to be, as Charles himself had always claimed, his most significant musical and personal influence. George Ives's musical musings were as advanced and sophisticated as other commentators had suspected.[26] Indeed, Ives's ambivalent embrace of obscurity, his self-imposed isolation from musical life, and even the specifics of his originality had their roots in psychodynamics that included the father, the image of the father, the wife, and other family relationships (e.g., with his Aunt Amelia and Uncle Lyman). Ives's career as a composer could be explained as a therapeutic working-out of the consequences of the father's untimely death in 1894 at the age of forty-nine. Charles Ives's creative patterns, illnesses, personal habits, eccentricities, and failure to write music after the early 1920s all could be accounted for as a case history. The intensely protective and insular marital bond sustained by Harmony Twichell Ives only added legitimacy to the psychologizing of Ives as a *sui generis* phenomenon. Psychohistory once again returned Ives to the status of an anomaly.[27]

By contrast, even though Mahler once consulted Freud and possessed what contemporaries and others since have accepted as the quintessentially neurotic fin-de-siècle artistic personality, Mahler's extensive public life, his close relations with leading figures in the worlds of music, literature, and art, and his notoriously troubled and nearly catastrophic marriage have made him a surprisingly poor subject for convincing psychobiography. Simply put, he was too much a member of the self-referential and dominant musical establishment, too evidently part of the public culture of his age and tied to the events of his day and age, to be separated, methodologically, from history and politics.

Despite the inherent anti-historical allure of psychobiography as a mode of inquiry, the net effect of revisionist scholarship has been to suggest that Ives's music did not spring forth *ex nihilo* or largely from within a closed family circle. As in the case of Mahler, Ives's music owed a great deal to the work of predecessors and to the culture and politics of his time.

The legitimacy of a comparison between Ives and Mahler is not merely a function of the politics of cultural reception from the late 1960s on. Although Ives was fourteen years younger than Mahler (exactly the age difference between Schoenberg and Mahler), their creative periods overlapped. In terms of their compositional output, they were almost exact contemporaries. Mahler died in 1911. Ives stopped writing music only a decade-and-a-half later. Ives was in New York during the years Mahler conducted at the Metropolitan Opera and served as music director of the New York Philharmonic. Mahler was an important and powerful presence in the city. There is reason to suspect that Mahler took an interest in the Ives Third Symphony.[28] Ives was aware of Mahler. He reported that in "1910 or '11" he found, coming back from a concert Mahler had conducted, that "listening to concert music seemed to confuse me in my own work . . . enough to throw me off somewhat from what I had in mind." Given that Ives went on to describe the same experience after hearing music by Max Reger, Ives may have been referring to hearing Mahler's own music, rather than Mahler as an interpreter of the music of others.[29]

It is possible that hearing Mahler's music around 1910 had an impact on Ives's subsequent compositional work, particularly the reworking and creation of the large orchestral pieces, from *Three Places in New England* on. Ives may have heard either Mahler's *Kindertotenlieder* (performed on 26 January 1910 at Carnegie Hall and on the 28th in Brooklyn) or the Fourth Symphony (performed on 15, 17, and 20 January 1911 at Carnegie Hall). During the crucial years of Ives's creative period in New York, it was Mahler the composer (whose music had been introduced to America as early as 1904) whose work may have unnerved and perhaps inspired Ives.[30]

Not only were Ives and Mahler contemporaries, but their attitude to the acoustic environment and outdoor music that surrounded them and their use of thematic material and other fragments from so-called banal, popular, and vulgar music amounted to more than a random coincidence.[31] In their music they both self-consciously reflected on the everyday sound experiences encountered by listeners and composers in modern life and compared those experiences with their own personal memories. Ives might even have known about the interview Mahler gave in Philadelphia in 1911 (published in the popular music journal *The Etude*) on the role of the folk song in art music. Ives would have been sympathetic to Mahler's professed eclecticism and debt to folk materials.[32] As Ives himself noted, "eclecticism is part of [a man's] duty."[33] Although Ives would have contested Mahler's view that there was no real American folk music apart from the African-American, he shared Mahler's doubt that African-American materials could serve as the basis of any distinctive future American music.

Both composers explored and utilized music as a dimension of memory and recollection. They worked with the idea that using elements recognizable and familiar to the listener but not normally associated with concert music added something crucial to the act of listening. They knew that the literate listeners they encountered used ordinary language to construct and document the past and their feelings toward it in such written forms as letters and diaries. The spread of literacy during the nineteenth century allowed the long-standing oral tradition of autobiographical story-telling to flourish in a different vein through the art of writing.

In a similar fashion, musical culture had spread sufficiently to enable the modern composer to use music in an analogous narrative manner: as a constituent of remembrance organized into a coherent communicable form. The popularity of the novel, the memoir, and short prose writing among educated contemporaries was not lost on Mahler and Ives. Musical memories could be exploited in the construction of musical narration. Unexpected aural recognitions and jarring associations within new music generated a confrontation between the memory of the familiar and its transformation within unexpected formal contexts. This juxtaposition, utilizing new sounds, forced a deeper and perhaps more self-reflective and self-critical act of listening.

This ambition regarding listener apperception became integral to the strategies of Mahler and Ives. Along patterns created by prose writers of the late nineteenth century, they used familiar places, landscapes, and historical events and individuals in their music. What they sought to do in their compositions is what Tolstoy, Mann, Schnitzler, Dreiser, and James did in narrative fiction.[34]

The manipulation of fragmentary moments of familiarity and memory by Mahler and Ives within original works of art served to force the audience to transcend the ambitions and habits associated with the public culture of concert music of the late nineteenth century. The character of the musical use of the familiar reflected what each composer perceived as the salient predicaments of modernity. One easily might hear in the music of both composers the clash between an idealized world and culture associated with an embattled rural landscape of the past and the urban, industrial, and technological facts of modern times. In the Postface and annotations to the score of *Washington's Birthday*, written between 1913 and 1919 and revised in the 1920s, Ives made clear that the gap between a "younger" and older generation and the evocation of memory of times past, even through "hearsay," was central to the character of the music.[35]

In the Postface to *Central Park in the Dark*, written around 1914, Ives referred to an incident which apparently took place in 1906, shortly before Mahler's arrival in New York. Ives wrote:

> This piece purports to be a picture-in-sounds of the sounds of nature and of happenings that men would hear some thirty or so years ago (before the combustion engine and radio monopolized the earth and air), when sitting on a bench in Central Park on a hot summer night. The strings represent the night sounds and silent darkness—interrupted by sounds [the rest of the orchestra] from the Casino over the pond—of street singers coming up from the Circle singing, in spots, the tunes of those days—of some "night owls" from Healy's whistling the latest or

the Freshman March—the "occasional elevated," a street parade or a "breakdown" in the distance—of newsboys crying "uxtries"—of pianolas having a ragtime war in the apartment house "over the garden wall," a street car and a street band join in the chorus—a fire engine, a cab horse runs away, lands "over the fence and out," the wayfarers shout—again the darkness is heard—an echo over the pond—and we walk home.[36]

Compare Natalie Bauer Lechner's account of a walk with Mahler near Klagenfurt six years earlier, in 1900. They came upon some Sunday festivities:

Not only were innumerable barrel organs blaring out from the merry-go-rounds, swings, shooting galleries and puppet shows, but a military band and a men's choral society had established themselves there as well. All these groups, in the same forest clearing, were creating an incredible musical pandemonium without paying the slightest attention to each other. Mahler exclaimed: "You hear? That's polyphony, and that's where I get it from! Even when I was quite a small child, in the woods at Iglau, this sort of thing used to move me strangely and impressed itself upon me. For it's all the same whether heard in a din like this or in the singing of thousands of birds; in the howling of the storm, the lapping of waves, or the crackling of the fire. Just in this way—from quite different directions—must the themes appear; and they must be just as different from each other in rhythm and melodic character (everything else is merely many voiced writing, homophony in disguise)."[37]

Mahler's explicit emphasis on childhood memory is Ivesian. As Hermann Danuser has observed, Mahler's comments also resemble Ives's explanation of *Tone Roads*, particularly the remembrance of marching bands coming from different directions.[38] There are many points of comparison with Mahler from within Ives's work: the sequential juxtaposition of diverse elements, the layering of different tunes with contrasting rhythms, or tunes in differing tonalities—the mastery of polyrhythm and polytonality—and the use of extremes in sound character and registration to create the illusion of spatiality. Last but not least, for Ives the conventional approach to counterpoint shared by his contemporaries failed to challenge a static conception of tonality. The potential of polyphonic writing to create tonal diversity was overlooked or undermined. This point of view has its parallel in the role of polyphony in Mahler's compositional technique.[39]

In turn, examples from different periods in Mahler's career, from the Third Symphony (1893–96) and *Das Lied von der Erde* (1908–9), invite comparison with Ives. In the Third Symphony, in the first movement, two sections are quite like Ives. Mahler piles contrasting themes one upon another, using non-blending orchestral timbres, fragmenting the material, and employing altered repetitions to build up a cumulative, nearly chaotically complex orchestral sound.[40] Even the self-consciously folk- and dance-like themes of the first movement are Ivesian in character. The much-debated "Posthorn" episode in the third movement is an example of how Mahler uses acoustic distance the way Ives often does, even in the well known *The Unanswered Question*. The posthorn (like Ives's trumpet in *The Pond*) evokes not only historical nostalgia but also aural memory. The manner in which Mahler uses the posthorn to frame the intervening material also can be compared to Ives's placement and use of recognizable, borrowed themes in the *Concord Sonata*.[41]

In Ives and Mahler orchestral sound becomes an integral medium of composition, particularly through the use of contrast in registration and the elaborate use of band-like sounds and percussion. The layering of themes and abrupt changes in sound in Mahler offer listeners a distinctly Ivesian narrative in which distortions and unexpected transformations created by the composer force them to reflect on the current experience and the memory of prior listening.[42] In this way each listener can supply an individualized sense of significance beyond compositional intent quite different from the experience of listening to Beethoven or Brahms.

In *Das Lied von der Erde* one might hazard a comparison between the structure, opening, and close of "Der Abschied" and the last movement of Ives's Fourth Symphony (ca. 1914–23).[43] In both works, the composer concludes with an elaborate scheme of stretching out the pulse and settling into a static, simplified tonally centered sound. Endings in Mahler and Ives merit close comparison. The end of the last movement of the *Second Orchestral Set* (ca. 1915–29), which builds to a forceful, multi-textured statement of the hymn-tune theme and then dissipates to a quiet close, suggests how Ives, like Mahler in the Third Symphony, extends tension and employs rapid shifts within a closely argued structure and then brings the material to a triumphant resolution, however brief and ultimately ambiguous. One thinks of the role of the fifth movement and the transition between the end of the fifth movement and the beginning of the sixth in the Mahler Third Symphony. The affecting chorus fades out after a blazing affirmation, only to lead directly into the calm lyricism of the opening of the sixth movement.

Adorno's seminal analysis of Mahler highlighted dimensions in Mahler's music that suggest points of departure for the study of Ives: the intentional mix of naiveté and sophistication; the disruption of the surface and the undercutting of the stabilizing function of tonality; the aspect of longing and mourning; the conflict with "experts" in music; and the desire to connect life and the work of music in a new way.[44] There was something at work for both composers in terms of their engagement with musical traditions and the place of music in contemporary existence that links them together as contemporaries facing comparable environments with respect to musical culture. The first movement of Ives's Third Symphony can compare with Mahler in the evocation of tradition and its distortions, in the neo-baroque opening and in the integration of hymn and quasi-folk material. The second movement of that work is Mahlerian in its tonal shifts and juxtapositions of material. The last movement compares with the sixth movement of the Mahler Third Symphony particularly in the calculated employment of the lyrical as a rhetorical means of establishing grandeur. Simple lyricism is exploited as a didactic strategy and functions in both expositions and resolutions alongside massive sonorities and complex textures. In Ives as in Mahler, the ear is led into the radical and innovative by means of rhetorical gestures suggestive of the familiar—an almost teasing concession to conventional expectations of continuity and consonance.

But it is precisely because of apparent likenesses that sharp contrasts become equally significant, not the least of which are cultural.[45] Adorno claimed that Mahler's music "holds fast to Utopia in the memory traces from childhood, which appear as if it were only for their sake that it would be worth living. But no less authentic for him is the consciousness that this happiness is lost, and only in being lost becomes the happiness it never was." Adorno's claim fits Ives even though the actual childhoods, the imagined memories, and the senses of utopia and happiness diverge.[46] Although Mahler focused on his mother's pain and suffering and its transfiguration through love (e.g., in the Fourth Symphony), both Mahler and Ives expressed nostalgic ambivalence about the world of their childhood—the natural surroundings, the visual memories. The present seemed more grim. As Mahler put it in 1900, "I am beginning to think more and more that only the deaf and blind are fortunate, being shut out of this miserable world."[47]

Ives—for all his attention to the past—was imbued with a combative American energy and a feisty optimism that things might improve along the "highway" of "social progress." At the same time, even Ives's proposals to empower the masses and his willingness to redistribute private property do not mask the centrality of nostalgia.[48] Nostalgia is frequently allied with pessimism and skepticism. For Ives, a belief in the inexorability of historical change—particularly progress in externals (e.g., health, education, technology, and commerce)—was combined with a sense of the loss of cultural values. Historical change reduced the likelihood of replicating past virtue. By changing fundamental conditions, progress creates barriers against any project of restoration. Therefore, in his politics, his business career, and his music Ives came to realize that quite radical means—strategies adequate to the altered conditions of contemporary life—were required if past virtues were to be sustained or revived. Maintaining established conventions and practices would not accomplish the task.

Both Ives and Mahler understood the real and potential audience and the dynamics of the music business (including concert life, publishing, and journalism) in their day and age. They shared a nostalgia for a more musical time located in the past, when music meant more and enriched lives significantly. At the same time they recognized progressive changes in the size of the audience and the range and character of the music to which listeners had become accustomed. These factors fueled and complicated their determination to confront compositional conventions and listener expectations.[49]

Consider for example Ives's views on the issue of repetition in music. In comparing 1790, when Beethoven was writing, to 1890 when Tchaikovsky dominated the scene, Ives observed that in 1790 the "ear was tougher." Beethoven had to "churn" to make his message carry. Repetition, particularly when something novel was at stake, seemed essential. But by 1890, the audience—exposed to Wagner and Brahms—seemed more adept superficially at comprehending complex music. The kind of "clarity and coherence" Tchaikovsky developed, however, relied on repetition. In modern times, this worked directly against the sort of spiritual potential inherent in music most evident, for Ives, in the example of Beethoven's attack on the reigning listening habits of his day. If Ives was to make his own message carry, he needed to undercut the historical process of routinization.

What had once been a useful musical strategy—classical repetition—had become unexceptional and in fact a barrier to getting under the skin, so to speak, of listeners. Tchaikovsky merely manipulated the Beethovenian tradition for superficial effect. The progress of musical culture and the accompanying easy familiarity with musical works brought with it a loss in spiritual contact with music. The modern ear was less "tough" but more complacent. It had become attached to compositional and performance uniformities heralded as evidence of either refined taste or the sort of rational progress associated with the widespread and, for Ives, deleterious acceptance of standardized equal temperament in tuning.[50]

The consequences of nostalgia in both Mahler and Ives were that they believed that they had to confront tradition by a mix of affirmation with respect to recognizable conventions (such as the use of symphonic form) and a deliberate undercutting of those conventions. Coherence was redefined, as was the use of musical time. In turn, the appearance of fragmentation—elusive quotations, quick shifts in tonality, and breaks in the continuity of the line—had to be transcended by the use of the very diversities in sound and style to create an overriding structural logic within the basic outlines of traditional compositional practice.[51] Among the most salient elements in this regard linking the two composers was the overt non-blending use of instruments in orchestral music to open up aural space and highlight autonomous lines. In this context each distinct familiar element was used as a lure by which the composer could communicate a critical aesthetic and cultural political commentary through music specific to the historical moment in which he lived.

As the revisionists have argued, Charles Ives was indeed not so exceptional as was once thought. The historical categories of conservative and avant-garde, reactionary and progressive, demand reconsideration in the context of the art, culture, and politics of the early twentieth century. Ives's nostalgia for a rapidly vanishing spiritual world and landscape made him conservative and reactionary. Yet his faith in progress and humankind and his commitment to the power of music led him to transform his nostalgia into experimentation and an avant-garde aesthetic.

Ives's music mirrors a strain in early-twentieth-century modernism, evident as well in the music of Mahler, that was obsessed with the moral fabric of contemporary politics and culture. Ives, like his European counterparts Mahler and Schoenberg, engaged in aesthetic experimentation and innovation in search of a moral force adequate to the dangers of modernity.[52] Even though the spiritual content and the desired impact on the listener were defined by a retrospective sensibility—the idea that past values needed to be reclaimed for modern life—historical progress demanded that the aesthetic means not be conservative. In Ives's view the conservative music written by his contemporaries possessed no power beyond its capacity to entertain and seduce. Owing to so-called cultural progress, music had become all too affirmative, too pleasing, and too uniform. It was spiritually irrelevant. The right path had to take into account the society's growing surface sophistication so that a healthy spirit could be restored in contemporary life.

Mahler and Ives lived in the age of Leo Tolstoy and Matthew Arnold. They were contemporaries of Oscar Wilde and Gabriele d'Annunzio.[53] Ives was concerned with the prevalence of mere sensuality in art. His critique of Debussy and Tchaikovsky was that, as quintessential modern urban artists, they were unable to penetrate even the surface of nature (to which both composers turned for inspiration) to express its inner truth.[54]

Ives certainly was aware of the scandal that surrounded and followed the American premiere of Strauss's *Salome* in New York in 1907.[55] He was keenly aware of a debate in his own time about decadence and degeneracy. Tolstoy was not alone in his disenchantment with the aesthetic and his disgust that art, including music (which Tolstoy loved), was not only powerless against the rise of immorality but complicit in the modern age by celebrating spiritual and moral corruption and bankruptcy. Modern progress in economic and social life and spiritual decline seemed to go hand in hand. The task of the artist and musician, for Ives, was to use the aesthetic as an instrument of spiritual rebirth and moral recognition.

Tolstoy, like Ives, idealized the simple rural individual and life. Where they diverged was that Tolstoy ultimately abandoned the making of art. As Ives put it, Tolstoy became "helpless to himself and to us, for he eliminates further."[56] Ives, in contrast, withdrew only from the role of the public artist, detaching himself from the commerce and blandishments of a career. He recalled, "I began to feel more and more, after seances with nice musicians, that, if I wanted to write music that, to me, seemed worth while, I must keep away from musicians."[57] Tolstoy donated the proceeds of his last novel, *Resurrection*, to a utopian community. Ives gave his music away free and refused to assign copyright or gain income from his works. After 1902 Ives tried his hand at writing music in a new way—albeit derived from the ideas of his father—in an effort to use the modern in the struggle against modernity.

III. Religion and Art: The Emerson Connection

A distinctly American ideology, that of transcendentalism as expressed in Emerson and Thoreau, led Ives away from the path taken by Tolstoy. The basic starting point for both men was fundamentally the same: an allegiance to Christianity. The key to Ives's aesthetic strategy after 1902—his way of getting his "message" across through music—is the religious background and character of American transcendental thought. Unlike Emerson, Ives did not reject organized Protestantism.

Ives's lifelong relation to religion took many forms. He functioned in the institution of the church as parishioner, organist, and composer. Ives's life and work as a composer of music and as a writer of prose were dominated by religion, both in its institutional form and in its generalized and secularized philosophical presence. He was a man of religious ideas and faith and a citizen who mused on the relationship between religion and civic and democratic life.

Ives's output, from the String Quartet "From the Salvation Army" (1898–1902) to the Fourth Violin Sonata (ca. 1914)—quite apart from the volume of music written explicitly for use in church—all derived from his fascination not with doctrine per se, but with the consequences of faith and the way Americans collectively, past and present, engaged in religious expression. The last movement of the *Second Orchestral Set, From Hanover Square North*, written between 1915 and 1919 and scored in the 1920s, depicts an occasion when people on a commuter train platform gradually joined in singing a gospel hymn, *In the Sweet Bye and Bye*, in memory of those who had perished in the sinking of the *Lusitania*. This was the twentieth-century secular equivalent of the collective sensibility of the nineteenth-century camp meeting whose memory Ives cherished. That movement conveys the sense that the mass aggregate of humanity—Ives's majority—was spontaneously, morally, and divinely privileged. Its collective memory of a gospel song, however, was decisive. Any genuine contemporary expression of spiritual recognition seemed to require some connection, however residual, to religion.

The aesthetic realm (in Ives's case, music) needed to offer a necessary bridge between a secularized modern world and the values formed in a past dominated by religion. Although the music Ives wrote in this work might well strike audiences as strange and off-putting, it was written in the belief that—precisely owing to its innovative character—it uniquely could generate a positive sense of mass spiritual empathy in the face of a particularly amoral modern cruelty: the sinking of a ship in war using a technology which shattered time-honored conventions about the rules of naval engagement.

Emerson's thought provided the basis for a reconciliation between Ives's assumptions about historical evolution and progress and his doubts about the spiritual and moral state of contemporary life and culture. It did so by encouraging the idea that moral strength in modern art could triumph over satisfaction with mere aestheticism, understood by Ives as manner or skill in the sense possessed by Richard Strauss. But morality, for Ives, remained inextricably tied to and derived from Christianity. Morality needed to be found in art, in the form of "spiritual sturdiness" and as an antidote to industrialization and urbanization. Ives opposed the idea of sending American composers to Rome to help raise the standard of American music. A day in a "Kansas wheat field," Ives wrote, "would do more . . . than three years in Rome."[58] For Ives, as for Emerson, Europe did not represent a model for America. At best it offered an instructive but not exemplary past. For Ives it also displayed a decadent present.

The task of holding on to essential American virtues—the sort celebrated by Emerson—framed for Ives the task of the artist. Ives feared the "scattering" and "vanishing" in the modern world of communities for whom the commitment to freedom and an allegiance to the Emersonian oversoul and underlying unity of life had once been sacred. Easy listening was a modern habit associated with the comforts of affluent urban middle- and upper-class life. The enemy—soft armchair music—was "feminine" in Ives's mind in the sense that spiritual faith and moral clarity were "masculine" virtues.[59] Ives identified the feminine with the degenerate, the undisciplined, the self-satisfied, and an immoral attraction to mere "manner."

Ives's prejudices were characteristic of a dominant strain in turn-of-the-century thought.[60] Ives's nostalgia led him to search for an alternative reminiscent of a more virtuous rural America of the past. Ives shared with Emerson and Thoreau their well-known mistrust of the city. Ives knew that Emerson contrasted the rural landscape as the proper place for the cultivation of spiritual clarity with the city as the location of falsity, betrayal, and artificiality.[61]

Art music therefore worked dialectically against the consequences of history as a counterforce. Art had to play a didactic role in the evolution of moral and political culture. Music, as a collective and participatory art in the modern city, could serve to counteract the inexorable mechanization and standardization of the soul which urban life brought by stimulating, among the majority, its "spiritual conscience."

A genuine and experimental modern music—the consequence of evolutionary progress—might rekindle the spirituality of lost rural existence. At the end of *Essays Before a Sonata*, in the Epilogue, Ives wrote,
"Could the art of music, or the art of anything, have a more profound
reason for being than this?" The "this" referred to a phrase from
Sidney Lanier: "music, *rightly developed* [italics: Ives] . . . will be found
to be a late revelation of all gospels in one."[62]

That Ives's religious impulse was tied to a particular Christian tradition and its secularized philosophical outgrowth, American transcendentalism, becomes clearer through the comparison with Mahler.
Mahler did not identify with any organized religion. His link to
Judaism was marginal and his attitude to Catholicism distant, at best.[63]
Certainly there was nothing approximating the family and community linkage to church life that dominated Ives's life. Although both
men idealized nature as opposed to urban civilization in a manner
reminiscent of Rousseau, Mahler was not nearly as philosophically
suspicious of the city per se. But like Ives Mahler was, as Ferdinand
Pfohl claimed, "a mystic, a God seeker. His imagination circled inces-
santly around these matters, around God and the world, around life
and death, around spiritual matters and nature. . . . He wanted to
believe—belief at any price."[64]

Mahler also wished his audience to respond spiritually to his
music, well beyond the realm of aesthetic judgment. Mahler's ambivalence concerning so-called programmatic statements—evident in his
initial acceptance of written programs early in his career and his later
disavowal of them (notably after his symphonic paean to nature, the
Third Symphony)—is an indication of his struggle (comparable to
that of Ives) with the question of whether music without programmatic narratives could succeed in transmitting its own essential spiritual content to the audience.[65]

Mahler's 1895 program for the Third Symphony (which he ini-
tially entitled "Pan"),[66] expressed in a letter to Friedrich Löhr, speaks
of the work's intention to express "the hierarchy of organisms . . . ; my
feelings towards all creatures, which . . . is gradually resolved into
blissful confidence. Summer is conceived in the role of the victor—
amidst all that grows and flowers, creeps and flies, thinks and yearns,
and finally, all that of which we have only an intuitive inkling
(angels—bells—transcendental)."[67] Compare this to Emerson's claims
about the hierarchy of nature in his essay "Culture" and to Ives's talk
of "the lessons of evolution, which Nature has been teaching men
since the days of Socrates."[68] In a similar vein, Ives quoted from
Emerson's essays *Nature* and *Poetry and Imagination* in his prose accom-

paniment to the first movement of the *Concord Sonata*. Emerson wrote, "for although the works of nature are innumerable and all different, the result . . . is similar and single. . . . A leaf, a sunbeam, a landscape, the ocean, make an analogous impression on the mind; And when life is true to the poles of nature, the streams of truth will roll through us in song."[69]

The proto-religious philosophical and perhaps ideological commonality between Ives and Mahler has an unexpected shared source. Emerson was crucial for Ives. A key inspiration for the young Mahler, apparent in the Third Symphony, was Friedrich Nietzsche (whose *Die fröhliche Wissenschaft* inspired one of Mahler's first titles for the Third Symphony). Mahler's conceit regarding the inner spiritual significance of his own work has its root in Nietzsche. Nietzsche's *Die fröhliche Wissenschaft* revealed, among other things, his extraordinary and perhaps unique regard for Emerson. Throughout his life Nietzsche read and re-read Emerson's *Essays*. Emerson's "over-soul" even suggested the formulation for Nietzsche's "Übermensch."[70]

There is no evidence that Mahler read Emerson. But the indirect connection, through Emerson, between Nietzsche and Mahler on the one hand and Ives on the other, is substantive and not coincidental. It underscores the significance for Ives of the turn-of-the-century debate regarding the moral and spiritual crisis of modernity. Ives knew something quite conventional and critical about Nietzsche. For him, Nietzsche was one of the chief architects of the moral and cultural decline of modern times. As Ives's disparaging parenthetical reference to Nietzsche in his critique of Richard Strauss suggests, it is unlikely that Ives read Nietzsche.[71]

Yet Nietzsche's attack on the "religion of comfortableness," on the self-satisfied, soft, and conventional notions of happiness in his day and age—even Nietzsche's critique of Wagner—have uncanny parallels in Ives.[72] Like Nietzsche, Ives recalled once being taken in by Wagner and later sensing "something commonplace—yes—of make-believe. . . . An unearned exultation—a sentimentality deadening something within—hides around in the music." Likewise, Ives's use of the feminine with respect to his critique of conventional taste and spiritual weakness is similar to Nietzsche's views expressed in *Die fröhliche Wissenschaft*.[73]

The Nietzsche that Mahler found alluring was the Nietzsche who wrote that Emerson's "spirit always finds reasons for being satisfied and even grateful; at times he touches on the cheerful transcendency." This idea was at the root of Mahler's project in writing the Third Symphony.[74] The projected last and seventh movement, which turned into the final movement of the Fourth Symphony, Mahler termed "humorous" in the sense Nietzsche had once located in Emerson a "cheerfulness which discourages all seriousness."[75]

The Nietzsche who inspired Mahler in the 1890s was the Nietzsche who found in Emerson a focus on the present and on man's capacity for renewal, collectively and individually. Emerson shared with Nietzsche a hostility to the abuse of history and the past that condemned modernity to a "worship of the past" and to being "a retrospective age." Both men dwelled on the hidden suprahistorical unities of life and attacked the abstract pose of detachment and objectivity characteristic of empirical science.

These ideas found their way into Ives's beliefs. His dedication to writing innovative music after 1902 mirrored the Emersonian conviction that even modern man—by his own actions, particularly through his creative will—could escape the seemingly inexorable negative logic of historical change transforming American society. The modern artist could make connections to the deeper and overarching logic of life. Ives was not alone among his American contemporaries in locating Emerson's significance in this idea. As William James put it, Emerson's "insight and creed" was that "the great Cosmic Intellect terminates and houses itself in mortal men and passing hours." This was the Emerson whom Ives described as having written "symphonies of revelation [that] begin and end with nothing but the strength and beauty of innate goodness in man, in Nature and in God—the greatest and most inspiring theme of Concord Transcendental philosophy."[76]

It is ironic that even the "death of God" argument that appeared in *Die fröhliche Wissenschaft* and formed the cornerstone of *Zarathustra* contains similarities to Ives's version of Emerson. Ives's critique of what he termed the by-then cliché-ridden "rebel of the twentieth century" (and perhaps he did have a popularized version of Nietzsche in mind), who "confuses God with a name" and who "in the keenness of his search, . . . forgets that 'being true to ourselves' is God," reads much like the Zarathustra of the Prologue and First Part of *Also Sprach Zarathustra* who castigates the superficially educated and modern intellects of his own time.[77] Even Nietzsche's use of the analogy of improvisation has parallels in Emerson and Ives.

Ives and Emerson, in their belief in a universal spiritual truth and continuum, can be compared with Nietzsche. Nietzsche's notion of "eternal return," particularly as presented by the animals in the second section of the thirteenth chapter of Part III of *Zarathustra*—a source of Mahler's conception of the natural cosmos as mirrored in the Third Symphony—owes a debt to Emerson's concept of the over-soul.[78]

No doubt Emerson, whether directly, or indirectly through Nietzsche, offered the crucial philosophical assumption shared by both Ives and Mahler. No matter how different their music may be, both composers accepted (albeit implicitly in the case of Ives) the Nietzschean notion of the unique potential of the aesthetic, his assessment of music and its potential effect on the listener as privileged. In the Nietzschean hierarchy, given the diagnosis of the age in which he lived and his critique of the "Houses of Wisdom" in *Zarathustra*, the true artist was superior, particularly in his capacity, through music, to make "the happiness of Homer" available to modern man. Ives and Mahler framed their sense of purpose and ambition as makers of music along these lines.[79]

God, in Ives's sense, resided in man and nature. Ives thought, as did Emerson, that the divine was not located in the doctrinal God of Christianity. Nietzsche's rejection of the moral language and world view of Christianity led him in a parallel fashion to celebrate the possibilities of man. A key difference between Emerson and Ives on the one hand and Nietzsche on the other lay in the latter's condemnation of democracy and contempt for the "superfluous" masses and the focus on the rare and exceptional individual.[80] In Nietzsche, the wisdom of Zarathustra displaced the internalized logic and psychology of Christianity, which devalued man, the body, and mortal existence and turned man against his own possibilities.

Ives parted company with Nietzsche and Nietzsche's version of Emerson by not accepting the radical transvaluation of values through which the entire moral structure inherited from Christianity was set aside. It is precisely the extent to which many turn-of-the-century modernists embraced the Nietzschean abandonment of moral categories and the delegitimation of secularized Christian ideas of good and evil that alarmed Ives and helped to focus his aesthetic project after 1902. Ives's position had its parallel in Mahler's turn away from Nietzsche after 1901 in search of a more affirmative credo. For both composers, the Nietzschean stance prevalent at the turn of the century ultimately could not serve as a basis for making new music.

Ives stressed Emerson's links to an earlier tradition of American theology rather than his overt rejection of Christianity.[81] In this way Ives tied Emerson to notions of faith and morality derived directly from Christianity. In contrast, Nietzsche stressed Emerson's departure from Christianity and the direction of his thought which lent support to the rejection of the language and dichotomies of conventional morality and ethics. Ives understood Emerson's rejection of doctrine, particularly Unitarianism. Indeed, Emerson had followed in the wake of an earlier American theological critique of a doctrinal dependency on the epistemology of Locke.[82] Rational understanding and empirical knowledge were accused of exercising an excessive hegemony with respect to the foundations of faith. Emerson's ideas grew out of the work of Jonathan Edwards and George Ripley, who helped redefine the notion of reason to include feeling and intuition.[83] The presence of a universal spiritual realm in each individual was vindicated by the fact of human consciousness. This in turn justified art as a human expression of the divine imagination. Writing in 1834, Emerson argued that "Religion, Poetry, Honor belong to the Reason. . . . Reason is the highest faculty of the soul—what we mean often by the soul itself; it never reasons, never proves, it simply perceives; it is vision." Reason, for Emerson, was a faculty not of argument but of spiritual and religious recognition cast in an aesthetic act. It was, as he argued (and Ives would have agreed), "potentially perfect in every man."[84] In contrast, intellectual calculation—understanding—was not. Music therefore was ideally suited to the project of appealing to the individual and collective Emersonian Reason in modern man.

Ives's spiritual universalism was clearly indebted to Emerson's faith in an underlying metaphysical unity. Ives's sense of "great primal truths" that transcend history, visible in even the smallest detail of individual life and nature as well as in the "majority," descended, as did Emerson's, from a religious impulse. It was the generous Emersonian sense of the cosmic spirit which prevented Ives from losing faith in modern politics, an arena for which Nietzsche had only contempt. Ives focused on the salutary role religion and religious feeling could play in political and social life.

Ives's view of the role of art as it relates to religion becomes clearer when one compares his self-image with respect to the power of music in his own time to the views of another American contemporary, George Santayana. Santayana argued in 1900 that "religion and poetry are identical in essence." Indeed, Ives resisted what Santayana decried as "the liberal school which attempts to fortify religion by minimizing its expression . . . it subtracts from faith that imagination by which faith becomes an interpretation and idealization of human life."[85]

The crucial point of difference with respect to Ives as opposed to Mahler or Nietzsche is one that is therefore characteristically American. The Emerson whom Ives revered and the philosophy Ives formulated out of Emerson paid constant homage to the roots of transcendental philosophy in American Christian theology. Neither Nietzsche nor Mahler can be accused of attempting to confront his audience or address the perils of their age—whether in politics or art—from within Protestant Christianity.

Much has been written on the role played by Emerson's writings and philosophy on Ives. J. Peter Burkholder has argued that the encounter with Emerson came relatively late and that the view—most directly argued by the Cowells—that Ives can be understood within the framework of American transcendentalism is exaggerated. Burkholder argues against any particular childhood and familial acquaintance (despite Ives's claim of one) with Emerson and places the direct encounter in Ives's Yale years.[86] Indeed, Ives recalled submitting an essay on Emerson in his senior year.

It may still be that the influence and image of Emerson—as understood even secondhand—during the 1880s and 1890s was crucial to Ives's early intellectual development despite the absence of direct biographical evidence. In the role of ideas in history, it is frequently not the original texts but rather the popularized and often bowdlerized versions that exercise the greatest influence. It seems clear, however, that Emerson's role was decisive in shaping the manner in which Ives defined his task as a private composer after 1902.

Ives was not a philosopher. At the same time, Stuart Feder's dismissal of Ives's prose as confused and comprehensible only from a clinical vantage point is off the mark.[87] Ives's conception of transcendentalism changed little after college, and his view of Emerson was remarkable in that it paralleled views held by three distinguished American philosophers and contemporaries—William James, George Santayana, and John Dewey—particularly with respect to the theological roots and political implications of Emerson.

William James referred to the "intensely religious character of his total thought."[88] The secularization of Emerson, so evident in Nietzsche's reading of him, is absent in these three American turn-of-the-century commentators. Ives shared Santayana's reading of Emerson as "a Puritan whose religion was all poetry"; the greatest incarnation of the "Psyche of Puritanism," who discarded literal beliefs in doctrine, "withdrew, without rancor and without contempt, from the fellowship of the church," and "assumed an attitude hardly less cool and deprecatory toward the enthusiasms of the new era."[89]

Santayana's description of Emerson might easily have fit Charles Ives the man and musician: "a Puritan mystic with a poetic fancy and a gift for observation and epigram, and he saw in the laws of Nature, idealized by his imagination, only a more intelligible form of the divinity he had always recognized and adored." What was peculiarly American about Emerson's brand of mysticism was that it was "kept within bounds" because his sincerity allowed his "imagination" to remain "near to experience." Ives shared the notion that this faculty of "imagination" was linked to real human life and nature. This was Emerson's overriding theme, even though his heart was fixed on the idea of unity and the single soul—on "eternal things." Key to both Ives's and Santayana's reading of Emerson was the notion that the aesthetic imagination manifested man's "moral vitality in the bosom of nature." Like Santayana's Emerson—as opposed to Nietzsche's—Ives remained a moralist.[90]

Perhaps more significant was the overriding view, circa 1900, that Emerson was an artist, not a philosopher. One is reminded of John Dewey's rejoinder to Emerson's critics in his 1903 Emerson lecture. Dewey wrote that Emerson was "more than a philosopher. He would work, he says, by art, not by metaphysics, finding truth." For Dewey, Emerson broke barriers, and let philosophy and poetry combine.[91] In James's Emerson essay from the same anniversary year, Emerson became "an artist whose medium was verbal."[92] Ives's commitment to music may have been inspired by the idea—echoed also by Santayana—that in the main, language in words and arguments had become inadequate to Emerson's unique capacity to inspire in his auditors "a truth that was inexpressible . . . the inaudible highest notes of his gamut, too pure and thin for common ears." Likewise, James spoke of the "souls of men" being "strengthened and liberated by the noble and musical pages" Emerson produced.[93] Given the direction of history, the right kind of music might function where once language—in Emerson's hand—had succeeded.

Ives's post-1902 view of Emerson was in line with Dewey, who believed that "the coming century may well make evident what is now dawning, that Emerson is not only a philosopher, but that he is the 'philosopher of Democracy.'" For Dewey and Ives, Emerson rendered the insights of philosophy "true of life, of the common experience of the everyday man."[94] Likewise, James stressed Emerson's view of the democratic character of the divine. Dewey's emphasis on the democratic aspect of Emerson further indicates the extent to which Ives's political interpretation of Emerson was shared among his contemporaries.

But it was William James's contrast between Whitman and Emerson that points to the peculiar affinity between Ives and Emerson. James argued that in contrast to the expansive optimism of Whitman,

Emerson demanded the "transfiguration" of the individual fact. Unmediated everyday experience betrayed "squalor," which required the interjection of the "Moral Sentiment." For James, Emerson was a moralist who believed that anything at all could be "suffused with absolute radiance." But any one of these "worthy specimens" could become so only through a connection with morality.[95]

Taken as whole, the turn-of-the-century American interpretation of Emerson explicitly supported Ives's notion of a useful synthesis between secularized religion and modern art. The obligations of the Emersonian artist toward the public fit Ives's own overt lifelong allegiance to a Christian legacy. Furthermore, Ives found outlined in Emerson a strategy that pointed to a manner through which the composer could realize precisely the moral transfiguration of the commonplace to which James alluded. As Ives wrote of the *Holiday* movements, they were morality tales: "attempts to make pictures in music of common events in the lives of common people (that is, of fine people)."[96]

The embrace of the present day and the possibilities of modern art and expression in one of Ives's favorite Emersonian writings, "The American Scholar," offered a precise account of the task of the artist as instrument of moral affirmation and renewal:

> This time, like all times, is a very good one, if we but know what to do with it. . . . I read with some joy of the auspicious signs of the coming days, as they glimmer already through poetry and art. . . . Instead of the sublime and beautiful; the near, the low, the common, was explored and poeticized. . . . The literature of the poor, the feelings of the child, the philosophy of the street, the meaning of household life, are the topics of the time. It is a great stride. It is a sign—is it not?—of new vigor, when the extremities are made active, when currents of warm life run into the hands and the feet. I ask not for the great, the remote, the romantic; what is doing in Italy or Arabia; what is Greek art, or Provençal minstrelsy; I embrace the common, I explore and sit at the feet of the familiar, the low. Give me insight into to-day, and you may have the antique and future worlds. What would we really know the meaning of? The meal in the firken; the milk in the pan; the ballad in the street; the news of the boat; the glance of the eye; the form and the gait of the body;—show me the ultimate reason of these matters; show me the sublime presence of the highest spiritual cause lurking, as always it does lurk, in these suburbs and extremities of nature. . . . One design unites and animates the farthest pinnacle and the lowest trench.[97]

The task of the modern composer, for Ives, was to demonstrate the "sublime presence" in everyday life even in its less ideal contemporary urban forms. This demanded the moral transformation of vernacular material through art, designed to reach and startle the contemporary listener. This ambition accounts for the increasing modernism and dissonance of Ives's work during the second decade of this century. Art through contemporary sounds took the place of political and religious exhortation in the form of speech. Before 1902, in the organ loft, the young Charles Ives sought to do what the profession of preachers—including his future father-in-law—within his community seemed to struggle to accomplish: moral elevation within modern democratic culture. After 1902, Ives's memory of camp meetings led him to an Emersonian search for a much-needed modern vehicle of spiritual transformation adequate to his own time.

Ives was not sure that he had succeeded. His inability to compose further and his turn to writing prose in the 1920s, analyzed in psychological terms by Feder and others, may have been a result of a sense of failure regarding the efficacy of music (and perhaps his work in insurance as well) in terms of its moral and political imperatives. For Ives, as for Tolstoy, withdrawal from public life, in art and business, had emerged as the only alternative.

IV. Ives and Modernism in New York

It has been suggested, most persuasively by Carl Schorske, that Ives and Mahler shared an ideological radicalism at odds with the political arrangements of the day.[98] In Mahler's case, universal suffrage and fundamental political rights as well as social justice in the Habsburg Monarchy were at stake. For Ives, the failures of modern democracy as well as extreme economic inequality inspired a political critique. The longest piece of Ives's prose, *The Majority*, and the works for unison chorus and instruments from 1912–20 are testimony to this.

However, it may be that what Ives saw himself as doing at the peak of his activity as a composer had less to do with politics per se and more to do with a sense of cultural and moral decline. Too often twentieth-century modernism has been analyzed retrospectively purely in terms of formalist aesthetics. The rebellion against inherited conventions—for example the emphasis both Ives and Schoenberg placed on the avoidance of repetition as a technique by which to achieve structural coherence or their shared rejection of notions of dissonance—may suggest comparisons that reveal historical common-alities. But the intent to displace a reigning stylistic paradigm often has motivations that are not formalist or aesthetic.

Undercutting the hegemony of an existing elite within a profession was the ambition of other radical artists at the time, as in the struggle of painter Robert Henri and the New York "Eight" against the National Academy of Design.[99] But this was not the primary ambition of either Ives or Mahler. No doubt both men had contempt for the prominent critics and pedagogues of their day. But Ives's modernism, like Schoenberg's, was steeped in its own curious cultural conservatism. Although Ives assumed the notion of historical progress, he sought to find a way to sustain historic American virtues against modernity. The consequences of progress in industrialization, mechanization, and urbanization were not good. Consider, for example, Ives's recollection of his experience in England making a recording in a studio: "Now what has all this got to do with music? . . . A man may play to himself and his music starts to live—then he tries to put it under a machine, and it's dead!"[100]

Ives's suspicion of modernity stemmed not only from a concern for the vanishing landscape and the future of democracy. Ives did not particularly like the popular music of his adulthood, particularly after he married.[101] He constantly railed against how music might become "soft in muscles and spirit, and die" even though over time, complex rhythms—progressive technical change—would become, as a function of progress, easier for subsequent generations.[102] But insofar as modern art—aesthetic modernism—thrived on its flaunting of supra-historical spiritual truths, including traditional morality, and justified itself purely in terms of a rebellion against aesthetic conventions, Ives took a stand against it. "The trouble with modern music is that [it's] somewhat too intellectual—the brain has [been] working a little more than that bigger muscle underneath (what you may call it, spirit, inner blast, soul?)."[103]

Mahler and Ives asked of music that it stand for more than mere rebellion *within* art. In part because of his adoption of Schopenhauerian and Wagnerian conceits that privileged the aesthetic realm (particularly music), Mahler understood music as filling the vacuum created by the decline in the prestige and power of conventional religion. His music could serve as a counterforce against what he perceived as widespread cultural and moral philistinism. In Ives's case, the transformation of everyday life through things he disliked telephone, gramophone, radio, airplanes placed nature, intimacy, community, and the spiritual at risk. "The most harmful element is commercialism, with its influence tending towards mechanization and standardized processes of mind and life (making breakfast and death a little too easy)."[104] Music needed to "stimulate" creativity, morality, and spirituality in "these days of automatic, readymade, easy entertainment" which is "deadening."[105]

In order to counter the threat to the "spiritual presence," an aesthetic strategy was required that was not restorative or rigidly conservative in an academic sense. But neither could it be akin to Walt Whitman, particularly in William James's sense, in whose work the celebration of the contemporary and vernacular seemed unlimited.[106] The emphasis in Mahler and Ives was not on the embrace of the modern or the common per se but on its transformation. The desire to use art (in this case music) to help achieve a moral agenda influenced the actual character of the modernist solution.

In the case of Ives this can be seen best in his striking non-relationship to the main contemporary events in art, particularly in New York during the period of his greatest creativity, the years from 1898 to 1920. Ives's relative isolation during his years in New York has been well-documented. As his critique of Strauss and collection of scores (which includes works by MacDowell and Reger) indicate, he did keep abreast of music.[107] But one must be suspicious of how little notice Ives seems to have taken of the most important and controversial events in the early history of modernism in New York. He seems to have been unaware of the legendary February 1913 Armory Show and the notoriety surrounding the 1908 Macbeth Galleries exhibition of what later would be the "Eight" of the Ashcan School. Furthermore he seems to have been oblivious to the presence of Alfred Stieglitz and his gallery at 291 Fifth and the early Dada movement in New York, particularly the circle of artists around the Arensbergs in New York after 1915.[108]

Ives's silence is not altogether trustworthy. In the first place, despite his allergy to newspapers, the controversy over the Armory Show and Marcel Duchamp's 1912 *Nude Descending a Staircase* would have been hard to avoid, given the extensive press coverage.[109] Even Theodore Roosevelt commented on the Armory Show. The same was true for the Eight, who, unlike Stieglitz, "exploited the news-hungry press. . . to alert the interest of the man-in-the-street."[110] The Eight, from the time of their break with the National Academy in New York, were prominently covered in the daily press. Even if Ives had never seen any of the work of the Ashcan painters, he could not easily have avoided reading about them and seeing newspaper reproductions.

Ives's own account of his train ride with a painter makes one suspect that indeed Ives had thought about the Ashcan school and the work in the Armory show. Most revealing in that memorandum is Ives's moralistic criticism of the use of nudity and the way in which the so-called moderns of the day were seeking to establish their originality.[111] Modern visual artists, Ives thought, were too interested in the form and "outer" content of their work and not on "the effect on the ideals of the inner conscience."[112] Ives's critique is somewhat similar to that leveled in Vienna by Karl Kraus and the young Arnold Schoenberg against Secession artists posing as radicals whose work betrayed merely a stylistic flair, pretension, and the exploitation of sexuality. Their art was not about ideas, but about style and decoration. This dichotomy, related to Adolf Loos's distinction between ornament and structure and Schoenberg's contrast between style and idea, mirrors Ives's distinction in the *Essays Before a Sonata* between manner and substance.[113]

Indeed, it was precisely the Ashcan approach to modernism that Ives explicitly sought not to emulate. On the surface, Robert Henri's break with the establishment seemed Ivesian. He declared himself, Joan Sloan, and William Glackens as uniquely American. In an early defense of the Eight, one critic asked, "Why copy continental themes when the United States offered a rich variety of subjects . . . even provincialism was not without merit?"[114] Like Ives, these painters (and with them George Bellows) celebrated the everyday and the vernacular. City life was their subject. Sloan's "Six O'Clock Winter," depicting the New York elevated trains, was done just a few years before Ives's Hanover Square movement. Glackens's *May Day, Central Park* from 1905 and Maurice Prendergast's watercolor *Central Park* from 1903 are proximate to Ives's own work *Central Park in the Dark* and depict activity and spatiality in ways that bear comparison to Ives.

Furthermore, these painters, in their choice of subject matter, were sympathetic to Ives's politics.[115] They depicted the poor and the ordinary citizen. George Luks painted immigrant orphans and crowded tenements. John Sloan, in an Ivesian way, parodied the insensitive rich and documented the harshness of city life for the lowest strata. What separated them from Ives and failed to impress him were several qualities: the relative absence of formal innovation in the composition and brushwork and either a moral neutrality with regard to the imagery or a stance that might have been construed by Ives as a celebration of decadence, as in Robert Henri's 1909 *Salome* and Sloan's *Three A.M.* and etchings in the series "New York City Life." Everett Shinn's 1902 *The Singer* celebrated exactly the kind of seductive and suggestive entertainment from the stage for which Ives had contempt.[116] Most of all, Ives seems to have taken a dislike to the self-appointed role of rebellion that involved the assumption of a bohemian style designed to discredit common-sense morality. The moral implications of the New York modern painters concerned Ives much the way the underlying moral and ethical consequences of the aesthetic conceits of the Viennese Secession and Young Vienna writers outraged Karl Kraus.

Ives's silence on the 1913 Armory show was repeated with respect to the April 1917 New York exhibit of the Society of Independent Artists. This latter exhibit was twice the size of the Armory show. Much in line with Ives's own prejudices, this was an American show without a jury or prizes. But like the Armory show, in works by Beatrice Wood and George Lathrop, nudity and sexuality—the attack on morality—was an overt dimension. Once more there was extensive New York press coverage (not to speak of gossip and talk), which Ives could not have failed to miss. What is most interesting in the cases of the Armory show and the 1917 Independents is that much of the work revealed an experimental aesthetic modernism absent from the Ashcan artists. Abstraction, collage, and cubism, as well as the early constructions of Man Ray and works by Francis Picabia and Duchamp, had been part of the New York scene—and objects of heated debate—in the years between 1913 and 1917.[117]

The visual art in New York that made headlines after 1913 was redolent with analogies to the sort of experiments and strategies on which Ives was working as a composer. The use of found objects, their transformation as part of larger formal structures, and the fragmenting and subverting of the illusion of a comfortable painterly realism were all in evidence. These innovations parallel the layering of lines, the juxtapositions of tonalities and sonorities, the experimentation with quarter tones, and the combination of competing rhythmic patterns in Ives's music from the same period. Varèse's association with the Arensbergs and Picabia and Joseph Stella's and Marsden Hartley's fascination with music further suggest formal and compositional parallels.[118] The experimentation with space and multidimensionality—one of Ives's great achievements—is striking in the visual art shown in these years in New York.

The reason for Ives's silence, distance, and implicit distaste for the modernist movement in the visual arts lies in his commitments as a Christian and as a moralist. For him, experimenting in music was justified because the "soft" conventional music failed to communicate spiritual and moral truth, particularly in churches. When the St. Louis

Star took on modernism in art in 1921, it asked, "Did you ever see family portraits like these?"[119] The key to the negative American reaction to Dada and Ives's silence is precisely the moral and societal implications of the aesthetic innovation apparent in modern art. The explicit amorality and nihilism portrayed in a *New York Evening Journal* article on Dada in 1921, with quotes from Duchamp and Stella, was horrifying to someone of Ives's views. If Jacobi's critique of Kant's Idealism was a defense of moral emotion, and Schleiermacher's embrace of music was on account of music's power to inspire inner religiosity, Emerson's defense of art as a dimension of reason was comparable. Likewise, for Ives, art was linked to an ethical spiritual sensibility.

The problem was that in "nice" music—in tune, with regular rhythms and no dissonances, which started and ended in the right keys with proper cadences and highly integrated blended instrumentations (the kind Parker and his lessers wrote)—no one was moved. Each of Ives's major works, from songs such as *General William Booth Enters Into Heaven* to the Second Orchestral Set and the Third and Fourth Symphonies, has written into it the expectation that for the listener hearing the music, precisely because of its radical surface, its novelty, and its tantalizing manipulation of familiarity and recognition, a Christian or moral verity—a democratic and spiritual sensibility—will be communicated. Modernism in music was therefore an instrument directed against the complacency of the present—the same complacency Ives railed against in business and politics—and against the decadent and immoral aestheticism of what the twentieth century and modern urban industrialized society seemed to be producing in the name of modern art. Ives was intent on reaching the amateur and the professional so that the function of listening could approximate the task of the preacher. As Wallach has noted, Ives developed a discourse in music, in part in imitation of the rhetorical strategy of Emerson's prose.[120]

The structural ingenuity with which Ives utilized quotation and borrowings, often with coherent final statements in works opened by subsidiary themes and fragments, is one example of how the need to make a moral claim lay beneath a choice of formal strategy.[121] Ives's use of stylistic diversities and abrupt shifts, often resulting in striking reconciliations even of competing rhythmic patterns, has its explicit moral overtones and analogies in the reconciliation of diversity in democracy.[122] Ives, through modern music, dethroned antimonies and demonstrated underlying unities. The mixture of fragments of memory becomes integrated into the larger form, just the way ephemeral, disparate details unify within the individual soul. False distinctions are exposed and superficial unity—the sort that appears in neat, well-composed, "soft" music—is discarded. Ives assumed, as did Mahler, that he created a cathartic process through sound, which at the end inspired a sense of humanity, brotherhood, and spiritual unity. Only by engaging the toughness of modern life, with its sense of loss, and not sweetening it, could music function as more than decoration.

V. Music and Morals

If Mahler had an affinity for Ives, or if there is a compelling, shared extramusical impetus behind the work of these two composers, it is this moral agenda that seems most convincing. When Alphons Diepenbrock heard the Third Symphony of Mahler he noted, in contrasting Mahler and Strauss, that the Mahler "is modern in every way. He believes in the future . . . his music appears to be granted the ability to 'transform people' and to give the experience of 'Katharsis.'"[123] Indeed, in the massive opening movement the raw power of nature in the form of summer, with its outdoor music, overwhelms the human in an inspiring fashion. It reminds one of the passage from *Zarathustra* Part I in which Zarathustra exhorts his disciples to "let the future and the farthest be for you the cause of your today." Indeed, Mahler's own postscript to the first movement expressed much the same notion: "To him who will get there! To those who will be there."[124]

Although commentators have had their doubts about Mahler's Eighth Symphony, here, too, Mahler sought to reach a large public with an experience comparable (despite the formal differences) to the Beethoven Ninth Symphony and the Mendelssohn *Lobgesang*.[125] Like Ives, Mahler sought to demonstrate, both in the duration and structure of the work and in its complex sound world, the essential unity and grandeur of the universe. The work was an affirmative summation of a credo and an aesthetic tradition dating back to Bach. The final transfiguration of Faust and the opening movement, with its appeal to the creator to endow humankind with illumination and love, were written to assert the opposite of decadence and cultural pessimism about the human possibility. Mahler brought the modern listener's awareness of the entire musical tradition to bear in this massive effort.

Ives's *Universe Symphony* had three parts, the first representing the past in creation; the second, the present, dominated by evolution in nature and humanity; and the third, the future, in which all would rise "to the spiritual." Ives's aspiration for a spiritual revival in the open air through music explains his curious comments about music sounding and not sounding, his disregard for expert renditions, his tolerance (derived from his father's attitude) of out-of-tuneness, and his expectation that over time historical progress would result in the widening of the range of so-called acceptable sounds. Music needed to break out of its self-referential limitations as cultivated entertainment to encompass all of life.

Since the Mahler Eighth Symphony is widely held to be less classically "Mahlerian" and Ives's *Universe Symphony* is unfinished, one might wish to turn rather to *Das Lied von der Erde* and Ives's Fourth Symphony. The sense of eternity and the spiritual repose that they bring to the listener, as distance is created in sound from parting, loss, and death at the end of both works, invite a comparison. In these works, the innovations with which the listener is faced speak to each composer's project to rescue modernity from itself. In Mahler's case, music sought to "transform life into art," as Donald Mitchell has eloquently observed, so that the experience of everyday life could be transcended for others.[126]

The renewal of life in nature—the affirmation of the beauty of the everyday beyond death—lies at the essence of the final lines of Mahler's text. In the Fourth Symphony Ives appropriated a traditional form—the fugue—as if to evoke not only "the reality of existence and its religious experience" but its continuity, despite change.[127] In both works the closing bars transmit a magical simplicity and clarity after an intense and complex journey. Ives and Mahler deliver the aesthetic anti-thesis—that of a yet unimagined new sound world and experience—of the philosophical and moral nihilism they most feared in the modern world.

NOTES

1. I would like to thank J. Peter Burkholder for his invaluable editorial and substantial assistance and many suggestions, and also Laurence Wallach, Paul De Angelis and Robert Martin for their help. See the discussion of these issues in Larry Starr, *A Union of Diversities: Style in the Music of Charles Ives* (New York: Schirmer Books, 1992), 68–70.

2. The significance of the formation of self-referential groups in art in the development of styles and the interaction of art with society is discussed in the work of Niklas Luhmann. See "The Autopoiesis of Social Systems" and "The Work of Art and the Self-Reproduction of Art" in Niklas Luhmann, *Essays on Self-Reference* (New York: Columbia University Press, 1990), 1–20 and 191–214. Ives's ambivalent relationship to the established self-referential community of musicians was, as will be argued later, crucial to his work and its reception.

3. Arthur Foote, *Arthur Foote 1853–1937: An Autobiography,* ed. Wilma Reid Cipolla (New York: Da Capo, 1979). There are other ironic parallels between these two composers. Both Ives and

Foote had one child, a girl. They both lost parents while still young. Both had close family ties to members of the clergy. Foote's music is not well known, and his posthumous reputation has suffered. There are good works however, including a fine concerto for violoncello, Op. 16, completed in 1893.

4. This essay relies on the standard modern accounts of Ives's biography. The most important documents describing Ives are in Vivian Perlis, *Charles Ives Remembered: An Oral History* (New York: W. W. Norton, 1976). See Frank R. Rossiter, *Charles Ives and His America* (New York: Liveright, 1975), David Wooldridge, *Charles Ives: A Portrait* (London: Faber, 1975)—originally published as *From the Steeples and Mountains*—and Stuart Feder, *Charles Ives, "My Father's Song": A Psychoanalytic Biography* (New Haven: Yale University Press, 1992). See also Robert M. Crunden, "Charles Ives's Place in American Culture," and Frank R. Rossiter, "Charles Ives: Good American and Isolated Artist," in *An Ives Celebration: Papers and Panels of the Charles Ives Centennial Festival-Conference,* ed. H. Wiley Hitchcock and Vivian Perlis (Urbana: University of Illinois Press, 1977), 4–28.

5. See Judith Tick, "Charles Ives and Gender Ideology," in *Musicology and Difference: Gender and Sexuality in Music Scholarship*, ed. Ruth A. Solie (Berkeley: University of California Press, 1993), 83–106.

6. See the common ground between Mason and Ives, despite differences in their music, in Mason's writings, especially about Emerson and his view of the "masses" and the state of the music business, in Daniel Gregory Mason, *The Dilemma of American Music* (New York: Macmillan, 1928), 96–98. See also the comparison between Mason and Ives in MacDonald Smith Moore, *Yankee Blues: Musical Culture and American Identity* (Bloomington: Indiana University Press, 1985), 1–63. See also Charles E. Ives, *Essays Before a Sonata, The Majority, and Other Writings*, ed. Howard Boatwright (New York: W. W. Norton, 1970), hereafter cited as *Essays*, 94–95.

7. John Cornelius Griggs, *Studien über die Musik in Amerika* (Leipzig: Breitkopf und Härtel, 1894), 2–5.

8. Ibid., 81–84.

9. Ives knew and played Buck's music and took organ lessons from him and from Buck's student, church musician and organist Harry Rowe Shelley, who was also a student of Dvořák's. See Gayle Sherwood, "The Choral Works of Charles Ives: Chronology, Style, Reception" (Ph.D. diss., Yale University, 1995), 92–100.

10. Griggs, *Studien über die Musik in Amerika*, 90–91. Griggs's views parallel those of Horatio Parker. See J. Peter Burkholder, *Charles Ives: The Ideas Behind the Music* (New Haven: Yale University Press, 1985), 101.

11. Vassar College Archives, programs from 1899, 1905, and 1907.

12. Charles E. Ives, *Memos*, ed. John Kirkpatrick (New York: W. W. Norton, 1972), hereafter cited as *Memos*, 52, and *Essays*, 79 and 94–95.

13. See J. Peter Burkholder, *All Made of Tunes: Charles Ives and the Uses of Musical Borrowing* (New Haven: Yale University Press, 1995). The typology and detailed analysis in this book make clear the extent to which Ives both knew and commanded classical compositional forms and developed complex formal strategies for his own work.

14. On the Second Symphony, see ibid., 102–36. On Ives's change of focus after 1902, see also Victor Fell Yellin's perceptive review of a 1974 recording of *The Celestial Country* by Harold Farberman (to whom much credit needs to be given for recording so much of Ives's music so well more than two decades ago) in *The Musical Quarterly* 60 (July 1974): 500–501.

15. See Perlis, *Charles Ives Remembered*, 155–68.

16. See Henry Cowell and Sidney Cowell, *Charles Ives and His Music*, 2nd ed. (New York: Oxford University Press, 1969); see also Leonard Bernstein, liner notes to the Ives Second Symphony in CD DGG 429220-2 (Hamburg 1990).

17. Cowell and Cowell, *Charles Ives and His Music*, vi, 131–32, 159, 163, and 217–18.

18. Frank R. Rossiter, "Charles Ives and American Culture: The Process of Development 1874–1921" (Ph.D. diss., Princeton University, 1970), 295.

19. Leonard Bernstein, liner notes, op.cit. *The Unanswered Question*, the Second Symphony and *Central Park in the Dark* emerged in this period as the most often played Ives works. Given Bernstein's comments, it should be noted that once (but no longer) Grandma Moses was a celebrated figure, precisely in the 1960s when things that were "folk" were highly prized. That Ives survived this phase itself suggests how wrong the notion of Ives as a charming "primitive" was.

20. The discussion of Ives and Mahler that follows owes much to the fine essay by Robert P. Morgan, "Ives and Mahler: Mutual Responses at the End of an Era," *19th-Century Music* 2 (July 1978): 72–81. See also Gianfranco Vinay, "Charles Ives e i musicisti europei: Anticipazioni e dipendenze," *Nuova revista musicale italiana* 7 (July–December 1973): 417–29.

21. See Vladimir Karbusicky, *Gustav Mahler und seine Umwelt* (Darmstadt: Wissenschaftliche Buchgesellschaft, 1978), 22–66; Henry A. Lea, *Gustav Mahler: Man on the Margin* (Bonn: Bouvier, 1985), 19–42; and Carl Schorske, "Gustav Mahler: Formation and Transformation," *Leo Baeck Memorial Lecture No. 35* (New York, 1991).

22. This comment is descriptive of a perception. The distinction between "music itself" and "extramusical meaning" is not shared by the author as useful or historically valid for either composer. The growing attention to Ives's music after 1970 may have also benefited from what was dubbed "the counter-culture": the so-called return to nature and the glorification of pre-modern rural folk traditions.

23. See Maynard Solomon, "Charles Ives: Some Questions of Veracity," *Journal of the American Musicological Society* 40 (Fall 1987): 443–70. Ives's chronology has recently been placed on a firmer footing by Gayle Sherwood, "Questions and Veracities: Reassessing the Chronology of Ives's Choral Works," *The Musical Quarterly* 78 (Fall 1994): 429–47, and Sherwood, "Choral Works," 1–82 and 306–70.

24. See Burkholder, *Charles Ives*, 58–82, and J. Peter Burkholder, "Ives and the Nineteenth-Century European Tradition," in *Charles Ives and the Classical Tradition*, ed. Geoffrey Block and J. Peter Burkholder (New Haven: Yale University Press, 1996), 11–33.

25. Ann Besser Scott, "Medieval and Renaissance Techniques in the Music of Charles Ives: Horatio at the Bridge?," *The Musical Quarterly* 78 (Fall 1994): 448–79, and Sherwood, "Choral Works," 117–53.

26. See Carol K. Baron, "George Ives's Essay in Music Theory: An Introduction and Annotated Edition," *American Music* 10 (Fall 1992): 239–88. I am indebted to my colleague Laurence Wallach and to his fine dissertation: Laurence D. Wallach, "The New England Education of Charles Ives" (Ph.D. diss., Columbia University, 1973).

27. Feder, *Charles Ives;* see also Carol K. Baron, "What Motivated Charles Ives's Search for Time Past: Review Essay," *The Musical Quarterly* 78 (Spring 1994): 206–19. See also the insights contained in Carl Schorske, "Mahler and Ives: Populism and Musical Innovation in Austria and America," unpublished typescript. I am grateful to Prof. Schorske for the use of this version of his previously published Ives paper, cited in note 98 below.

28. Wooldridge, *Charles Ives*, 150–51. Most of the Mahler literature repeats this story. Ives himself suggested that Mahler saw the score and took it; see *Memos*, 55 and 121. Wooldridge's surmise that Mahler performed it in Munich seems implausible in part because his account of a German musician's recollection is among other things linguistically dubious. *Ausführung* is used quite inappropriately and uncolloquially. Nevertheless it is understandable that Mahler would have been truly fascinated with any music that resembled, even superficially, his own work. This certainly was the case with his 1900 re-reading of Hans Rott's remarkable symphony. See Natalie Bauer Lechner, *Recollections of Gustav Mahler*, trans. Dika Newlin, ed. Peter Franklin (Cambridge: Cambridge University Press, 1980), 146.

29. *Memos*, 137.

30. Knud Martner, *Gustav Mahler im Konzertsaal: Eine Dokumentation seiner Konzerttätigkeit 1870–1911* (Copenhagen: By the author, 1985), 123 and 145.

31. Donald Mitchell, *Gustav Mahler: The Wunderhorn Years* (Berkeley and Los Angeles: University of California Press, 1975), 169–71. Mahler, in contrast to Ives, seems not to have made much serious reference in his music to parlor music or the European equivalents of Stephen Foster.

32. The text of the *Etude* interview can be found in Zoltan Roman, *Gustav Mahler's American Years 1907–1911: A Documentary History* (Stuyvesant: Pendragon Press, 1989), 442–45. Compare this to Ives's statements in the *Essays*, 78–81, and Griggs's views in his dissertation.

33. *Essays*, 79.

34. Theodor W. Adorno, *Mahler: A Musical Physiognomy*, trans. Edmund Jephcott (Chicago: University of Chicago Press, 1992), 61–74. Adorno also suggested a comparison to Flaubert. One thinks of *Madame Bovary*, even in the layering of the interior and exterior, public and private events, in a single scene. Ives's intensive relationship to prose fiction and reading (with his wife)— including the work of Jane Austen—and his efforts to write music based on literary personalities all fit in with this observation. David C. Birchler discusses Mahler's reminiscences of his own earlier works as a means of constructing an autobiography in "Nature and Autobiography in the Music of Gustav Mahler" (Ph.D. diss., University of Wisconsin–Madison, 1991). The use of music in the formation of narrative, particularly autobiography—an issue for both Ives and Mahler—is also discussed, in the case of Mahler, in the context of Arthur Schnitzler's relationship to music and his attitude toward Mahler. See Marc A. Weiner, *Arthur Schnitzler and the Crisis of Musical Culture* (Heidelberg: Winter, 1986), 30–35.

35. Charles Ives, *Washington's Birthday*, ed. James B. Sinclair (New York: Associated Music Publishers, 1991), ii and iii; also *Memos*, 96–97, note 1.

36. Charles E. Ives, "Note," in *Central Park in the Dark*, ed. Jacques-Louis Monod with notes by John Kirkpatrick (Hillsdale, N.Y.: Boelke-Bomart, 1973), 31.

37. Bauer Lechner, *Recollections of Gustav Mahler*, 155–56.

38. Hermann Danuser, *Gustav Mahler und seine Zeit* (Laaber: Laaber, 1991), 299–301.

39. See Morgan, "Ives and Mahler," and his "Spatial Form in Ives," in *An Ives Celebration: Papers and Panels of the Charles Ives Centennial Festival-Conference*, ed. H. Wiley Hitchcock and Vivian Perlis (Urbana: University of Illinois Press, 1977), 145–58. See also *Memos*, 67 and 105, and the comments of Otakar Zich about Mahler's use of polyphony, written in 1911 and cited in Karbusicky, *Gustav Mahler und seine Umwelt*, 129–30.

40. For Mahler's Third Symphony see the score (Vienna: Universal, UE 950); see the sections leading up to rehearsal no. 28, and particularly the transition to reh. 29 and the passage between reh. 32 and 34; and the section from reh. 44 to 55, all pp. 40–78. Following on the Mahler example, one can also compare Ives's larger orchestral works to Shostakovich, particularly the Fourth Symphony from 1935–36.

41. See the Mahler Third Symphony, 154–73. On the *Concord Sonata*, see Burkholder, *All Made of Tunes*, 350–57.

42. Richard Specht, *Mahler, III Symphonie: Thematische Analyse* (Vienna: Universal, n.d.); Paul Bekker, *Gustav Mahlers Sinfonien* (Tutzing: Schneider, 1921/1969), 103–36; Bauer Lechner, *Recollections of Gustav Mahler*, 40–41 and 58–67; Mitchell, *Gustav Mahler*, 311–62; Friedhelm Krummacher, *Gustav Mahlers III. Symphonie: Welt im Widerbild* (Kassel: Bärenreiter, 1991); Peter Franklin, *Mahler: Symphony No. 3* (Cambridge: Cambridge University Press, 1991); Bernd Sponheuer, *Logik des Zerfalls* (Tutzing: Schneider, 1978), 135–82; Hans Heinrich Eggebrecht, *Die Musik Gustav Mahlers* (Munich: Piper, 1982), 169–98; William McGrath, "'Volksseelenpolitik' and Psychological Rebirth: Mahler and Hofmannsthal, "*Journal of Interdisciplinary History* 4 (Summer 1973): 53–71.

43. See Hermann Danuser, *Gustav Mahler: Das Lied von der Erde* (Munich: Fink 1986), 83–110, and the score in the pocket edition Phiharmonia No. 217 (Vienna: Universal, 1962).

44. Adorno, *Mahler*, 35, 84–88 and 134; *Memos*, 28–34.

45. There is, for example, no equivalent in Mahler of Ives's wit and sense of playfulness, evident in his songs and college music.

46. Adorno, *Mahler,* 145. I am indebted to Peter Burkholder for bringing my attention to an article on this subject by James Hepokoski, *"Temps Perdu," The Musical Times* 135 (December 1994): 746–51. Hepokoski argues that the fade-outs which often follow the closing statements of themes in Ives denote the loss of a "cherished past." As Burkholder has pointed out, this strategy has many parallels in nineteenth-century composition. Furthermore, some works by Ives that are explicit in their reference to childhood end strongly (e.g., *Putnam's Camp*), and some with fade-outs were inspired by adult experiences (e.g., *The Housatonic at Stockbridge* and *From Hanover Square North*). This suggests rather Ives's view that modernity was itself inadequate. Childhood represented a solid, healthy, and affirmative past. Modern life was, by comparison, unstable. Spiritual firmness encountered in adult life was fleeting. Communicating the consciousness of a spiritual crisis in modern times by comparison with the past may explain better Ives's use of fade-outs. Burkholder therefore is right when he suggests that Ives's use of cumulative settings signals the "value of a usable past," not its loss. See Burkholder, *All Made of Tunes,* 469, note 70. The argument being made here points rather to such works as Ives's *Decoration Day*.

47. Bauer Lechner, *Recollections of Gustav Mahler,* 148.

48. *Essays*, 34; see also p. 73 and his essay "The Majority" and proposal for a constitutional amendment on pp. 139–214. For a view that rejects the word "nostalgia" while supporting other aspects of the argument articulated here, see Joseph W. Reed, *Three American Originals: John Ford, William Faulkner, and Charles Ives* (Middletown, Conn.: Wesleyan University Press, 1984), 54–55, and Burkholder, *All Made of Tunes,* 311 and 478, note 10.

49. On Mahler's relation to the audience, consider his reforms at the Vienna Opera, which included darkening the house and banning late comers, and his recognition that, for example, a Beethoven symphony had become so familiar that it demanded breaking with tradition and resisting the "Procrustean bed of insipid interpretation" (Mahler gives an example from Beethoven's *Eroica*). Bauer Lechner, *Recollections of Gustav Mahler,* 106–7 and 111–12.

50. *Essays*, 99. Ives's critique of Toscanini (in particular his reading of the *Eroica*) and Ives's overall critique of contemporary musical habits mirror Mahler's attitude toward conductors, performance traditions, and audience expectations. See Arthur Hall's recollections and Bernard Herrmann's account in Perlis, *Charles Ives Remembered,* 91 and 159. Ives's contempt for experts and the self-styled connoisseur and critic is distilled in his character named Rollo, who appears in *Memos*, 26–32. See also ibid., 108–10, on tuning.

51. This is the basic argument regarding Ives made in Larry Starr, *A Union of Diversities*.

52. This issue has been widely explored. See for example the collection edited by Robert B. Pynset, *Decadence and Innovation: Austro-Hungarian Life and Art at the Turn of the Century* (London: Weidenfeld and Nicolson, 1989).

53. Ives had written an Arnold overture, mentioned in *Memos*, 76. Ives was aware of Tolstoy's views. He also mentioned d'Annunzio, critically, concerning a self-conscious arrogance about idealism. Ives's attack betrayed a mix between an old fashioned moralism about doing things on account of their "intrinsic" value and a Nietzschean contempt for the pursuit of fame in the modern world. Ives's negative assessment of Debussy is in part made clearer if one considers Debussy's collaboration with d'Annunzio and the music he created in 1911 for d'Annunzio's play *Le Martyre de Saint Sebastien*. See *Essays*, 4–5 and 87–88.

54. Cowell and Cowell, *Charles Ives and His Music*, 88.

55. John Dizikes, *Opera in America: A Cultural History* (New Haven: Yale University Press, 1993), 315–16.

56. *Essays*, 5.

57. *Memos*, 71.

58. *Essays*, 93.

59. *Essays*, 101, and *Memos*, 133–36.

60. See the brilliant book by Bram Dijkstra, *Idols of Perversity: Fantasies of Feminine Evil in Fin de Siècle Culture* (New York and Oxford: Oxford University Press, 1986).

61. Morton White and Lucia White, *The Intellectual Versus the City* (Cambridge, Mass.: Harvard and MIT Press, 1962), 21–35.

62. *Essays*, 96. Editorial brackets by Boatwright.

63. The literature on this matter is extensive, beginning with Dika Newlin, *Bruckner, Mahler, Schoenberg* (New York: W. W. Norton, 1947/1978). See the Mitchell volumes cited here and the three-volume Mahler biography by Henri Louis de la Grange. One scholar, however, sought to argue Mahler's "Christian" character. See Zdenek Nejedly, excerpts from his 1912 essay "Gustav Mahler," reprinted in Karbusicky, *Gustav Mahler und seine Umwelt*, 134–35.

64. Cited in Norman Lebrecht, *Mahler Remembered* (New York: W. W. Norton, 1988), 94.

65. See for example a contemporary account of this in Arthur Elson, *Modern Composers of Europe* (Boston: Page, 1904), 36–37; see also Constantin Floros, *Gustav Mahler III: Die Symphonien* (Wiesbaden: Breitkopf und Härtel, 1985), 75–101.

66 Bauer Lechner, *Recollections of Gustav Mahler*, 63.

67. Knud Martner, ed., *Selected Letters of Gustav Mahler* (New York: Farrar, Straus and Giroux, 1979), 164–65.

68. Ralph Waldo Emerson, *Essays and Lectures*, ed. Joel Porte (New York: The Library of America, 1983), 1033; and Ives, *Essays*, 34.

69. See *Essays*, 244.

70. Friedrich Nietzsche, *The Gay Science*, trans. and with commentary by Walter Kaufmann (New York: Vintage Books, 1974), Translator's Introduction, p. 11. The standard Kaufmann translations of Nietzsche are cited here, rather than the German text.

71. *Essays*, 83.

72. See Friedrich Nietzsche, *Der Fall Wagner* and *Nietzsche contra Wagner*, in Nietzsche's *Werke*, vol. 2, ed. Karl Schlechta (Munich: Hanser, 1966), 901–38 and 1035–62; also *Essays*, 72–73.

73. Nietzsche, *The Gay Science*, 317–19. Mahler's later rejection of Nietzsche is well-documented and may have to do with his disagreement with this aspect of Nietzsche's thought.

74. Nietzsche, *The Twilight of the Idols* (1889), reprinted in *The Portable Nietzsche*, ed. and trans. Walter Kaufmann (New York: Penguin, 1976), 522; see also Nietzsche, *The Gay Science*, 191.

75. *Selected Letters of Gustav Mahler,* 165. See also William J. McGrath, "Mahler and Freud: The Dream of the Stately House," in *Gustav Mahler Kolloquium 1979: Beiträge*, ed. Rudolf Klein (Kassel: Bärenreiter, 1981), 40–51.

76. William James, *Essays in Religion and Morality* (Cambridge, Mass.: Harvard University Press, 1982), 111; and *Essays*, 35.

77. Nietzsche, *Thus Spoke Zarathustra* in *The Portable Nietzsche*, ed. and trans. Walter Kaufmann (New York: Penguin 1976), 122–24; and *Essays*, 19.

78. *Zarathustra*, 328–33; and Ives, *Essays*, 30–36.

79. Nietzsche, *The Gay Science*, 302.

80. *Zarathustra*, 161 and 174–75.

81. *Essays*, 18–21.

82. This discussion owes much to Morton White, *Science and Sentiment in America: Philosophical Thought from Jonathan Edwards to John Dewey* (New York: Oxford University Press, 1972), 71–119.

83. Ives was aware of this history. See *Essays*, 17–24.

84. Quoted in White, *Science and Sentiment in America*, 77.

85. George Santayana, *Interpretations of Poetry and Religion* (New York: Scribner's Sons, 1900), v and vii.

86. Burkholder, *Charles Ives*, 36–41; see also Wallach, "New England Education," 291–310.

87. See for example Feder, *Charles Ives*, 263.

88. James, *Essays in Religion and Morality*, 112.

89. This reads like an echo of Ives; Santayana, *Interpretations of Poetry and Religion*, 231.

90. Ibid., 230, 226, and 225.

91. John Dewey, *The Middle Works 1899–1924*, vol. 3: *1903–1906* (Carbondale and Edwardsville: Southern Illinois University Press, 1977), 185.

92. James, *Essays in Religion and Morality*, 110.

93. Ibid. 115.

94. Dewey, *The Middle Works*, 190.

95. James, *Essays in Religion and Morality*, 114.

96. *Memos*, 97.

97. Emerson, *Essays and Lectures*, 68f.

98. See Carl Schorske, "Mahler et Ives: Archaisme populiste et innovation musicale," in *Colloque Internationale Gustav Mahler 1985*, 87–97. Schorske, unlike Michael Broyles, understands Ives's politics within the rubric of populism. See Broyles's essay in this volume.

99. See Elizabeth Milroy, *Painters of a New Century: The Eight and American Art* (Milwaukee: Milwaukee Art Museum, 1991).

100. *Memos*, 81.

101. Ibid., 93, and *Essays*, 47.

102. *Memos*, 136.

103. Ibid., 78.

104. Ibid., 133.

105. *Essays*, 8 and 47.

106. James, *Essays in Religion and Morality*, 114–15.

107. See Vivian Perlis, ed., *Charles Ives Papers*, Yale University Music Library Archival Collection MSS. 14 (New Haven: Yale University Music Library, 1983), 186–95. For example, Ives is quite articulate about Richard Strauss. His critique even shares much in common with Adorno's discussion of Strauss. When Ives critiques Strauss (as in the *Essays*), it becomes clear that Ives had the *Sinfonia Domestica*, Op. 53, in mind when he made reference to "thoughts and memories of childhood" (*Essays*, 83). Ives must have been in attendance when Strauss was in New York in 1904 to conduct at Carnegie Hall and at Wanamakers, where he premiered the *Sinfonia*. Ives was more in touch with current musical events than one might suspect. He seems also to have followed modern poetry, setting recent poems by Louis Untermeyer, Vachel Lindsay, and others. See also Ives's views on the superiority of indigenous art, *Essays*, 83–86, and *Memos*, 79, 89, and 137.

108. The discussion and the reproductions of the paintings are drawn from Francis M. Naumann, *New York Dada 1915–1923* (New York: Abrams, 1994); Rebecca Zurier, Robert W. Snyder, and Virginia M. Mecklenburg, *Metropolitan Lives: The Ashcan Artists and Their New York* (New York: W. W. Norton, 1995); Milroy, *Painters of a New Century*; and Milton W. Brown, Sam Hunter, Naomi Rosenbaum, John Jacobus, and David M. Sokol, *American Art* (New York: Abrams, 1978).

109. See the *New York Tribune* article of September 12, 1915, reproduced in Naumann, *New York Dada*, 36.

110. Cited in Milroy, *Painters of a New Century*, 45.

111. Cited in Rossiter, *Charles Ives and His America*, 161–62. Ives noted, "The human anatomy can never be and has never been the inspiration for a great work of art. . . . I have felt that if a great painter could catch the radiance we see in some faces, be it homely or beautiful . . . and then gradually make invisible the things we have to look at—the eyes, the nose, the mouth, the cheeks—leaving in the picture the influence and benediction of the tender, strong and beautiful soul the metamorphosis between earth and heaven would be now nearly understood. It never will be by painting the human body" (p. 162).

112. *Essays*, 77–78.

113. The literature on this aspect of Schoenberg is immense. For an account of the cultural politics of Schoenberg's aesthetics in relation to Vienna, see Leon Botstein, "Music and the Critique of Culture: Arnold Schoenberg, Heinrich Schenker, and the Emergence of Modernism in Fin-de-Siècle Vienna," in *Constructive Dissonance: Arnold Schoenberg and Transformations of Twentieth-Century Culture*, ed. Juliane Brand and Christopher Hailey (Berkeley: University of California Press, 1996); "Arnold Schoenberg: Modernism, Language and Jewish Identity," in *Austrians and Jews in the Twentieth Century*, ed. Robert S. Wistrich (New York: St. Martin's Press, 1992); and *Judentum und Modernität* (Vienna: Böhlau, 1991). For a comparison between Ives's dichotomy of manner and substance and Schoenberg's dichotomy of style and idea, see Keith C. Ward, "Ives, Schoenberg, and the Musical Ideal," in *Charles Ives and the Classical Tradition*, ed. Geoffrey Block and J. Peter Burkholder (New Haven: Yale University Press 1996), 87–104.

114. Milroy, *Painters of a New Century*, 28.

115. The one key political difference concerns immigration and the growing presence of non-Anglo-Saxon populations in New York City. Ives's political and cultural nostalgia as well as his isolation reveal a distance and perhaps a distaste for the new ethnic poor. Ives clearly had no prejudice toward the older German or Irish immigration. In the case of turn-of-the-century New York, the question points more to the Italian, Eastern European, and Jewish immigration. Ives's silence may signal simple neutrality. But it is clear that unlike some of his contemporaries, he was neither intrigued by nor drawn to this new powerful facet of New York's life and culture. Ives's America of the past, as Rossiter and Wallach have pointed out, dated from before the great wave of immigration. Ives's project of moral restoration therefore may have been inspired by the hope of using music to communicate the essence of a past to a diverse America without its own memory of that particular past. Modernism offered a way for new populations to appropriate an American legacy (the virtues of Protestant New England traditions) they themselves did not inherit. Ives's discomfort and insularity with respect to the changing social structure of New York City does help explain his lack of interest in the Ashcan School. His mistrust of the European also sheds light on his disregard for the Armory show.

116. Private Collection (Mr. and Mrs. Robert Hurst). Reproduced in Christie's Auction *Catalogue*, May 28, 1992, Lot 218.

117. Naumann, *New York Dada*, 22–96.

118. On Hartley and Stella, their attitude to music, and their admiration for it as a model for abstraction, see Barbara Haskell, *Marsden Hartley* (New York: New York University Press, 1980) and *Joseph Stella* (New York: Harry N. Abrams, 1994).

119. Naumann, *New York Dada*, 213.

120. Wallach, *New England Education*, 95–109.

121. See the discussion of cumulative settings in Burkholder, *All Made of Tunes*, particularly pp. 245–53.

122. See Starr, *Union of Diversities*.

123. Quoted in Franklin, *Mahler: Symphony No. 3*, 28.

124. Nietzche, *Zarathustra*, 174; Franklin, *Mahler: Symphony No. 3*, 90.

125. Donald Mitchell, *Gustav Mahler: Songs and Symphonies of Life and Death* (Berkeley: University of California Press, 1985), 520–49.

126. Ibid., 430–32.

127. Quoted in John Kirkpatrick, "Preface," in Charles E. Ives, *Symphony No. 4* (New York: Associated Music Publishers, 1965), viii.

Ives's Concord Sonata and the

Texture of Music

DAVID MICHAEL HERTZ

One of the focal points of Charles Ives's oeuvre, his Piano Sonata No. 2, "*Concord, Mass., 1840–1860*" is a dense and challenging work that incorporates a variety of material drawn from earlier musical compositions, including Ives's own. Tracing the similarities of the earlier textures for keyboard music that Charles Ives knew in relation to the great *Concord Sonata* he created shows how Ives absorbed and rebelled, nourished himself and created himself in relation to the great masters of keyboard composition. In his manner, he is uniquely Emersonian, displaying a brilliant optimism and scope as he allowed his ear to roam the musical worlds of the humble and the refined, drawing them together in the mammoth achievement that is the *Concord Sonata*.

Ives is situated in music history in a position parallel to Walt Whitman's in literary history. Ives had American precursors, but they were as mediocre or as nondescript as were Whitman's indigenous precursor-poets, and they are now forgotten. In his massive cultural biography of Whitman, David S. Reynolds describes some of Ives's precursors: Richard Hoffman, Charles Grobe, and Anthony Phillip Heinrich.[1] They were antebellum composers who had already displayed Ives's predilection for blending American popular music with European art music. Whitman, who knew of their work, was more capable than they of inventing a powerful expression of the American dualism connecting popular and elitist art.

The strongest precursors for Ives's keyboard music—Beethoven, Liszt, Chopin, Scriabin, and Debussy—were in Europe. The Europeans were great keyboard masters who had pushed the instrument and the virtuoso to new limits. And Ives knew their work. His *Concord Sonata* is an Emersonian assertion of musical independence written in a way that situates it as a keyboard masterpiece in its own right, as a work that takes its deserved place alongside the achievement of these earlier composers.

Musical texture is recycled just as words are recycled in language. Writers capture words and place them in their personal constructions, where they reside for a time. The same words may be used again, recaptured by another writer in another literary construction. Original writers instigate a Lucretian swerve of literary atoms, as they play against the works of their creative forebears, troping new meanings out of older ones. A *trope* is a turn of meaning that positions itself in relation to an earlier meaning. It is an act of both reinterpretation and creation. All creative life depends upon such turns and swerves in response to earlier material.[2] Meanings may change, as clever writers may turn their meanings by troping against earlier usages. But nobody owns words, and they travel to other writers and other times and places. The same goes for the textures of music, which are composed of all sorts of sound materials. Among the many kinds of musical phenomena that travel from composer to composer are sonorities, melodic patterns, voicings of chords, rhythms, motivic details, arpeggiated textures, and methods of stringing together musical ideas. These are encoded in the notated dance of the hands, as composers have inscribed them in keyboard scores through the last three centuries.

The history of the keyboard and its music cannot be reduced to a narration of the vast and brilliant literature written for it or a descriptive sequence of technological developments in the construction of instruments; the two evolved together. Keyboard music also traces a history of the human hand and its connection to the mind. The texture of music for keyboard reflects the history of the imagination, for it is the imagination of ingenious composers that shaped movement for the hand in relation to the possibilities of the keyboard. The great piano works of Charles Ives are a significant part of this history.

The appropriation of musical quotations from music by others is a procedure for which Charles Ives is famous. It is the most obvious example of the many ways in which musical texture flows from composer to composer, and Ives is a famous example of a musical quoter. By no means is he the only one among the great composers. Studying the traces of music by others in Ives's *Concord Sonata* shows how the texture of earlier music yields to the craft of a later master composer. But Ives was a master who lived and wrote in Danbury and New York City, not Vienna or Paris. He worked mostly in isolation, rarely hearing a performance of his musical compositions until well after he stopped composing actively. Not content to work in an established musical style developed by others, Ives was also a musical explorer intent on pushing back the frontiers of sound to claim new territory for musical understanding and measurement.

The *Concord Sonata* was more gigantic and more ambitious than any previous keyboard sonata. Like many of its European precursors, it is written in four movements. Each movement of the *Concord Sonata* has a programmatic title: "Emerson," "Hawthorne," "The Alcotts," and "Thoreau." In terms of style, mood, and the overall architectural placement of the series of movements, each movement corresponds roughly to the plan of the European sonata, a formal arrangement of musical structure widely used from Beethoven through Hindemith. "Emerson" corresponds with the first movement sonata allegro; "Hawthorne" with the second movement scherzo; "The Alcotts" with the standard slow third movement; and "Thoreau" with the quicker finale-rondo (which also customarily could be in first movement allegro form or a theme and variations). While Ives retains some features of this format, there are crucial differences that make the *Concord Sonata* unlike any of its precursors.

Although Ives clearly used various European sonata forms as his models, he also developed something so new and revolutionary that it overshadows any amount of appropriation from earlier music for his own artistic ends. In fact, Ives's musical borrowings serve to make his revolutionary notion comprehensible and distinct, heightening his originality rather than diminishing it.

Ives's revolutionary idea was the conception of cumulative form. It is the master trope of his work as both composer and philosopher of music, for it changed his relationship to the entire history of music and enabled him to embrace a wide variety of precursor materials in a highly complex but flexible new form. Its importance has recently been demonstrated by J. Peter Burkholder in *All Made of Tunes: Charles Ives and the Uses of Musical Borrowing*.[3]

In Europe, the musical ideas of the sonata were presented first and then developed in a clear system. They were then repeated in a distinct summation, which lucidly reiterates ideas presented earlier. In one of his typical movements written in cumulative form, Ives does away with this pattern of organization, and instead presents the development first, saving the statement of the main theme until the end. He thus allows themes to emerge out of great masses of sounds, causing our ears to slowly recognize the familiar buried among strange and challenging clusters of musical material. This is Ives's Emersonian undoing of stodgy tradition, and its importance in the *Concord Sonata* cannot be underestimated. As far as I know, there is nothing like cumulative form in the works of composers that Ives rewrites into his *Concord Sonata*, even in the piano works of the revolutionary premodernists such as Debussy or Scriabin who were active around the turn of the century.

The *Concord Sonata* is written in a type of cumulative form slightly more hybrid in its nature than the purer examples of the form Ives used for, say, his four violin sonatas. In the *Concord Sonata*, the thematic process of accumulation involves all four movements, not just one, and the themes emerge with greatest clarity at the conclusion of "The Alcotts," which is the penultimate movement, not the last one. Here, at what might be thought of as the focal crux of the work, one finds the sharpest crystallization of its principal themes.[4] Nevertheless, all four movements show procedures common to Ives's cumulative form. Three of them—"Emerson," "The Alcotts," and "Thoreau"—have the culminating appearance of clearly expressed thematic material in the coda sections.

For a clear introduction of thematic material without the competition of cadenza textures, the listener has to wait. Ives always prefers to suppress—and perhaps repress—the true expression of his lyrical nature, forcing the listener (and himself) to work for its arrival, to earn its pleasures through hard aural exertions. By the time we have the gratification of hearing a full flowering of the thematic material in the *Concord Sonata*, our ears have been exposed to hidden or submerged material, expressed in fragmented form, buried in other masses of sound for over thirty minutes.

In addition to his ambitious score, Ives wrote the thoughtful and complex *Essays Before A Sonata*, a series of Emersonian literary meditations that accompany the musical work. While the *Concord Sonata* was probably written over a long period of time, chiefly between 1909 and 1919, the *Essays* were primarily written from 1919 to 1920 (although some of the material on Emerson may go back to Ives's student days at Yale, when he studied Emerson with William Lyon Phelps).[5] Both the sonata and the *Essays* were published in 1920. Since the *Essays* were conceived so closely to the sonata, it is not surprising that they are crucial to any serious understanding of the latter. And since he worked on both of them during the most fertile period of his composing career, they are seminal to any serious understanding of Ives's music.

Far from serving as a mere programmatic statement in the high Romantic style, the *Essays* contain many clues about Ives's method and purpose, important statements on Ives's general aesthetic position, and his specific views of music by other composers. *Essays Before a*

Sonata consists of seven sections. There is an essay for each of the four movements of the sonata. In addition, Ives adds an "Author's Preface," a "Prologue" and an "Epilogue." Although each section is important, and all of them should be read together as a whole, the three added sections contain perhaps even more secrets to Ives's method than the four sections named for each movement.

Ives was part of a vast cultural shift in musical history which is first clearly marked by Debussy's swerve from the *Gesamtkunstwerk* of Wagner in the 1880s. Ives's achievement, like Debussy's, contributes to move art music away from older architectural models toward newer psycho-perceptual models of musical composition. We find evidence of this in the Author's Preface (xxv),[6] in which Ives uses the word "impression" four times while attempting to give an overview of what he is doing:

1. "the whole is an attempt to present (one person's) impression . . ."
2. "in impressionistic pictures of Emerson and Thoreau . . ."
3. "composite pictures or impressions . . ."
4. "far from accepted impressions . . ."

Rather than create an architectonic structure in which every note is related to every other note in a taut interrelationship, Ives clearly is out to do something else—to capture the musical expression of psychological experience in measured sound.

Following Ives's statement of purpose in his preface, the Prologue is an enigmatic meditation on the relation between music and representation. In it Ives wonders how nostalgia, memory, experience, and emotion coalesce in musical expression. The unconscious and the conscious are viewed as part of a larger understanding of the mind, which enables artistic intuition to flow into musical sound. Ives considers the extremes of program music and abstract music as opposite ends of the same musical spectrum, and he ponders the unique communicative process of music and the variety of responses it can create.

Ives has little to say about other composers that is flattering. But when he discusses the music of others, including his most powerful European precursors, he is exposing many of the anxieties and struggles that were crucial to the formation of his aesthetic stance as a composer and musical theorist. For this reason, the Epilogue is a major essay on style and originality as they pertain to Ives's own method. Here Ives's lively statements on music by other composers—among them Beethoven, Wagner, Chopin, Brahms, and Debussy—expose his artistic uneasiness with significant musical influences, and he considers issues ranging from popular culture to European art music while at the same time reflecting on the value of the metaphors of "evolution" and "progress" for changing musical styles.

Studying *Essays Before A Sonata* together with Ives's score clarifies the important role in which Emerson served: as a defense against the European models Ives wished to subsume. Emerson gets not only an important chapter of his own in the *Essays*, but he returns as a unifying factor in the Epilogue, as Ives summarizes his views. Ives's Emersonianism helped him devour the earlier works of European composers precisely where those passages in the *Concord Sonata* resemble the works of those composers.[7] As Ives writes in the penultimate paragraph of his Epilogue to the *Essays*,

> No true composer will take his substance from another finite being—but there are times when he feels that his self-expression needs some liberation from at least a part of his own soul. At such times, shall he not better turn to those greater souls, rather than to the external, the immediate, and the "Garish Day"? (102)

Ives understood well that there are two poles in the Emersonian dialectic of creative originality. One is to "insist on yourself," which is best expressed in Emerson's "Self-Reliance." The other is that "all minds quote." This message is most clearly found in Emerson's "Quotation and Originality," one of his lesser-known works.[8] It is the reconciliation between the two that fascinates Ives in his own *Essays*. Emerson helped Ives see that quotation is useful and appropriate to the composer of real talent. (Ives would describe himself as a composer of "substance," not "manner.") The quotation from a composer who worked in the past used by a composer working in the present functions just as nature does when its own materials are recycled through its processes of decay and regeneration:

> Every book is a quotation; and every house is a quotation out of all forests and mines and stone-quarries; and every man is a quotation from all his ancestors. . . . The Past is for us; but the sole terms on which it can become ours are its subordination to the Present. . . . The Profound apprehension of the Present is Genius.[9]

The strong personality understands the present moment and makes the old material work in the needed new context. Music of the past must serve the present and the future. In Ives's view, the composer of genius understands this rhythm. This is more of an essential aspect of creativity, which Ives sees as a synthesizing process, than the need to invent totally new ideas.

Ives shows his understanding of Emerson's notion of originality clearly in his own "Emerson" essay, in which he paraphrases Emerson's words:

> If we would stop and trust heavily on the harvest of originality, he [Emerson] shows us that this plant—this part of the garden— is but a relative thing. It is dependent also on the richness that ages have put into the soil. "Every thinker is retrospective." (15)

Along with inspiration, Emerson may have given Ives a more specific and pragmatic formal plan for his cumulative form, for he noted that Emerson's "codas often seem to crystallize in a dramatic though serene and sustained way the truths of his subject—they become more active and intense, but quieter and deeper" (25). According to Ives, the clearest expression of Emerson's thought typically comes at the end of his essay, where there is a moment of clarifying summation. Ives used similar language to describe his own music. In the program note for the 1917 premiere of his Third Violin Sonata, Ives described his own coda as a musical space for crystallization and final clarification: "The last movement is an experiment: The free fantasia is first. The working-out develops into the themes, rather than from them. The coda consists of the themes for the first time in their entirety and in conjunction."[10]

In choosing cumulative form over more standardized European sonata forms, Ives was making a conscious aesthetic choice that amounted to a musical declaration of independence. He explicitly expresses his dissatisfaction with the European sonata model in the Epilogue of the *Essays*. He discusses it in terms of a jaded musical critic who has been on the beat for so long that he no longer really listens to the dull procedure of sonata form while he hears it:

> A critic has to listen to a thousand concerts a year, in which there is much repetition, not only of the same pieces, but the same formal relations of tones, cadences, progressions, etc. There is present a certain routine series of image-necessity-stimulants, which he doesn't seem to need until they disappear. Instead of listening to music, he listens around it. And from this subconscious viewpoint, he inclines perhaps more to the thinking about than thinking in music. If he could go into some

other line of business for a year or so, perhaps his perspective would be more naturally normal. The unity of a sonata movement has been long associated with its form, and to a greater extent than is necessary. A first theme, a development, a second in a related key and its development, the free fantasia, the recapitulation, and so on, and over again. Mr. Richter or Mr. Parker may tell us that all this is natural, for it is based on the classic song form; but in spite of your teachers a vague feeling sometimes creeps over you that the form-nature of the song has been stretched out into deformity. (98–99)

The orderly European presentation of musical materials had become a sterile procedure for Ives. He rarely used it after his early work, and he chose a very different path for the *Concord Sonata*.

Ives's new path enabled him to absorb a tremendous variety of musical materials culled from the works of earlier composers. Among the subsumed or co-opted earlier works in Ives's *Concord Sonata* are Beethoven's "Hammerklavier" Sonata, Op. 106 (1819), and Liszt's Sonata in B minor (1852). In his *Memos*, Ives dismisses Chopin as a composer who wore a skirt, but there are clear traces of the French-Polish composer as well, and I will discuss some of them. Debussy and Scriabin were more closely competitive contemporaries. Not only did Ives own personal copies of scores by these composers, but there are traces of their personalities in Ives's music, and their proximity to Ives's position in the unfolding history of art music made them far more dangerous to Ives's delicate sense of his own originality.[11]

What does it mean to co-opt a piece of music? To masterfully take over what is useful in it and use this useful material for music that is new and just as powerful and original. The new material forces its presence into the world of musical expression, resounding backwards into musical history, just as the older material resounds forwards. The new material tropes against the older creation, supplanting its primacy, pushing it into a lesser position. The older music is finally sublimated into the newer material, carefully reworked through the imagination of the later composer until mastery is obtained and what was original once before becomes original once again.

Ives carefully sublimated the opening motive of the Fifth Symphony (Figure 3.1) and the opening motive of the "Hammerklavier" Sonata (Figure 3.2), two of Beethoven's most famous musical ideas, into the central lyric theme of the *Concord Sonata*. The clearest crystallization of this theme occurs at the concluding climax of "The Alcotts," the third movement, shown in Figure 3.3.[12] Ives calls it the "human-faith-melody":

> All around you, under the Concord sky, there still floats the influence of that human-faith-melody—transcendent and sentimental enough for the enthusiast or the cynic, respectively—reflecting an innate hope, a common interest in common things and common men—a tune the Concord bards are ever playing while they pound away at the immensities with a Beethoven-like sublimity, and with, may we say, a vehemence and perseverance, for that part of greatness is not so difficult to emulate. (47–48)

Figure 3.1: Ludwig van Beethoven, Symphony No. 5 in C minor, mm. 1–2

Figure 3.2: Beethoven, Sonata in B-Flat Major, Op. 106, "Hammerklavier," mm. 1–2

The full flowering of the human-faith-melody is a highly complex idea, involving a reworking of material from two Beethoven masterworks and at least two popular hymn tunes from Ives's own native culture. The two hymns, Charles Zeuner's *Missionary Chant* (Figure 3.4) and Simeon B. Marsh's *Martyn* (Figure 3.5), have musical features that are far too close to the Beethoven motives to be anything other than carefully calculated choices. Ives obviously wanted to blend the famous motives that a European composer had used to erect huge, magisterial musical edifices with the humbler material of hometown church chorales. Radically altered and reset in slow motion, the four notes of the Fifth Symphony and the similarly brief motive of the

"Hammerklavier" Sonata nevertheless resound throughout the *Concord Sonata*.

Figure 3.3: Charles Ives, Human-Faith-Melody as it appears at the end of "The Alcotts," *Concord Sonata*, p. 57, systems 4–5

Figure 3.4: H. Charles Zeuner, *Missionary Chant*

Figure 3.5: Simeon Marsh, *Martyn*

In the *Concord Sonata*, Ives sought to create a towering musical challenge of gigantic length and extreme technical difficulty. Beethoven was the European master most noted for this type of composition. There was an aural machismo in Beethoven's music for Ives: "Beethoven had to pull the ear hard and several times" (99). Beethoven's massive "Hammerklavier" Sonata is certainly the most glaring precedent in art music that Ives faced. It is a work of incredible daring and almost overwhelming length, consisting of four movements and a short transitional section. Ives chose a similar four-movement plan for the *Concord Sonata*. Twentieth-century listeners who take Beethoven's compositions for granted as standard classics must remember that nothing like the "Hammerklavier" Sonata existed before Beethoven wrote it. Ives outdid him, expanding the nature and scale of the tendency toward gigantism for keyboard composition.

"Hawthorne," which Ives described as a scherzo, has a precursor in the scherzo of Op. 106. *Scherzo* means joke in Italian, and it originated as a short diversion in the classical sonata of the eighteenth century. Beethoven was the first classical composer to incorporate the scherzo into the keyboard sonata, replacing the stately minuet with a form that accommodated his more uproarious humor. But in the nineteenth century the jest of the scherzo became macabre and ironic, and resulted in extended forms. Beethoven's great scherzo for the Op. 106, certainly the hugest written at the date of its composition (1817–18), contains abrupt contrasts in dynamics and sudden changes in tempi. Most notable is the surprise ending, which features an abrupt departure from B-flat major, the sudden ebbing of the tempo into a D major reverie, and then the jarring return—worked out with almost Lisztian octave unisons—to the principal B-flat major tonality of the composition. The abrupt contrast in dynamics and texture was one of Beethoven's trademarks, but here it is exaggerated to an especially extensive degree. The huge fugue of the last movement also contains a surprise chorale in D major, which creates another startling contrast to the driving contrapuntal texture that dominates the movement. Both of these D major surprises, however, are prepared by a more conservative and obvious modulation to the submediant tonality in the first movement, a plan that, as Charles Rosen has shown, is similar to those Beethoven used elsewhere in his thirty-two sonatas.[13]

Ives extends the practice of the Beethovenian surprise to new extremes, creating far more abrupt variations in dynamics, tempo, and texture. The contrasts of the Op. 106 scherzo echo in "Hawthorne," in which Ives shapes musical ideas into paradoxical contradictions that even Beethoven could never have predicted. In Beethoven's work the surprise D major sections are clearly distinct from the preceding B-flat sections, however abruptly introduced and startlingly varied from the earlier music. In Ives's work, tranquil new music appears to overlap with the turbulent outerlayers of "Hawthorne," as if this music were an embracing underlayer of celestial tranquility that had been going on all the time and was only temporarily drowned out. Another dimension of musical sound seems to have existed in a parallel universe. It is Ives's trope on the *Martyn* hymn, which, appearing in fragmentary form here, seems to be intoning under the music like the chorale of harmonies under the dissonances in Ives's *Unanswered Question*. When the great roar of "Hawthorne" abruptly ceases, as in Figure 3.6, the ear detects the harmonious chords, a blend of *Martyn* and Beethovenian triads, revealed as if they had been resounding both before and after, and even during, the entire movement of "Hawthorne." Nicolas Slonimsky, one of Ives's important early interpreters, first described this uniquely Ivesian device as "sonic exuviation."[14]

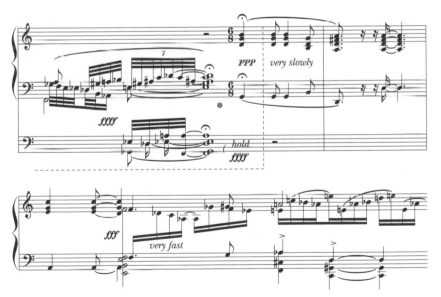

Figure 3.6: Ives, "Hawthorne," *Concord Sonata*, p. 33, systems 1–2

The manner of manipulation of musical material in the *Concord* is more like Liszt's great Sonata in B minor than the large-scale works of any of the other keyboard composers of the nineteenth century. As a close reading of the two scores reveals, Liszt was Ives's closest precursor in terms of developing musical structure. Ives must have known this famous work, but he uses Liszt's technique to his own advantage and in an entirely fresh way. In the music of both Ives and Liszt, thematic fragments that at first seem insignificant assume great structural importance as they turn up in a great variety of contexts, gradually asserting a sort of hermetic unity. The full implications arrive later. The great variety of dramatic contexts in which Liszt manages to use his fragmentary motives is still startling today. Ives achieves a similar effect, but he carries it to a much greater extent.

Liszt actually offers a precursor version of Ives's cumulative form. Liszt's material at first appears in fragmentary form and then accrues greater wholeness and visibility while the meaning of the ideas becomes more apparent as the piece proceeds. The concluding pages of Liszt's work offer the clearest expressions of his material, similar to the conclusions of Ives's cumulative forms.

Liszt's method should be contrasted with the periodic structure of Haydn, Mozart, and Beethoven, in which musical ideas are clearly stated early on and in clear symmetrical phrases with demarcated beginnings, middles, and ends.[15] It is true that their musical ideas are also developed in fuller expressions, but for them development meant a breakup and expansion of clearly stated musical materials that had been expressed at earlier points in their compositions. For Ives and Liszt, clear thematic expression did not need to precede such developmental procedures.

Four principal motivic kernels generate the Liszt sonata, as illustrated in Figures 3.7a and 3.7b. Additional material is added in the slow section of the work. The motives are continually developed in an increasingly wide variety of contexts, and the various major sections—large enough to be separate movements—are connected without pause. "Emerson" has a similar number of principal motives, shown in Figure 3.8, and a similar pattern of continuous development. The great variety of materials and moods also gives the impression of combining different movements in a single large entity.[16] Some of this material also turns up in other movements of the *Concord Sonata*, linking all four movements as the themes accumulate shape and clarity.

Figure 3.7a: Liszt, Sonata in B Minor, mm. 1–15

Liszt holds back his Grandioso theme in D major until well into his sonata. Ives makes a similar move with his main contrasting theme, which first appears in its full incarnation on page five of "Emerson." This theme has an open, quasi-pentatonic quality; its full entrance is marked by a change in tempo; and it has a clear tonality. These features set the main contrasting theme apart clearly from the three other principal motives that occur on the first page, although its opening notes also appear, buried in fragmentary prefigurings, within the dense opening bars of "Emerson."

Figure 3.7b: Liszt, Sonata in B Minor, mm. 105–108 (Grandioso theme)

Ives would have noted the various odd extremes in changing tempi of the second principal motive of the Liszt sonata.[17] The motive first appears in its faster versions, and then in dreamier incarnations in augmented form, or with a light textural filigree, or rewritten in octave exclamation. The motive emerges into full melodic implications near the end of the sonata, as if it had been accumulating the necessary energy to do so all along. Here Liszt achieves something similar to the cumulative form of Ives, with the final brilliant burst of octaves for right hand and left hand achieving a full symmetrical flowering of the material. This moment, which is the climax of the Liszt sonata, occupies a spot parallel to the cumulative expressions of thematic material at the ends of "Emerson," "The Alcotts," and, especially, "Thoreau." All of these are codas of crystallization, in which the listener is rewarded with a clear and fully shaped version of thematic material that has already appeared in fragmentary form in earlier musical textures.

Figure 3.8: Ives, "Emerson," *Concord Sonata*, p. 1, systems 1–4. The principal motives are indicated.

Beethoven, Op. 106

Figure 3.8, continued

A similar heaping up of themes occurs in the climax-before-the-close of each of the two works, creating the effect of a kind of culminating summation, followed by a hushed and meditative conclusion. The main strands are finally sewn together in clear, fully formed realization. Near the end of the Liszt sonata (Figure 3.9), there is a presto reprise of the first motive. Next, the second motive, reorchestrated in octaves, actually becomes a symmetrical period of eight bars. As opposed to its initial occurrence, in which it outlined a diminished seventh chord, it finally outlines a stable major chord. Then the left hand responds to echo the right-hand octaves for six bars. A cascade of chromatic octaves follows, leading directly to the grand and final pronouncement of the Grandioso theme.

Figure 3.9: Liszt, Sonata in B Minor, cumulative climax, mm. 673–703. The motives, transformed into varied shapes, are indicated.

Figure 3.9, continued

Ives similarly brings together the signature motive for "Emerson," the full human-faith-melody (containing the Zeuner and Marsh hymns, as well as the Fifth Symphony and "Hammerklavier" quotations), and a fragment taken from Stephen Foster's popular song "Massa's in de Cold Ground" at the end of "Thoreau." At the end of "Emerson," the Emerson motive, the principal motives of Beethoven's Fifth Symphony and Op. 106 (both fragments of the human-faith-melody), and the quasi-pentatonic theme are treated in an extended melodic form and diverse stretto configurations (Figure 3.10). Both

Figure 3.10: Ives, "Emerson," *Concord Sonata*, p. 18, systems 4 and 5, and p. 19, system 1. The various motives are indicated.

the Ives and the Liszt sonatas come to a hushed close shortly after
these culminating expressions of their main materials. Ives ends
"Thoreau" with a last quotation of the Fifth Symphony and a D major
seventh chord. Liszt ends his sonata with a B major chord, sounded
three times to create an intensely mysterious pianissimo.

There are crucial differences in the two works which become more
obvious once their familial similarity is noted. In the Liszt sonata, the
diverse components or fragments are introduced in clear sequence. Their
importance becomes more apparent in the music that follows as they recur
and blend into many varied textures. They first appear in rapid sequence,
but one clearly follows the other, without interruptions or overlapping.

What is strange and new in the opening staves of "Emerson" is that
all three motives are hidden in a dense thicket of sound masses; the
ear has to take them in almost simultaneously because they are buried
in a heap of free, unregulated sounds. Actually, they too appear in
sequence. First comes a fragment from the human-faith-melody, then
the famous four notes from Beethoven's Fifth Symphony emerge with
two overlapping entries, then the Emerson motive appears, and
finally Beethoven's Fifth Symphony returns. All of this occurs within
the first two systems. But there is a great deal of additional music
going on as well. In the Liszt sonata there is no such interference from
conflicting sounds. The thematic material of the work appears in a
clear, unobstructed sequence. Ives seems to be using musical form to
express the simultaneity and complexity of experience, a preoccupation that did not yet concern Liszt. In this sense, Ives displays a tendency common to many modernist artists working in a variety of
media in the early years of the twentieth century.

The musical texture of a number of specific passages in "Emerson"
relates to some of Liszt's work, such as the Andante sostenuto section
of the Sonata in B minor. Ives was probably attracted to the texture of
a sustained melodic line over a widely spaced harmonic pattern and
the mixture of long notes and rapid configurations. The two fugues—
one two-thirds into "Emerson" and the other at roughly the same
point in the Liszt sonata—create similar effects in the two works. Both
initiate new momentum after a slow middle section, creating tension
that leads to a climactic denouement. Elsewhere in Ives's huge sonata,
there are similar textural configurations that remind a practicing
pianist of Liszt. In "Hawthorne," for example, swirling passages create a musical texture that is prefigured in the transitional sections at
the exposition and recapitulation of the Liszt sonata.

The quasi-pentatonic theme of "Emerson" and the broad D major
theme of the Liszt sonata occur in parallel places in each work. In the

heart of his sonata, Liszt varies his broad D major theme by rewriting the long notes of the melody with rapid improvisatory notes. Liszt also uses similar techniques as he resets the third motive of the work in the more melodic incarnations of D, A, and B major, transforming the tiny musical unit into a broad lyrical pattern. In the Quasi Adagio section of the Liszt sonata the contrast between the augmented version of the third motive in its lyrical expansion and the rapid improvisatory notes that punctuate this statement are particularly effective, as shown in Figure 3.11. Ives achieves similar effects with his quasi-pentatonic

Figure 3.11: Liszt, Sonata in B Minor, mm. 347–55. Note the A major treatment of the third motive, now transformed into a lyrical phrase punctuated by rapid notes.

theme in "Emerson," adding rapid notes as he reorchestrates the theme, which is still clearly recognizable but now worked out with greater dissonances. On p. 7, systems 1–2 of "Emerson," shown in Figure 3.12, he suspends his quasi-pentatonic theme in long notes under rapid arpeggiated patterns requiring both right and left hands.

After this rather Lisztian maneuver, the left-hand arpeggios support the long climbing lyrical line in a manner resembling the broad arpeggiated patterns elsewhere in the more tranquil middle section of the

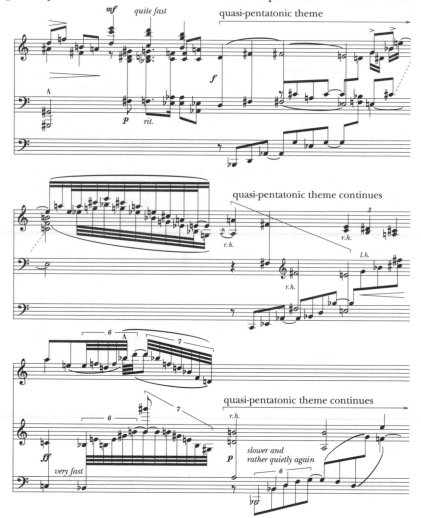

Figure 3.12: Ives, "Emerson," *Concord Sonata*, p. 7, systems 1–2

Liszt. In the bottom system of page seven of "Emerson," Ives alternates between a low A and a high C♯, harmonious but broadly spaced, which intone like ringing Concord bells (Figure 3.13). Between them rapid thirty-second notes race by, as if complex dissonances are meant to be captured in the embrace of broad consonance. Perhaps it is not a coincidence that Ives chose this arrangement, for he was clearly aware of his Romantic precursor, Liszt, who uses A major for the similar passage in his sonata. But once again, Ives has added something new, creating an effect of superimposing rapid improvisatory notes upon a widely spaced and consonant melodic pattern, whereas the earlier composer could only think of treating them in sequence. As Ives well knew, Emerson wrote that "only an inventor knows how to borrow."[18] Ives borrowed, absorbed, and added significantly to the method of Liszt.

Links between Ives's *Concord Sonata* and the work of Frédéric Chopin are stronger than Ives's comments about Chopin might suggest. Ives ridiculed Chopin as a composer who wore a skirt, but one, he admits, Chopin "made himself."[19] Yet underneath Ives's attempt to dismiss Chopin as a sissy composer lies a begrudging admiration.

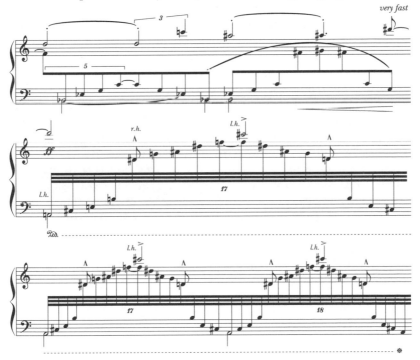

Figure 3.13: Ives, "Emerson," *Concord Sonata*, p. 7, systems 3–4

Chopin had perhaps the greatest gift for melodic writing for the keyboard in the entire nineteenth century, and Ives, too, was a gifted melodist. Not surprisingly, there are echoes of the French-Polish composer in the *Concord Sonata*.

Most particularly of interest are Chopin's Ballades, Opp. 23 and 52 (1836 and 1843), and the C minor Etude (1833), Op. 10, No. 12 ("Revolutionary"). Chopin's two great piano sonatas, Opp. 35 and 58, are also written in the four-movement plan that serves as a model for Ives's *Concord*. Ives certainly was aware of them, probably finding the most intrigue with the more uncommon Op. 35 (1840), which includes the famous "Marche funèbre" and a unique last movement presto. Chopin wrote four independent scherzi for solo piano and two others incorporated within the larger four-movement architecture of his sonatas. Including the two scherzo movements of the two sonatas, there are a total of six scherzi that Ives would have noticed. In the Preludes (1839), the pianist also finds passagework that foreshadows movements of the hand articulated in the *Concord Sonata*.

The scherzino passages of the Opp. 23 and 52 Ballades are obvious links to "Emerson," with its rich rhythmic complexity and syncopation. These scherzini are interludes, offering relief from Chopin's method—a unique innovation in his ballades—of reiterating thematic material in increasingly complex and ever more dramatic contexts. Ives's "Poetry" interlude in "Emerson" (pp. 8–11) serves a similar purpose to the Chopin scherzini in these two ballades. The left-hand passagework of the Etude in C Minor, Op. 10, No. 12 (Figure 3.14), is so close to Ives's music here that one suspects that Ives practiced it. In Ives's work the more modern incarnation of Chopin's revolutionary étude (revolutionary also in the way in which the human hand is used to achieve the desired effect) reappears in C Major, not C Minor, but it is a blues-like, irregular expression of the musical idea, creating a new and modern exuberance that is not in the Chopin étude itself (Figure 3.15). Another similar spot that any pianist would recognize is the left-hand pattern in "Emerson," p. 10, system 3 (Figure 3.16). Here the Ives texture plays in the hand like an altered version of the Chopin Prelude in G Major, Op. 28, No. 3 (Figure 3.17).

Figure 3.14: Chopin, Etude, Op. 10, No. 12, "Revolutionary," mm. 10–12

Figure 3.15: Ives, "Emerson," *Concord Sonata*, p. 9, system 4

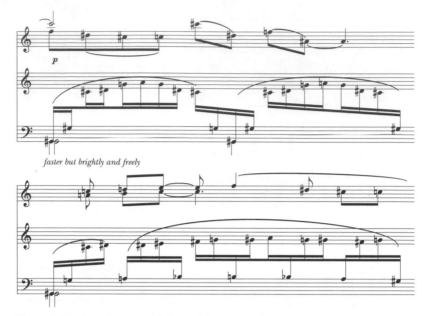

Figure 3.16: Ives, "Emerson," *Concord Sonata*, p. 10, system 3

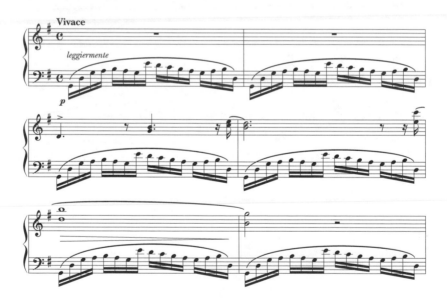

Figure 3.17: Chopin, Prelude in G Major, Op. 28, No. 3, mm. 1–6

The idea of a scherzo as a great dramatic rush of spun notes, played at great speed, is first presented by Chopin, in his great B minor Scherzo, Op. 20 (1835). This piece, already long popular among the virtuosi of Ives's era, would certainly have been echoing in Ives's inner ear as he composed in seclusion. Compared to the wild liberties of "Hawthorne," however, Chopin's scherzo is written in rather conservative eight-bar periods, with a simple ternary form, a folk melody for a middle section (possibly modeled on a Polish Christmas Carol), and a decisive coda. While Ives obviously noticed Beethoven's "Hammerklavier," the texture of music in "Hawthorne" is far closer to the texture of the Chopin scherzo than it is to the simple rhythmic patterns of Beethoven's scherzo in Op. 106. Another model may have been the presto of the Op. 35 Sonata, which is made up of rapidly moving unison voices played by both right and left hands. It is highly dissonant and features ascending diminished seventh chords which precede each entry of its principal B-flat minor theme. Its radical nature could have influenced Ives's notion of texture in "Hawthorne." Chopin's B-flat minor sonata was so popular among the virtuosi of the early twentieth century that the musical satirist Erik Satie chose to lampoon it in his *Embryons desséchés* ("Dried-up Embryoes"). Surely Ives knew it well.

The great mountain range of sound that is the *Concord Sonata* is not modeled on the structural norms of German classicism. It is closer to the sound pictures of the first musical modernist, Claude Debussy. *Arabesques* (1888), *Estampes* (1903), *Images* (1905 and 1907), and many other Debussy titles for musical works are visual in orientation.[20] Debussy's rebellion is already implied in these words. A florid design, a print, or an image are hardly typical words used for titles of sentimental Romantic works. Debussy and Ives were aware of the sensory complexity of psychological perception and how this activity melds with memory. Music taps into the subtleties of mental process, and both composers created a music that was far closer to this activity in orientation than, say, the more architectural plans of Bach, Beethoven, or Mozart. Ives, who deals with such issues in the *Essays,* expresses an uneasy admiration for Debussy. While Ives admits that Debussy esteems the beauty of nature in *La Mer* (1905), Ives debunks Debussy as merely a city composer who makes weekend flights to the country. Debussy, who was extremely close to the French Symbolist poets, was also commonly linked with the Impressionist painters. Both the Impressionists and the Symbolists were experimenting with ways to allow the flexible character of the natural process of perception to achieve a privileged and central status in the construction of their art works. In this sense, both Symbolists and Impressionists might be relabeled as *perceptionists*.[21]

Ives's numerous claims in his *Essays* that he is attempting to create "impressions" links him clearly to his French artistic precursors, as well as to other contemporaries such as Freud, Bergson, and Wittgenstein. Ives's notion of his *Concord Sonata* as a project to render "musical impressions" should be remembered in relation to the image of the human mind that emerges in the combined European oeuvre of Freud and Proust, produced at around the same time. We should also not forget that William James (1842–1910), Ives's fellow American, focused new attention on phenomenological experience, rather than on a priori categorization for an understanding of the mind, and invented the term "stream-of-consciousness." Both James and Ives give us a more flexible understanding of mental process as it negotiates experience and memory. Ives does so in his sound collages, James in his philosophical tracts.

Debussy was the composer chiefly responsible for destabilizing diatonic key relationships in favor of investigating sounds as a free phenomenon in musical scores. Ives continues this trend, taking the implications of Debussy's work much further than the French composer would have imagined was possible (or desirable). At times, Ives uses devices for which Debussy was famous. Examples are the pentatonic and whole-tone scales, or nondiatonic clusters of seconds and thirds. All of these are used profitably in the *Concord Sonata*.

For example, in "Hawthorne" Ives uses a fourteen-and-three-quarter-inch board to make pentatonic sound masses in the right hand, while a Debussyean melody appears in the lower register. If an adventurous pianist would like to try an experiment that would have thoroughly annoyed both Ives and Debussy, he or she might try playing the first eight bars of Debussy's *Hommage à Rameau*, from *Images*, Book I (Figure 3.18a), followed by p. 25 of "Hawthorne" (with left hand and board) from the top of the page until the bar line in the fourth system (Figure 3.18b), then the first eight bars of *Hommage à Rameau* again. The whole makes a delightful little A B A form that fits together extremely well.

In "The Alcotts," whole-tone scales are used to prepare for the climactic presentation of the cumulative expression of the principal themes in a manner reminiscent of Debussy's *L'Isle joyeuse* (1904) and some of his other keyboard works. In "Thoreau," the parts of the music that seem to convey the notion of Thoreau meditating in the woods are closely reminiscent of two Debussy piano preludes, *Des Pas sur la neige* and *Bruyères*.[22] The textures of some of Debussy's études are reminiscent of passages in "Hawthorne." One particular instance is the "arpeggio" étude of 1915, a work that begins much like one of the more euphonious sections of "Hawthorne." In fact, the first few bars of the étude segue smoothly into "Hawthorne," p. 42, system 3 (Figure 3.19).

Figure 3.18a: Claude Debussy, *Hommage à Rameau*, mm. 1–8, from *Images,* book I

Figure 3.18b: Ives, "Hawthorne," *Concord Sonata*, p. 25, systems 1–4

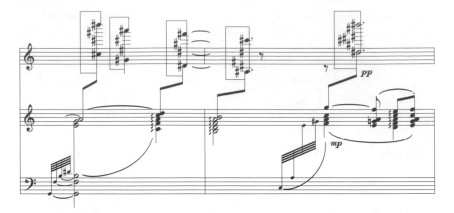

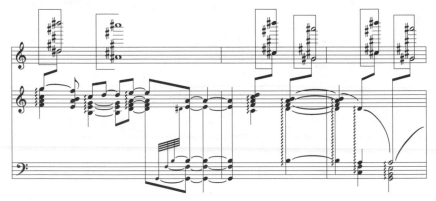

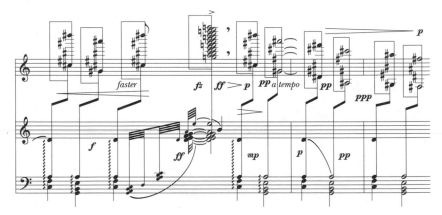

Figure 3.18b, continued

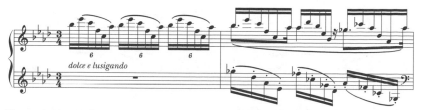

Figure 3.19a: Debussy, *Etudés*, Book 2, No. 11, "Pour les arpèges composés," mm.1–2

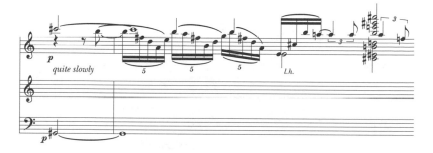

Figure 3.19b: Ives, "Hawthorne," *Concord Sonata*, p. 42, system 3

Ives also mentions Scriabin in the *Essays* (26) and he owned copies of Scriabin's Fourth, Fifth, Eighth and Ninth Sonatas.[23] From the Fifth Sonata onward, Scriabin leaves his complex oedipal relationship with Chopin in the distant background, taking flight in the odyssey of his own unique musical development. Because of this, I will concentrate on a few important nodes of intersection between Ives's work and Scriabin's later piano sonatas.

At times in "Emerson," Scriabin seems almost to have entered into the work, offering a hand in setting the quotations from Beethoven's Fifth Symphony. His presence is most particularly welcomed in the post-"poetry" section of "Emerson," where the Fifth Symphony motive enters in various registers, at varying speeds, all couched in a Scriabinesque chromatic texture (Figure 3.20). Beethoven's symphony certainly reappears here with numerous entries, but this is Ives's Beethoven, fully absorbed and recast into a languid atmosphere of meditation. Scriabin created many similar instances of such a mood in his scores for piano solo. One excellent illustration of this is the languido section of the Fifth Sonata, Op. 53 of 1907, which Ives certainly could have played at home, since he owned the score. As in many instances of Debussy's piano music, Scriabin's music for the languido section flows attractively from the Ives excerpt (Figure 3.21).

Figure 3.20: Ives, "Emerson," *Concord Sonata*, p. 12, systems 1–3

Another point of intersection between Scriabin's Fifth Sonata and Ives *Concord Sonata* can be found in the similar splashes of color achieved with rapid movements of all five fingers and a turn of the hand. This is most apparent on the opening pages of Scriabin's Fifth Sonata (mm. 1–11), recurring in ritornello fashion later in the work as well, and in "Hawthorne," p. 24, where the great rush of sporadic outbursts of five-note groups, best achieved with five fingers and the aid of the opposite hand, prepares for the Debussyean hand-and-board section, which follows shortly after.

Figure 3.21: Scriabin, Fifth Sonata, Op. 53, mm. 13–24

Scriabin's Eighth Sonata achieves a juxtaposition of contemplative or meditative sections with più vivo sections in a quasi-rondo pattern that has an affinity with "Thoreau." In "Thoreau," Ives varies his impressionistic sections with rag rhythms. Scriabin uses various kinds of syncopations and delayed accents to create his more vigorous sections. The many falling passages of parallel fourths in the Eighth Sonata are also similar to various instances of parallel fourths in the right hand in "Hawthorne." Both composers, too, look back to Debussy for halcyon effects created by pedal tones and open intervallic relationships of octave, fifth, and fourth.

There is no biographical proof that Ives studied Scriabin's Tenth and last sonata for piano, Op. 70, but there is nothing in this last great instance of Scriabin's sonata forms for piano that is not implied in the steady evolution in the nine sonatas that preceded it. And there is no proof that Ives *never* saw or heard the score. Scriabin finished this last of his sonatas in 1912, before Ives completed his sonata. Whether or not Ives knew this work, there is a fascinating similarity of the chromatic and melodic treatment of the inner voices in both "Emerson" and in the tenth Scriabin sonata. Both the *Concord* and Scriabin's Op. 70 display a similar propensity to sustain outer voices that outline a vast musical space, with plenty of room for the pianist to project haunting *espressivo* dissonance and lyrical chromaticism in various inner voices. This trait of Ives's music is more typical of Scriabin than Debussy, who has a softer palette for sonorities, however experimental. Ives and Scriabin show a harder-edged tonal vocabulary.

One of the most effective moments in the *Concord Sonata* is the coda of "Emerson." Here the texture of the music suggests thick dynamic colors to emphasize the melodic line in the inner voices, with lesser emphasis on the outer textures. Apparently Ives intended the long descending chromatic line on p. 19 (system 1) to be played on the piano by the thumb and second finger of the left hand, not on a viola; he probably marked it "viola part" to indicate the instrument that played this part in the original orchestral version of the movement (Figure 3.22). If the pianist manages to play this (and it is well worth the challenge), the connection between this great moment and Scriabin's Tenth Sonata becomes quite plausible (Figure 3.23). Both works masterfully achieve a projection of inner voices against distant outer textures, as if to indicate that traditional harmony had been

Viola part (ad lib) **pp**—*if played*—*but bringing out accent.*

Figure 3.22: Ives, "Emerson," *Concord Sonata*, p. 19, system 1

fractured, exposing vibrant instances of organic musical life pulsating between the limits demarcated by the old norms of nineteenth-century harmonic outlines.

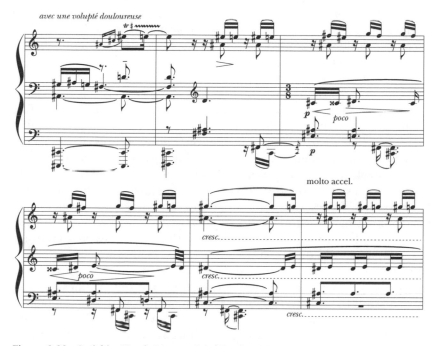

Figure 3.23: Scriabin, Tenth Sonata, Op. 70, mm. 124–28

It is now commonly understood that Ives altered much of his music as he reworked his scores over the years. Perhaps he could have seen this Scriabin score during the many years before he published his sonata and *Essays*, or while making changes in the *Concord Sonata* score after 1920. But in Scriabin's last sonata, he sounds as much like Ives as Ives sounds like Scriabin. In the works of both composers, there is a remarkable exploitation of harmonic ambiguity and chromaticism that undermines the tonal conventions of the nineteenth century. Both composers follow Chopin and Debussy in their love of pianistic color. This results in audacious enrichments of conventional harmonies. For example, Scriabin and Ives are especially fond of supplementing triadic chords with both major and minor thirds of the chord superimposed, one on top of the other, in complex chords of the seventh, ninth, and even thirteenth. This creates a blended sound, implying quarter tones that the conventional piano does not offer. But

Ives is even more adventurous. Partly by deconstructing the norm of the octave unison and substituting parallel movements of major sevenths and minor ninths and partly by superimposing distant key relationships in layers of polytonality, Ives provides new directions for keyboard music that imply, not merely quarter tones, but quarter tonalities and extra dimensions of musical space. Ives's music also features a less delimited implication of closure to both shorter phrases and larger musical shapes.

Scriabin's structure is highly unusual, but it has more customary patterns of expository presentation, development, and recapitulation than does Ives's structure. Scriabin neatly wraps up the closure of his sonata form, as it concludes in the recapitulation style, stating material that was clearly stated in the beginning of his work. While Scriabin's achievement is remarkable for 1912, Ives's score is even more revolutionary and unique, even for 1996. In Scriabin's work, the music comes to a close because it is restated after it has been worked out. In Ives's work, music culminates because it is fully revealed after a momentum of accumulation.

No study of the precursor textures to the *Concord Sonata* diminishes its unique place in the literature. Among American composers, who else but Ives would have had the audacity to confront the tradition of art music with a new kind of cumulative form that undermines the very premises of the architecture of European art music? There are no similar figures in music. Only Whitman and Emerson existed in literature, and in my view, their voices are as essential as the voice of any musician in understanding Ives. They mapped out the poetics and ideology that Ives needed to find his musical voice. Aided by their examples as pioneers in their own fields, Ives was able to discover his musical innovations and demarcate his unique place in musical history.

I hear Ives as the Walt Whitman of American music. Walt Whitman knew well that the waves of the Atlantic Ocean have a powerful rhythm and yet do not wash up upon the shore in perfectly symmetrical meter. Charles Ives also knew this. Both Whitman and Ives created an entirely fresh rhythmic exuberance that is unconstrained by the norms of European patterns of organization. Both poet and musician display an Emersonian awareness of natural phenomena as they occur in the American landscape. Both valorized the unique nature of individual perception and meditation in response to this new environment.

Ives's total disdain for meter and bar line is reminiscent of Whitman's casting off of poetic meter. In the work of both artists, the line is exactly long enough to suit the immediate length of the phrase, not more or less, and the irregularity of length is remarkable in relation to the overall unity of ideas for both of them. Ives described the scherzino interlude of "Emerson" (pp. 8–11) as an approximation of Emerson's poetry. Actually, it is far more like the work of Whitman, who invented a new form of prosody to fit his unique message.

The Ives scherzino is characterized by repeated C pedals and repetitions of a simple five-note pattern that is repeated and extended in various ways. Anaphora, a rhetorical device using repeated groups at the beginning of the poetic sentence (or musical phrase), links Ives's style to Whitman's. Whitman similarly tends to anchor his poetic line by beginning phrases with the same word groups. Long chains extend from these repeated word groups:

> Smile O voluptuous cool-breath'd earth!
> Earth of the slumbering and liquid trees!
> Earth of departed sunset—earth of the mountains misty-topt!
> Earth of the vitreous pour of the full moon just tinged with blue!
> Earth of shine and dark mottling the tide of the river!
> Earth of the limpid gray of clouds brighter and clearer for
>   my sake!
> Far-swooping elbow'd earth—rich apple-blossom'd earth!
> Smile, for your lover comes.[24]

In other words, symmetrical impositions come at the beginning of Whitman's line, not at the end, as was the custom before *Leaves of Grass* (1857) made its impact on the world of poetry. Ives, who knew Whitman's poetry, and wrote a song about him which contains an excerpt from *Leaves of Grass*, similarly changes the rhythmic length and meter frequently in the "poetry" scherzino for "Emerson," where eight different meters are specified. Finally, the scherzino ends as the music subsides into the dreamier 2/4 so akin to Scriabin's music. Ives frequently changes the meter to allow for different phrase lengths, just as Whitman varied the length of his poetic line.

In the *Essays*, Ives weighs the importance of popular culture for the art music composer, but he tries to dismiss its fertilizing impact too emphatically. He seems to prefer that his listeners ignore the trail leading toward the rich indigenous music of ragtime, just as he would conceal the path leading back to Debussy (93–95). Actually the rhythms of ragtime and other popular American music brought more richness to his music than he would have us know.

Aside from the Fifth Symphony quotations, the popular culture sources in Ives's *Concord* are better known than the underlayers of texture culled from European art music. Rather than signs of a weak imagination, they are marks of Ives's creative strength as he struggled to create a new way to compose music. They are of extreme importance in Ives's creation of his new style. Ives never borrows and recycles his material in whole chunks, as some of his mediocre American precursors did. This would have created more of a medley effect, which Ives always avoided. Instead Ives absorbs the musical material and deconstructs or decomposes it into different kinds of musical fragmentation. Usually the borrowed fragments are portions of a melody recollected as if from a remote corner of the remembering mind, pulled up from the subconscious. Ives perfects his technique of fragmentation at the same point in the twentieth century when the modernist painters were breaking apart natural forms into fractured prisms of painterly space. In the *Concord Sonata*, Ives performs the same kind of operation on "Columbia, the Gem of the Ocean," or Stephen Foster's "Massa's in de Cold Ground." Also, the hymns *Martyn* and *Missionary Chant* offer material that roughly matches augmented versions of Beethoven's opening motives for the Fifth Symphony and Op. 106, as if these fragments from European art music are recast in slow motion to suit the popular culture sound of a nineteenth-century parlor piano in the house of the Alcotts.

Other kinds of popular music in the *Concord Sonata* are vaudeville; rag (in decomposed wrong-note versions in "Emerson," "Hawthorne," and "Thoreau"); a blues progression (the I to IV progression in the "Emerson" poetry section is recognizable to every American schoolboy); and the re-created "old Scotch song" in "The Alcotts." By the end of the *Concord Sonata*, the two popular songs, the two hymn themes (*Missionary Chant* and *Martyn*), and the vaudeville, rag, and blues sounds merge to exist on equal footing with the Fifth Symphony and the "Hammerklavier" sonata; popular culture and high-status European art culture are blended to create a new musical synthesis of culture. The rhythmic life and melodic richness of popular culture are captured by the composer, who incorporates them into a larger and more comprehensive sound structure.

Mikhail Bakhtin's well-known term *heteroglossia* is particularly apt for describing the great multiverse of Whitman's ear and the American pluralism his poetry implies. Heteroglossia is the simultaneous existence of diverse voices in a literary text, so that the many components exist in a polyphony of diversity, without reconciliation. Whitman seems to have come up with Bakhtin's concept himself when he wrote:

> Do I contradict myself?
> Very well then I contradict myself,
> (I am large, I contain multitudes.)[25]

It is a good concept to help us grasp what Ives was up to as well. In their creative works, both Whitman and Ives used the high and low sounds of the salon and saloon, street and concert hall. Heteroglossia provides a concept for understanding how diverse voices may be present in a work and never fully reconciled. Full reconciliation was not necessary to Ives. It was more important for him to create in music a full account of his experience.

Certainly the patches in the *Concord Sonata* that remind the educated pianist of precursors and rivals are charged nodes allowing us to momentarily jump backwards and sideways into musical history. But they do not diminish the massive achievement of the *Concord Sonata*. They place it in relation to the other great challenges for the keyboard by other major composers and help us retrace Ives's own steps as he traveled along his way. They tell us as much about who Ives is as they do about their importance as sources.

Taken together, the *Concord Sonata* and the *Essays* expose a shift in musical practice from the patterned linearity of German classicism to the coloristic explorations of Romantic form to the new model of music as a massing of acoustic perceptions that provoke psychological meditation. Although Ives is a chief initiator of the last of these musical stances, his work is syncretic and sums up the implications of earlier styles, as Bach's work did in the eighteenth century. Ives's work contains all three of these basic views of musical poetics. Whitman's new form gave him a voice that was vast and expansive, a voice that seemed to encompass an entire mind and a burgeoning civilization. Ives's cumulative form enabled him to embrace diverse musical cultures and a wide range of aural predilections, as in, for example, the accumulated significances of the four notes of Beethoven's Fifth Symphony in the *Concord Sonata*. These famous notes accrue meanings as they are reheard in terms of their Zeuner counterpart, fashioned across the ocean. The motives from Beethoven and Zeuner coalesce and crystallize, combining cultural diversity; revealed at first partially, then fully, they are heard in full consummation at the culminating moment of climax and clarity.

Ives's revolution is clearer if we ask ourselves a few simple questions. During which hearing can the listener take in the dense mass of musical material that is the *Concord Sonata*? When can one achieve an understanding of the work? Mozart had a legendary ability to totally recall his first hearing of a musical work and then transcribe it perfectly onto paper. Even an ear as gifted as his would probably be stymied on first hearing the *Concord Sonata*.

During the twentieth century, comprehension became much more elusive as music became more complex; Ives's music obviously requires many rehearings. In the work of the great German masters like Beethoven and Schubert, the architectonic nature of the musical design made comprehension much more available on the first hearing. The European sonata was characterized by an orderly presentation of simple materials, which were heightened by the contrast of modulation. These sound events were followed by development and recapitulation. Ives smashes apart this model, proposing a new psychological process of meditation and comprehension, and he creates a great personal challenge for both performer and listener. It is this bold proposition that enabled Ives to borrow from the models of the past to make his new style of musical composition understandable to performers and interpreters. It is this bold proposition that makes the *Concord Sonata* such a unique moment in the history of music.

NOTES

1. David S. Reynolds, *Walt Whitman's America: A Cultural Biography* (New York: Knopf, 1995), 176–93.

2. I have written on this topic in my *Angels of Reality: Emersonian Unfoldings in Wright, Stevens, and Ives* (Carbondale: Southern Illinois University Press, 1993), 164–73. Lucretius first writes of the swerves of atoms in *De Rerum Natura*, but the modern critic who first applied this concept to an intricate Freudian theory of poetry was Harold Bloom. Bloom's ideas on literary influence are most concisely presented in *The Anxiety of Influence* (New York: Oxford University Press, 1973). The reader may also wish to consult Bloom's *The Breaking of the Vessels* (Chicago: University of Chicago Press, 1982) and *A Map of Misreading* (New York: Oxford University Press, 1975). See also Bloom's teacher, Walter Jackson Bate, *The Burden of the Past and the English Poet* (Cambridge, Mass.: Belknap Press, 1970). Joseph N. Straus has applied Bloom's theories to twentieth-century music history in *Remaking the Past: Musical Modernism and the Influence of the Tonal Tradition* (Cambridge, Mass.: Harvard University Press, 1990).

3. J. Peter Burkholder, *All Made of Tunes: Charles Ives and the Uses of Musical Borrowing* (New Haven: Yale University Press, 1995), 137–266.

4. "The Alcotts" begins roughly twenty-nine minutes into the composition, which runs, on average, about forty-five minutes. The concluding bars of "The Alcotts," the moment of the clearest lyrical expression of the thematic materials in the sonata, occurs at roughly thirty-five minutes into its performance.

5. J. Peter Burkholder, *Charles Ives: The Ideas Behind the Music* (New Haven: Yale University Press, 1985), 74–76.

6. All quotations taken from the *Essays* are to be found in Charles Ives, *Essays Before a Sonata, The Majority and Other Writings*, ed. Howard Boatwright (New York: W. W. Norton, 1970). Page numbers are in parentheses in the text.

7. Hertz, *Angels of Reality*, 31–34 and 93–116.

8. Ralph Waldo Emerson, *The Complete Works of Ralph Waldo Emerson* (Boston: Houghton Mifflin, 1903), vol. 2: 83 and vol. 8: 178.

9. Emerson, *The Complete Works,* vol. 8: 200, 202, and 204.

10. Charles Ives, *Memos,* ed. John Kirkpatrick (New York: W. W. Norton, 1972), 69. See also the discussion in Burkholder, *All Made of Tunes,* 159–60, and the analysis of "cumulative setting" in the last movement of the sonata on pp. 154–61.

11. In *Angels of Reality,* I have demonstrated that Debussy was the major European innovator who prefigured Ives. See pages 93–113.

12. All quotations from the *Concord Sonata* are from the second edition (New York: Arrow Music Press, 1947), as reprinted by Associated Music Publishers.

13. Charles Rosen, *The Romantic Generation* (Cambridge, Mass.: Harvard University Press, 1995), 241–42.

14. See Nicolas Slonimsky, *Music Since 1900,* 4th ed. (New York: Charles Scribner's Sons, 1971), 1491. Robert P. Morgan also describes this Ivesian device in "Spatial Form in Ives," in *An Ives Celebration: Papers and Panels of the Charles Ives Centennial Festival-Conference,* ed. H. Wiley Hitchcock and Vivian Perlis (Urbana: University of Illinois Press, 1977), 151–52.

15. I have discussed this difference in *The Tuning of the Word: The Musico-Literary Poetics of the Symbolist Movement* (Carbondale: Southern Illinois University Press, 1987), 1–31.

16. See Burkholder's discussion of the *Concord Sonata* in *All Made of Tunes,* 350–57, which has helped me clarify my recent thinking on this work.

17. One may profitably compare the shape of the opening antecedent section of the human-faith-melody and the second motive of the Liszt sonata. The intervals are slightly different but the contour of the falling antecedent and rising consequent are surprisingly similar, and there is a similar fall and rise in the cumulative forms of each. Ives may well have used the Liszt motive as a model, although his motive is sufficiently different to establish it as an entirely independent creation.

18. Emerson, "Quotation and Originality," in *The Complete Works*, Vol. 8: 204.

19. Ives, *Memos*, 135.

20. While Schumann wrote an *Arabesque* as well, that title is not typical of the many poetic titles the composer chose for his numerous character pieces, most of which were inspired by his readings of Jean-Paul Richter or E. T. A. Hoffmann.

21. For Symbolism, see my own *Tuning of the Word,* 1–84, and Anna Balakian, *The Symbolist Movement* (New York: New York University Press, 1977). For Impressionism, see Paul Smith, *Impressionism: Beneath the Surface* (New York: Harry Abrams, 1995); and Robert L. Herbert, *Impressionism: Art, Leisure, and Parisian Society* (New Haven: Yale University Press, 1988).

22. See my discussion of this in Hertz, *Angels of Reality,* 103–111.

23. See Vivian Perlis, ed., *Charles Ives Papers,* Yale University Music Library Archival Collection, MSS. 14 (New Haven: Yale University Music Library, 1983), 193.

24. Walt Whitman, *Leaves of Grass,* ed. Sculley Bradley and Harold Blodgett (New York: W.W. Norton, 1973), 49.

25. Whitman, *Leaves of Grass,* 88.

Charles Ives and the American Democratic Tradition

MICHAEL BROYLES

Democracy and patriotism were at the core of Charles Ives's work. His political views were a principal source of his creativity and inspired some of his most important compositions as well as some of the most bizarre events in his life.[1] Political fervor lay behind much of what he did, and unlike many other aspects of his life, it did not fade with his aging, greater isolation, and decline in creativity.[2]

In spite of the acknowledged importance of politics to Ives's art, a reconsideration of the roots of Ives's political beliefs is long overdue. Musical issues, such as questions of dating, style, structure, and musical sources, have dominated recent Ives scholarship.[3] Politics, when dealt with at all, has been addressed from the perspective of postmodernism.[4] The postmodern approach, however, raises serious methodological questions, principally because it repeats unchallenged many clichés about Ives's political roots which become assumptions in a dialogue whose very foundation is undermined by questionable historical connections. Musicologists have enriched their field greatly by embracing other disciplines, particularly philosophy and literary theory. They have, however, ignored much historical research of the past twenty years. As a consequence many interpretations of Ives are based on outdated or even naive historical premises. Ives's relationship to his time assumes a very different shape when his political ideas are examined in the context of modern historical research.

For example, I will demonstrate that Ives's early years in the insurance business shaped his personal philosophy in ways no scholar has addressed, because Ives's position during the Armstrong insurance investigation was not what has been assumed, and because the later establishment of his own agency with Julian S. Myrick did not happen as generally reported. Further, musicological scholarship has completely ignored several notions or myths about the American past that were prevalent in Ives's time. The presence of these myths fundamentally affects any interpretation of Ives and his past.

One point about Ives is clear: his political views cannot be separated from other aspects of his life. His prose writings, his business career, and his music must be examined as a unit. More than one person who knew Ives observed that Ives's experience in the life insurance business shaped his political philosophy. In regards to his music: practically every piece that Ives wrote was rooted in time and place, sometimes very specifically, as when recalling an individual event or experience; at other times topologically, as when recreating a more general but no less real activity such as a holiday celebration. But his pieces are seldom introspective, at least on the surface; Ives does not plumb his emotional self and present deep raw emotions from within his own psyche. His music rather is a commentary on life, the past, the social order, the world about him as observed from his highly idiosyncratic perspective.[5]

Ives lived at a time of fundamental change in American society, and his creative work mirrors those changes. In particular Ives gives voice to the pervading mixture of anxiety, nostalgia, and revolution that did much to shape the late nineteenth and early twentieth centuries.[6] He is an important historical source, sometimes ignored, frequently oversimplified. His relationship to the past was complex at every level— personal, psychological, political, and artistic. But to many writers Ives fits all too easily into two of the most powerful political movements of his time: populism and progressivism. J. Peter Burkholder, who associated transcendentalism directly with Ives's political beliefs, presents succinctly the standard interpretation of Ives's political thought.

> Ives's Transcendentalism has long been linked with his political beliefs, and it was likewise soon after his marriage that he began to express strong populist or progressive political ideals in his memos, in his music on the subjects of abolition and the Civil War era, and in topical political songs. . . .

> In the first years of his marriage to Harmony, there is a clear shift of topic in Ives's chosen texts towards spiritual, Transcendentalist, and later populist or progressive political ideals, coinciding with the composition of the Concord Sonata and the beginning in the 1910s of Ives's applications of Trancendentalist issues.[7]

Burkholder's statement leaves many points unresolved. For instance, what precisely was Harmony's role? Ives did become interested in politics shortly after his marriage, and Harmony certainly was an important intellectual influence on him, but there were other serious developments, indeed crises, in his life at this time. And what precisely was the link between transcendentalism and his political beliefs? Finally, and most important, was Ives either a progressive or a populist?

The last question is the most problematic, yet has gone unchallenged in Ives scholarship. Virtually all Ives scholars have applied these labels unhesitatingly, without considering fully their complexity and nuances.[8] I will argue that Ives was neither a populist nor a progressive, and that his political roots draw on quite different traditions, which were prevalent in late nineteenth-century America but have been totally ignored in Ives scholarship.

Except for a campaign song supporting McKinley in 1896, Ives's overtly political statements began in 1912 with a song fragment, *Vote for Names*. Ives himself wrote the text, as he did for many of his political songs. It reveals a deep-seated cynicism with the political process:

Vote for Names! Names!
All nice men!!
Three Nice Men:
Teddy, Woodrow and Bill.

After trying hard to think
what's the best way to vote I say:
Just walk right in and grab a ballot
with the eyes shut and walk right out again.[9]

From 1912 to the early 1920s, when his compositional career by and large came to an end, Ives composed several other political songs. The most specific was *An Election*, or *Nov. 2, 1920*, in which Ives voiced his bitterness over the election of Harding and the implicit repudiation of the League of Nations. He also wrote several about the First World War, which he originally opposed. *He is There!* is a stirring justification of the war to establish freedom and build "a world where all may have a 'say.'" In the style of a patriotic march, it is designed to rouse patriotic sentiment for the fight. Other World War I songs, such as *In Flanders Field* and *Tom Sails Away*, focus on the tragedy and personal sacrifice of the war. They are, like many Civil War songs, essentially anti-war. Others of Ives's songs had more general but nevertheless overt political themes.[10]

Several of Ives's instrumental pieces deal with political issues either directly or indirectly. For instance, in the orchestral work, *From Hanover Square North*, Ives seeks to capture the mood of the crowd on the subway platform where he was standing on the day the news broke about the sinking of the Lusitania. This event was important to Ives, who at that time was moving from a position of pacifism to become a supporter of Wilson.

Ives's most important and remarkable political statement comprises the song and the essay entitled *Majority*.[11] In the essay, written 1919–20, he elaborated his views on how to reorganize the political structure. Fifty-seven pages long in the printed version, it is Ives's most complete account of his political beliefs. The song, entitled "The Masses" when Ives originally wrote it as a piece for unison chorus and orchestra in the late 1910s, does not seem to relate to the essay directly. The text is more general, an almost mystical description of the people. Yet when Ives revised it for piano and voice in 1921 for *114 Songs*, he changed the title to *Majority*, and placed it as the first song of the collection.[12] On closer examination the two turn out to be closely related statements of similar political beliefs, their differences a reflection of Ives's sensitivity to the nature of the two modes of expression. Taken together they allow a deeper and more complete understanding than otherwise possible of Ives's political orientation and its connection with nineteenth- and twentieth-century thought.

Ives originally wrote the essay as a dialogue and produced several heavily annotated typescripts before the final version.[13] Other statements of similar ideas go back to 1916 at the latest, and other iterations, including his proposed twentieth amendment to the Constitution, followed the essay.[14] The principal points of the essay thus occupied Ives's thought for some time. They are: (1) the notion of direct democracy, by referendum; and (2) a limitation on property or wealth.

Ives wished to replace representative government with direct democracy. He envisioned first a "suggestive, or formative ballot, in the nature of a general survey" several months before an election, which would "relate to general economic business, internal and international questions" excepting those necessitating emergency measures. Congress's job would be two-fold: first, to take these ballots and refine them, eventually framing a set of more detailed questions for the electorate to decide; second, after the people had spoken, to pass necessary technical legislation to enable or specify further what the people had mandated. Ives believed that as the years went by and the will of the people was heard more and more clearly, this second function would diminish. In general Ives saw the role of both Congress, which he called the "clerical machine of the people," and the President as technical. He allowed that the President might be head of the "Foreign Department," but recommended that congressional membership be "subject to Civil Service examinations," rather than "territorial elections."[15]

If important or emergency measures came up between these general ballots, the people would be polled in a mass referendum. The government would provide "bureaus of information" to disseminate the facts, allowing the people to make an informed choice. Ives believed that new technology, particularly electronic technology, would allow the people to express themselves directly in a way that had not been possible before.[16]

The second major theme running through the *Majority* essay was that private wealth should be limited. Ives did not want to abolish it. He did not object to people living comfortably or accumulating a fair amount of wealth; he opposed gross concentration of wealth and the exorbitant incomes of some in the gilded age and after. Specific amounts he wished to leave up to the majority, but suggested a weekly income below $150 ($7,800 annually), and total property of below $150,000. In 1995 dollars that would be the equivalent of an annual income of $136,000 and a property value of $2,400,000.[17] Ironically the income he himself reported on his tax return in the year he wrote the tract was $41,000 or the 1995 equivalent of $656,000.[18]

Ives has been called a populist because of his interest in direct democracy (specifically the referendum) and his antipathy to the wealthy. Unfortunately this label does not fit. Ives was writing at a time in which the political movement called Populism and its formal political party were past history. More importantly, many of Ives's ideas are not consistent with populism as a philosophy, which it should be noted was quite different from progressivism.

An acute class consciousness pervaded historical Populism, which was first and foremost a labor movement. Populists comprised two disaffected groups, the small poor farmers of the South and Midwest and working class laborers. The farmers felt pinched by big business interests and land speculators, and the laborers were fighting for the very right to organize. They did not occupy a middle ground. Populist support of labor and their condemnation of those who accumulated or hoarded capital was unequivocal.[19]

Ives's roots were in New England, and he spent his professional life in New York City. He never showed any interest in rural America, other than in his idyllic vision of having a country home, which he eventually did in West Redding, Connecticut. That of course is hardly the rural America of Populism. Populist thought and Ives's thought differs most clearly, however, on the question of class. As many writers have pointed out, the class element is strikingly absent in Ives's thought. In that sense his views were pre-industrial. Ives saw a homogeneity of interests among all men, and considered universal the male middle-class sense of responsibility on which the insurance industry was built.

Though Ives does not fit the mold of a populist, was he a progressive? This question is more important because Ives has been associated with progressivism more than with any other political movement. It is also more complex, in no small measure because the meaning of progressivism itself is elusive. Few historians have agreed on a definition, and some have found progressivism sufficiently unclear to doubt its usefulness as a historical label entirely.[20] Others have interpreted progressivism so broadly that Ives is a progressive mainly because he was born between 1854 and 1874. Associating progressivism with Ives thus means trying to pin a shifting, protean label onto an elusive, paradoxical target. This has not, however, discouraged historians from the attempt.

Robert Crunden's 1982 book, *Ministers of Reform*, makes the most elaborate and sweeping case that Ives was a progressive. Crunden's study consists of biographical vignettes of twenty-one persons whom he considers progressives, including Ives. Crunden does not necessarily discuss progressivism as a political movement. He admits that progressives "shared no platform, nor were they members of a single movement." To Crunden progressivism was characterized by "the existence of a dominant mood," a state of mind "brought about by shared family and cultural experiences."[21] These included a strong but not excessively doctrinal Protestant background, association with the Republican Party, a veneration of Lincoln bordering on the reverential, attendance at a small denominational college, and a general dissatisfaction with the relatively narrow career choices traditionally associated with this heritage coupled with an inability to throw off the sense of duty and service that this heritage instilled.

Even within Crunden's own framework, Ives does not fit the model very well. His family was certainly Protestant, and even though Ives himself had a deep, non-doctrinal religious belief, there is no indication that his choices as a young man were determined by religious conviction. Ives chose Yale because of family tradition and a desire to succeed professionally, and Yale in the 1890s could no more be termed "a small denominational college" than could Harvard or

Princeton. Spending much more energy on social than scholarly or intellectual pursuits, Ives seemed to have recognized the principal value of a Yale education: to make the proper connections to insure a successful business career. In that sense he was successful, as both his election to the Yale secret society known as Wolf's Head and his later professional life confirm.

Yet the most important problem with Crunden's advocacy of Ives as a progressive is his definition of progressivism itself. For most scholars, practical efforts at social and political reform constituted the very core of progressivism. Daniel T. Rodgers attempted to provide an umbrella definition of progressivism that takes into account the seeming absence of any coherent centralizing element. He found that in spite of the many contradictions that historians encountered, progressives shared "three distinct clusters of ideas": "the rhetoric of anti-monopolism," "an emphasis on social bonds and the social nature of human beings," and "the language of social efficiency." Rodgers further described progressivism as an issue-oriented movement characterized by a fundamental shift in politics at the end of the nineteenth century, as parties gave way to a multitude of pressure groups ranging from civic leagues to special interest lobby groups, and voters formed a "slimmed-down electorate of highly specific loyalties."[22]

Yet Ives stands outside even this definition. Various measures such as initiative, referendum, and recall were specific, controlled, and limited tools for curbing the power of legislators; they gave the people the equivalent of an appeals mechanism. The emphasis in most progressive agendas was for more government control and intervention, not less. The direct democracy movement, an important part of progressivism, was motivated by the attempt to restrain the influence of an invisible government, the political bosses who operated behind the scenes, unaccountable to the public, manipulating the legislators. Realizing that most legislators, from municipalities to Congress itself, were especially vulnerable to such manipulation, the most common progressive solution was to strengthen the hand of the executive branch. Whether a mayor, city manager, or governor, executive power provided a counterbalance to an easily swayed legislature.

Progressivism also sought to use the methods of social science to address problems: analyze a specific problem, and here the emphasis is on the word specific; determine a practical solution, usually one that necessitates more government intervention; and then campaign to get it approved. It is a targeted approach, using government as a solution, rather than attempting to undermine the role of government itself.

This targeted approach is utterly at odds with Ives's proposals. Ives's political ideas, on the surface highly specific in calling for direct democracy, are in fact so sweeping, vague, and unrealistic as to defy practicality. Ives's proposed reforms are really about government reinventing itself in an utterly idealistic manner. Ives did not want to fine tune the body politic; he wanted to bury the corpse and begin anew. Ives had in mind nothing less than the entire destruction of the legislative process that had evolved from the founding of the Constitution. Nothing in progressivism remotely resembles that.

Were Ives not such a famous musician, he could simply be dismissed as another fringe thinker prone to writing eccentric letters to the editor. And had Ives's politics not affected his music fundamentally, it would be only a biographical curiosity. But Ives of course is one of America's premier composers, and his political beliefs shaped some of his most important compositions. Because of this, the song *Majority* promises a type of insight into Ives's political thought that cannot be obtained by examining only the prose in the essay that accompanies it, even though the essay is much longer and more specific. I believe that the song provides the key to understanding Ives's political views, including the question of their sources, and that an analysis of the song not only reveals a close connection with the essay, but explains the essay itself. The song *Majority* is Ives's most personal and deep-seated statement of his political views. It goes far to explain not only his politics in the narrow sense, but many other aspects of his life, as well as a number of other compositions whose political themes are less obvious.

The song itself addresses no political goals. It is an incantation, a mystical statement of belief in the masses or the people. The text, written by Ives, consists of five verses, each beginning with a statement of action by the masses, followed by a final verse, in the nature of a coda, taken from Robert Browning. The structure of the song resembles a Psalm in which the same text is repeated with minor changes, usually in key words:

The Masses have toiled;
   Behold the works of the World!
The Masses are thinking;
   Whence comes the thought of the World!
The Masses are singing;
   Whence comes the Art of the World!
The Masses are yearning;
   Whence comes the hope of the World!

The Masses are dreaming;
   Whence comes the vision of God!
God's in his Heaven;
   All will be well with the World!

When comparing the final and the original version of the song, two places stand out. The first is the ending. The text of the last verse is no longer Ives but a quotation from Robert Browning. It is an abrupt change in thought and in tense, breaking the incantation pattern that had prevailed up to then. Musically the ending itself is unusual, two major triads in a descending fifth progression, preceded by an unusual variety of sonorities (see Figure 4.1): a series of triads that ascends to D♭ by half-steps so rapidly that it creates the effect of a chromatic blur, bare octaves on F♯ (including the voice), a dominant thirteenth on A with both the raised and lowered forms of the ninth, and then the two final triads. By 1921, Ives rarely ended a piece with two major triads in a seeming dominant-tonic relationship, particularly in a piece so dissonant throughout.

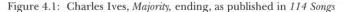

Figure 4.1: Charles Ives, *Majority*, ending, as published in *114 Songs*

The two major triads at the end are a deliberate simplification of the 1914 version, shown in Figure 4.2. There the second violins, divided into six parts, enter on the second beat with an F-sharp major triad that moves to a C-sharp major triad. Ives marked the part with four p's, while the rest of the orchestra holds a fortissimo F major chord. Ives commented: "last 6vs, This C♯ chord to be heard just a second after CM. . . . Almost as a 3. Not only [?] dying away but together." This effect, an "amen" reminiscent of the closing of the *Housatonic at Stockbridge* or *Decoration Day*, puts a sheen to the final chord quite different from the *114 Songs* version. Yet as we will see below, both versions are consistent with the broader meaning of the song.

Figure 4.2: Charles Ives, *The Masses*, ending, original choral-orchestral version

The second major change that Ives made was to eliminate two verses, which occur in the original between the fourth and fifth verses, after "Whence comes the hope of the world." His reasons were probably both textual and musical. The eliminated text reads:

> The masses are as legion,
> as the rain drops falling together make the Rivers
> And for a space become as one
> So men seeking common life together for a season become
>   as one
> Whence comes the nations of the World.
> As the tribes of the ages wandered and followed [sic] the stars,
> whence comes the many dwelling places of the world.

Each of the other verses refers to the masses in some sort of action, mostly mental. These verses are different. They are longer, and they discuss more fully who the masses are. The verses are more a commentary on the song than part of the song itself. They are also not Psalm-like. They not only interrupt the momentum gained from the parallel structure but also inject a note of reality that is inconsistent with the abstractness of the rest of the song.

In the margin to the eliminated verse, shown in facsimile in Figure 4.3, Ives wrote two of his most quoted comments. The first explains the musical design:

> The plan of this, in the orchestra parts, is to have each in different rhythm group complete the 12 notes (each on a different system and end and hold last of 12) as finding its star.

The second comments on and seems to reject the original plan on aesthetic grounds:

> Occasionally something made in this calculated, diagram, design way may have a place in music, if it is used primarily to carry out an idea or as part of a program subject matter as in the above, but generally or too much or alone as such it is a weak substitute for inspiration or music. It's too easy—any high-school student (unmusical) with a pad, pencil, compass and logth [logarithm] table, and a mild knowledge of sounds and instruments (blown or hit) could do it. It's an artificial process without strength, though it may sound busy and noisy. This wall-paper design music is not as big as a natural mushy, ballad.[23]

Kirkpatrick associated Ives's first idea for this verse and the subsequent comment with the twelve-tone row, a point Rossiter and others have repeated.[24] Ives obviously wrote the second comment later since it was a rejection of the first, but how much later? The handwriting differs enough to suggest some separation of time, although it is not the "snake tracks" of Ives's later years.[25] Ives probably wrote the second comment in 1920–21 when he was revising the song for

Figure 4.3: Charles Ives, *The Masses*, choral-orchestral version, verse omitted in *114 Songs*

Figure 4.3, continued

114 Songs, although he could have written it anytime in the 1920s. Whether Ives's comment refers to the twelve-tone system is uncertain, but he clearly had nothing in mind similar to the twelve-tone system when he composed the choral version of the song. His plan was programmatic, some very literal tone painting on the words "And for a space become as one." As shown in Figure 4.3, Ives wrote in the score: "On 2nd note in Cho. voices take all tones (semi or even less from B Bass to A sop & go as a group wave to W[ord] one in the sense of a 'Wan.' Voices: E, e, e¹, e².”[26] Music for the following line, "So men seeking common life together for a season become as one," consisted of a held E, with the single comment above, "chant." All twelve tones are present because Ives essentially wrote a tone cluster on the words, "and for a space become as," which dissolves into a unison on the word "one." As a highly descriptive musical effect this passage resembles Penderecki more than Schoenberg. It would obviously be difficult for a solo singer to reproduce it, however. Although Ives did suggest a chorus sing this song, he was not precluding solo performance in the final version.

The tone clusters in the piano at the beginning of the song, shown in Figure 4.4, are analagous to the choral cluster Ives wrote into the eliminated verse five. They function similarily, to create a general level of dissonance or a mass of notes. The choral manuscript confirms that they are Ives's way of rendering the same idea on the piano. The second page of the choral manuscript contains directions to the orchestra quite similar to those of the chorus in the fifth verse: "The ins[trumental] players arrange among thems[elves] to cover as many notes as possible (to have it as strong as a ham[mer]." This comment occurs precisely where tone clusters appear in the piano score.

Both Larry Starr and Stuart Feder associate the dissonances with the masses themselves. Starr argues:

> The enormous tone clusters [in the introduction] serve as a virtually literal portrayal of "masses," and they form the basis of accompaniment when the voice enters at last, proclaiming that very word. As the text continues to reveal the importance and the capabilities of the human masses, the tone clusters disappear, yielding place to a series of well-differentiated musical idioms.[27]

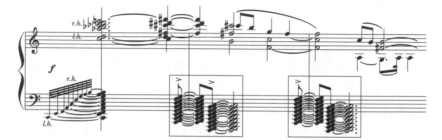

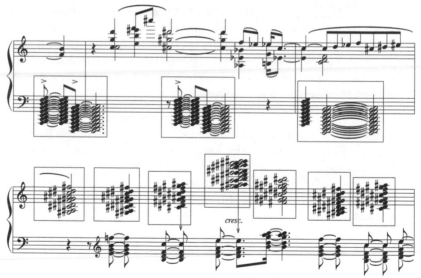

Majority. © 1935 by Merion Music, Inc. Used by Permission.

Figure 4.4: Charles Ives, *Majority*, beginning, from *114 Songs*

The changes that Ives made in the *114 Songs* version do support Starr's thesis of moving from density to simplification. In fact had Ives not eliminated the two verses, the presence of the clusters in them would have undercut that directionality. Starr is not entirely clear, however, about the overall meaning of this in relation to the text. If the dissonances at the beginning represent the masses, which equals the majority, the people, what happens to them? Is the message that they disappear? I would like to offer another suggestion, hinted at by Starr: that in this song we have a progression from the past to the present to the future, and simultaneously a sublimation of the masses as they move from the realm of the earthly into the spiritual. And that spiritual clearly connects with the past. The verbs of the text reflect that: from toiling to thinking to singing to yearning to dreaming. The dissonances refer not to the masses themselves but to "toil," and the masses are already beyond that after the first verse. Toil is the only verse in the past tense.

The final couplet, from Browning, is anything but representative of progressivist reform. It is a dream. Ives has moved from the world of reality, the world of toil, through the world of thought, song, yearning, and finally to the world of dream. He has also changed Browning's verb from "is" to "will be." The vocal line itself becomes diatonic, descending in the most traditional scalar pattern, 3–2–1. And the strange, sudden cadence is less a full cadence on F than an incomplete plagal cadence; as Starr points out it is a truncated amen of a nineteenth-century hymn.[28] Ives has retained the distant, chromatic, dissonant Amen of the earlier version and brought it much more into the foreground.[29] As such the ending is open-ended, the musical counterpart of a transcendental future tense, in which past, present, and future are collapsed. And as the amen cadence suggests, Ives has basically sanctified the masses in this song. In his odd retreat from reality the masses are no longer a political entity but rather something broader and more universal.

If we go back to the essay we discover that the masses assume the same transcendent quality they acquire by the end of the song. Ives uses the terms masses, the majority, and the people synonymously with such terms as the Majority consciousness, the Majority mind, the Majority giant, and the Universal mind. In such a context the essay becomes even more divorced from political reality, but it also becomes more consistent with the song as an idealistic statement.[30]

In spite of his idealism and the tenuous hold on reality the essay suggests, Ives does articulate thoughts and beliefs of some historical importance. His views may be exaggerated, naive, and hopelessly impractical, but he was not out of touch with his time. Ives's idealism connects with several strains of thought prevalent in the late nineteenth and early twentieth centuries, and his statements provide unique insight in understanding an important turning point in American history.

    Ives's politics have at their root two forces recently discussed by
historians. The first is "collective memory," as Michael Kammen has
outlined it: the commemoration and the glorification of a nation's
past. The "memory industry," which Kammen calls official attempts in
some countries to manipulate historical symbols, was less a centralized
industry in America than a vast amalgam of independent agents, publishers, politicians, and others acting to create a collective consciousness revolving around certain episodes, figures, or ideals in American
history.[31] Ives had an acute interest in the past as remembered, and
he transmitted many American cultural myths: Concord,
Massachusetts and transcendentalism in the early nineteenth century,
American patriotism, the nineteenth-century New England town, and
a view of man as a moral, responsible agent. Most potent for him was
the Civil War, because it intersected so deeply with the myth of his
own father. In much of his music he commemorated the myths in very
specific ways. The most obvious of these are the orchestral works
based on patriotic holidays, which are essentially commemorations of
commemorations. *The Fourth of July* for instance captures the holiday
as a boy experienced it in nineteenth-century America, down to the
exploding fireworks.
    But driving Ives's politics and artistic creations is more than the
remembrance of things past. The second and more powerful force
Ives wished to recover was the values of the past. Later in life Ives saw
modern civilization itself as degenerating, and he responded with self-
imposed isolation. He refused to read newspapers or listen to radios,
and he fled New York City as soon and as much as he could.[32] With
his retirement from the insurance business he no longer had to stay
in New York, even part of the year. And the more he retreated to the
past, the more heated his political rhetoric became. Its tone directly
reflected his frustration and disillusionment with the present. It was
an expression of the tension he felt between the world in which he
lived and the past he wanted to reclaim. Ives's rhetoric was the conflict between memory and reality.
    Ives yearned for a simpler, preindustrial time. His artistic life and
political beliefs together constitute one of the purest and most clearly articulated expressions of the late-nineteenth-century tension
Robert Wiebe described twenty-five years ago, the desire to return to
village values in a changing industrial world. According to Wiebe,
America was a small-town society until the late nineteenth century,
"premised upon the community's effective sovereignty, upon its
capacity to manage affairs within its boundaries." Most Americans
still lived within these "personal centers" or "island communities"

and were at best vaguely aware that society had changed, while remaining puzzled about what was changing. Unable to comprehend what was happening to them, "they fought . . . to preserve the society that had given their lives meaning." But "it had already slipped beyond their grasp."[33]

At the national level Americans settled into a general indifference about politics, knowing that the best minds went into business and the moral idealists still went into the ministry. Ives was genuinely and passionately concerned about politics at a level larger than the small town. His views follow directly from his career. He decided to go to New York with apparently no thought of returning to Danbury. His own work in the insurance industry provided him a perspective on man broader than that of caring only for one's immediate neighbor. Ives's passion for humanity was genuine, although it is idealized and abstracted. Yet Ives's political solutions remained small-town, nineteenth-century parochial ones. Rather than expanding his nineteenth-century local view into a broader one that incorporated all humanity, he instead sought to cram all of humanity into a nineteenth-century town.[34]

Yet precisely to what past did Ives wish to return? From what material or experiences did he build his special vision? Scholars, particularly those that associate Ives with progressivism, have foundered on precisely this issue, but any revisionist interpretation of either Ives or his music must provide an alternative answer. I will argue that Ives's views of man and society derived from one major event in his life and two important nineteenth-century traditions, or more precisely myths.

The major event is the Armstrong insurance investigation of 1905. Important as it was, it has never been examined closely by Ives's biographers.[35] The New York State Assembly passed a resolution on July 20, 1905, creating an investigative committee chaired by Senator William W. Armstrong, to look into malpractice in the insurance industry. The committee itself was formed August 1, and hearings began on September 6. They lasted until December 20, and the Committee submitted its report to the legislature February 22, 1906. Much of the investigation centered around James Hazen Hyde, who had inherited control of Equitable Life from his father in 1899, managed it badly and dictatorially, employed questionable business practices, and spent company money on lavish entertainments. Mutual, Ives's company, came under fire for serious actuarial and accounting practices involving insurance policies as well as favoritism and nepotism. Richard A. McCurdy, Mutual's President, drew an extraordinarily high salary and had established his son Robert McCurdy as manager of the Raymond agency, to which Mutual not only channeled many large policies but paid unusually high commissions. The Armstrong Investigation came as no surprise to those in the insurance business; many had foreseen for a considerable time that something like it would occur, and rumors of trouble with the legislature had circulated for months before the actual hearings were announced.[36]

I should state here that the case for the importance of the Armstrong investigation to Ives is based on circumstantial evidence. Ives himself made little mention of it, ever. But the evidence that it was a crucial turning point in Ives's life is substantial. The Armstrong insurance investigation must rank with Ives's complex relationship with his father, including his awareness of his father's situation within the Ives clan, as one of the most important shaping factors in Ives's life. It was a harrowing experience for Ives, threatening his career, but also providing him the rhetoric about the life insurance ideal that became the basis of his political and much of his personal philosophy.[37]

The investigation occurred at a pivotal time in Ives's life. Between 1904 and 1908 Ives changed dramatically both artistically and personally. He suffered two major health crises, his business career nearly collapsed and then flourished in new, unexpected ways, his compositional style changed radically, and he married, ending his extended, almost desperate, attempt to sustain his college days in Poverty Flat.[38] For Ives these four years were a crucible, from which emerged the composer, thinker, and man that we know.

Ives's dark period began in February, 1904, when his uncle Lyman Brewster died. Brewster, a prominent attorney, was the most successful member of the Ives clan. He and his wife, Amelia, were childless and treated Charles and Moss, Ives's brother, as special. For many years after his father George's death Charles sought surrogate fathers, and Brewster apparently filled that role.[39] The extent to which Ives's memory of George, which was so intertwined with his own self, affected the relationship remains a mystery, but at the very least Brewster was an important role model for Ives.[40] Amelia Brewster certainly became the dominant mother figure in Ives's life, though his own mother Mollie was still living. Brewster made it possible for Ives to attend Yale, and Brewster's will made Charles and Moss his heirs after his wife Amelia, and designated the two brothers joint executors of the estate.

Ives's life was changing in other ways. Many of the original members of Poverty Flat had married and started their own families, and their careers were flourishing. Ives began to take an interest in Harmony at about this time, and her brief engagement to Walter Lowrie in late 1904 likely added to the distress of a young man very unsure of himself. Many years later Julian Myrick observed that Ives had many rivals for Harmony's affections in the early years of their developing relationship.[41]

Ives's first health crisis occurred in the summer of 1905, a physical or emotional breakdown about which details are lacking. He had been suffering depression.[42] Ives mentions a composer's slump "around 1905–06," which is confirmed by a relatively low musical output for early 1905.[43] He consulted his friend, Harmony's brother, David Twichell, who was a practicing physician. Ives visited Twichell in Hartford and was invited to spend a few weeks with him in August with the Twichell family on vacation at Saranac Lake in the Adirondacks. Ives extended his stay into September, almost certainly because Harmony came then. Amelia Brewster confirms that Ives's health was a concern. Expecting a summer visit from Ives she wrote him acknowledging the importance of his stay at Saranac: "We want you to get the *most good* possible out of your time and while you know we are always glad to have you home, your health is of the first importance and we wish you to do what is best."[44]

Ives was already weakened by his earlier bout of ill health when he returned from Saranac Lake in September, 1905, only to step into the Armstrong investigation, a much more serious and traumatic situation. Because of his relatively junior position he was not directly in the line of fire from the investigating committee. But as the investigation unfolded it came closer than has been realized. Coming under particular attack were the manner and extent of compensation for agents and agencies, with the Raymond Agency of Mutual singled out as the most egregious of the abusers. Ives not only worked for the Raymond Agency but was assigned to the section that dealt with agents.[45] His level of management is unknown, although he had acquired considerable experience as an in-house manager of agents by 1905. When he and Myrick formed their partnership Ives assumed charge of that part of the business and handled it as an experienced veteran. Whatever Ives did at Raymond, however, he was not only in the house but in the very room under heaviest attack.

Indirectly at least, Ives's business integrity, not to mention the future of his career, was at stake. But the investigation was getting even closer for other reasons. It also zeroed in on practices of nepotism in the industry. The following two excerpts indicate the tone of this line of inquiry and of the principal figures involved:

> The next on the list was Dr. Grenville [Granville] M. White, and Mr. Hughes asked if he was a relative of any of the other officers. The witness said that he didn't think so.
> "Is he a nephew of Mr. Grannis?" Mr. Hughes asked.
> "I don't think he is," said Mr. McCurdy. "I think his wife is a niece of Mrs. Grannis."
> While the laugh was still going around Mr. Beck jumped to his feet and declared with some dramatic emphasis:
> "If it is going to be declared a crime for a man to have a brother or cousin or a niece by marriage connected with him in his business it seems to me the President will have to modify his ideas on race suicide."
> "It isn't a crime," put in Chairman Armstrong. "It's only ridiculous," and Mr. Beck sat down.[46]

> When the question of Mr. Marsh was raised the witness said his impression was that the Mutual's Medical Examiner had married the sister of President McCurdy after he had entered the service of the company.
> "Who is P. Stuyvesant Pillot?" Mr. Hughes asked?
> "I suppose that it is his relation to Mr. Thebaud that you want to know." Mr. McCurdy replied. "He is a cousin to Mr. Thebaud, and has the title of Inspector of Risks."
> Q.—What does that mean.? A.— . . .
> Q.—How long has he held that position? A.—I really don't know; a number of years. . . . Six or seven, I don't know.
> Q.—What is his age? A.—I should say he was about 40.
> Q.—Was he connected with the company prior to that time, prior to the time he became inspector of risks. A.—Yes; his first connection with the company was with the metropolitan agency, as a clerk there, and after that he went into the home office. I think it was in the policy department, or somewhere else; I have forgotten.[47]

Ives must have breathed deeply when he read these excerpts, and since a detailed transcript appeared daily in the *New York Times,* he likely did. The position he took in 1898 as a clerk in the Mutual Office, at almost the same time as Stuyvesant Pillot, he not only acquired originally through nepotism, but through the very people named above, his cousins Granville H. White and Robert Grannis.[48]

Besides the embarrassment, the investigation gave Ives several causes for concern. It quickly became apparent that the Raymond Agency was slated for sacrifice. Ives would be out of a job. Exacerbating this threat, his relationship to Harmony was deepening. Here he was, a young man unsure of himself, in an industry rife with scandal, personally on the brink of having his career tainted, as his own position was originally dependent on the nepotism of those very cousins under fire for such on the witness stand. And just at this moment, the formidable spiritual leader of Hartford, Connecticut, the Reverend Joseph Twichell, loomed as a prospective father-in-law. Ives might continue with Mutual, but life insurance itself had been given a bad name. Ives was ever mindful of his reputation. Feder observed that Ives, who had decided to abandon music as a career by 1902, must have been haunted by the memory of his father's failures, and now he faced the prospect of failing in business.[49]

The investigation also took its toll on Ives's health. In late 1906 he suffered a second collapse.[50] A series of events occurred in its aftermath that profoundly shaped Ives's life. These events have become an integral part of the Ives legend and a stirring story of American business enterprise. But they are almost certainly inaccurate. Here is the story according to all previous accounts: when Ives suffered his second collapse in late 1906, the medical examiner at Mutual suggested that Ives take a vacation, and Ives spent the Christmas holidays at Comfort Springs, Virginia. Julian Myrick accompanied him. On this trip Ives and Myrick considered what to do about the imminent demise of the Raymond Agency. At this moment they conceived of forming their own agency, and on their return Washington Life gave them the opportunity. Associating with Washington put them at a considerable disadvantage vis-à-vis the "big three," Mutual, Equitable, and New York Life. Still, they made a go of it until Washington Life was bought out by Pittsburgh Life and Trust in 1908—at which time Ives and Myrick again found themselves out of a job. They were finally rescued when Mutual decided to take them back, and from there they went on to success.[51]

The above scenario is problematic in several respects. It does not take into account the relationship between Mutual and Washington Life, Ives's position at the Raymond Agency, the timing of the establishment of Ives's and Myrick's first agency in 1907, Mutual's sale of Washington in 1908, the reason that Myrick accompanied Ives to Virginia, and why the first agency was called Ives and Co. and the second Ives and Myrick. When these factors are considered, a very different pattern of events emerges, one that involves Ives much more closely in the aftermath of the investigation, although here I want to stress there is no evidence that Ives himself was engaged in illegal or unethical practices. Even though he was close enough to the flames to feel the heat, he was not fueling the fire. In fact the following alternative scenario is probable because, in the eyes of Mutual, Ives appeared relatively untainted.

First of all Ives's career was in no real danger. When the Raymond Agency disappeared, it was split into several other agencies. Ives's in-house work managing agents was an important position for which there were few qualified individuals. Most young men entering the industry were interested in being where the money was—in the field, selling. As office manager Ives could easily have gotten a job with another Mutual agency.[52]

The key to the alternative scenario is a little-known fact: The Washington Life Insurance Company began as a subsidiary of Mutual. Earlier Frederick Winsten, President of Mutual, had created it specifically to handle excess insurance.[53] The Armstrong Committee, concerned about the stranglehold that the "big three," New York Life, Mutual of New York, and Equitable, had on the insurance business, forced the larger companies to limit the amount of insurance they could carry. Washington Life became a convenient way for Mutual to shift large cases off their books. To what extent Mutual still owned Washington Life in 1906 is unknown, as, not surprisingly, practically all such records from this time have disappeared.[54] But in 1906 Washington Life was run by John Tatlock, who had moved into the presidency in 1905 directly from Mutual.

Ives's first agency was Ives and Co., and Myrick was Ives's assistant. Ives and Co. began operating Jan. 1, 1907, the day the Raymond Agency dissolved, less than a week after Ives and Myrick returned from Virginia.[55] In the standard scenario Ives and Myrick completed all the necessary details to establish the agency, including working out the agreement with Washington Life, in about a week. Were Washington Life a separate institution, would they not have first tried to negotiate with Mutual? The timing seems remarkable, indeed implausible. More likely Tatlock or someone at Mutual set Ives up before the trip to Virginia. Myrick's presence in Virginia strongly supports this thesis. Feder states that Mutual's doctors, who examined Ives, suggested that Myrick go with Ives, but I have found no evidence to substantiate Feder's claim. Rossiter simply states that he went. It turns out Myrick had been asked by upper-level management of the main Mutual office to accompany Ives.[56] Mutual executives may have been truly concerned about Ives, and knowing that he and

Myrick were friends, generously allowed Myrick to go with him. Yet it is difficult to imagine that upper-level management at the main office would have been that involved with or even aware of Ives's personal situation. A far more reasonable explanation for upper management to intervene and send Myrick to Virginia was for him to be there to help work out details of a plan that had already been decided.

By 1908, Washington Life could be sold because the heat from the Armstrong Investigation was off. The company had essentially outlived its usefulness to Mutual.[57] That Ives was quickly taken back into Mutual is thus not surprising, because he had never left it in the first place. In the two years, meanwhile, Myrick had proved his worth, and the company became Ives and Myrick. Many years later Myrick showed extraordinary generosity to Ives; that feeling of mutual respect and closeness may have come from Ives's generosity in this early stage.

In spite of the good fortune that eventually came to Ives from the Armstrong investigations, evidence suggests that the revelations were originally unsettling. After a compositional hiatus during 1905 Ives immersed himself in composition, writing in 1906 several highly original and experimental pieces, pieces that raise basic questions about the nature of music and its stylistic and structural possibilities. A new seriousness and philosophical questioning also pervades many of these works. The two most important in this regard are *In the Cage*, from the *Set for Theatre Orchestra*, and *The Unanswered Question*. *In the Cage* pointedly addresses questions about life and its potential.[58] With *The Unanswered Question* Ives began his investigation of the most fundamental questions of life and existence.[59] In 1906 Ives sought universal answers about life itself, answers that dealt in the broadest sense with the human condition.

Ives might retreat into music, but he could not escape his business world and all the moral questions that it raised. Particularly since he and Harmony were drawing closer, he had to come to terms with the world of insurance, philosophically as well as financially. Ironically the investigation itself presented Ives a solution at least to the moral dimension. On October 11, 1905 Richard A. McCurdy, President of Mutual Life, testified that life insurance as practiced by mutual companies was a philanthropic, eleemosynary enterprise, benefiting humanity at large, and that it had been wrongly understood as a moneymaking institution: "Every person ought to understand when he takes a policy of life insurance that he is not doing it solely for his own benefit, but he is participating in a great movement for the benefit of humanity at large and for every other person who comes in and takes a policy in that company, and in that way joins the great brother-hood."[60]

McCurdy went on to claim that Mutual was founded as a "great beneficent missionary institution," and that "profits were not thought of, were not dreamed of." He described his mission in evangelical terms, "to extend the benefits of life insurance as far as possible within the limits of safety and as far as practicable into every town and hamlet of this country."[61]

The extent to which this idealistic vision was part of the Mutual philosophy or was an ingenious invention in the box by a clever but unscrupulous businessman is unclear. The testimony itself was greet-ed with laughter and derision, which only continued when Hughes inquired whether this vision had figured in the literature of the com-pany. McCurdy replied that it had earlier, but in the last ten years, only "inferentially." McCurdy's own career was hardly a model of enlightened humanitarianism. He figured prominently in the investi-gation because of widespread allegations of questionable if not sleazy business practices. The philosophy he articulated was probably a the-oretical ideal, known but ignored by those in the industry. Regardless of its origin, however, McCurdy's testimony is an almost exact state-ment of the beliefs that would guide Ives's work in the insurance industry and by extension become part of his overall philosophy. McCurdy may have used them cynically; Ives embraced them fully and honestly.

Had Ives been familiar with this rhetoric earlier, it probably had little effect on him. As a young man Ives was highly impressionable but not prone to serious reflection. His work, music, and the social chaos of Poverty Flat all but precluded such. Harmony changed that. Her own idealism and sense of duty and service, as well as her more thoughtful, contemplative approach to life were not lost on Ives. She encouraged him to read and to reflect. In addition Ives must have felt not only the heat of his association with the Raymond Agency, but some shame from it. It was time to reconsider his profession and his role in it. From that emerged a philosophy of life, later translated into political beliefs. That it conformed closely with McCurdy's testimony is not coincidental. Even Ives's cousin Amelia Ives Van Wyck observed that his political outlook was based on a view of mankind derived from the ideals of the life insurance industry.[62]

Life insurance as a humanitarian enterprise accounts for much but not all of Ives's political philosophy. Ives did connect with several nineteenth-century traditions, but care must be exercised to distin-guish between superficial and significant connections. For example his idealistic vision of a social order based on direct democracy resembles some turn-of-the-century strains of utopian thought. Utopian thinkers such as Lester F. Ward, Simon Nelson Patten, Edward A. Ross, or Walter Rauschenbusch talked about society evolving in stages, from the smaller community into some sort of world-wide utopia, where peace, harmony, and in some cases Christian values would prevail. They spoke of the "Christian Commonwealth," the "Creative Economy," the "Free City."[63]

Like progressivism, these ideas resemble Ives's, but like progressivism, they differ fundamentally. Utopians were highly diverse, but most believed that society was evolving toward a more benevolent and classless state through the productive capacity of industrialization. Ives's thought, however, was essentially pre-industrial. To Ives the material benefit of industrialization is peripheral, and, as we have noted, the class structure that is an inevitable byproduct of industrialization is curiously absent from his thinking. As Rossiter and others have observed, Ives saw white, male, middle-class America (that is, the clients of Ives and Myrick's Insurance agency) as the social norm, the basis for his ideal town.

The "Majority" essay seems to embrace socialism. Ives believed in group management or direct majority management for large industries such as the railroads. The workers, workers equaling majority, participate collectively in running the business. Ives also advocated nationalization of some industries, but here the term had a special meaning. An industry was to be nationalized "when a group occupation becomes, in character and in size, a Majority business."[64]

On closer examination Ives remained very much a capitalist. He did not advocate socialism. He did not suggest that ownership of a majority business become public, although he is unclear about the plight of the owners. Ownership, like class, was unimportant for Ives. In the case of national industries Ives believed that if not only the owners and workers, but also those who used the product, participated in the management of the business, it would be a better business. His advocacy of an apparent socialist approach was based on abstract ideas of efficiency, not on issues of capital and ownership.

At about the same time that Ives became interested in political issues, *The Masses*, a socialist journal, appeared in New York. Founded in 1911, it at first espoused the vision of an idealistic community based on cooperation and the common good, ideas similar to Ives's. It supported high art as a means of inspiring and uplifting the worker. According to Rebecca Zurier, "*The Masses*' early editors assumed that if the proletariat could be taught to appreciate great works of art, these works would eventually exert an improving influence."[65] It is easy to imagine Ives being attracted to this philosophy.

Internal and external evidence suggest that Ives was familiar with *The Masses*. The original title of the song *Majority* was *The Masses*, and the text refers to the masses' thinking, singing, yearning, and dreaming as the source of the world's thought, art, hope, and vision. This is consistent with the idealism of the first incarnation of the journal. Moreover, the journal was supported by men in the insurance industry and by friends of Ives's. It was originally capitalized by Rufus Weeks, vice president of the New York Life Insurance Company, and later by Amos Pinchot, a socialist and friend of Ives from his college days.[66] The journal was probably the original inspiration for Ives's song, *Majority*.

Had Ives been interested in *The Masses*, however, he would not have remained so. The journal never caught on and after a seventeen-month struggle went out of business in August 1912, to be reborn in December 1912 under new ownership as a much more radical magazine. It is inconceivable that Ives would have reacted positively to the new *The Masses*. It was dedicated to a highly sharpened awareness of class struggle. Through a vivid, at times wrenching, portrayal of the workers as the victims of an evil capitalistic system run by greedy, rapacious exploiters, it loudly proclaimed socialism. Although Ives had plenty of vitriol for the "hog-mind," the greedy barons of the gilded age and beyond, the point of view in *The Masses* contrasted sharply with his belief that given the opportunity all men would work together putting the common good above personal greed.

But even if Ives could have somehow reconciled the socialist orientation of *The Masses* with his own idealistic political thought, his Victorian morality would have been even more repelled by *The Masses'* stances on art and love. *The Masses* strongly supported modern art, and reproduced many works within its covers that featured realistic representations of nudity. Frequently the nudity had a political purpose, as in Robert Minor's cartoon of Anthony Comstock, Secretary of the New York Society for the Prevention of Vice, published in the October–November 1915 issue and shown in Figure 4.5. Minor's cartoon depicts Comstock as a crazed pigmy attacking a voluptuous, prone nude, with an outlandishly oversized sword. Its Freudian content is obvious.

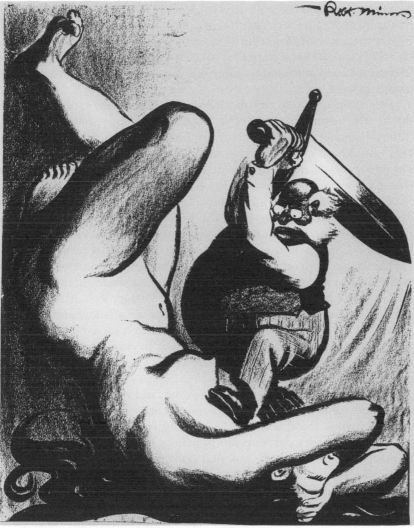

Figure 4.5: Robert Minor, *O Wicked Flesh,* published in *The Masses* 7, no. 1, (October–November 1915): 20

Ives opposed nudity even in painting, as he clearly revealed when he met by chance a friend from Yale who had become a painter. He commented in his diary, "The human anatomy can never be and has never been the inspiration for a great work of art. It's a medium to be used in Gods service and not stared at by Gods servants."[67] It is also hard to conceive Ives getting beyond his Victorian notions of sexual morality to react favorably to *The Masses'* sympathetic portrayal of prostitutes as further victims of the powerful capitalistic class. Prostitution was an issue that Ives would not discuss. In general both he and Harmony were noted for an extreme reticence on any matters that even hinted at sexuality. They felt such issues should remain completely private.

Ives and *The Masses* did share some goals, such as creating a society in which women were more equal. Their approaches, however, differed dramatically. One can only imagine the horror with which Ives would have greeted the proposal that marriage be eliminated, as *The Masses* advocated, because it consigned women to a subjective role. Charles and Harmony Ives were deeply committed to marriage as an important social institution. Ives's own commitment to the insurance business sprang from the same source. At the very core of Ives's beliefs, which include his deep-seated feelings about masculinity, was his fundamental sense of a man's responsibility to his family.

The Masses, a product of Greenwich Village, was in the words of William O'Neill, "a local institution reflecting some of the idiosyncrasies of the pre-war Village." Greenwich Village, well-established as a center of bohemianism by the 1910s, remained a "small and intimate place."[68] Ives did not find it congenial, although he lived close by. In fact it is remarkable that although Ives was in close physical proximity to many avant-garde artists in the village, he seems to have made no effort to interact with them.

Yet Ives's idealism, interest in the past, and deep sense of responsibility do connect him with two nineteenth-century political traditions or myths. Along with the Armstrong Investigation these are the two principal sources of his political beliefs. The first of these is republicanism. The second is the colonial revival.

I call republicanism a myth because, while it was a potent political philosophy in early America, it was an ideal never realized, even in the eighteenth century. Republicanism as a political philosophy is not to be confused with the Republican Party, although originally there were overlaps. Advocated by the eighteenth-century upper class, who saw in it a way to perpetuate their own hierarchy, republicanism was designed to maintain the existing social order.

Republicans believed in a homogeneous society, in which everyone kept their place and in which the arts could help establish social unity. The original version of *The Masses*, the journal, advocated the same role for the arts. Ives's belief in the people acting as an organic entity, his trust in the majority, his optimism about what he considered the common man, his opinions about direct town-meeting governance, and his lack of sympathy for anyone who got out of line, are eighteenth-century republican tenets. Central to Ives's political thinking is the notion that men are motivated by a willingness to place the interest of society above their own individual desires. That is the heart of republicanism.

Nowhere does Ives come closer to a republican position than in the closing of the "Majority" essay, when he considers what a dissenting minority is to do. Like the eighteenth-century republicans, Ives does not find the alternatives inviting: (1) "He can abide by the winner's terms . . .; (2) the Minority man can go to some other country whose laws are more congenial to him; or (3) he can begin to shriek, to get nasty, hysterical, and begin to throw things around—and then the Majority will strangle him—and treat him like a farmer treats a skunk who loses his self-respect."[69] This closely parallels eighteenth-century ideals of homogeneity; it also recalls the solidarity that characterizes the masses in the song.

Historians have taken republicanism on an extended journey in the last twenty years, and I will not retrace familiar landmarks.[70] Ives does provide a few interesting twists and turns. He comes closest to the republicanism narrative as defined by Jean Baker. Baker argues that by the late nineteenth century republicanism no longer appeared in conscious debate but had instead filtered down to the level of culture, or what Clifford Geertz calls "the point at which ideas become a layer of culture, and sentiments turn into symbols, ideas into habits." Republicanism was embedded in an elaborate set of symbols and rituals, enacted in the school, in the home, and in the political process. According to Baker "republican ideas were encoded into the institutional life of the community, not as precise postulates of formal doctrine, but as vague behaviors."[71]

Because of its very nature, music gave Ives an ideal vehicle to perpetuate republicanism as it had evolved by the late nineteenth century. Music's freedom from linguistic restraints, ability to arouse feelings of nostalgia, and potential for simultaneous presentation of multiple ideas permit juxtaposition and manipulation of symbols in a way possible with few other modes of communication. Ives could capture the basic essence of republicanism through an elaborate and often nondiscursive set of allusions, sentiments, and symbols. Many of his pieces that deal with the past, in particular the national past, do just that. Much of Ives's music is about the creation of myth: the myth of the majority, the myth of the patriot, the myth of collective responsibility. These together form the myth of eighteenth- and nineteenth-century republicanism.

Ives as well as many nineteenth-century intellectuals saw the Civil War as a crucial turning point, affecting the republican vision. Charles Eliot Norton recognized the emergence of a new nationalism from it. Norton was a nineteenth-century New England Brahmin intellectual in the fashion of Henry Adams or William James. With the Civil War as a powerful catalyst, old-guard New England republicans such as Norton began to see themselves more as Americans, or at least to define themselves in terms of the nation rather than New England alone. The "new nationality" which appeared was still based, however, on the classical premise of an individual's willingness to subvert his will to that of a broader good. Like Ives, Norton envisioned his nationality in the broadest humanitarian terms: the "sentiment of nationality" lifted people "out of narrow and selfish individualism into a region where they behold their duties as members of another, and as partakers of the general life of humanity."[72]

Ives's political vision, which sounds much like Norton's, also contrasts notably with it. A member of an elite New England family, Norton was one of the last direct descendants of the older republican tradition; for Ives, growing up later and in a different class, republicanism was neither real nor direct. A loose amalgamation of ideas rather than a unified political philosophy, it was neither the sole nor even the principal tradition from which Ives drew. And in contrast to Norton's ideas, Ives's republicanism seems to go from the village to all of humanity, skipping the nation as an entity. Ives is either universal or local, and admits little in between. His concept of nation is global. He provides little discussion of the nation as a state, and even less acknowledgment of a practical national government. In fact the reforms he proposed sought to enervate if not demolish the nation as a political entity. This tendency is only one more indication of Ives's distorted sense of reality, which contrasts notably with Norton's attempts at sound political theory.

The Civil War was important to both Ives and Norton, but for very different reasons. For Norton the Civil War was immediate, and his writings come directly out of his experience of it. For Ives it was a distant event made real by his own imagination. And what he remembered, more than anything else, was his father's imagined place in it. The Civil War, while actually remote, was to Ives close and personal, less a humanitarian cause than part of his own family myth.[73]

Because Ives viewed the Civil War as a personal rather than a political event, it had little effect on his principal source of inspiration, the pre-industrial New England village. Ives's idealization of the New England village is the most important factor shaping his political vision. It is the principal source of his political philosophy. But it was not an isolated or anachronistic quirk. It was part of an extensive movement in nineteenth-century New England, the colonial revival. The colonial revival is the second and by far the most powerful myth shaping Ives's philosophy, including his political beliefs.

The colonial revival was a typically New England response to the growing industrialization of America. It began shortly after the Civil War and was most visible in architecture, in attempts to restore and maintain in their original state New England towns. Old buildings were preserved and restrictions placed on the erection of new ones. But the colonial revival was more than an architectural movement. The restored village became the romanticized symbol of all that was best about early New England, and inferentially America, "an emblem of . . . stability, morality, and democracy."[74] As the movement caught on the revival had a major impact on literature. Writers such as Harriet Beecher Stowe and Henry Ward Beecher extolled the New England town, depicting village life, including its politics, in glowing, mythological terms.[75] Beecher and Stowe not coincidentally grew up in Litchfield, Connecticut, one of the most important of the colonial revival towns. By the late nineteenth century, small-town life in New England had become a favorite topic in many short stories and novels, and by the early twentieth century, according to Alan Axelrod, "the ubiquitous New England village was a popular subject for art, literature, and advertising and had become a stereotype in the American mind."[76]

Historians other than architectural historians have yet to investigate the colonial revival, particularly its political impact, but its importance to Ives is clear. Ives's creative life and work is the colonial revival in action. It transcended his politics, affecting every aspect of his art. Virtually everyone who has looked at Ives has been struck by the intensity of his memories of small town New England, which became the principal source of his creativity. How he hung on to those memories is remarkable, and why, in spite of his success in twentieth-century New York, has been a paradox. In the context of the colonial revival, this is no puzzle. The idealized New England village was constantly in the press and in literature around him.

For Ives the ultimate political paradigm was the New England town meeting. This New England tradition encapsulated all that Ives believed about man and his society: it encompassed his ideal of direct democracy, the principle of the "Majority" essay; it recalled Concord and the transcendental tradition; it took Ives back to an earlier, less complex, pre-industrial era; it celebrated a way of life dominated by homogeneity of interests; it had at its heart a staunch Yankee individualism; and finally, it placed the true seat of democracy itself in New England.

Ives, as the twentieth-century man desperately wishing to escape to a simpler, earlier time, could return to a classless New England village, in which all men, and I use that term with all its gender implications, worked together for the good of the village. Ives's commentary about his Second String Quartet articulates his political ideal. The movements are entitled: "Discussions," "Argument," and "The Call of the Mountains." In a sketch he wrote: "S.Q. for 4 men—who converse, argue (in re 'Politick'), fight, shake hands shut up—then walk up the mountain side to view the firmament."[77] Some years later, Nicolas Slonimsky apologized for a ragged performance of Ives's *Three Places in New England.* Ives responded with a direct reference to the town meeting: "Just like a town meeting—every man for himself. Wonderful how it came out."[78]

For Ives, growing up in Danbury, memories of small-town New England were real, and it is not surprising that his political views would be shaped by them. Ives seems completely unaware, however, that his idealized political philosophy had no basis of reality, even in his memory. In this case Ives's thought was not anachronistic. He was much a man of his time, buying fully into one of the more potent myths of his youth. The New England town meeting as the birthplace of American democracy was part of the colonial revival. It was a fabrication, a mythological creation of the late nineteenth century.

In reality governance in early New England towns was anything but democratic. Town meetings existed, and theoretically reflected a democratic process; elected officials had to listen to citizens and the majority prevailed. The meetings, however, were strictly controlled. Hierarchy was clear and constantly displayed. Town offices rewarded wealth and family status. Church pews were assigned according to a family's position in the hierarchy, and the church assembly was by far the most important social organization in the town. Colonial New England was a theocracy, with the minister's sermons, lasting upward of three hours, providing the intellectual foundation. And those sermons stressed authority, obedience, and terror for those who strayed. As Ronald Bushman noted, "The entire social structure, including the church, reinforced the doctrine of authority, and made it clear that those at the top of the pyramid were expected to govern, and that it would be a serious mistake for those who did not occupy such a position to try and do so."[79]

The town meeting was essentially the church service secular. The same congregation assembled, and even though the minister did not preside, the magistrate, who held a comparable position in the governmental structure, was the same figure of authority and majesty. Church, state, law, and moral authority merged to create one monolithic whole designed to discourage dissent in either religious or secular matters. Page Smith summarized this position, "For the town there was only one truth—its own." The franchise was broad, as most towns were governed by consensus, but consensus, not disagreement was expected, and through many subtle pressures, ruthlessly enforced.[80]

Idealization of the New England town as the seat of democracy occurred in the second half of the nineteenth century, between the Civil War and the 1890s, precisely correspondent with the colonial revival.[81] Two prominent multivolume nineteenth-century histories, one written mostly in the 1860s, the other in the 1890s, vividly illustrate the change in attitude. In 1858 John Gorham Palfrey published the first volume of his five-volume *History of New England*.[82] There and in the next two volumes (1860 and 1864) he discusses Colonial government, focusing almost exclusively on activities of the state government. References to town government are few and limited mainly to what the state records show, that town governments were subservient to the state and that mostly they maintained law and order. The closest he comes to extolling the town is by observing that the towns relate to the states as states do to the national government, with New England government being "the opposite of political centralization."[83]

In 1893 Charles Adams presented a very different picture.[84] He lauds the town meeting as the saving force in colonial life, and as the very seat of democracy itself. His language is romantic, his description mythological. He treats the records of those town meeting as sacred objects in the history of democracy, akin to the Magna Carta and the Declaration of Independence:

It is in the towns and town records of Massachusetts, therefore, that the American historical unit is to be sought. . . . The details are trivial, monotonous; and not easy to clothe with interest: yet the volumes which contain them are the most precious of archives. Upon their tattered and yellow pages the hardly legible letters of the ill-spelled words are written in ink grown pale with age; but they are all we have left to tell us of the first stages of a political growth which has since ripened into the dominant influence of the new world: nor is it too much to imagine that when the idea of full human self-government, first slowly welded into practical form in the New England towns, and as yet far from perfected, shall have permeated the civilized world and assumed final shape, then these town records will be accepted as second in historical importance to no other description or archives.[85]

Clearly between the time of Palfrey's and Adams's studies the town meeting assumed a very different place in the American democratic myth. The power of that myth can be found when Adams is forced into fanciful interpretation of evidence. Even Adams had to admit that the towns limited participation, as the records show. Nevertheless he surmised:

> But, though the law was thus restrictive, there is reason to believe the practice in town-meeting was far more democratic, and that from a comparatively early day all who were accepted inhabitants or householders were by tacit common consent, if not otherwise, admitted to an equal voice.[86]

Adams gives no support for this supposition. But for him to conclude otherwise would undermine the entire premise of New England as the cradle of American democracy.

If the town meeting myth was so powerful that Adams, a prominent historian who had contradictory evidence in front of him, could so easily dismiss that evidence, can it be any surprise that Ives, whose political beliefs were extremely idealistic and more than a little naive, would buy wholeheartedly into the concept? Ives's political ideas, like much of his music, were original, in some ways unique, but they came from sources much about him. And they are not anachronistic, at least at first. They are reflexive; they do look back to the nineteenth century, but those looks back were characteristic of that time when his ideas were formed.

There is a lag between the formation of Ives's ideas and their full-blown appearance in words or music. For this reason Ives appears anachronistic. Much of Ives's political vision was formed in those crucial years between 1905 and 1908, even though he did not express any direct interest in politics then or articulate fully his views until after the First World War.[87] By 1908 Ives had worked through his life insurance crisis and begun to see insurance as the concept of shared responsibility in practice. He had become disenchanted with the changed Danbury and was already planning his escape to West Redding, an idealized quest for an earlier New England. And he was becoming fascinated with the transcendentalists, seeing behind their flowering the remarkable pre-industrial town of Concord. To Ives Concord is as much a part of the transcendental tradition as Emerson, Hawthorne, or Thoreau. And soon thereafter he would begin work on his remembrances of shared patriotic holidays, the focus of late-nineteenth-century republican encoding.

Spurred by a desire to return to the values of the nineteenth century, Ives fused his ideals of life insurance, his beliefs in the republican concept of responsibility, and his vision of a pre-industrial New England town meeting into a political philosophy that burned inside him with an incredible intensity. As long as he believed it possible, it fueled much of his creativity. That belief crumbled, however, on November 2, 1920, with the election of Harding, its implicit rejection of the League of Nations, and Ives's embittered reaction. Within three years Ives was practically finished as a composer, although for several years he continued to revise previous works. His retreat into anger, cynicism, and isolation had begun.

But in the realm of politics Ives never stopped feeling and trying. He continued to send letters to politicians through the 1930s. And he continued to lobby well into the 1940s.[88] In the early 1940s Ives received an announcement of a meeting at the Redding Ridge School, organized by the Fairfield County Committee for a Declared War against Nazi Germany. They issued a pamphlet and a post card asking everyone to sign. The post card said "I am in agreement with the purposes of The Fairfield County Committee for a Declared War against Nazi Germany." Ives wrote, or had written on the post card:

> Yes, if it may be a bigger move than just war between two countries; that its fundamental aim be to help free the world from slavery and its cowardly brutality; and that the United States will do everything possible (and it probably will) to make this clear to all the world a move presaging the people's world police, and also one which may in some way help the people to build a World Union of Democratic States.

This statement was not simply a hasty note dashed off in a sudden burst of anger. Ives spent considerable time drafting this. In the Ives's material there are several pages of attempted drafts, in his daughter's Edith's hand.[89]

Ives's health problems undoubtedly had much to do with the end of his creativity, although it was not until 1926 that he acknowledged that his creative life was over. His health crisis of 1918 may have been precipitated by a meeting with one of Franklin Roosevelt's representatives. Ives was on a committee, chaired by Roosevelt, to sell Liberty Bonds. Ives wanted a fifty-dollar bond so more people could participate; Roosevelt scorned the notion of a bond so small. Ives had a heated argument with a Roosevelt representative, and according to Harmony's diary, he suffered a heart attack shortly after the meeting.[90] In any event, his song *Nov. 2, 1920*, underscores just how bitter Ives was over the 1920 election. There is a defiant, optimistic tone in it, Ives refusing to give up. But it is Ives's most savage and cynical work. Unlike many other songs, there is virtually no irony in *Nov. 2, 1920*.

Ives wanted his imaginary New England village to become global. With the 1920 election he knew that would not happen. To Ives humanity had given way to selfish national interests. He could neither understand nor accept that verdict, and with the election Ives in more ways than one went over the edge. The 1920 election closed a major chapter in Ives's life in much the same way that events of 1905–7 opened one, and Ives's disillusionment about politics contributed in no small way to the end of his creative life.

NOTES

1. Few episodes in Ives's life are as strange and at the same time touching as the sheer ineptitude of his endeavor to have a proposed twentieth amendment to the constitution distributed at the 1920 Republican National Convention. Ives recruited Darby Day, a Mutual Life Insurance agent in Chicago, to help him, but the material arrived only after the convention. See the Ives–Day correspondence in the Charles Ives Papers, compiled by Vivian Perlis, Yale University Music Library Archival Collection, MSS. 14, box 35, folder 5. Precisely how many political compositions Ives wrote depends on how broadly the term politics is defined.

2. As late as the 1940s Ives was still writing letters and notes expressing his political views. And one of his last acts of composition was to update the World War I song, *He Is There!*, to include references to Hitler and the situation in the early 1940s. Nothing better captures the fervor of Ives's politicial feeling than the well-known recording of it with Ives singing and playing the piano (*Charles Ives: The One Hundredth Anniversary*, LP M4 32504, Columbia Records, 1974).

3. The debate about the dates of Ives's compositions was touched off by Maynard Solomon, "Charles Ives: Some Questions of Veracity," *Journal of the American Musicological Society* 40 (Fall 1987): 443–70, although Kirkpatrick had observed in 1974, "All datings in Ives are problematical," in *An Ives Celebration: Papers and Panels of the Charles Ives Centennial Festival-Conference*, ed. H. Wiley Hitchcock and Vivian Perlis (Urbana: University of Illinois Press, 1977), 69. Other scholars who have addressed the question include J. Peter Burkholder, "Charles Ives and His Fathers: A Response to Maynard Solomon," in *I.A.S.M. Newsletter* 18, no. 1 (November 1988): 8–11; J. Philip Lambert, "Communications," *Journal of the American Musicological Society* 42 (Spring 1989): 204–9, followed by Solomon's response, 209–18; Carol K. Baron, "Dating Charles Ives's Music: Facts and Fictions," *Perspectives of New Music* 28, no. 1 (Winter

1990): 20–56; Stuart Feder, *Charles Ives: "My Father's Song": A Psychoanalytic Biography* (New Haven: Yale University Press, 1992), 351–57; Gayle Sherwood, "Questions and Veracities: Reassessing the Chronology of Ives's Choral Works," *The Musical Quarterly* 78 (Fall 1994): 429–47. Sherwood's article is adapted from her dissertation "The Choral Works of Charles Ives: Chronology, Style, Reception" (Ph.D. diss., Yale University, 1995). Significant books on Ives's musical style and structure include Larry Starr, *A Union of Diversities: Style in the Music of Charles Ives* (New York: Schirmer Books, 1992) and most recently J. Peter Burkholder, *All Made of Tunes: Charles Ives and the Uses of Musical Borrowing* (New Haven: Yale University Press, 1995).

4. Lawrence Kramer, "Cultural Politics and Musical Form: The Case of Charles Ives," in *Classical Music and Postmodern Knowledge* (Berkeley: University of California Press, 1995), 174–200.

5. Burkholder, *All Made of Tunes*, discusses Ives's use of quotation and programmatic material as a kind of commentary on these matters.

6. Peter Conn, *The Divided Mind: Ideology and Imagination in America, 1898–1917* (New York: Cambridge University Press, 1983).

7. J. Peter Burkholder, *Charles Ives: The Ideas Behind the Music* (New Haven: Yale University Press, 1985), 106–7.

8. Twice in the passage quoted above Burkholder seems to equate the terms populist and progressive. Frank Rossiter states that Ives "was obviously a progressive," because he was interested in what Rossiter considers progressive reforms, "the initiative, the referendum, and 'direct democracy.'" Frank Rossiter, *Charles Ives and His America* (New York: Liveright, 1973), 127.

9. Ives described the piano part as follows: "The same chord hit hard over and over. Hot Air election Slogan," which he called "a sad chord—a hopeless chord—a chord of futility." John Kirkpatrick, *A Temporary Mimeographed Catalogue of the Music Manuscripts and Related Material of Charles Edward Ives, 1874–1954* (New Haven: Library of the Yale School of Music, 1960), 195.

10. Other Ives songs or song fragments with political overtones are *The New River; Lincoln, the Great Commoner; Tolerance;* and *Sneak Thief.* Burkholder, *Charles Ives,* 106, describes several of these.

11. The song, in its final version, is entitled *Majority*; the essay "The Majority." The song appears in Charles Ives, *114 Songs* (Redding, Conn.: By the Author, 1922; reprint, New York: Peer International, Associated Music Publishers, and Theodore Presser, 1975), 1–5. The essay has been printed in *Essays Before a Sonata, The Majority, and Other Writings by Charles Ives*, ed. Howard Boatwright (New York: W. W. Norton, 1970), 142–99.

12. Although *114 Songs* is for solo voice, Ives suggested that a unison chorus sing this song because of the difficulty of a solo singer holding his or her part against the piano.

13. Charles Ives Papers, box 25, folder 1.

14. Ives's first dated comment on ideas in the "Majority" essay appeared in 1916, in a reply to a letter from H. P. Davison, dated January 1, 1916. This and the several drafts of the essay are in the Charles Ives Papers, box 25, folders 1 and 2.

15. Ives, *Essays*, 184–86.

16. Ives, *Essays*, 186. It is curious that as late as 1992 this idea was still being presented in presidential campaigns.

17. Ives, *Essays*, 172. Here and earlier he stated that he preferred a maximum property value of $100,000 but would allow up to $150,000. The 1995 equivalent amounts are based on the chart, "Consumer Price Index—1913 to 1995 (log scale)" published by Investec on the World Wide Web at http://www.investec.com/mocharts.html.

18. Ives's income tax records are in the Charles Ives Papers, box 38, folder 1.

19. The 1892 platform of the People's Party was considered the purest summary of Populist sentiment, for by 1896 the Populist program was being diluted, as the Populists aligned with William Jennings Bryan in the presidential election. The 1892 platform stressed class divisions wrought by the industrialization of America. That much Populist support was rural only reflects the extent that industrialization, particularly in the form of the railroads, affected all of America. The platform outlined labor, wealth, railroads, finance, transportation, and land as main topics. The first topic clarifies who they were: "That the union of the labor forces of the United States of America this day consummated shall be permanent and perpetual. . . ." The section on wealth stated that those who create it should own it. Railroads, the telegraph, and telephone systems were to be taken over by the state.

In addition to the platform, the 1892 platform committee reported a series of ten "resolutions expressive of the sentiments of this Convention." Many of these have to do with specific labor union issues, such as the condemnation of the importation of foreign labor, the use of "standing armies" such as Pinkertons (mentioned by name), sympathy with efforts to shorten work hours, and the fights of the Knights of Labor against the clothing manufacturers of Rochester.

Resolution Seven supported the initiative and referendum: "Resolved, That we commend to the favorable consideration of the people and the reform press the legislative system known as the initiative and referendum." This is the only part of the platform that bears any resemblance to Ives's thought, and it is not even part of the platform itself. This summary of the Populist position is taken from George McKenna, *American Populism* (New York: Putnam, 1974), 91–94.

20. The problems of progressivism as an historical term were raised particularly by John D. Buenker, "The Progressive Era: A Search for a Synthesis," *Mid-America* 51 (1969): 175–193, and Peter G. Filene, "An Obituary for 'The Progressive Movement,'" *American Quarterly* 22 (1970): 20–34. A list of the voluminous scholarly writing that followed Filene's and Buenker's essays is found in John D. Buenker and Nicholas C. Burckel, eds., *Progressive Reform: A Guide to Information Sources* (Detroit: Gale Research, 1980).

21. Crunden, Robert Morse, *Ministers of Reform: The Progressives' Achievement in American Civilization 1889–1920* (New York: Basic Books, 1982), ix and 274.

22. Daniel T. Rodgers, "In Search of Progressivism," *Reviews in American History* 10 (1982): 116–17 and 123.

23. Kirkpatrick, *Temporary Mimeographed Catalogue*, 126–27.

24. Charles E. Ives, *Memos*, ed. John Kirkpatrick (New York: W. W. Norton: 1972), 164; Rossiter, *Charles Ives*, 137; Solomon, "Charles Ives," 456.

25. After about 1930 Ives suffered sufficient tremor that his handwriting resembled what he called "snake tracks." See Feder, *Charles Ives*, 345.

26. By "wan" Ives is referring to the sound the chorus makes as it slides up the scale, "in a group wave," on the word "one."

27. Starr, *Union of Diversities*, 133–34. Feder is less direct than Starr: "The text is about the masses, and the music itself represents mass—indeed *has* mass. It is massive in space and in sound, as are many passages in Ives" (*Charles Ives*, 335).

28. Starr, *Union of Diversities*, 137–38.

29. Ives's original ending, although more chromatic and complex, incorporates the amen effect in a different way, as the second violins echo a distant amen in a remote key.

30. Ives, *Essays*, 146, 148, 151, and 199. The "Majority" essay has been characterized by Stuart Feder as the "central verbal document of this period of Ives's life," as well as a "ranting, vituperative dialogue," with "groping, rambling, and often irrelevant text," demonstrating that Ives's "hold on reality was tenuous" (*Charles Ives*, 298 and

301). Feder's assessment is psychological and may be a bit harsh, but Feder is entirely correct in one sense: the essay is not a realistic political statement in either tone or content.

31. Michael Kammen, *Mystic Chords of Memory* (New York: Alfred A. Knopf, 1991), 3.

32. Harmony Twichell, letter to Ives, January 15, 1908, quoted in Rossiter, *Charles Ives,* 127.

33. Robert Wiebe, *The Search for Order, 1877–1920* (New York: Hill and Wang, 1967), 44.

34. Rossiter, *Charles Ives,* 138, explicitly rejects the notion that Ives was engaged in the "search for order" that Wiebe found to be characteristic of professional men in the late nineteenth century. To the extent that the search for order was part of the progressive spirit of targeted reform, Rossiter is correct. And by the 1910s, when Ives was writing about politics, America had lived through the Roosevelt reforms and was coming to terms with a new, more interlocked industrial society. Yet even though Ives's nostalgia and desire to maintain the past is extreme and on the surface anachronistic, Ives's anxiety about the industrial future, often considered aberrant, admits another interpretation, that, in spite of reforms and war, or possibly because of them, a widespread anxiety about the disappearance of the village as the model of society persisted.

35. David Wooldridge, *From the Steeples and Mountains: A Study of Charles Ives* (New York: Alfred A. Knopf, 1974), 128–9, has the most extensive discussion. It is also mentioned in Rossiter, *Charles Ives,* 111, and Feder, *Charles Ives,* 179–80.

36. Shepard B. Clough, *A Century of American Life Insurance: A History of the Mutual Life Insurance Company of New York 1843–1943* (New York: Columbia University Press, 1946), 214.

37. Feder, *Charles Ives,* 180, rightly speculates that Ives was certainly aware of what was going on and that he probably narrowly escaped being implicated. How close he was will soon become apparent.

38. Poverty Flat was the name given a series of apartments that a group of former Yale students rented in New York City and where Ives lived between 1898 and 1908. The personnel and the location changed over the years, but a college atmosphere remained.

39. Feder, *Charles Ives,* refers to Brewster as a "second father" to Charles. There is no direct evidence about what Ives thought about this arrangement, other than a clear appreciation for the help that Brewster gave. Shortly after Ives's engagement to Harmony, and three years after Brewster's death, Ives wrote a letter to Harmony's father, Joseph Twichell, in essence requesting that Twichell assume the role of father figure. Letter of Charles Ives to Joseph Twichell, November 23, 1907, quoted in Ives, *Memos,* 260–1 and Feder, *Charles Ives,* 208–9.

40. Ives's memories of the two would sometimes blend together. Ives remarked, about Mark Twain, "It sort of reminds [me] of what Jermimah said to Father (or Uncle Lyman, I think) . . ." Ives, *Memos,* 193.

41. Julian S. Myrick interview, in Vivian Perlis, *Charles Ives Remembered: An Oral History* (New Haven: Yale University Press, 1974; repr. New York: W.W. Norton, 1976), 37.

42. Wooldridge, *From the Steeples and Mountains,* 124, states that Ives was depressed. Feder, *Charles Ives,* 183, states that it was "likely to have been frank depression."

43. Henry Cowell and Sidney Cowell, *Charles Ives and His Music* (New York: Oxford University Press, 1955), 71.

44. Letter of Amelia Brewster to Charles Ives, September 7, 1905, quoted in Feder, *Charles Ives,* 184.

45. Perlis, *Charles Ives Remembered,* 36.

46. "McCurdy Family Got $4,600,000," *New York Times*, October 7, 1905, p. 4

47. Ibid.

48. Amelia van Wyck, interview, quoted in Perlis, *Ives Remembered*, 10.

49. Feder, *Charles Ives*, 180.

50. There has been much speculation as to whether Ives had a heart attack at this time. Rossiter, *Charles Ives*, 111, says he did. Kirkpatrick states that Ives's heart had been "cause for anxiety" (in Ives, *Memos*, 270). Myrick states that Ives had "something of a heart attack" (Perlis, *Charles Ives Remembered*, 36). Feder, the most medically accomplished of the Ives's scholars, doubts it was a heart attack (*Charles Ives*, 198). Recent evidence confirms that it was not a heart attack. When Ives applied for a personal insurance policy in 1909, he was examined by the Mutual office. The report is extant. Signed by Hamilton Bisse, medical examiner, and Ives, it states that Ives was in good health, that he had no impairments or bodily malformation, and in response to the questions "what illnesses, diseases or accidents have you had since childhood," Ives mentioned only two incidents: in November 1908 he suffered a "slight bilious attack" and in June, 1909 a "sore throat," which was dismissed as "trivial." Even if Ives had wanted to cover up a possible heart attack, this was the same Mutual office that had examined him before, and it is unlikely that he would have succeeded in this attempt. Mutual of New York, Charles Ives Folder, New York archives.

51. Cowell and Cowell, *Charles Ives and His Music*, 46; Rossiter, *Charles Ives*, 111–12; Feder, *Charles Ives*, 199.

52. Much of this information about the organization of agencies is based on an interview with Charron Fullerton, archivist at Mutual of New York, conducted February 12, 1995. I would like to thank Ms. Fullerton for her generosity both in the interview and in making Mutual documents available.

53. Terrence O'Donnell, *History of Life Insurance in Its Formative Years* (Chicago: American Conservation Co., 1936), 541.

54. Fullerton, interview.

55. Ibid.

56. Perlis, *Charles Ives Remembered*, 36; Feder, *Charles Ives*, 198–99; Rossiter, *Charles Ives*, 111.

57. Fullerton, interview.

58. The text reads, "A leopard went around his cage from one side back to the other side; he stopped only when the keeper came around with meat; a boy who had been there three hours began to wonder, 'Is life anything like that?'" (Ives, *114 Songs*, 144). Ives later rewrote the piece as a song with the above text, but the text is in Ives's manuscript score of the orchestral piece.

59. Ives provided a lengthy programmatic explanation for *The Unanswered Question*, printed with the score (ed. Paul C. Echols and Noel Zahler [New York: Peer International, 1985], 10). In Ives's words the muted trumpet, which has the most prominent of the thematic layers in the piece, "intones 'The Perennial Question of Existence.'"

60. "Life Insurance Just Philanthropy," *New York Times*, October 11, 1905, 2.

61. Ibid.

62. Rossiter, *Charles Ives*, 136.

63. Lester Frank Ward, *Dynamic Sociology, or Applied Social Science, as Based upon Statical Sociology and the Less Complex Sciences* (New York: D. Appleton, 1883); Simon Nelson Patten, *The New Basis of Civilization* (New York: Macmillan, 1907); Edward A. Ross, *Foundations of Sociology* (New York: Macmillan, 1905); Walter Rauschenbusch, *Christianity and the Social Crisis* (New York: Macmillan, 1907). They are discussed in Wiebe, *Opening*, 140–44.

64. Ives, *Essays*, 167.

Michael Broyles

65. Rebecca Zurier, "*The Masses* and Modernism," in *1915, The Cultural Moment: The New Politics, the New Woman, the New Psychology, the New Art and the New Theatre in America,* ed. Adele Heller and Lois Rudnick (New Brunswick, N. J.: Rutgers University Press, 1991), 196. I would like to thank Judith Tick for suggesting the connection between the Ives song and the journal, *The Masses.*

66. Eugene E. Leach, "The Radicalization of *The Masses,*" in Heller and Rudnick, eds., *1915, The Cultural Moment:* 27. Henry F. May, *The End of American Innocence: A Study of the First Years of Our Own Time* (New York: Alfred A. Knopf, 1959), 315–16.

67. Ives diary entry, June 26 [1914], Charles Ives Papers, box 45, folder 12.

68. William L. O'Neill, ed., *Echoes of Revolt: The Masses, 1911–1917* (Chicago: Quadrangle Books, 1966), 20.

69. Ives, *Essays,* 197.

70. The two principal types of republicanism were those defined by Gordon S. Wood, *The Creation of the American Republic, 1776–1787* (Chapel Hill: University of North Carolina Press, 1969), and J. G. A. Pocock, *The Machiavellian Moment: Florentine Political Thought and the Atlantic Republican Tradition* (Princeton: Princeton University Press, 1975). For a summary of the multitudinous historical writing on republicanism see Daniel T. Rodgers, "Republicanism: the Career of a Concept," *Journal of American History* 79 (June 1992): 11–38.

71. Jean Baker, "From Belief into Culture: Republicanism in the Antebellum North." *American Quarterly* 37 (Fall 1985): 539. Material from Geertz is taken from Clifford Geertz, *The Interpretation of Culture: Selected Essays* (New York: Basic Books, 1973), 192–93 and 201.

72. Quoted from James Turner, unpublished draft of biography of Charles Eliot Norton, by permission of the author.

73. Feder, *Charles Ives,* 4–5.

74. Alan Alexrod, *The Colonial Revival in America* (New York: W. W. Norton, 1985), 20.

75. Harriet Beecher Stow, *Pagunuc People: Their Life and Loves* (New York: Fords, Howard and Hulbart, 1878); Henry Ward Beecher, *Norwood: Village Life in New England* (New York: C. Scribner, 1868).

76. Axelrod, *Colonial Revival,* 20.

77. Quoted in Kirkpatrick, *Temporary Mimeographed Catalogue,* 60.

78. Quoted in Cowell and Cowell, *Charles Ives and His Music,* 106.

79. Richard L. Bushman, *From Puritan to Yankee: Character and Social Order in Connecticut, 1690–1765* (New York: W. W. Norton, 1970), 10–12.

80. Page Smith, *As a City upon a Hill: The Town in American History* (New York: Alfred A. Knopf, 1966), 110–11; see also Michael Zuckerman, "The Social Context of Democracy in Massachusetts," in *Colonial America: Essays in Politics and Social Development,* ed. Stanley N. Katz (Boston: Little Brown, 1976), 284–97.

81. The germ of this idea is found in Tocqueville who paints a romantic picture of New England town governance; Alexis de Tocqueville, *Democracy in America* (1835; 12th ed., 1848, reprinted New York: Alfred A. Knopf, 1979). Tocqueville is prejudiced toward townships in general, which he considers the most universal and natural bodies of social organization. He holds an idealistic view of how the New Englander relates to his town: "Every individual is always supposed to be as well informed, as virtuous, and as strong as any of his fellow citizens. He obeys society, not because he is inferior to those who conduct it or because he is less capable than any other of governing himself, but because he acknowledges the utility of an association with his fellow men and he knows that no such association can exist without a regulating force" (p. 64). Toqueville also believes that New Englanders relate to their townships in an altruistic way: "the township of New England is so constituted as to excite the warmest of human affections

without arousing the ambitious passions of the heart of man" (p. 67). Tocqueville seems to be blind to the hierarchy that existed in New England: "In New England no tradition exists of a distinction of rank; no portion of the community is tempted to oppress the remainder" (p. 68). Most of his information, where cited, comes from the Laws of Massachusetts.

82. John Gorham Palfrey, *History of New England*, 5 vols. (Boston: Little, Brown, and Company, 1858–89). He died in 1881, leaving volume 5 unfinished; it was finished by Francis Winthrop Palfrey.

83. Palfrey, *History*, vol. 2, 12.

84. Charles Adams, *Three Episodes of Massachusetts History: The Settlement of Boston Bay; The Antinomian Controversy; A Study of Church and Town Government* (Boston and New York: Houghton, Mifflin, 1893).

85. Ibid., vol. 2, 813.

86. Ibid., vol. 2, 817.

87. A letter from Harmony Twichell to Ives dated "Wed. evening" and assigned a date January 15, 1908 by Rossiter implies that Ives had public affairs on his mind but was put off by attitudes in New York City: "No[body] is public-spirited in N. Y., it seems to me. When you get to living in Connecticut, you'll feel like going in to all sorts of things, I'm sure." Quoted in Rossiter, *Charles Ives*, 127.

88. Letter to Sir Norman Angell, June 21, 1938, Charles Ives Papers, box 27, folder 1; letter to Franklin Roosevelt, January 6, 1938, Charles Ives Papers, box 25, folder 8. In a letter from Sol Babitz regarding an edition of the Third Violin Sonata that Babitz was preparing, dated September 6, 1943, Babitz adds a P. S. "My wife was very interested in your material on national legislation." Charles Ives Papers, box 27, folder 2. In 1943 Ives received a pamphlet from his friend Charles Kauffman, *Universal Law and the Democratic Principle* (Bethel, Conn.: Warren Press, 1943), a rambling idealistic vision of democracy based on the principle of intuition. In a letter dated only 1943, Ives responded warmly to Kauffman's work, not only praising it but suggesting that he send a copy to the Friends of Democratic Society. Ives included the address of the society for Kauffman. Finally there is Ives's updating his World War I song *He Is There!*, with new words, to become *They Are There!*

89. Charles Ives Papers, box 25, folder 6.

90. Perlis, *Charles Ives Remembered*, 12.

Of Men and Mountains:

Ives in the Adirondacks

MARK TUCKER

The health of the eye seems to demand a horizon.
—Emerson

If only I could have done it. It's all there—the mountains and the fields.
—attributed to Ives

Every summer they roar up the Northway from Albany in cars loaded with tents and backpacks, fishing rods and bicycles, sunblock and citronella. Once inside the Adirondack Park, an area of upstate New York covering six million acres, nearly the size of Vermont, they scatter in all directions toward their favorite wilderness haunts. They flock to the region to breathe pristine air and soothe jangled nerves. Following tradition, they go to get healthy. As the Reverend William H. H. Murray noted in 1869, the year his book *Adventures in the Wilderness* sparked the first great tourist boom in the Adirondacks, "It is . . . a place to which not only the artist, and the lover of nature in her grandest aspects; but the business man and the professional man, weary and jaded by months and years of over work, can go and find in its recesses, rest and recuperation for body and mind."[1]

One who repeatedly headed north to the Adirondacks for these reasons was Charles Ives. Artist, lover of nature, and overworked businessman, he fit Murray's profile exactly. Ives discovered the Adirondacks while still in college, going there in August 1896 just before his junior year at Yale. Over the next twenty years he returned to the area another nine times, staying a week or two, sometimes longer, and making one last trip in October 1915 around his forty-first birthday (see the chronology in Table 5.1).[2] Like the modern-day Adirondack tourist, Ives packed such basics as warm clothing and hiking boots. Like others he enjoyed walking in the woods, boating on lakes, going on picnics, and soaking up glorious mountain scenery (see Figure 5.1). But Ives's essential Adirondack gear also included pencils and music manuscript paper. Vacations in the mountains gave him the freedom to enter fully into his private musical universe. Leaving behind the rhythms of daily routine, Ives could drift on the current of his creative energies—composing, sketching, revising, and copying, tending to old projects and dreaming up new ones.

Table 5.1
Ives in the Adirondacks: A Chronology

1896	12–29 August Visits Twichell family at Waldruhe, the cottage owned by C. O. Wood	**Keene Valley**
1903	Labor Day weekend Goes to Waldruhe with Del Wood	**Keene Valley**
1905	mid-late August–8 September Visits David Twichell, then at the Roberts camp (1–8 September) with David and Harmony Twichell	**Saranac Lake**
1907	August Visits David Twichell	**Saranac Lake**
1908	19 November–5 December Harmony and Ives take first vacation at Lower Saranac Lake	**Saranac Lake**
1909	20 August–12 September Vacation with Harmony and members of Twichell family	**Elk Lake**
1910	12 August–7 September Vacation with Harmony and members of Twichell family	**Elk Lake**
1911	16–26 September Vacation with Harmony and members of Twichell family	**Elk Lake**
1912	September Ives and Harmony on vacation, visit David and Ella Twichell	**Lake Kiwassa (Saranac Lake)**
1915	October Ives, Harmony, and Edith with Joseph and Sue Twichell on the Dunham plateau	**Keene Valley**

Figure 5.1: Elk Lake, 1909. Left to right: Harmony Twichell Ives, Charles Ives, Sarah Dunham Twichell.

The two decades during which Ives visited the Adirondacks coincided with his main period of musical productivity,[3] and the record suggests he worked well in the mountains. According to his annotations on manuscripts, while vacationing in the Adirondacks he wrote the *Three-Page Sonata*, the songs *Mists* and *William Will*, and *The Innate*, a movement for piano and string quartet and later a song; he finished the Third Symphony and began the Fourth; he orchestrated *The Rockstrewn Hills Join in the People's Outdoor Meeting* for the *Second Orchestral Set*; he sketched the third movement of the Fourth Violin Sonata and worked on the *Robert Browning Overture*. In the Elk Lake wilderness of the Adirondacks Ives turned his thoughts to old New England, conceiving the idea for the *Concord Sonata* and sketching the "Hawthorne" movement. Most notably, while staying on "the plateau" in Keene Valley in 1915, Ives made extensive sketches for the *Universe Symphony*, the unfinished work that obsessed him until the end of his life and that drew inspiration from the rugged mountainous landscape Ives had come to know as a frequent Adirondack visitor.[4]

New England played such a dominant role in Ives's personal history and musical imagination that it is difficult to picture him composing in the wilds of upstate New York. On a map the Adirondacks appear close to New England, rising out of the Lake Champlain valley only a few miles west of the Vermont line (see the map in Figure 5.2). But the Adirondacks are a world apart. Travelers entering them

Nancy A. Bernstein

Figure 5.2: Map of the Adirondacks and New England. The border around the Adirondacks indicates the present-day boundary (or "Blue Line") for the Adirondack Park.

from Vermont find a place where mountains are higher, forests denser, people scarcer, and mosquitoes fiercer. In Ives's New England—especially that part of southwestern Connecticut around Danbury and West Redding—natural and human features seem harmoniously balanced. Farms, ponds, woodlands, and villages interlock to form a tight patchwork design. A cozy sense of containment prevails, with picturesque towns encircled by low hills or nestled snugly in river valleys. The Adirondack landscape, by contrast, gives the impression of vastness and distance, of wilderness untamed, unknowable, unending. Nature rules and residents struggle to survive on the margins. In history and literature, New England boasts rich cultural traditions and vital communities, from Plymouth Plantation to Peyton Place, Brook Farm to Grover's Corners. The Adirondacks are remote, slightly forlorn: Cooper's hero Natty Bumppo roaming alone in the woods, Edmund Wilson isolating himself in Talcottville, and Clyde and Roberta, in Dreiser's *An American Tragedy*, meeting their fate on a lonely northern lake.[5]

The wild character of the Adirondacks resulted not just from terrain and settlement patterns but from legislation passed just prior to Ives's first trip there in 1896. An Adirondack Forest Preserve was created in 1885 by the New York State legislature, which proclaimed that the lands would be kept "forever wild," thus safeguarding them against logging, sale, and future development. Boundaries for an Adirondack State Park—encompassing both the state-owned Forest Preserve and private lands—were established in 1892; two years later the "forever wild" clause protecting the Forest Preserve was written into the New York State constitution.[6]

These legal measures to protect the Adirondacks came about just as a thriving tourist industry was developing. Many hotels, lodges, resorts, and private camps sprang up in the 1870s and 1880s, following the interest generated in 1869 by Murray's *Adventures in the Wilderness*. The area soon became a fashionable destination for industrialists and urban aristocrats, such as the Tiffanys, Astors, Stuyvesants, and Biddles who stayed at the Prospect House, a luxury hotel in the middle of the woods that had steam-generated electric light, an elevator, bowling alleys, and a two-story outhouse.[7] The young Theodore Roosevelt spent three summers in the 1870s at Paul Smith's, a popular resort north of the village of Saranac Lake where Dr. Edward Livingston Trudeau arrived in 1873 to convalesce from tuberculosis. The famous sanatorium later founded by Trudeau in Saranac Lake brought another wave of visitors to the area, people who came not to hunt deer or socialize in the "Great Camps" but to recover from illness.[8]

In addition to attracting wealthy vacationers, hunters and fishers, and invalids, the Adirondacks drew intellectuals seeking to unwind in the solitary of the wilds. Ralph Waldo Emerson and a group of prominent friends from Cambridge and Boston—among them Louis Agassiz and James Russell Lowell—had made a trek to Follensby Pond in 1858, later celebrated in Emerson's poem "The Adirondacs" and William J. Stillman's painting, *The Philosophers' Camp in the Adirondacks*.[9] In the 1870s William James began spending part of each summer near the town of Keene Valley, staying in a rustic house co-owned with several others and known as Putnam Camp. James wrote to a friend in France about the appeal of his simple existence there:

The virgin forest comes close to our house, and the diversity of walks through it, the brooks and the ascensions of hilltops are infinite. I doubt if there be anything like it in Europe. Your mountains are grander, but you have nowhere this carpet of absolutely primitive forest, with its indescribably sweet exhalations, spreading in every direction unbroken. I shall stay here doing hardly any work till late in September. I need to lead a purely animal life for at least two months to carry me through the teaching year.[10]

Like James, Felix Adler, the psychoanalyst and founder of the Ethical Culture Society, was an avid hiker drawn to the country around Keene Valley; today one of the main trails up Noonmark Mountain, the peak looming over the village, bears Adler's name. Landscape painters, too, found this area inspiring. Eminent figures from the Hudson River School—among them Asher B. Durand and John Kensett—visited Keene Valley in the mid-1800s, while lesser-known artists such as John Fitch, Roswell M. Shurtleff, and Alexander Wyant kept returning to the place, helping a small art colony develop there. To be sure, Keene Valley was no Montmartre or Greenwich Village, with poets and painters spilling out onto sidewalk cafés in the evenings, talking politics and sipping espresso. But it did attract artists and academics who found the place physically restorative and spiritually uplifting.[11]

Within the history of the Adirondacks, then, Ives represented a familiar type: one of the many city-dwellers who joined the yearly northern exodus, an intellectual, a person of privilege. For Ives, though, the Adirondacks came to mean something more than a favorite vacation spot. The place proved conducive to creative work. Its tranquil environment promoted contemplation. Its mists, valleys, and mountains made a direct impact on some of his compositions. It was, also, a region indelibly associated with a family that provided some of his richest emotional experiences: the Twichells of Hartford, Connecticut, among them Harmony Twichell (whom he married in 1908), her brother David Cushman Twichell, and their father Joseph Hopkins Twichell. Ives spent time in three different Adirondack communities—Keene Valley, Saranac Lake, and Elk Lake—always in the company of Twichells. When he first journeyed north to Keene Valley in 1896, he was visiting a place Joseph and his wife Julia Harmony Cushman Twichell had been coming to for thirty years.

Mark Tucker

In the Valley

The Reverend Joseph Hopkins Twichell (1838–1918; see Figure 5.3) belonged to a group of Connecticut clergymen who discovered the charms of Keene Valley in the latter half of the 1860s. Dubbed the "Climbing Clerics" because of their passion for hiking, these ministers went there in the summers to walk, read, fish, and relax. Occasionally they preached in a small schoolhouse in the middle of the village. The building still stands, now used as a men's locker room for the Keene Valley Country Club. A plaque under its front eave commemorates the group to which Twichell belonged:

> This building was erected for a
> District School House in 1850 and was
> framed by Orson S. Phelps. Divine worship
> was for many years held here by
> Thomas Watson, Pastor.
> Horace Bushnell
> James B. Shaw
> Noah Porter
> William H. Hodge
> Joseph H. Twichell
> William L. Kingsley.

Two of these men were close friends of Joseph Twichell: Dr. Horace Bushnell, like Twichell a Hartford minister and an "indefatigable tramper"; and the Reverend Noah Porter, president of Yale from 1871 to 1886.[12] Twichell, Bushnell, and Porter, according to Adirondack historian Alfred L. Donaldson, were "specialists in good-fellowship" who formed "a notable triumvirate."[13] Their annual pilgrimages to Keene Valley underscored a point made in *Adventures in the Wilderness* by Murray (yet another Connecticut cleric at the time he began writing about the Adirondacks):

> If every church would make up a purse, and pack its worn and weary pastor off to the North Woods for a four weeks' jaunt, in the hot months of July and August, it would do a very sensible as well as pleasant act. For when the good dominie came back swarth and tough as an Indian, elasticity in his step, fire in his eye, depth and clearness in his reinvigorated voice, wouldn't there be some preaching! . . . The preacher sees God in the original there, and often translates him better from his unwritten works than from his written word.[14]

Keene Valley Library

Figure 5.3: The Reverend Joseph Hopkins Twichell

Twichell and his fellow ministers from Connecticut were attracted by Keene Valley's scenic beauty and varied hiking opportunities. Many were led on their expeditions by Orson "Old Mountain" Phelps (mentioned above on the schoolhouse plaque), a legendary guide who made his home in the village. Contemporary guidebooks to the Adirondacks singled out Keene Valley as an exceptional site to visit:

Within the Town of Keene the Adirondack Range reaches its loftiest culminations, and Keene Valley is one of the wildest and most enchanting of all the nooks in this region of wildness and beauty. No place commands more glorious panoramic views. The entire horizon is grandly serrated with mountain pinnacles. . . . The narrow district possesses, perhaps, with its environs, a richer variety of natural beauties in the way of lake, mountain, chasm and cascade, than any other section of equal extent within the boundaries of these "Northern Wilds."[15]

Joseph and Julia Twichell took their first Keene Valley vacation in 1866, boarding at the farm owned by Otis Estes (later bought by Livingston Taylor and named Rivermede). That summer, as Joseph Twichell later noted in his scrapbook, they grew close to another family from Hartford—that of Charles Dudley Warner, editor of the *Hartford Daily Courant*. When Warner returned to Hartford in the fall, he described his trip to the mountains in the pages of the *Courant*. "Keene Flats," he wrote, using an earlier name for Keene Valley, "is a charming interval among the mountain meadows of the AuSable [River], a sandy road strung with farm houses and a post office with mail twice a week" (see Figure 5.4).[16] Warner drew a picture of the easygoing life he and the Twichells had found there:

> One of the first things to do, when you are installed in a farm house at Keene Flats, is, nothing. It is about the only thing that does not require a guide. . . . Of excitement and thrilling adventure at Keene Flats there is not much of note. You may climb Hopkins' Peak and look at all creation, or walk a few miles to see a water-fall two hundred feet high and not very broad; there was the excitement of mail night, the wonder what we should have for dinner. . . . The people here are nearly all wealthy.[17]

Figure 5.4: View of the town of Keene Valley from Spread Eagle Mountain, pre-1910

When Ives first traveled to Keene Valley from New Haven in 1896, he found a town with a sizable contingent of summer folk from Connecticut (still true a century later, in fact). The invitation to make the trip came from David Twichell, fourth oldest of nine children, and a Yale classmate Ives had met two years earlier after attending a lecture by Joseph Twichell.[18] Writing to "Charlie" in Danbury on 4 August 1896, David sent directions on how to reach Keene Valley:

> There are two ways to get here: one, the way we always come via Hartford via Springfield via Albany via Saratoga to Westport. We leave on a train from Hartford at 5:52 a.m. That would mean your spending the night in Hartford. The train arrives in Westport at 5:42 p.m. There you will take a stage for Elizabethtown, where you spend the night. From Elizabethtown to Keene Valley there is a stage, which gets here around noon. . . . [Twichell then itemizes the total cost of the trip: $15.75.]
>
> The second way to come is by New York, which I have never been so know nothing about. You come via New York via Albany via Saratoga to Westport. When you come over in the stage ask for Wood's cottage. You better telegraph me when you start, so I can be on the lookout for you. It seems to me the best time for you to start, will be Tuesday Aug. 11. I do hope that date will suit you, for I want you up here as soon as possible.[19]

Wood's cottage, where David and his family were staying that August, was owned by C. O. Wood. One of Wood's sons, Howard Ogden Wood, had married Julia Curtis ("Judy") Twichell, Harmony's older sister; another son, Cornelius Delano "Del" Wood, was a Yale friend of both Ives and David Twichell. The "cottage" was a roomy two-story house in the south end of Keene Valley (see Figure 5.5). Perched on the lower slopes of Hopkins Mountain, surrounded by pines, and commanding a spectacular view of the Ausable River rushing over rocks below, Wood's cottage was aptly named Waldruhe, "Wood's Rest." It had been built in the mid-1870s by Alexander Wyant, one of the painters in Keene Valley's artist colony. Of classic Adirondack design, it featured two separate structures: the main house with sitting rooms below, bedrooms on the upper floor, and a wraparound porch overlooking the river; and next to it, a smaller building with dining room, kitchen, and work area for service staff.

David J. McDonough

Figure 5.5: Waldruhe, C. O. Wood's Cottage in Keene Valley where Ives stayed in 1896 and 1903

Ives stayed at Waldruhe for just over two weeks, from 12–29 August 1896. There he joined a large group made up of the Twichells, Woods, and assorted friends. David's younger sister Harmony was there, too. As Joseph Twichell recalled the scene later in his diary:

> At Keene Valley as guests again of Judy's father-in-law Mr C O Wood, in his cottage Waldruhe. All the family, except Judy, were there, part of the time also, Fred Ware and Bartlett Yung, whom we count of our number, and in the course of the season several young men and women friends of Harmony and Dave. We had plenty of delightful company, and never enjoyed a season more.[20]

Amidst the convivial crowd at Waldruhe, Ives wrote *William Will*, a campaign song for Republican candidate William McKinley. He collaborated with Yung—a member of Yale's Banjo Club—on an arrangement of the song for banjo and piano,[21] probably performing it for the Waldruhe guests. On August 26 Ives received a telegram from his brother Moss bidding him to come down from the mountains: "Grandmother wants you home. Start Saturday if possible. Nothing serious."[22] Thus ended Ives's first trip to the Adirondacks and his introduction to the extended Twichell family.

On Ives's next known visit to the Adirondacks, which occurred over Labor Day weekend, 1903, he was again invited to Waldruhe in Keene Valley. Five years out of college, Ives was now living with the Poverty Flat group in New York City and working for the Charles H. Raymond Agency, a division of the Mutual Life Insurance Company. His friend David Twichell, meanwhile, had graduated from both Yale and Columbia's College of Physicians and Surgeons, and had taken a position in June at Trudeau's sanatorium in Saranac Lake. Ives mentioned his short trip to Keene Valley in a letter that fall to Twichell:

> Del Wood took me to Keene Valley over Labor Day. We didn't seize any panthers, but had [an] agreeable time! Though I am afraid I was a disturbing element being full of malaria, . . . opinions and whisky at the time.[23]

In the same letter Ives sent Twichell news about Pine Mountain, near Danbury: "We finally succeeded in placing that shanty on the mountain in Ridgefield. . . . It makes a good young camp."[24]

Although far removed from upstate New York, Pine Mountain in Connecticut deserves mention as an important rural retreat for Ives. David Wooldridge has called Pine Mountain a "catalyst for many new ideas," and Stuart Feder described it as "one of the outdoor locales Ives loved best, a precursor to later favorite places in the Adirondacks."[25] Henry and Sidney Cowell wrote that Ives often went there with his brother Moss but also liked "to camp alone, composing or just sitting, absorbed in the mountains. Then back to New York and the 18-hour days he imposed on himself."[26] Unlike the boisterous social scene of Waldruhe, Pine Mountain offered solitude. There, according to annotations on his manuscripts, Ives wrote (or finished) *Overture and March "1776", Halloween*, and two pieces now lost, the *Orchard House Overture* (the basis for the "Alcotts" movement of the *Concord Sonata*) and *An Autumn Landscape from Pine Mountain*; he made sketches for the Piano Trio and began the first Piano Sonata; and he produced a fully scored first version of the Third Symphony which, in David Wooldridge's romantic characterization, "breathes the clear air of Pine Mountain."[27] There, too, Ives found ways to translate intense responses to nature into tones. He was fascinated by hearing sounds from a distance and sought to recreate the effect in *An Autumn Landscape from Pine Mountain*, a piece written for strings, woodwinds, and cornet—the last of these muted and described by Ives as "heard from Ridgebury."[28]

Ives's much-discussed interest in the spatial and physical properties of sound derived not from abstract theories but from real life experience—walking along a river and hearing hymn-singing from the other side (*The Housatonic at Stockbridge*), or sitting in a Manhattan apartment and perceiving street sounds below (*Over the Pavements*).[29] Up on Pine Mountain Ives could gaze upon distant hills, listen to the wind, and compose without interruption.

Weekend stints on Pine Mountain must have been refreshing breaks in Ives's hectic life as a businessman. When he began going regularly to the Adirondacks, in 1905, he would find other natural settings where he could work productively.

By the Lake

In 1903, the year Ives placed his camp on Pine Mountain, two of the Twichell children moved to the Adirondacks. David, as already mentioned, became one of the staff physicians at Trudeau's sanatorium at Saranac Lake, while Harmony—who in 1900 had graduated from the Hartford Hospital Training School for Nurses—began serving as companion and nurse for a family friend, Sarah "Aunt Sally" Dunham, in Keene Valley.[30] That September Harmony traveled the thirty miles northwest to Saranac Lake, where she joined her brother at the sanatorium, working as a nurse there until November 1904. The following spring Harmony was hired as the companion of Mrs. Dean Sage of Albany, another friend of the Twichells. Mrs. Sage, too, turned out to have Adirondack connections—at least Harmony visited her there at Hewitt Lake (or Pond), near Minerva, New York, in the summer of 1907.[31] Between the summer of 1903 and spring of 1907, Harmony Twichell shifted her geographic locus from Connecticut to upstate New York. Ives, too, drew closer to the Adirondacks after an important encounter with Harmony at Saranac Lake in September 1905.

It seems fitting that both David and Harmony Twichell found their way to the village of Saranac Lake. As Stuart Feder has observed, these were the Twichell children who "most surely carried their father's healing touch," two individuals whose "idealism led to a life of service."[32] Since Edward Livingston Trudeau had opened his "Adirondack cure cottage" in 1884, Saranac Lake had developed into a major center of tourism, attracting not only short-term vacationers—like Mark Twain, who came in the summer of 1901 to rest up from a world tour—but year-round sanatorium patients and others seeking the supposed health benefits of Saranac's cold winter air. One of the latter was writer

Robert Louis Stevenson, whose respiratory problems took him to Saranac Lake in 1887. Unlike Twain, who actually rested at Saranac, Stevenson worked intensely there, turning out articles for *Scribner's*, writing hundreds of letters, and progressing with his novel *The Master of Ballantrae*. Béla Bartók followed Stevenson's disciplined example when he went to Saranac in 1943 for leukemia. In a period of less than eight weeks he wrote his *Concerto for Orchestra*, later telling a friend: "Through working on this concerto, I have discovered the wonder drug I needed to bring about my own cure."[33]

Ives's visit to Saranac Lake in the summer of 1905—like his first trip to the Adirondacks nine years earlier—was prompted by an invitation from David Twichell. But the timing was propitious, since Ives now needed the health-restoring experience for which Saranac had become famous. Working for the Raymond Agency, Ives may have been under stress—as Stuart Feder hypothesizes, and Michael Broyles explains elsewhere in this volume—due to the Armstrong committee's investigation into corruption in the life insurance business. Feder also speculates that Ives fell into one of his creative "slumps" around this time, characterized by "a periodic and generalized sense of depression."[34] Whatever the symptoms of Ives's weakened condition—partly exhaustion from his hard-driving regimen—a vacation in the Adirondacks with his good friend promised relief. He went up to Saranac Lake some time in August and stayed into September. For Ives, the Saranac "cure" of 1905 had two salutary effects: it renewed his creative drive, and it brought him together again with Harmony. Meanwhile, back in Connecticut Ives's Aunt Amelia Brewster expressed concern, hoping the change of scene was helping: "We want you to get the *most good* possible out of your time and while you know we are always glad to have you home, your health is of the first importance and we wish you to do what is best."[35]

In August 1905, while staying with David Twichell at Saranac Lake, Ives worked on several pieces. One was a setting for cornet and strings of the gospel hymn *The Beautiful River*. This was "a tune Dave was very fond of," Ives noted in the *Memos*, often sung at camp meetings in Danbury's Brookside Park. Coincidentally Ives heard it performed at a "prayer meeting" he attended in the town of Saranac Lake.[36] Ives arranged another hymn, *Watchman Tell Us of the Night*, for horn and strings, which later evolved into the first movement of the Fourth Symphony. During that same month he finished the *Three-Page Sonata* for piano. Ives's idea of recuperation at Saranac, like that of Robert Louis Stevenson before him and Bartók after, was to immerse himself in creative work.

Adirondack Collection, Saranac Lake Free Library

Figure 5.6: A typical cottage or small camp on Lower Saranac Lake, similar to ones in which Harmony and Charles stayed in 1905, 1908, and 1912

Adirondack Collection, Saranac Lake Free Library

Figure 5.7: Camp Carmigeo on Lake Oseetah, near Saranac Lake. A property owned by the realtor W. F. Roberts, from whom David Twichell leased a camp in 1905.

Figure 5.8: Interior view of Camp Carmigeo, from an ad placed by W. F. Roberts in the *Adirondack Daily Enterprise*, 25 May 1911.

Ives extended his stay at Saranac into early September, when Harmony came up from Albany to visit her brother. For the occasion David had leased a camp from W. F. Roberts, one of the leading real estate men in Saranac Lake who specialized in cottage and camp rentals.[37] The camp may have been on Lower Saranac Lake (see Figure 5.6), but more likely was on one of the smaller lakes near the village—Lake Kiwassa, Lake Flower or Lake Oseetah—that had been developed for tourism (see Figures 5.7 and 5.8). This encounter between Harmony and Charles was a signal event in their lives, sparking the romance that would lead to marriage three years later. The week of 1–8 September 1905 at the Roberts camp formed the first entry in "Our Book," the diary kept by the couple. Harmony also recalled this time in a letter written two years later:

Dear Charlie,
    I'm sitting right where you and I sat so many hours—on the ground looking at the marsh where the sun sets up at the

Roberts camp—do you remember? . . . This is the first time I've been here since you and I were here that last precious evening of the hunt—it's as lovely as ever and a beautiful day—The wind is blowing quite hard and makes a pretty nice noise in the pine trees. . . . It doesn't seem right to be here without you and I wish you were along.[38]

Taking in the view formed a major part of Ives's Adirondack vacations. Rather than vigorously hiking trails or paddling canoes, getting "swarth and tough" like Murray's pastors on holiday, Ives enjoyed contemplating the landscape. Harmony alluded to this pastime in another letter recalling their rendezvous at the Roberts camp in 1905: "That day we went up to Saranac seems almost a miracle—I remember saying then, as we looked across the lake to the mountains at sunset that I didn't think Paradise could be any more beautiful."[39] Back in Manhattan, opportunities for reverie must have been rare for Ives, caught up in the mad rush of business and furious stints of composing at Poverty Flat. Yet they abounded in the Adirondacks, where Ives worked and rested in Saranac, regaining health and discovering his feelings for Harmony.

Those feelings intensified over the next several years. With Ives based in New York City and Harmony in Albany (until the summer of 1907), the Adirondacks took on a special resonance for their relationship. When Ives went to Saranac Lake in August 1907 to visit David and his wife Ella, Harmony was spending time with her family at Pell Jones's lodge at Elk Lake, located deep in the mountains in a remote area ten miles south of Keene Valley. From Elk Lake Harmony sent Charles her poem "Spring Song," which he adapted to an earlier piece. Later that month Harmony went to Saranac for a temporary nursing assignment at Trudeau's sanatorium, by which time Ives may have gone back to New York. Although Harmony could have stayed on in Saranac for the coming year, she chose to move home to Hartford, notifying Charles that she would "probably be in N.Y. sometime."[40] That fall of 1907—two years after their time at the Roberts Camp—she and Ives became formally engaged, and the following June they were married. They spent their honeymoon in the Berkshires of Massachusetts, but late in November returned to the Adirondacks, taking their first vacation together at a camp on Lower Saranac Lake. As was customary by now, Ives seized time in the north country to compose, on this visit writing the movement for piano and string quartet, *The Innate*. In "Our Book" Harmony noted the name of their guide—Gilbert Whiteman—which suggests outings on the lake and in the woods. Her brief comment on the experience: "comfortable cabins and good weather."

For Ives, Saranac Lake became a place intimately associated with Harmony. Over the next several years, a more secluded spot in the Adirondacks—Elk Lake—helped integrate him into the Twichell family and fire his musical imagination. He and Harmony went to Elk Lake for two and a half weeks in 1909, for nearly a month in 1910, and for three weeks in 1911. The Twichells had discovered the place as early as 1902.[41] According to Joseph Twichell's granddaughter, "When it began to get noisy in Keene Valley . . . they started going to Elk Lake."[42] Surrounded by forest and ringed by mountains, Elk Lake offered exceptional wilderness solitude. It still does today; thousands of acres around Elk Lake Lodge remain untouched by development, and the place conveys a haunting sense of isolation and remove from civilization.

Elk Lake began attracting visitors in the late nineteenth century when it was known as Mud Pond. E. R. Wallace's 1875 *Descriptive Guide to the Adirondacks* referred to a "sylvan resort at Mud Pond run by John Moore." Unlike some of the grander resorts further to the west, Elk Lake remained modest and off the beaten track into the 1900s; in 1914 the entry for it in Stoddard's *Standard Guide to the Adirondacks* only states: "A small hotel furnishes entertainment."[43] The place may have been successful enough not to need to advertise, though, depending on visitors and families who returned. When the Twichells began visiting the resort in 1902, the "Elk House" was run by Henry Pelletier "Pell" Jones on a lease arrangement from the Finch Pruyn Paper Company (which had bought the surrounding land in 1891). Ives usually referred to the place in his manuscripts as "Pell's" (with or without apostrophe); since the 1950s the resort has been called Elk Lake Lodge.

The present-day Elk Lake Lodge, close to the south shore of the lake, was finished in 1906, three years before Ives arrived. It was built on a modest scale: a small sitting room with vertical pine-log siding and a stone fireplace, a tiny dining area, and six bedrooms upstairs. Charles and Harmony may have stayed in one of these rooms, or possibly shared with the Twichells the large lean-to-like structure situated closer to the lake in front of the lodge, on a raised piece of land now called Mt. Tom.[44] The single most stunning feature of Elk Lake is the view of the High Peaks looking north across the lake from the lodge (see Figure 5.9). Noted Adirondack writer Paul Jamieson has called it "the noblest of wild prospects in the entire region," describing the semicircle ring of mountains as forming "a gentle rhythmic outline

Courtesy of Margot Paul Ernst

Figure 5.9: View of Elk Lake and the High Peaks beyond

against the sky."[45] There are many vistas of peaks and lakes throughout the Adirondacks, but Elk Lake combines the best of both: an
enchanting wilderness lake, dotted with islands of pine and tamarack,
and an imposing wall of mountains stretching across the horizon.

Of Ives's three places in the Adirondacks, Elk Lake proved most
inspirational. A private forest preserve, it offered rest and healthy
exercise. Typical activities included boating and taking short expeditions; in "Our Book," Harmony recorded two picnics in September
1911, one to "Strays pool" (probably on one of the many streams on
the property), the other to West Inlet, directly across the lake from the
lodge, accessible most readily by boat. A number of snapshots in "Our
Book" show Ives and the Twichells at Elk Lake, posing stiffly for the
camera in proper outdoor clothes (see Figure 5.10). But one of them
from 1909 captures Harmony and Charles at ease (see Figure 5.11).
They lean against a cabin, shielded from the bright sun by umbrellas.
Harmony appears to be reading. Charles, clean-shaven, sits in jacket
and tie, clenching a pipe in his teeth and propping his jodhpurs up
on a bench. A well-thumbed book rests on the arm of his chair, but he
focuses on the sheaf of orchestral score paper he holds. Absorbed in

The Charles Ives Papers, Yale University Music Library. Used by permission.

Figure 5.10: Ives and members of the Twichell family at Elk Lake, 1909. Left to right: Charles Ives, Harmony Twichell Ives, Will Cooke (brother of David Twichell's wife, Ella), Burton Twichell, Esther Twichell (wife of Joseph Hooker Twichell), Joseph Hooker Twichell, Edward Carrington Twichell ("Deac"), the Rev. Joseph Hopkins Twichell, Sarah Dunham Twichell, Harmony Cushman Twichell.

his music, Ives looks both relaxed and fully concentrated. Together the couple seems to have realized the wish Harmony expressed in a letter written before their marriage: "We must plan to have times for leisure of thought & we must try & read a lot, the best books—we can live with the noblest people that have lived that way—& we will have your music."[46]

At Elk Lake Ives carried out two kinds of musical work. One involved revising earlier pieces. In the summer of 1909 he rescored one of the *Ragtime Dances* to become *The Rockstrewn Hills Join in the People's Outdoor Meeting* in the *Second Orchestral Set*. That summer (and in the ones following) he also worked on a third version of the Third Symphony. Harmony may have been referring to this in an entry in "Our Book:"

> Aug. 20. To Elk Lake Found there Dad & Mother Sue Burt. Ed & Will Cooke [brother of Dave Twichell's wife Ella] came Aug 22 for two weeks. Perfect vacation. Charlie working on the symphony. Fine weather & the place as beautiful & re-creating as ever. Home again Sept. 13.[47]

The Charles Ives Papers, Yale University Music Library. Used by permission.

Figure 5.11: Harmony and Charles Ives at Elk Lake, 1909

During the summer of 1910 Ives made sketches for the Fourth Symphony's first movement, based on the *Watchman* hymn setting he had devised while staying with David Twichell at Saranac Lake. Back in New York that fall, Charles wrote to Harmony in Hartford: "I have finished the score of the 1st movement and I feel fairly satisfied with it. Its free from extraneous substances & closely woven & the product of our summer at 'Pell's.' "[48]

A number of new pieces begun by Ives at Elk Lake had literary origins. In the song *Mists* (1910) he set a poem by Harmony that touched on the grieving process—her mother had died a few months earlier, and her absence from the Twichell family gathering at Elk Lake must have been keenly felt:

Low lie the mists; they hide each hill and dell;
The grey skies weep with us who bid farewell.
But happier days through memory weave a spell,
And bring new hope to hearts who bid farewell.[49]

Oscillating whole-tone formations and hushed dynamics convey the mysterious atmosphere, with only a momentary break in the clouds at "happier days" before chromatically descending augmented chords lead back to the opening fog-shrouded landscape (see Figure 5.12).

Mists. © 1933 by Merion Music, Inc. Used by permission.

Figure 5.12: *Mists* (1910), mm. 11–19

Charles and Harmony's reading program during these summers may have rekindled interest in his "Men of Literature" series of overtures. In October 1911 at Elk Lake, Ives worked on the *Robert Browning Overture*, begun three years earlier. Ives also traced the origins of the *Concord Sonata* to Elk Lake around this same time: "Shortly after 1911, at Pell's, I got the idea of a Concord sonata—and finished Emerson as a sonata [movement in] 1912—took the common themes from the Alcott [overture] and 'Fate knocking'."[50]

The wilderness setting of Elk Lake provided a sympathetic landscape for Ives's conception of works devoted to such literary heroes as Browning, Emerson, and Thoreau. In describing thematic treatment in the *Robert Browning Overture*, for example, Ives employed metaphors of discovery and exploration, of a person blazing new trails in unknown territory: "the themes themselves, except the main second theme, were trying to catch the Browning surge into the baffling unknowables, not afraid of unknown fields, not sticking to the nice main roads, and not so exactly bound up or limited to one key or keys (or any tonality for that matter) all the time."[51] Ives compared Browning to a hiker of philosophical bent—similar, really, to his father-in-law Joseph Twichell and other notables who summered in Keene Valley (William James, Felix Adler, Noah Porter). Musical exploration, like challenging hikes, inspired gendered images: "Browning was too big a man to rest in one nice little key, his inward tough[ness] & strength he walked on the mountains not down a nice proper little aisle. . . . His mind had many roads, not always easy to follow—the ever flowing changing, growing ways of mind & imagination—over the great unchanging truths of life & not death!"[52] Underlying Ives's belief in the salutary effects of dissonance and experimental techniques was a quality Robert M. Crunden has identified with progressives like Teddy Roosevelt. As Crunden points out, Ives's well-known comment to "use your ears like a man" carried echoes of "Roosevelt in the Dakota badlands, or on his famous, muscle-stiffening hikes, while he was President, to demonstrate to effete bureaucrats the virtues of the strenuous life."[53] Ives expected the listener to follow Browning, like some mountain guide, into the wild regions of the imagination, ever upward to the summit. "Great things are done," he would agree with Blake, "when Men & Mountains meet."[54]

Beyond bold tonal exploration, another aesthetic property Ives associated with Elk Lake was the effect of hearing sounds from a distance—which he had earlier sought to capture with muted trumpet in *An Autumn Landscape from Pine Mountain* and *The Pond*, and muted strings in *The Unanswered Question*. Later, when he finished the "Thoreau" movement from the *Concord Sonata*, Ives wrote: "Walden Sounds—Ch Bells, flute, Harp (Acolian) to go with Harmony's Mist . . . Elk Lake 1910."[55] In a footnote on the last page of "Thoreau," Ives noted that two treble clef chords "are but distant echoes over the lake," with one of them to be "scarcely audible." *Mists*, too, sought to convey the perception of sounds coming from varied points of distance; the vocal line and low supporting bass notes were marked *p*, the piano's middle-register augmented triads *pp*,[56] and the upper-register ones indicated by Ives as *ppp* and to be "scarcely audible" if played at all. The left-hand accompaniment evokes gently lapping water heard from the shore, the right-hand echoing it from a point further away.

If Concord represented for Ives, as Stuart Feder has stated, "the ultimate 'place in the soul,' somewhere between Olympus and Danbury," Elk Lake provided the prospect for bringing it within sight of Ives's imagination. Camped out on the shore of his own Walden, seeking to shed his urban skin and embrace a simpler existence, Ives was ideally positioned to commune with the spirits of his transcendental literary heroes: through the mist coming off the water he could hear the sound of Thoreau's flute, metamorphosed into the loon's eerie cry; on the distant peaks to the north he could see Emerson leading his readers closer to God and Heaven; and above it all, where the mountains touched the sky, blazed Hawthorne's Celestial City, bright and glorious.

In August 1912, after visiting Elk Lake during each of the past three years, Ives bought a parcel of land in West Redding, Connecticut, close to his home town of Danbury, on the slopes of Umpawaug Mountain and within sight of Pine Mountain. The following year construction started for Ives's own mountain retreat. This event marked the beginning of the end of Ives's Adirondack experiences. From 1913 on, he and Harmony would spend summers at Redding, going up from Manhattan when the weather became warmer and staying into the fall before returning to their townhouse on Manhattan's Upper East Side. The house at Redding is where the Iveses met the child Edith Osborne, whom they first sponsored through the Fresh Air Fund and eventually adopted in 1916. In later years it became their retirement home, as Ives played the role of "the transcendental and crotchety old man on his mountaintop, a Bronson Alcott philosophizing while his wife took care of the practical details of life."[57]

After buying the land in West Redding in 1912, Charles and Harmony paid a visit in September to David and Ella Twichell at Saranac Lake. Staying in a cottage at Lake Kiwassa, near the village of Saranac Lake, Ives worked on *The "St.-Gaudens" in Boston Common*, the first movement of *Three Places in New England*. A note on the manuscript reads: "Franklin Carter Esq. asked me to whistle this measure—

no smile Saranac Lake NY Sep 14, 1912."[58] Around the same time
Ives may have been working on *Decoration Day*, second movement of
the *Holidays Symphony*. Ives's contact with the Twichells that fall may
have prompted his dedication of the song *Lincoln, the Great Commoner*
to the idealistic physician he admired: "To Dr. David Cushman
Twichell."

September 1912 was Charles and Harmony's last recorded visit to
the Saranac Lake area; apparently they never returned to Elk Lake.
But they would go up to the Adirondacks once more, in the fall of
1915, ending up in Keene Valley—the site of their first meeting
nearly twenty years earlier. This final time, though, Ives had the benefit of an entirely different perspective.

On the Plateau

In the early days Keene Valley was known as Keene Flats, a name
attributed to Orson Phelps and reflecting its geological origins as the
"bed of a great lake."[60] Around the lake bed's edges small plateaus
formed. One rises just south of town along Route 73; villagers refer
to it as the Dunham (or Cheney) plateau. On top is a grassy
meadow encircled by pines, with two old cottages at either end. It
was in one of them that Ives stayed in October 1915 when he made
his extensive sketches for the *Universe Symphony*.[61]

Ives was nearly forty-one. He and Harmony now spent much of
the year at West Redding. Visiting Joseph Twichell and his daughter
Susan in Keene Valley that October, they brought along young Edith,
not yet two, and not yet legally adopted by the Iveses. At seventy-
seven, Joseph Twichell was fading. In the winter of 1912 he had gone
into a sanatorium at Brattleboro, Vermont and later was forced to
resign his position as minister at Hartford's Asylum Hill Church. He
would die in December 1918 after a "quiet, steady ebbing."[62]

The two cottages on the Dunham plateau have a long history
with summer residents from Connecticut. The one to the north in
which Charles and Harmony stayed had been built around 1873 by
Austin Cornelius Dunham, together with Joseph Twichell and
Hartford Courant editor Charles Dudley Warner.[63] "Uncle Cornelius"
was a close friend of the Twichells who gave Harmony a European
trip as a present for graduating from nursing school; his sister was
Sarah ("Aunt Sally") Dunham, whom Harmony was hired to care for
in 1903.[64] Harmony's brother Burton Twichell later remembered
staying on the Dunham plateau as a boy in the 1880s. After his par-

David J. McDonough

Figure 5.13: "On the plateau": the Dunham cottage, Keene Valley, where Ives worked on the *Universe Symphony* in October 1915. Porter Mountain is visible through the trees.

ents had boarded for a period at Rivermede farm, he recalled, "for a number of summers [they] were privileged to rent the larger house on the Dunham plateau."[65]

The two-story, green-shingled cottage (see Figure 5.13) faces east, looking across the valley to the upper slopes of Giant Mountain. A roofed porch with supports of unfinished pine begins on the east side and continues around to the north. From this vantage there is a dramatic view of the open rock face of Porter Mountain, not a distant shape but powerfully near. The mountain was named after the Reverend Noah Porter, Joseph Twichell's climbing companion.[66] Inside the cottage is a living room with fireplace and bay windows opening out toward Porter, a dining room and kitchen, and four bedrooms upstairs. The roofed porch makes the interior somewhat dark, but the place has the plain rustic comfort and solid woodworking craft typical of Adirondack summer dwellings.

In the *Memos*, Ives linked his final visit to the Adirondacks with the genesis of the *Universe Symphony*:

> When we were in Keene Valley, on the plateau, staying in the
> fall of 1915 with Sue and Grossie—and with Edie (and Edie's
> second mother)—I started something that I'd had in mind for
> some time.[67]

Ives described two distinct musical sections in the piece, one representing "the sky or tops of the trees," another "the earth and land." (One of the titles he considered for the work was "The Earth and the Heavens.") Within the densely contrapuntal fabric of the *Universe Symphony*, different lines associated with the earth would depict "the ledges, rocks, woods, and land formations—lines of trees and forest, meadows, roads, rivers, etc.—and undulating lines of mountains in the distance that you catch in a wide landscape." Above this, played simultaneously but moving in its own orbit, the "heavens" music would unfold in cycles of "chordal counterpoint." Ives claimed he was "trying out a parallel way of listening to music, suggested by looking at a view," in which one shifts focus between sky and land but always remains aware of the other part.[68] To carry out the idea, he envisioned two "huge orchestras" performing the different parts, positioned "across from each other on mountaintops overlooking a valley."[69] Never finished, the *Universe Symphony* continued to haunt Ives into his later years. According to Christine Valentine (née Loring), who worked as Ives's typist in Redding, he "once stood looking out the picture window toward the mountains . . . humming and singing bits of music," then said, "If only I could have done it. It's all there—the mountains and the fields." He told her he was referring to the *Universe Symphony*.[70]

On the Dunham plateau Ives contemplated the scene before him and tried to write music to capture the eye's way of seeing. He looked not down upon the village but up to the gentle slopes and steeper mountain faces, to the open rock of Porter and distant summit of Giant. One of the notes he wrote on Section A of the *Universe Symphony* described a sight very much like that of Porter viewed from the plateau:

> sharp jagged edges of rock going up, up up to the heaven all is
> rough and different lines yet as the eye contemplates the [great
> spaces &] clouds, the seething moving earth becomes a huge
> foundation of eternity[71]

Other notes Ives jotted on the *Universe* sketches capture the distinctive mountain landscape that had drawn painters to the Keene Valley region: "the wide valley & the clouds are one accord & the horizon distant hills are as the clouds their roots from earth then into heaven/The soaring lines of mountains, cliffs & pinnacles sent from the moving veins of Rocks."[72] If Ives's theme was universal—the unfolding of geologic history from the "Formation of the waters and mountains" to "Earth, evolution in nature and humanity" to "Heaven, the rise of all to the spiritual"—the inspiration was local and immediate, as Ives folded together the view from the Dunham plateau with other mountain memories: the panoramic vista of Elk Lake, the paradisiacal sunset he and Harmony had seen at Saranac, and the view from Pine Mountain in Connecticut.

For psychoanalyst and biographer Stuart Feder, the *Universe Symphony* is a mid-life fantasy of omnipotence, a childlike creation myth devised by Ives to combat a host of anxieties: fear of aging, recognition of "increasing mental instability and of physical illness," and "awareness of failing creativity," in turn associated with "impotence, emasculation, and the imminence of death."[73] Feder makes the *Universe Symphony* seem the act of someone both desperate and frustrated—and Ives may have been both as he struggled with it. But the *Universe Symphony* also can be viewed as the culmination of Ives's nature-inspired works, part of a line including the *Concord Sonata* and the Fourth Symphony (both conceived in the Adirondacks), songs like *The Housatonic at Stockbridge* and *Maple Leaves*, and experiments in sound travel like *An Autumn Landscape on Pine Mountain* and *The Pond*. The *Universe Symphony* reflected Ives's profound awe at the miracle and mystery of life on earth. "It was to be religious (a paean of praise, I believe he said)," as his typist recalled.[74] Like his father-in-law Joseph Twichell and the other Connecticut divines who came to Keene Valley to worship Nature, Ives found God in the mountains. The *Universe Symphony* would be his gloss on the Book of Genesis— and as William H. H. Murray had remarked on the impact of the Adirondacks upon vacationing ministers, "Wouldn't there be some preaching?"[75]

But if Ives's *Universe Symphony* connected him to other nineteenth-century Adirondack visitors who had intense Romantic responses to the region, his own relationship to the mountains was rather different. For "indefatigable trampers" like Joe Twichell, Horace Bushnell, and William James, mountains were meant to be scaled, offering a physical and spiritual reward for those who made it to the top. For Ives, mountains were objects to contemplate, best viewed from afar and below. They stood as a record of geological creation, also as a symbol of endless human striving. Just as mountains were dwelling places of the immortals in Greco-Roman mythology and the Taoist tradition

of China—"staircases to the celestial," in Simon Schama's phrase[76]—
so for Ives they were sacred places where men could come close to
heaven and God.[77] One didn't need Orson "Mountain Man" Phelps
for a guide: Art could perform the service. Browning "walked on the
mountains," and Emerson was a "mountain-guide" who "stood on a
summit at the door of the infinite, where many men do not care to
climb, peering into the mysteries of life, contemplating the eternities."[78] Similarly Ives's music, like Browning's poetry and Emerson's
philosophy, offered the challenge of an exhilarating ascent.
Negotiating its rugged dissonance, rough terrain, and twisted paths
required stamina. It was not for the "lily pads" and faint of heart. But
those who pushed on to the summit could consider themselves sound
in body and spiritually fit. They could come back down from the
mountain having glimpsed, like Thoreau in the wilds, "proof of
immortality."[79]

The tendency to identify Ives exclusively with New England has
obscured the role played by the Adirondacks in his personal history
and compositional career. His relationship to this northern region
changed over the years. At Waldruhe he enjoyed *gemütlich* gatherings
familiar from his Yale experience, relaxing with sons and daughters
of Connecticut families like the Woods and Twichells. Later in Saranac
Lake he renewed creative energies and recovered health in the company of "healers" like David Twichell and his sister Harmony. Out of
the solitude and sublime landscape of Elk Lake came the great
creative visions of the Fourth Symphony and the *Concord Sonata*.
These mountain-inspired projects culminated in the *Universe
Symphony* sketched by Ives on the Dunham plateau in Keene Valley.
On the surface, Ives's trips to the Adirondacks resembled those of
other privileged northeasterners who went to the woods seeking
escape from the everyday. But like the "climbing clerics," landscape
painters, and philosophers who had come before him, Ives found in
the Adirondacks spiritual sustenance and subjects for his art. Taking
the wilderness tonic of Adirondack forests, lakes, valleys, and mountains, Ives joined Emerson and Thoreau in their own quests for truth
and beauty in nature. Sitting by Elk Lake or on the Dunham plateau,
he could smoke his pipe, dream, and compose, becoming the
Everyman he described in the "Postface to *114 Songs*"—a figure who
would "look up over the mountains and see his visions in their reality," and who would "hear the transcendental strains of the day's symphony resounding in their many choirs, and in all their perfection,
through the west wind and the tree tops!"[80]

In their biography of Ives, Sidney and Henry Cowell described him in old age at his retreat in West Redding: "Beyond the immediate hills are the Berkshires—a view Mr. Ives seems never to tire of contemplating."[81] As Ives gazed north, his thoughts may have strayed back to the Adirondacks of his youth. Once a place of love, art, and ideas, the great mountains were now remote, outside his field of vision. But perhaps he still heard their music floating down from afar, echoing faintly in mists of memory.

NOTES

My thanks to Richard Beamish, Margot Ernst, H. Wiley Hitchcock, Carol J. Oja, Peter Burkholder, and Wayne Shirley for reading an earlier draft of this essay and offering helpful comments and corrections. I am grateful to a number of others for their assistance: in the Adirondacks, Janet Decker and Barbara Parnass (Saranac Lake Free Library), Dorothy Irving (Keene Valley Library), Reid Larson (Essex County Historical Society), Jerold Pepper (The Adirondack Museum, Blue Mountain Lake), Alice Cheney, Emily Neville, Margaret Twichell Jones, Chas Twichell, Chase Twichell, photographer Dave McDonough, and map-maker Nancy Bernstein; at Yale, Public Services librarian Suzanne Eggleston, Elizabeth Bergman, and Tom Owens provided information from the Ives Collection.

The Emerson epigraph can be found in his essay "Nature," in *Nature, The Conduct of Life and Other Essays* (London: J.M. Dent, 1963), 7. The epigraph attributed to Ives is quoted by Ives's secretary Mrs. Rodman S. Valentine (née Christine Loring) in Vivian Perlis, *Charles Ives Remembered: An Oral History* (New Haven: Yale University Press, 1974), 117.

1. William H. H. Murray, "The Adirondacks," in *Adventures in the Wilderness*, ed. William K. Verner (Syracuse: Syracuse University Press/The Adirondack Museum, 1989), 93. The quoted passage is from an article published 23 October 1869 in the *New-York Tribune*, in which Murray answered critics of his enthusiastic accounts of the Adirondacks in *Adventures in the Wilderness*.

2. The subject of Ives in the Adirondacks was first elaborated upon by David Wooldridge in *From the Steeples and Mountains: A Study of Charles Ives* (New York: Alfred A Knopf, 1974). Drawing mainly upon information presented by Wooldridge, Joe Jillisky pieced together the main outlines of the story in "Charles Ives in the Adirondacks," *Adirondac*, May 1987, 8–11. More recently Stuart Feder has discussed the region's significance for Ives in *Charles Ives, "My Father's Song": A Psychoanalytic Biography* (New Haven: Yale University Press, 1992); see especially 292–97.

3. "[My] things [were] done mostly in the twenty years or so between 1896 and 1916." From notes by Ives quoted in Henry Cowell and Sidney Cowell, *Charles Ives and His Music*, 2nd. ed. (New York: Oxford University Press, 1969; reprint ed., New York: Da Capo, 1983), 75.

4. Place names jotted down on manuscripts by Ives make it possible to link individual works to his stays in the Adirondacks—for example, when he writes on the *Three-*

Page Sonata score, "Fine at Saranac L." John Kirkpatrick recorded much of this marginalia in his edition of Ives's *Memos* (New York: W. W. Norton, 1972) and in *A Temporary Mimeographed Catalogue of the Music Manuscripts and Related Materials of Charles Edward Ives 1874–1954* (New Haven: Library of the Yale School of Music, 1960).

As for verifying the dates when Ives worked on or completed pieces—a famously difficult exercise in Ives studies—I am interested in the topic only peripherally here. My main concern is to explore the nature and dimensions of Ives's relationship with the Adirondacks, sifting together biographical, historical, and musical evidence with impressions drawn from my own summers spent in the region.

5. Evocative descriptions of the Adirondacks abound in Paul Jamieson, ed., *The Adirondack Reader* (Glens Falls, New York: The Adirondack Mountain Club, 1982). Christine Jerome comments on the distinctive character of the region in her preface to *An Adirondack Passage* (New York: HarperCollins, 1994), xviii–xix.

6. A detailed account of legislation affecting the Adirondacks is given by Alfred L. Donaldson in his still-essential *A History of the Adirondacks*, 2 vols. (1921; reprint ed., Port Washington, N.Y.: Ira J. Friedman, 1963), II: 163–256.

7. William Chapman White, *Adirondack Country* (New York: Alfred A. Knopf, 1967), 127.

8. For the story of healing at Saranac Lake, see Edward Livingston Trudeau, *An Autobiography* (Garden City, N.Y.: Doubleday Page, 1916), and Robert Taylor, *Saranac: America's Magic Mountain* (Boston: Houghton Mifflin, 1978).

9. See Jamieson, *The Adirondack Reader*, for Stillman's reminiscence of this journey and an excerpt from Emerson's "The Adirondacs" (74–85).

10. Letter to Charles Renouvier, 5 August 1883, in Jamieson, *Adirondack Reader*, 110. For more letters by William James about the Adirondacks, see Josephine Goldmark, "An Adirondack Friendship," *The Atlantic Monthly*, September 1934, 265–272 (Part I) and October 1934, 440–447 (Part II).

11. For the history and cultural life of Keene Valley, see Edith Pilcher, *Up the Lake Road: The First Hundred Years of the Adirondack Mountain Reserve* (Keene Valley, N.Y.: Adirondack Mountain Reserve, 1987).

12. The descriptive phrase for Bushnell is from Donaldson, *A History of the Adirondacks*, II:46. Bushnell helped secure Joseph Twichell's post of minister at the Asylum Hill Church in Hartford (Ives, *Memos*, 259). Twichell later wrote a memoir of his outdoor experiences with Bushnell, "Dr. Bushnell in the Woods," *Outlook* 65 (2 June 1900): 261–65. For the impact of Bushnell's sermons and thought upon Ives, see J. Peter Burkholder, *Charles Ives: The Ideas Behind the Music* (New Haven and London: Yale University Press, 1985), 103–4 and 111. Today, Bushnell Falls, located on John's Brook on one of the trails up to Mt. Marcy, commemorates the Hartford minister's time in the Adirondacks.

Joseph Twichell's poignant memoir of Noah Porter appeared in *Noah Porter: A Memorial by Friends*, ed. G. S. Merriam (New York: Scribner's, 1893); it is excerpted in Jamieson, *The Adirondack Reader*, 471–73.

13. Donaldson, *A History of the Adirondacks*, II:45–46.

14. Murray, *Adventures in the Wilderness*, 23–24. Twichell makes the same point in his memoir of Horace Bushnell. One evening, Twichell recalled, while camping by John's Brook and listening to Bushnell pray in the "sanctuary of nature . . . with a tone as soft and melodious as the low murmur of the stream beneath, . . . I found every other feeling swallowed up in the thought that God was there" ("Dr. Bushnell in the Woods," 265).

15. E. R. Wallace, *Adirondack Guidebook* (1872), quoted in Pilcher, *Up the Lake Road*, 15.

16. From an article by Warner published in the *Hartford Courant* 24 November 1866, quoted by Burton P. Twichell in "Mr. and Mrs. Twichell's Early Days in Keene Valley," typescript of a talk given before the Keene Valley Historical Society, 3 August 1938, in Twichell family vertical file, Archives of the Keene Valley Library. Known to the Twichell children as "Uncle Charley," Warner was remembered after his death in 1900 by Harmony as "a great and good man" and "a sure and dear guide for young people" (Ives, *Memos*, 276).

17. Warner, article from 24 November 1866 *Hartford Courant*, quoted by Joseph Twichell in his "Scrap-book," 6; Joseph Twichell vertical file, Archives of the Keene Valley Library.

18. Wooldridge, *From the Steeples and Mountains*, 95. The Twichell children, from oldest to youngest, were: Edward Carrington ("Deac"), Julia Curtis ("Judy"), Susan Lee ("Sue"), David Cushman, Harmony, Burton Parker ("Burt"), Sarah Dunham ("Sally"), Joseph Hooker ("Joe"), and Louise. All but Sue and Sally married. Interview with Margaret Twichell Jones (daughter of Burton Twichell), Keene Valley, 18 August 1995.

19. Letter from David Twichell to Charles Ives, 4 August 1896, transcribed by John Kirkpatrick. In John Kirkpatrick Papers (box 87, folder 797), John Herrick Jackson Music Library, Yale University, New Haven.

20. Quoted in Wooldridge, *From the Steeples and Mountains*, 95. Bart Yung, another Yale undergraduate and part of Keene Valley's Connecticut contingent—his parents were neighbors of the Twichells in Hartford—would later become one of Ives's Poverty Flat roommates in New York City, as would David Twichell.

21. Wooldridge, *From the Steeples and Mountains*, 113.

22. Ives, *Memos*, 260.

23. Letter from Ives to David Twichell, September or October 1903, Ives Collection (box 32, folder 10), John Herrick Jackson Music Library, Yale University, New Haven.

24. John Kirkpatrick located Pine Mountain "three miles southwest of Danbury" and roughly two miles east of Ridgebury (Ives, *Memos*, 159); it lies within the township of Ridgefield (thanks to H. Wiley Hitchcock and Cynthia Farris for their help with Connecticut geography).

25. Wooldridge, *From the Steeples and Mountains*, 121; Feder, *Charles Ives*, 182.

26. Cowell and Cowell, *Charles Ives and his Music*, 41.

27. Wooldridge, *From the Steeples and Mountains*, 121.

28. Ives, Memos, 159. Kirkpatrick believed *An Autumn Landscape* might have been an early version of *The Pond* (1906), which later became *Remembrance* in *114 Songs* (Kirkpatrick, *Temporary Mimeographed Catalogue*, 42).

29. For more on Ives and musical space, see Robert Morgan, "Spatial Form in Ives," in *An Ives Celebration: Papers and Panels of the Charles Ives Centennial Festival-Conferences*, ed. H. Wiley Hitchcock and Vivian Perlis (Urbana: University of Illinois Press, 1977), 145–58.

30. Ives, *Memos*, 276.

31. Ibid., 277.

32. Feder, *Charles Ives*, 202. David Twichell's life was tragically cut short in 1924, at the age of forty-nine, when he committed suicide in Keene Valley at the Whispering Pines resort (one of the places where Joseph Twichell boarded summers with his family). Interview with Chas Twichell (son of Burton Twichell), Keene Valley, 25 July 1995.

My account of Charles and Harmony at Saranac Lake has been strongly influenced by Feder's interpretation in *Charles Ives*.

33. Quoted in Taylor, *Saranac*, 264.

34. Feder, *Charles Ives*, 183. For more on the Armstrong committee's investigation and its effects on Ives, see the chapter by Michael Broyles in this volume.

35. Quoted in Feder, *Charles Ives*, 184.

36. Ives, *Memos*, 72. The 1905 setting of *The Beautiful River* later became the basis for the third movement of Ives's Fourth Violin Sonata, and from that movement he arranged the song *At the River* (*114 Songs*, no. 45).

I have tried unsuccessfully to uncover information on prayer meetings held in Saranac Lake in 1905. Researching this period of the town's history is difficult, since a fire in the 1950s destroyed most of the back run of the main newspaper, *The Adirondack Daily Enterprise*. The Saranac Lake Free Library has only scattered issues of the *Daily Enterprise* on microfilm from the 1890s up to the time of the fire (personal communication, Janet Decker, 5 December 1995.)

37. Roberts had settled in the Saranac Lake area in the 1880s. An article about him in the *Northern New Yorker*, vol. 2 (Carnival, 1907), stated that "for the last sixteen years he has awakened interest in Adirondack real estate to a greater degree than any living person." In 1904 his agency handled one hundred forty cottages and camps in the Saranac Lake area; by 1907 the number had grown to over three hundred. Thus "Robert's [sic] Camp" was not the Twichell's "family retreat" at Saranac Lake, as Feder states (Feder, *Charles Ives*, 184), but a short-term rental David Twichell had arranged.

The term "camp" in Adirondack usage can mean anything from a primitive shanty without running water to an extensive lakeside compound (like Marjorie Merriwether Post's Camp Topridge on Upper St. Regis Lake). The Roberts camp stayed in by Charles and Harmony was probably a modest cabin, comfortably appointed, with two to three bedrooms and perhaps a screened porch (like the one in Figure 5.7).

38. Harmony Twichell to Charles Ives, 21 September 1907, uncatalogued letter, Ives Collection, John Herrick Jackson Music Library, Yale University, New Haven.

39. Harmony Twichell to Charles Ives, 24 March 1908, quoted in Feder, *Charles Ives*, 185–86.

40. Harmony Twichell to Charles Ives, 17 September 1907, quoted in Feder, *Charles Ives*, 205.

41. Ives, *Memos*, 276.

42. Interview with Margaret Twichell Jones, Keene Valley, 17 August 1995.

43. Stoddard, *Standard Guide to the Adirondacks* (1914), 145. A chronological history of Elk Lake Lodge has been compiled by Margot Ernst, one of the current owners. I am grateful to her for generously sharing with me a copy of the chronology, and for patiently fielding my inquiries about Elk Lake.

44. The August 1909 diary of Roberta Ernst, grandmother of present owner John Ernst, states that during the week of 19 August 1909 the Twichells stayed "on Mount Tom." From the same summer, she noted other Twichells vacationing at Elk Lake, among them Burton, Susan, and Sarah Dunham Twichell.

45. Paul Jamieson, "Wild Prospects," *Adirondack Life*, September/October 1994, 26 and 28.

46. Harmony Twichell to Charles Ives, February 1908, quoted in Burkholder, *Charles Ives*, 100.

47. "Our Book," Ives Collection (MSS. 14, box 45, D7), John Herrick Jackson Music Library, Yale University, New Haven.

48. Charles Ives to Harmony Twichell Ives, 18 October 1910, quoted in Feder, *Charles Ives*, 218. It is possible that Ives referred to the first movement of the Third Symphony, not the Fourth.

49. Ives may have finished the song after leaving Elk Lake. According to H. Wiley Hitchcock, who has closely studied song manuscripts as part of his work on an edition of Ives's songs, one of the manuscript pages for *Mists* reads: "(last mist at Pells Sep 20 1910/H— Poeta." If the 20 September date is correct, this setting might have been completed—or worked on—after the Elk Lake vacation, which apparently ended 7 September 1910 (*Memos*, 329).

50. Ives, *Memos*, 202, n. 23 (bracketed emendations by Kirkpatrick). The dating is problematic. Kirkpatrick notes that Ives was at Elk Lake in 1911 but not the following year (i.e., "shortly after"). Also, earlier sketches for the *Concord Sonata* apparently date from 1910 ("Hawthorne," at Elk Lake, see *Memos*, 329) and from 1907 (Wooldridge, *From the Steeples and Mountains*, 131). Despite these discrepancies, it seems clear that by the time Ives came to write the *Memos*, in the early 1930s, he traced the conception of the *Concord Sonata* to the Adirondacks—Elk Lake in particular.

51. Ives, *Memos*, 76.

52. Annotations on Ives's full score of the *Robert Browning Overture*, quoted in Kirkpatrick, *Temporary Mimeographed Catalogue*, 32.

53. Robert M. Crunden, "Charles Ives's Place in American Culture," in *An Ives Celebration: Papers and Panels of the Charles Ives Centennial Festival-Conference*, ed. H. Wiley Hitchcock and Vivian Perlis (Urbana: University of Illinois Press, 1977), 6–7.

54. The Blake quotation appeared on the title page of Carl Ruggles's *Men and Mountains*, published in the first issue of Henry Cowell's *New Music Quarterly* (October 1927). Rossiter has noted Ives's admiration for Ruggles's piece, writing that "Ives himself had long used the symbol of the mountain to suggest spiritual transcendence and the hard and lonely way of truth" (Frank R. Rossiter, *Charles Ives and His America* [New York: Liveright, 1975], 269). As an example Rossiter cites a statement in the *Memos*: "Even today probably about 83% of the so-called best musical programs . . . lean more to the mollycoddle than the rough way up the mountain" (134).

For a searching and subtle discussion of Ives and the culture of masculinity, see Judith Tick, "Charles Ives and Gender Ideology," in *Musicology and Difference*, ed. Ruth A. Solie (Berkeley: University of California Press, 1993), 83–106.

55. Cited in Feder, *Charles Ives*, 269.

56. According to H. Wiley Hitchcock, the *ppp* designation for this part in *114 Songs* is an engraver's error.

57. Rossiter, *Charles Ives and His America*, 178.

58. Kirkpatrick, *Temporary Mimeographed Catalogue*, 15.

59. Feder, *Charles Ives*, 231.

60. Donaldson, *A History of the Adirondacks*, II:47.

61. The caption under a photograph in *From the Steeples and Mountains* reads: "Keene Valley Plateau" (between pages 178 and 179). Jillisky reproduces the same image and titles it, "The Keene 'Plateau' as Ives knew it in the early 1900s" ("Ives in the Adirondacks," 10). But the photo is not of the "plateau"—rather, it shows the village of Keene Valley, looking north. Seeing this photo, Chas Twichell surmised it had been taken by a photographer *standing* on the Dunham plateau (Interview, Keene Valley, 25 July 1995). The incorrectly labeled photos give the impression of a plateau both expansive and thickly settled; in fact it is quite small, and the slight elevation gives it a feeling of being removed from the town itself.

62. Ives, *Memos*, 261.

63. *Keene Valley Houses*, vol. 3, Archives, Keene Valley Library. The source leaves it unclear whether these three Hartford gentlemen actually "built" the house or contracted the work out and owned the property jointly. Later the cottage was owned by Sarah

Dunham Rowley, niece of A. C. Dunham; it is now occupied summers by her daughter Alice Rowley Cheney.

64. Ives, *Memos*, 276.

65. Burton Twichell, "Early Days," 2.

66. Pine trees now prevent seeing the top of Porter from the house itself. In 1915, when the area around Keene Valley had fewer trees and was much more open, the view was probably unobstructed.

67. Ives, *Memos*, 106. "Grossie," as Kirkpatrick explains in a footnote, was short for Grosspapa (Joseph Twichell) and Edie's "second mother" was Harmony. While claiming that he "started" the *Universe Symphony* during the fall of 1915, Ives also referred to sketches "made a few years before," and Kirkpatrick noted that one of the addresses on the manuscript (37 Liberty, a lower Manhattan location for the Ives & Myrick company) dates it before February 1914 (*Memos*, 163). Nevertheless, Ives's account in the *Memos* makes it clear that he associated work on the *Universe Symphony* with his 1915 visit to Keene Valley.

68. Ives, *Memos*, 106.

69. Perlis, *Charles Ives Remembered*, 117.

70. Ibid. Ives's unfinished *Universe Symphony* has held a powerful attraction for scholars and devotees of his music. Foremost among them is composer Larry Austin, who began studying the sketches in the mid-1970s, has written four original works based on Ives's musical material, and "realized" a performance score of the *Universe Symphony* recorded in 1994 (*Charles Ives: Universe Symphony*, Centaur CD CRC 2205). For an altogether different approach, there is *In the Universe of Ives*, a five-minute, partly-improvised setting arranged by jazz mallet-player Mike Mainieri, scored for six overdubbed xylophones, bass marimba, alto clarinet, bass, and percussion (*An American Diary*, NYC CD 6105-2).

71. Ives, *Universe Symphony* sketches, section A, negative q2757+3256, frame number f6897. (Note: the frame number refers to the master microfilm of Ives's music manuscripts in the Ives Collection, John Herrick Jackson Music Library, Yale University.)

72. *Universe*, sketches, section A, negative q3027, frame number f1830.

73. Feder, *Charles Ives*, 294–96.

74. Perlis, *Charles Ives Remembered*, 117. In *Essays Before a Sonata*, describing how music might reflect a spiritual response to nature, Ives invoked Thoreau: "the music may have been influenced strongly, though subconsciously, by a vague remembrance of certain thoughts and feelings, perhaps of a deep religious or spiritual nature, which suddenly came to him upon realizing the beauty of the scene, . . . perhaps some such feeling as of the conviction of immortality that Thoreau experienced, and tells us about in *Walden*. 'Ah! I have penetrated to those meadows . . . when the wild river valley and the woods were bathed in so pure and bright a light as would have waked the dead. . . . There needs no stronger proof of immortality.'" (*Essays Before a Sonata, The Majority, and Other Writings*, ed. Howard Boatwright [New York: W. W. Norton, 1971], 5.)

75. Murray, *Adventures in the Wilderness*, 24. Stuart Feder goes further, claiming that Ives's labor on the *Universe Symphony* "paralleled the work of God in Genesis" (*Charles Ives*, 294).

76. Simon Schama, *Landscape and Memory* (New York: Alfred A. Knopf, 1995), 411. See 385ff for a discussion of mountains in the western imagination.

77. Ives worked this idea into his programmatic description of the Second String Quartet, a piece which he characterized as a work for "4 men—who converse, discuss, argue in re "Politick", fight, shake hands shut up—then walk up the mountain side to view the firmament" (Kirkpatrick, *Temporary Mimeographed Catalogue*, 60). Thanks to H.

Wiley Hitchcock and Wayne Shirley for reminding me of "The Call of the Mountains," the quartet's third movement.

It should be noted that in Ives's time, virtually all the noted mountain climbers in the Adirondacks were men, whether athletically inclined intellectuals like Twichell, William James, and Felix Adler, or hardy locals like Orson "Mountain Man" Phelps. The latter expressed a severe—though perhaps not atypical—view of the place of women in the wilderness: "Women . . . never ought to come into the woods. There was a lot of 'em I took up [Mt.] Marcy last summer, went gigglin' all the way up, talking of their beaux, and ribbons, and when they got up didn't see nothing. I wanted to kick 'em off the mountain" (quoted by Joseph Twichell in his "Scrap-book," 20; Archives of the Keene Valley Library). In *Adventures in the Wilderness*, Murray does not rule out women visitors to the Adirondacks—in one section he discusses what ladies should wear there—but seems to be addressing men as his primary readers, relating anecdotes that show males bonding while hunting, fishing, or sitting around the campfire.

78. Ives, *Essays Before a Sonata*, 12.

79. Ives, *Essays Before a Sonata*, 5. In one section of Ives's "Memos about the Concord Sonata," he compares the unfolding of musical form to a mountain hike: "A natural procedure in a piece of music, be it a song or a week's symphony, may have something in common [with]—I won't say analogous to—a walk up a mountain. There's the mountain, its foot, its summit—there's the valley—the climber looks, turns, and looks down or up. He sees the valley, but not exactly the same angle he saw it at [in] the last look—and the summit is changing with every step—and the sky. Even if he stands on the same rock at the top and looks toward Heaven and Earth, he is not in just the same key he started in, or in the same moment of existence" (*Memos*, 196; bracketed emendations by Kirkpatrick).

80. Ives, *Essays Before a Sonata*, 128–29.

81. Cowell and Cowell, *Charles Ives and His Music*, 125.

Part II

LETTERS

Selected Correspondence 1881–1954

EDITED BY TOM C. OWENS

This cross-section of Ives's correspondence presents only a fraction of the material preserved in the Ives collection in the John Herrick Jackson Music Library at Yale University.[1] These previously unpublished letters span the period from his earliest family letters of the 1880s to letters commenting on his death in 1954 and cover music, politics, family life, patronage, and a host of other subjects. Through these letters we can sharpen and refine our image of Charles Ives and examine his works within a broader historical context. One prominent theme is Ives's substantial presence in the lives of those with whom he came into contact. His correspondence is replete with examples of the effect—musical, intellectual, financial, spiritual—that he had on others' lives. This influence extended to people whom he knew only through their letters as well as to those whom he had met in person. Although Ives was ill and lived in seclusion for much of his later life, the correspondence reveals that his actions and his music were a vital, present force in the lives of many people.

Childhood and Education

In the few surviving letters from Ives's childhood, later personality traits and habits are already apparent. For instance, in his desire to show mastery of grammar in the letter of 25 May 1886, Ives foreshadows the revisions that would be so common in the sketches for his music and later letters. His sense of humor is also evident early on. His postscript in the same letter is one of several humorous references to his duties as custodian of his Aunt Amelia and Uncle Lyman Brewster's chicken coop. In another letter, he refers to himself as "your humble chicken waterer."

September 1881, Charles Ives to Lyman Brewster

DEAR UNCLE LYMAN,
  MOSSIE AND I HAVE JUST HAD OUR BATHS. I WENT TO HARRY FLINT'S AND DROVE HIS GOAT. KISS GRANDMA AND AUNT AMELIA FOR CHARLIE.[2]

> GOOD BYE
> CHARLIE

25 May 1886, Charles Ives to Amelia Brewster

Dear Aunt Millie
  Mossie and I stayed down to your house Saturday. In bed Mossie pulled my hair and I dreamt about it, I dreamt that Will Greely and Art Ballard pulled my hair. I was just awake enough to feel Mossie pull it and I dreamt about [it] and it is true. Uncle Lyman has got home safely and I am staying down here to supper. I was going to stay all night but U. Lyman is going to burgeses meeting. I thought I would not stay. I am going to stay some other night. Uncle Lyman went to Burgeses meeting last night too. Mamama and Papa and Moss are all well and so am I and Uncle Lyman. Ask Sarane how her Mikado is getting on and tell her to write to me. There is not no any school Friday. Uncle did not have to tell [me] to cross off no and put any I did it myself. I want to learn grammar. There is a cirus [circus?] Saturday. With love to you all I must close.

> Yours truly
> Charlie

P.S. The chickens are all right.

•

While at Hopkins Grammar School (1893–94), and then during his freshman year at Yale, Ives wrote frequently to his father George. Their correspondence reveals the complex and sometimes uncomfortable relationship developing between the two as Ives established his own identity and moved away from paternal control. The musical bond between the two is clear in these letters, which reflect Ives's activity as a listener, as a composer, and as a practical musician, trying to adapt to a new performance environment.

The letter of 24 October, four days after Ives turned twenty and only eleven days before his father's unexpected death of a stroke at forty-nine, provides vital information about the art music Ives heard at Yale. This letter also gives us a sense of Ives's desire to succeed in Yale society by playing football and submitting an article to the *Yale Literary Magazine*.

4 February 1894, Charles Ives to George Ives

Dear Father,
Received your letter with checks, and also the one with newspaper slip. How did Ashmall happen to send the "America" home, did you write for it? I think he did write to me before about [it], but just mentioned some places which I could cut or clear out, and didn't say anything about publishing it, as I remember.[3] I didn't call for that copy of it as I have one here. I went to the Glee and Banjo concert Monday, but was rather disappointed.[4] Some of the tenors flatted quite often, and the one that did the [illegible][5] solo sharped so badly that he was nearly a whole tone higher than the club at the end. The banjo club was good, I thought. I heard that [Adelina] Patti was coming to New Haven but not sure when. Will send receipt as soon as I get it. How is Grandmother and all the folks?

Yours truly,
Chas E. I.

24 February 1894. Charles Ives to George Ives

Dear Father,
Have just written to Uncle Lyman. Received the "Eagle" today.[6] There is a choral service at the church to morrow. During Lent all the chants that are sung are founded on the Gregorian tones. The choir sings them in unison, and so I have to change the harmonies. It is rather awkward to do as the air has to be kept on the top. The best way I have found to do is to use diminished chords in the same key, or go to the 1st and a # remove. . . .[7] It is very cold here today, the coldest this year. I hope all the folks are well. With love to all.

Yours very truly,
Chas

24 October 1894, Charles Ives to George Ives

Dear Father,

Yours received last evening. The man that makes them ought to know best about the cards. The dis[tance] between the window frames for the pole or rod is 3 ft. 4 1/2 in. I should think some colored stuff would [be] better than white, something like that in the music room.

I have bought a ticket of Mr. Hume for the series of chamber concerts, this winter, Kneisel, Beethoven quartets, etc., $2.50. I hope to hear the Symphony concert Tues.[8] When you get this please send Garrison some more lessons, if only a little. We can go over them together.[9] Also please send the man[uscript] of the march I was fixing just before I left. When you send the cushions, curtains, etc., then send my black hat also. . . .

I began playing football a little the other day. I go out regularly, from 2:00–3:00, on Tues., Thurs., and Fri. every week. The other days they have games. It's pretty good exercise as they make us run in and out, to the field, which is [a] little over a mile. There is not much fun in it, as I thought at first there would be, especially as I won't play in the games, but think I will keep it up for a while anyway as I feel much better for it.[10] They take us in the gym and give us a rub down after it.

Mr. Parker gives an organ recital this evening in Battel.[11] I have made arrangements with the blower for every day except Tues. and Fri. as I have recitation at that time. I sent some old copies of the "Lit." [of] which Mullaly's brother was editor, and which Mandeville will probably be on before he gets through his college course. If Moss wants to try to see what he can do, he might write something and hand it in under my name, which is alright.[12] If he writes anything, it must be some good sensible piece. He must know thoroughly what he is writing about, not only to have it sound good, but it must mean something, and above all it must be original but not in an *egotistic* way. Some little short stories are good too. There is no harm in trying, as if it isn't published, they will return it with suggestions etc. The "Lit." is the best and largest paper in college, and to get on it is even a bigger thing than to make the football team (at least some consider it so). . . .

Yours Very Truly
C. E. Ives

A letter of 20 January 1895 is one of the few surviving letters
from Ives to his mother. It reflects his daily life and demonstrates the influence of his friend, John C. Griggs, the choirmaster at Center Church where Ives played the organ. Ives
clearly considers his reputation as an organist when he writes of
the importance of studying with prominent organist and composer Dudley Buck.

20 January 1895, Charles Ives to Mollie P. Ives

Dear Mother,

Received your's and Aunt Amelia's letters. I finally found the
landlady in and paid her $10.00. I told her about the mistake in the
bill etc. and she said she [would] make out another one and have it
ready next week. The chairs haven't arrived yet. Are they coming by
express or freight? We supposed they would come by freight so we
asked a carman [to] look out for them. I will say before I forget it that
Garrison was much pleased with his hat, he says it fits him better than
any hat he ever had. The commons bill was 13 weeks instead of 12.
It began Oct. 13 Thur. which week I had to pay for as I went in
before the 22nd. Mullaly also owes about $6.00 as he went in on a
guest ticket with me before he was admitted as a regular member. I
spoke a little while ago about me taking a few lessons this winter with
Dudley Buck.

As I haven't taken any lessons at all for quite a while, I think it
almost necessary that I should and if I don't get any other good from
it, just being a pupil of Buck's would be very helpful. I think I can go
about every 3 wks until about March or April. I think he charges $4.00
a lesson. Mr. Griggs who advised me to do it has made arrangements
for next Thurs. at 5:00. I can leave here about 1:30 and get back
about 8:30 or 9:00.[13] I have more time than I did, and no recitations
Thurs. afternoon. So I will go down anyway next Thurs. unless I hear
to the contrary from you.

Please ask Moss to go up to Lizzie Raymond and ask her for the
copy of "Rock of Ages" which I wrote some time ago. . . . [14]

Yours very truly,
Chas

Courtship

After his father's death, Ives seems to have written home less frequently, or perhaps his letters were not saved as often as before. The next large body of Ives's correspondence centers around his courtship of Harmony Twichell and their marriage on 8 June 1908. These letters, many more of which survive from Harmony than from Charlie, paint a touchingly personal portrait of the relationship between the two who were to be so completely devoted to each other for the next forty-six years.[15] The two frequently discussed music as in the letter below and collaborated on musical projects, such as the song *Autumn* (1908).

29 September 1907, Harmony Twichell to Charles Ives

Dear Charlie—

Please don't think it was thoughtful or kind of me to write you from the camp for it was nothing but selfish indulgence on my part.[16] I wanted to. I am glad you think of that time we were there as a good time for I do too and am sure times like that will come again.

Miss Fites is staying away an extra week and I now expect to get home the eleventh so plan to come that next week and can't you come Wednesday or Thursday and stay over Sunday.—[17] If we have only one day to count on it will surely rain or do something unpleasant— please try. I can hardly wait to see you.—

I did see that about Greig in the *Outlook*.[18] What was it you were particularly struck with in it? It seemed to me very true that his music is individual rather than National or general—lyric rather than epic. It generally seems as if the song of Greig I hear is meant exactly for me.— The more I try to think what that Swan Song is the more it seems what said—"the elves in the bushes" that scare the poor swan might well be the indifference and unappreciation that check expression, don't you think so?— And still it might mean something different to everyone who reads the words.

Wasn't it nice to meet your brother as you did? I'm glad you had a visit and hope he won his case.— That office joke of yours is rather splendid.

. . . It's a pouring day and a great luxury to be able to stay in and hear the storm.— If I had several such days I might get at the *Kimiash Hills*. . . .[19]

Good by—I shall be glad to talk to you in place of writing.

> Yours as ever,
> Harmony T.

•

By the end of October, 1907, Harmony and Charlie had become more serious about their relationship, and Harmony's tone takes on the ecstatic quality of newly declared love.[20] Her letter of 27-28 October shows her literary bent as she compares her love to that of famous past lovers and mentions a poem she has written about "last Tuesday," the probable day of their engagement.[21] Her thoughts of George Ives suggest Ives's devotion to his memory and the amount that Ives must have talked about him.

On 17 November Harmony's father recorded the couple's request for his blessing on their marriage in his diary.[22] In her letters to Ives of early November, Harmony makes an impassioned case that the ceremony take place as soon as possible. Despite his financial worries, she is consumed with a desire to share Ives's every experience.

25 October 1907, Harmony Twichell to Charles Ives

Dear—

I never wrote a love letter and I don't know how. If I don't mail this today you won't get mail until Monday, and I can't wait that long to have you see in my writing what you've seen these perfect days in my face—that I love you, and love you, and love you and no numbers of times of saying it can ever tell it. But *believe* it and that I am yours always and utterly—every bit of me.

> Harmony

26–27 October 1907, Harmony Twichell to Charles Ives

Only *best* beloved—my dearest—anything—everything—I haven't any thoughts except that I love you and I've been thinking of all the "grandes passiones" in history and I know neither Francesca nor Beatrice nor anyone was ever more possessed than I am. I'm such a surprise to myself—and it's all *you*. My, what a time we've had and it's only the beginning. I went and did my errands after you left and made only one mistake so providence was looking after me I think. . . .

27–28 October 1907, Harmony Twichell to Charles Ives

Sunday Afternoon
  Dear—I wrote these lines down just as they came of course, now I have the idea in any shape I can put it into some other order and it would be better rhymed or more rhythmical, wouldn't it? Do you think it seems like last Tuesday at all—from the cliff?
  I found these kodaks which may amuse you—haven't you any of yourself? Don't think you have to keep them. . . .
  I've had a wonderful day only my feelings and thoughts are so much too much for my heart and brain that I don't know what I'm going to do. What do you think? In Church I thought all of a sudden of your father—so intensely that the tears came into my eyes and I thought how much I love him—actually as if I'd known him—I almost *felt* him and I am sure he knows all about this and how dearly I love you and that your welfare is my happiness.— And I thought of other things I can't write about.— I'll tell you my best beloved when I see you. . . .

Harmony

7 November 1907, Harmony Twichell to Charles Ives

You darling and best beloved person in the world.— I'm so glad to have a letter from you.— My others are in my trunk, and that hasn't come yet. I was utterly lonesome without even them. I'm so glad I had the picture which I assure you lay very near my heart all night long.
  Charlie Dearest, I don't want you ever to do anything in regard to me that your best judgement doesn't recommend but I truly think it is best for us to be married as soon as we can.— It's really a hardship for me to be away from you.— I want to do the big things for you and

all the little everyday things too and it isn't as if I hadn't always lived very simply.— I shouldn't feel deprived of things I never wanted to have—I wouldn't *mind feeling deprived* but it just happens I couldn't. For my wants are few and my tastes not fancy.— If we were ten years younger it would be different too. When you can "get a line" on things we will talk it all over.— But I really feel as if it were getting to be a duty to each other, as well as the most heavenly pleasure to be together—I'm not myself without you—I go lame.

When I got home last night I wished *more* acutely—what I'm always wishing unconsciously and acutely—that you were with me.— The house was so quiet and peaceful and all the sort of things that is busying Howard and Burt so far away and so much less important than higher and better things that it would have rested you as it did me.— I do so hope we can make a home that will remind people who come to it of the same sort of things. I think we can for I truly believe the highest and best things are the most important and you do.— That is why I can love you in the absolutely beautiful and sacred way I do—my best beloved.

My trip yesterday wouldn't have been bad if it hadn't been leaving you.— How I hated to and I'm glad you kissed me. . . .

Be sure and write me every day, even if it's only a line to say you are alright. My dearest I love you in every way as hard as my heart can.— And it loves so hard it *aches* and even then it doesn't do it all some how or other.

> Good by blessed one
> Harmony

8 November 1907 A.M., Harmony Twichell to Charles Ives

My Dearest—
. . .Yesterday Morrison and I took a perfectly splendid ride and all the time I was nearly ready to cry to think of what *you* were doing.— Dear heart of course it isn't any of the things you wonder to contemplate. My enduring any hardships with you.— I am quite sure things will come right in a few years anyway but what people regard as hardships would be robbed very much of their bad features if I had the satisfaction of being with you and caring for you I *know.* And look at my point of view.— Can't you see how it seems to me that I *must* be with you these days when you are working hardest and coming home

tired—you may never need me more in your whole life—and as soon as I can come and not be a burden to you I'm coming. . . .

8 November 1907 P.M., Harmony Twichell to Charles Ives

Dearest—you must think I am very impractical to say the least to have written you as I have since I came from New York. What I really mean tho', is *this*—that I don't think we have to wait to have a whole house and a servant etc. to get married. I don't mean to be foolish about it, but I am impatient to be with you—you dear. . . .

Every Lovingly
Harmony

•

Ives's letters also show the strain of separation on the pair. Faced with the difficulties of his business, he is eager to accept the support Harmony offers in her letters. His request for more letters and joyful reaction on receiving mail from Harmony are evidence that he shares the frustration evident in her letters. He is also ready to begin their life together as his question about "our book" demonstrates. This book was a private record of their collective life. Ives wanted Harmony to record their walk on the wood road to Farmington of 22 October as the official beginning of this book they would "keep together," thus to inscribe the day as "the greatest event in the history of this country."

22 November 1907, Charles Ives to Harmony Twichell

Darling little old Harmony,

Another dark day outside but very bright *inside*—and that's all on account of Harmony the only *cause* and *reason* for me now in anything and everything. Your letters are beautiful and have such a wonderful effect—so lasting and so strong. I wonder if it would be too much to ask you to divide your letters (because I don't like to ask you [to] write two letters every day. I know how much you have to do before you come to N.Y.)—but if you would just send me a line so I could have one to help me start the day and then know all day long that I'll find one waiting for me when I come home. It gives me courage and more ability all day long. Letters are weak substitutes for you—best beloved—but they're absolutely essential for me now. Could you do that until I see you? Just a line with your name *would* do—and a little something else.

I'm sorry your aunts etc. annoy you. If it would be easier for you, just tell them. Tell any one you think best to if it will make it any less of a strain on you. I know it's much harder for you being at home than it is for me. Anything that you want to do about anything will be what I want too. I can't tell you why it is that way but it *is*. Aunt Amelia enjoyed you so much I can tell by the way she acted. I'm sorry you didn't find her in—what right had she to be out in the rain? . . . Will take this up to the flat and finish this evening.

Home—such as it is—and to find your letter here!— Harmony— blessed girl—how did you know I *had* to hear from you tonight, to make things endurable. When I started this letter and told you the day was dark, I didn't mean that business wasn't as good as could be expected or that anything bad had happened—only meant that little annoying things had happened, as they always do and always will— business good or bad—lack of activity is the principal thing I guess that makes it hard. Our business I really think is on a solid basis, and is not suffering any more and not as much as most firms are. The hardest thing during the whole day is to feel that I haven't you—at hand—to get your encouragement in the morning and your sympathy at night. I wonder if that is selfish—it seems as though I were wanting you for something you could give me. Well—Harmony—I guess it's all one and the same thing . . . every bit of happiness and help I receive from you must be reflected back to you.— That's one of the wonderful things about our love—we always understand each other and always will.

This is November 22—a month after October 22 and the greatest event in the history of this country though the populace doesn't know it—poor souls! Our wedding day can't be any greater than that—as we really gave all that was best to each other then. Next time we are in Hartford let's try to go out to that wood road again and we must at least once every year.

I'm thankful and grateful to God and everything that helped make it possible for your dear mother and father to feel as they do about it all. I'd rather give up anything else in the world—*except you*—than to ever have them disappointed in me.

Good night—God bless and keep you. I'll have to stop writing now or you may not get this in the 1st mail tomorrow.

Did you get our book that we may put down all the perfect days?
Please start it October 22 and bring it to New York and [we] will keep it together.

God bless you,

My *dearest dearest*
and very best beloved
Chas

26 November 1907, Charles Ives to Harmony Twichell

Dearest Dearest Girl,

Have just hung up the receiving end after hearing your voice without being able to be *with you*—I feel all wrong again. It was so kind and considerate of you to call me. I didn't intend to give you that trouble. I *had* to telephone this morning as I couldn't go through the day not *knowing* how you were. I received two letters this morning—both of them beautiful and wonderful helps to me. Don't worry because the mail-man works on the wrong system, but I want this to reach you tonight.

With all my heart and love and all I have,

Chas

This is not a letter, will write more later.

•

Harmony's letters of 11 and 12 December hint at the physical dimension of the relationship and recall the walk to Farmington.

11 December 1907, Harmony Twichell to Charles Ives

Darling—It's cold enough to light my fire again and I'm rather glad for its company—my, but I'm lonesome! I feel today as this were all a dream and can hardly persuade myself that I actually have *you* my love for you never seem a dream but that you love me that I've had you here and in my arms and kissed you seems almost unbelievable *dearest* heart! My quiet days make little to write of.— The family comes in and out—tho' the well ones are out of the house most of the time. . . .

I wish you wouldn't scratch out *the unspeakable* parts of your letters.— It's quite hard to decipher thro' the scratches and it's always quite important.— I can generally tell what you *would* say.— Scratchings are better than a perfectly lame ending anyway— that's what *I* do— Start to say something inexpressible, find I can't and put down some perfectly feeble word. I hope you've had a good day.— Be sure and tell me always whether it's good, bad, or casual.— I can't *do* anything about it but I like to know. . . .

Good night Charlie dearest
Your loving H.

12 December 1907 P.M., Harmony Twichell to Charles Ives

Dearest—
    . . . I wish we could be planning to take a walk to Farmington over our wood road. I have thought very much today of that hour there and it seems like Paradise.— How beautiful everything was and when you said to me what you did it seemed to me I was swept into a flood and I can't remember much else.— Bless you darling—that moment can never be changed or lost.— It is one of the *supreme* moments of existence isn't it? I had almost said *the* supreme moment but there are others that reach it I am sure. . . .

Harmony

Attempts at Recognition

Soon after his marriage, Ives began attempts to reach an audience for his music. His letter of 14 December 1911 to conductor Walter Damrosch represents both a desire to interest a prominent conductor in his work and the more basic need to hear his music performed. Although Damrosch had conducted a reading of three movements of Ives's First Symphony in 1910 at Ives's expense, he never showed any interest in the other scores Ives sent him. Ives wrote Damrosch to ask about these scores, clear ink copies of the Second and Third

Symphonies, in June 1915 and again around 1936, but they were never returned to him.

14 December 1911, Charles Ives to Walter Damrosch

Dear Mr. Damrosch:—

You were kind enough to say, at the time my manuscript was tried over last year, that you would look at it again later.

Since then I have finished another score in symphony form, which I think better in many ways than the former and would greatly appreciate your looking at it.[23]

If similar arrangements could be made to have it played over at a rehearsal it would be a great help to me—at any rate I hope you may not find it inconvenient to let me show you the score.

The themes for the most part are suggested by tunes and hymns that have always been familiar to us New Englanders and for that reason I feel that it may be more interesting than the other.

Very truly yours,
[Charles E. Ives]

•

A letter from the spring of 1914 shows Ives balancing the demands of family, business, and music. Charles and Harmony were settling in at their summer home in West Redding, Connecticut. Ives's discussion of his aging horse Rocket and the "small automobile" he and Harmony had just purchased demonstrates the effects of the advance of technology even in Ives's rural retreat.

23 May 1914, Charles Ives to Amelia Brewster

Dear Aunt Amelia:

. . . We expect now to be settled in Redding on June 3rd or 4th. Louise and John leave for East Hampton next Thursday, and Harmony will have her hands full with housecleaning and moving. Rocket has been so lame during the last six weeks that we are afraid that he cannot be driven to Redding. We have a small automobile which will be a necessity in Redding, as I am to commute all summer.

It is quite easy to run. We are getting to be quite experts with it (Harmony especially). We go as slow as we can.— And even at that it's a great time saver. Neither of us enjoy riding in it—per se—we use it as a matter of business. Will see you sometime week after next.

> With love,
> Chas

•

Prompted by a sharp decline in his health in 1918, Ives began to make much broader attempts to reach the musical public. In 1920 Ives had his Second Piano Sonata, *"Concord Mass., 1840–1860"* and the book *Essays Before a Sonata* printed and sent to friends and prominent musicians; he followed this in 1922 with his collection of *114 Songs*. Replies to this series of works that Ives had "printed and thrown at the music fraternity—chancing that a few may be interested" varied widely.[24]

A typical response to the *114 Songs*, and one that must have been especially meaningful to Ives considering his background as a band musician, is the following letter from renowned band leader John Philip Sousa. Ives left no comment on this letter but must have taken solace in the fact that Sousa seems, at least, to have read through the songs. Many responses to the *Concord Sonata* and to *114 Songs* thank Ives for his generosity but indicate that the recipient of the volume has not yet had time to examine it.

1 June 1923, John Philip Sousa to Charles Ives

My Dear Mr. Ives:

Permit me to thank you for your kindness in sending me your volume of *114 Songs* of which you are the composer. Some of the songs are most startling to a man educated by the harmonic methods of our forefathers.

> Yours sincerely,
> John Philip Sousa

•

An important early positive response to the *Concord Sonata* came from Henry Bellamann, dean of Chicora College for women in Columbia, South Carolina. Bellamann's excitement over the sonata and the possibility of seeing other works must have been extremely rewarding for Ives, especially in light of the many non-committal thank-yous and decidedly negative responses he received from others to whom he had sent the sonata.

10 April 1921, Henry Bellamann to Charles Ives

My Dear Mr. Ives:

Recently I received a copy of your second piano sonata. I have either you or your publisher to thank. I have just recently had time to go over it several times and I want to tell you how remarkable a piece of work it is. Miss Purcell, who is my assistant and who plays a great many modern works for the various lectures I give thru the year on such composers as Casella, Malipiero and Schönberg, is very delighted with the sonata and we purpose making it the subject of an evening's lecture recital in our series for next year.

I should be very interested to know the *first* sonata and any other music of yours. May I have also any information you care to have give[n] audiences about you. I shall value any material you can give me to render an estimate of your music intelligible to the music club audiences to whom I speak thru the year.

An extraordinary work. One feels very happy to know that a creation of such calibre on an American subject may be done in America—tho I must say truthfully that I am not much interested in the geography of any work of art.

My sincerest and most interested congratulations and with every good wish I am,

Cordially,
H. H. Bellamann

•

Bellamann's letter and intention to present the *Concord Sonata* in a lecture recital with pianist Lenore Purcell delighted Ives. He was so encouraged that he sent Bellamann a copy of the *Essays Before a Sonata* and suggested that the two give the lecture in New York at his expense. Ives's letter also shows his reluctance to accept praise without a veil of self-deprecation.

Undated answer to 10 April 1921, Charles Ives to Henry Bellamann

My Dear Mr. Bellamann:

I regret that Illness kept me, upon the receipt of your letter of April 10th, from doing nothing more than formally acknowledging it. I appreciate your kindness in writing and thank you warmly for your interest. Your proposal to include the Concord Sonata in your lecture-recital programs shows more courage than most musicians care to show. But I am afraid it (at least the first two movements) will arouse little enthusiasm with most audiences (except perhaps in the form of refined abuse or expressive silence). The first movements I find are severe tests for the listener as well as the player. But it is not so difficult to make the "Alcott" and "Thoreau" acceptable to the average audience. Possibly passages from the Emerson or Hawthorne movements selected in ways that may suggest themselves to you could be played separately,—without losing too much of the general impression which I've tried to present,—for instance, in the "Emerson," his free-sweeping way of throwing one from the many-colored aspects towards the underlying thought— the breadth of his philosophy. However, I want you and Miss Purcell to feel free to make any changes or revisions which meet your best judgement; there are some passages that were not exactly intended to be played literally—at least by two hands. I shall be much interested to know what comes of the adventure. If your efforts in my behalf meet with enough success, that is, artistically (measured by *your* standards—not necessarily by that of others, the press or the audience), possibly Miss Purcell and you may find it practicable to give the lecture in New York sometime. If the later you should think this advisable I would insist upon seeing that you both are adequately compensated for your time and efforts, and also paying all the expenses. However, this is just a thought that occurs to me while writing—it may not appeal to you at all.

Perhaps by this time you have decided that to undertake my music will be a too arduous and thankless job,—perhaps you have already relegated me to the "bench"; but in any event I am grateful for the interest and sympathy of one who I hear has done much valuable and unselfish work for the advancement of serious music in this country. Thanking you again for your letter, I am

Sincerely Yours,
Charles Ives

P. S. Under separate cover I am having sent a copy of the "essays" which were intended to be a "part with the music," whether for better or worse is an open question.

•

The publication of Bellamann's review of the *Concord Sonata* in the New Orleans magazine *The Double Dealer* prompted Ives's second letter reacting to Bellamann's interest in his music.[25] Ives again exhibits reluctance to accept Bellamann's favorable impressions of the work. He also characteristically casts his compliments for Bellamann as a reviewer in the voice of Mrs. Ives. This use of voices other than his own to present his opinions becomes a very common feature in the correspondence, especially after 1930. Perhaps the most revealing aspect of this letter is Ives's acknowledgment of the responsibility implied in public acclaim for his work. While much of his creativity as a composer lay behind him in 1921, this sense of responsibility must have influenced Ives as he prepared works for publication and tried to organize his unruly manuscripts.

15 November 1921, Charles Ives to Henry Bellamann

My dear Mr. Bellamann:
    Yesterday, I saw your review in the "Double Dealer" which I found in a bookstore here,—the copies I sent for, probably went to Redding and were not forwarded, though we receive mail from there regularly, at least I hope so.
    It is hard for me to tell you how I felt upon reading the article, or to thank you as I want for the interest and care you have given. I'm by no means certain that all of what you say— the favorable part of the impression, is justified; but I am certain of this,—that you have strengthened and deepened in me the sense of responsibility towards future work. I have a wider vantage-ground to rise from, thanks to your sincere and thoughtful help. Mrs. Ives says that the keen insight

you have shown, in the personal feeling and thought behind it all—in what I have tried to do but haven't done,—amazes her.

We hope that we shall see you in New York this winter. We are counting on it and don't want to be disappointed.

Sincerely yours,
Charles E. Ives

P. S. If the sonata has gone on a program I hope it has not brought disastrous effects in its wake; if it has don't let it bother you—at least on my account.

•

As Ives encountered the first widespread reaction to his work in the correspondence surrounding the publication of the *Concord Sonata,* he was composing and compiling the *114 Songs.* Considerable correspondence in relation to this work survives. Much of it involves reactions to the songs such as the one above from Sousa. More interesting, in terms of the composition of the songs themselves, is the following letter of 20 August 1921 to the author of the text for *The Greatest Man.* Here is Ives's brief characterization of the text and the song, and an intimation of the process by which Ives chose the texts he set.

20 August 1921, Charles Ives to Anne Collins

Dear Madam:

I am having a collection of some manuscript songs printed, under one cover; and would like to include in this one composed to your verses—"The Greatest Man"—which I saw in the "Evening Sun" (N.Y.) a few months ago. Your words had my interest and admiration immediately (as they did the rest of the family). It seems to me that you've caught a boy's unconscious pride and love for "dad,"—the sentiment is true and appealing, without being sentimental, and I've tried to catch this spirit in the music.

I will be glad to compensate you for the use of the verse, if you will let me know what that should be.

My manuscript is indistinct, and I'm having Schirmer's engraver strike off a clearer copy, which will be sent you when it is ready. This, of course, will not be used if you are not entirely willing—but I hope you will be.

The songs are to be privately printed and are not to be sold. I expect to send complimentary copies of the book to friends and some musicians who may be interested—and to those who have been kind enough to let me trespass on their words.

Sincerely,
Chas E. Ives

•

Although it was not made publicly, Clifton J. Furness's long letter responding to *114 Songs* is a reaction to the songbook similar in scope to Bellamann's review of the *Concord Sonata*. Furness, a Whitman scholar and musician, approaches the songs from both poetic and musical viewpoints and provides a balanced though essentially positive evaluation of twenty-one of them. Ives's response shows his gratitude for such extensive consideration of his work.

11 August 1922, Clifton J. Furness to Charles Ives

My dear Mr. Ives:

Your song-offerings which recently came to me here were a welcome reminder of my pleasant chat with you last spring when I was in New York. Thanks for remembering me.

I'll try only to slip you a few of my initial reactions: later, when I see you, I should like to take up some of the points at close range—writing on such matters seems much more inaccurate and unsatisfying than talking, because so much more one-sided and therefore indirect.

First, if Harmony Twichell Ives is your wife, allow me to congratulate both her and "her husband" on the real literary validity of some of the song poems! The unusual and charming blending of certain Victorian touches—(and I mean here "Victorian" in the better sense)—with up to the minute incisive diction; the close-ups of Nature at first hand, often intimately welded with the thought to be expressed in a way that makes one think, almost, of the symbolist-imagist technique—(but the result much more strong, healthy, near to the soil and vital than in the more attenuated French)—; the pragmatic socialism (?), transcendental spirit-ism shining thru many of the simple straightforward lines; the pure white ecstasy of "There is a Lane" and the "Spring Song," (and most of all "To Edith,") unbelievable almost in its poignance and *Innigkeit*); all this, and above all, thru all, the union of fine feeling with forceful expression, makes me overlook largely some of the defects (I mean what appear to me to be such) in the setting of some of the poems, for I cannot believe that so just a faculty of discrimination in word-values would be evident without a more or less complementary sense of tonal selection. Therefore, what I can *hear* (with either mental or physical ear) I appraise to my own satisfaction; the few which I cannot, I leave to the good Lord and the composer to reveal to me at some future time in their significance.

There are at least a half dozen that hold me, and I think will do so permanently. "The White Gulls" is as clean of bit of writing in the new vein (of song) as I know. It has Geoffrey O'Hare's "O Men Coming up from the Fields," (of which I somehow thought in connection with it), backed off the map! A flame, truly. "West London" gets me somewhat in the same vein, tho with not quite so irresistible a sweep. The way it plays about diatonic-feeling without arriving, is tantalizing—perhaps intentionally so? "The Housatonic" I'm inclined to place very near the top—at least the first three pages. For sheer atmospheric sheen it grips me as much as the "Mists," almost; altho I think the latter holds together better as a whole, and is somehow more satisfying—organic unity perhaps? The "aura" effect of upper-strings in both of these I am particularly fond of. The harmonic effects with the pedal-points in the low register in "Mists" have an almost Scriabinish timbre (I hope you don't object to my comparisons and allusions; I admit they are a lazy and inexact method of characterization, for the most part). I hope you'll forgive me for liking the "Spring Song" and "Songs My Mother Taught Me" inordinately; even tho juvenilia, I'm sure they possess more than historic significance. Among late acquisitions, "The Greatest Man" has equal forthrightness, commensurate to the text. I've already spoken of "To Edith"—should I capitulate as completely to the original of this tone-portrait, I fear I'd be tempted to steal her quite away. —I get a pounding thrill from "The Swimmers," altho my fingers prove unequal to the task and I have to depend on my eye and ear to supplement them. It certainly has the requisite wallop. The utter simplicity of greatness characterizes "Remembrance," and in equal degree, (despite conventionality) "Ilmenau." "Mirage" is a real consummation of the union of thought and tone; your setting has not violated the immaculate conception of the poem. "Autumn" occupies a pleasing middle-ground between the old and new, with its subtle rendering of word-values and emotional nuances. —"The Old Mother" I forgot to mention in the earlier group. I was frankly (and pleasantly) surprised to find how fully you could orient yourself in this typical German Lieder-Ton, upon occasion.

The two most disappointing (but tentatively so?) are the Whitman and Paracelsus fragments. That they are a sincere and forth-right outburgeoning of cosmic import I can't doubt,—knowing you and the words. "Walt Whitman" I don't agree with, I don't know why, exactly. (Perhaps our divergence of opinion as to the original?—to me he seems more god, to you more man). Paracelsus I simply don't get. I don't believe it's because I demand "easy-chair" harmonies that I fail to swallow "Majority"—the words are so direct and powerful that I'm sure there must be some explanation for the apparent "wordiness" of the music. I anxiously await an alibi for this and "Nov. 2, 1920,"—also "Lincoln," etc. No doubt it's significant that the ones I'm most anxious to register because of the spirit-sweep of the words (as above, of your own (?), and likewise "Religion," "Tolerance," etc.), are the ones I do not find convincing. The more vital the thought, the more essential it is to understand the idiom.

Of all this, more later. I'm writing some music myself this summer— a "dance-poem" in the new style of dancing. I don't know how it will turn out yet. "Vibration-music" in the making is a rather uncertain quantity, to say the least.[26] It's extremely difficult to bring anything thru clean from the mental conception—so deucedly hard to keep from getting mixed up with the usual conventional clap-trap. If one could only compose in a vacuum! —But then the vital spark would be lost, the spiritual current grounded doubtless. At any rate, it's great sport!

My best wishes for the health of yourself and your potato-patch.

Cordially,
Clifton Joseph Furness

P.S. My Father is much interested in your proposed constitutional amendment—may I have a copy of the article you mention? He is also so much interested in some of your songs that I am going to leave the extra copy you sent me with him, at his request. . . .

C.J.F

Undated Sketch for Charles Ives to Clifton Furness

It was fine to get your letter; we both enjoyed it. Your impressions are not only a help to me but they have a literary color which is good to look at.— And some made me ponder—which is a good thing to make a man do. Your characterization is more interesting than some of the songs you comment about.

Bring in your new sound music when you come next. I'm interested to hear it.

Let us have your N. Y. address as soon as you know it,—will stay here as long as we can in the fall, but we want you to learn the way to our home as soon as we get back to 72nd St.

I'll be glad to have books sent to the two addresses you gave and will also send the article your father asked about.

Hoping to see you soon,

Mrs. Ives wants me to say that pragmatic socialism that may be found in the book is not hers. Therefore, it's mine—or it isn't—I'm not sure.

Friendships

Spurred by mutual interest, Furness and Ives formed a long-lasting friendship and corresponded frequently well into the 1940s. Indeed, Furness was one of the few people who visited Ives in Redding from time to time. Ives gave Furness important financial and professional help and made loans and wrote recommendations for Furness's father as well. Subjects of the Ives–Furness correspondence ranged from Scriabin, Brahms, and Schoenberg to Whitman and Emerson. The discussions of Scriabin are especially interesting: from them it is clear that Ives and Furness played through a Scriabin symphony in July 1923 and attended a performance of Scriabin's *Poeme d'Extase* in April 1924.[27]

Ives's relationship with author Henry Dwight Sedgewick was also based on a philosophical affinity. Although Ives was not as close to Sedgewick as he was to Furness, the Iveses did rent Sedgewick's house in New York from 1917 to 1926, and Ives quoted him in the "Postface" of the *114 Songs*.[28] Ives's sketch for a letter to Sedgewick of 19 May 1923 demonstrates the breadth of Ives's intellectual interests and emphasizes the importance that transcendentalist philosophers such as Thoreau had assumed in Ives's thought by the early 1920s.

Second sketch for 19 May 1923,
Charles Ives to Henry Dwight Sedgewick

This is our first day in the country,—almost the first warm and beautiful May day—but the occasion is memorable for a far greater reason, *Edie* has *Susanna* with her, *in Redding* for the first time. . . . Edie's excitement in showing Susanna her room, her old dolls, her favorite walks in the woods, "the secret bench," "landmarks of her long life," and S[usanna]'s enthusiasm are all "in the same span."[29] Why do children in moments like this bring back everything we want bro't back and nothing we do not. We brought the *Pro Vita Monastica,* with us—which I'm just finishing. I like to make a book like this last,—and turn to it as we do to our north window when certain lights and shadows are there.—

[We] have enjoyed it all—its quiet beauty and the kind of help which comes with it—it strengthens something that ought to go on in all purposes of life.

You break the legs (his head is blow-proof) of a kind of cynic—the worst kind, I think,—"the perfect reasoner," who builds his all on "reason" without knowing, as you say, that "reason is born of things without reason," "that the origin of life lies far back of reason," who crowds out imagination—spiritual meditation—and so, faith,—without knowing that they are crowded out.

I don't agree with you, when you say you are "quite unmusical." In many of your pages I hear the music of César Franck and of Palestrina, and of some like them. There is a kind of rhythm and sensitivity to melodies moving together (harmony) chord-vibrations which play around in prose (Thoreau's is a good example) that will be caught sometimes in a vibratory-medium,— what it all is I don't know, except that it is music,—for it sounds out and carries one high. Yet an old aunt of mine who knew somebody who knew Thoreau said that he was "tone deaf"—couldn't carry a tune etc.— She meant he was "interval" deaf—in preconceived intervals,— That his arithmetic of music didn't measure up with Jadassohn. I thank you for the book. Mrs. Ives joins me in that and many other things we have to thank you for.

Edith and Susanna send their love.

Ives

•

Composer and critic T. Carl Whitmer wrote Ives upon receiving a copy of the *Concord Sonata* and *Essays.* In his evaluation of the Sonata, Whitmer shows the same fluidity of approach to words and music that characterizes Ives's writing.

15 March 1921, T. Carl Whitmer to Charles Ives

Dear Mr. Ives,

You could not have found a more ready listener than my-self to whom to send your very fine, original and altogether interesting Piano Sonata. I thank you for it. May I send you in return my latest book The Way of My Heart and Mind? Kindly send me your exact address and I shall take pleasure in sending it. It is one of three books and in the appendix you will see the names of my musical works.

I think your text preceding the music is rarely lovely and suggestive. It is hard to say whether the author loves words or music the more. I think you handle words with more economy and less waywardness than music. I am in complete sympathy with the modernism expressed but am aware of the presence of a purely extempore form and the absence of applied contrapuntal criticism. There is an ingenuity of pianistic idioms which delight me and a grasp of 'atmospheric music' which is exceptional.

I brought myself up on Emerson and wish that your interpretation of him had followed his concise hitting off of effects. It has rather the length of his life than of his sentences, but surely gives me the breadth of his philosophical thought.

Perhaps from the composition side I am more interested in your originality of rhythmic use. I do not refer to your absence of time markings, which I consider only a barrier imposed, making it urgent that a sincere player find all your many rhythms and making an insincere one throw the work aside. But I do think that when one really looks within he finds that you have given much more rhythmic variety than most moderns who seem so inclined to handle the harmonic side ultra-modernly that their rhythms are uninventive.

I do not pretend to have found the depths of your work just yet, but I hope to. I showed the thing to a friend and said that the Alcott section showed you could write simply when the mood suggested it. The others may be simple relatively but that ought to show a conservative that an advanced style was a real expression. I hope I may have the opportunity to hear you play this sonata sometime. It would give me genuine pleasure to get at your personal view more certainly than I feel I have it.

With highest regard and appreciation of your sending me the Second Pianoforte Sonata, I am,

Sincerely,
Carl Whitmer

•

Built on this foundation, the Ives-Whitmer correspondence was long and spirited. Whitmer and his wife were also among the small set of friends whom the Iveses saw occasionally. The span of the conversation between Ives and Whitmer is evident in the following letter from 24 March 1929. Ives writes Whitmer to thank him for his review of the second movement of the Fourth Symphony in *The Musical Forecast*. However, the letter soon turns to other subjects.[30]

24 March 1929, Charles Ives to T. Carl Whitmer

Dear Mr. Whitmer:

We are looking back to your visit. It was fine to have you with us again. Next year Mrs. Whitmer we hope will be with you. You must enjoy her enthusiasm for her new work and the youthful minds. I thank you and appreciate your article and criticism. It isn't an easy job to write up a thing like that and make it interesting. But you do it well. I hope it will stand up to some of the things you say. That's quite an idea of yours—"musical gasses."[31] I hope they don't produce flatulency in any body—they did in one man. Could you have a dozen or so copies sent me and ask them to send the bill with it?

I've been thinking about "Nietzsche." It shows what prejudice does to people. Before the war I was quite an admirer of his, but when those "soft headed war lords" made him their mouthpiece, it threw me all out.

As I remember back, his "superman" was neither physical nor imperialistic. I used to think he was in sympathy with Emerson— perhaps influenced somewhat by him. You see I'm trying to let myself out!

Edie is much better and has gone to Danbury and Redding for her Easter vacation and we hope to go up next week.

Please remember us to Mrs. Whitmer.
Hoping to see you next summer

> I am
> Sincerely
> Chas E. Ives

•

One of Ives's closest friends throughout his adult life was his business partner Julian Myrick. Ives was almost certainly closer to Myrick than to anyone outside of his family. The two men formed a highly efficient and successful partnership in life insurance. Their mutual admiration is clear in their correspondence, in Myrick's laudatory article on Ives's retirement in the *Eastern Underwriter*, and in Ives's dedication of *The Fourth of July* to Myrick. Ives's decision to retire on 1 January 1930 prompted several touching letters of respect and concern between the two men. After his "heart attack" in 1918, Ives's health slowly but inexorably declined.[32] Ives's gradual mental and physical deterioration forms a subtext in the correspondence for the rest of his life.

Ives's sketch for a letter to Myrick from July 1929 touches on the subject of the coming retirement and gives one of the clearest descriptions in the whole correspondence of Ives's physical and mental condition. Ives plainly describes a period of depression compounding his physical difficulties. This mental disturbance is literally unnameable for Ives; he refers to it enigmatically through his doctor's diagnosis, "n   x." In spite of his obvious and acknowledged disability, Ives maintains his optimism and plans to return to work briefly before officially retiring. Ives retained this optimism, a belief that his health would soon improve, throughout much of the rest of his life; it is one of the most resilient aspects of his character.

Early July 1929, Sketch for Charles Ives to Julian (Mike) Myrick

Dear Mike,
    H[armony] wants to acknowledge receipt of the Trustee check that Watson forwarded.— And I want to send the enclosed check for any extra expenses, as traveling, luncheons, etc. that you had paid person-

ally. I remember just before I left you gave a lunch to the field club men. If the enclosed isn't enough for these items please let me know. If it happens to be more please keep the bal[ance] till needed. It's an uncomfortable enough feeling to be drawing full profits and not be able to be on the job, without having you put to any expense which I don't share in. That's one reason it's a relief to have the future plans settled as they are and it's also well to have some time for readjustment. I realize fully now that I could not keep going for another year,—though I always want to do anything I can to help you and the office ex-officio from next year on ad infinitum. My main regret is entirely one of sentiment—for you. But as Harmony says, we may have more time to see each other than we have in the last few years.

I don't know exactly what to say about myself. For 3 or 4 days at a time, I feel quite well, then come periods when I certainly don't. However, I'm better than I was during the last two months in NY, when I was apparently in worse shape than I thought. I couldn't do anything physically or mentally. Wells said it was a kind of n   x over the usual physical condition and is trying to get the weight up etc.[33] I won't bother you with more details except to say that I couldn't possibly have written a letter as long as this a month ago and so I hope to be able to get down for a few days at a time when you are away, the last of August or Sept. and by Oct. I want to be able to finish strong on the home stretch just for the satisfaction of it if nothing else. It won't have any great effect on the years bus[iness] I have some things in mind to suggest for the fall, but haven't got down to work on them yet—expect to soon.

I hope you are keeping well and are not taking on so much that you're kept under a strain. . . .

Edie and Harmony are in fine shape this summer. They send kindest regards to you and the family,

Sincerely,
Chas

Retirement, Patronage, and Recognition

Ives's normal letter writing procedure changed several times as he aged. His earliest letters are handwritten; those from the first three decades of the century are often typed by a secretary.[34] Around 1 January 1930, the date of Ives's retirement from his insurance firm, Ives and his wife Harmony began using a new method of writing letters. Ives's chronic illness made it a burden to answer the correspondence he received in increasing amounts during the 1930s. A tremor in his arms and hands made Ives's handwriting very unsteady; using a fountain pen exacerbated the problem. It was frustrating and difficult to write, so Harmony began to answer many letters for Ives. The shift was not immediately complete; Ives continued to write directly to some correspondents for several years. Nevertheless, 1 January 1930 is a useful date to mark the change to the new method of correspondence.

The new procedure was as follows. Charles sketched each letter—often on sheets from a legal pad. Harmony, or the Iveses' adopted daughter Edith, wrote the final copy of the letter and mailed it. Charles took into account who would write the final draft of the letter and sketched accordingly. In doing so, he displaced his own personality and consistently referred to himself in the third person. As Frank Rossiter observes, few of Ives's correspondents knew how deeply he was involved in writing the letters bearing Harmony's signature.[35]

The typical letter begins with an apology from Mr. Ives, mentions that he is not well enough to write, and explains that, consequently, Harmony or Edith will write for him. This formula is so common in the sketches that Ives abbreviates it: "I am writing—." In the finished letter, this sentence would read, "I am writing for Mr. Ives, who is not at all well, and cannot attend to things as he would like to." After these preliminaries, Ives conducts the business of the letter. If he wishes to speak directly, he writes: "Mr. Ives says that, ' . . . ,'" and then continues carefully in the third person. Letters in this format, which I call mediated correspondence, comprise the bulk of Ives's letters after 1930. As a result, many letters survive as sketches. Surviving pairs of sketches and realized letters indicate the fidelity normally maintained in the transcription process: the copies were very often exact but in a much clearer hand. So, while the process of sketching and transcription was a manifestation of a vexing disability, the drafts it left behind are a boon to the historian.

By the 1930s Ives was gaining wider notoriety. Nicolas Slonimsky conducted *Three Places in New England* in Town Hall, New York City, on 10 January 1931 and went on to perform the piece in Boston, Havana, and Paris. One of the people to whom Ives sent tickets for the Town Hall performance was his old apartment mate from Poverty Flat, George A. Lewis.[36] He attended the concert and wrote Ives to thank him for it on the following day. Lewis's response includes a fair measure of Yale spirit, as in the "cheer" he invents in closing. The most interesting aspect of the letter, however, is Lewis's appreciation of the music. Here is a person of similar age and background to Ives, a listener who has some appreciation of music but is not a professional musician. Lewis nearly embodies Ives's ideal audience, and his appreciation of the piece is revealing. Lewis hears the work programmatically and notes Ives's use of atmospheric effects. The way in which Lewis describes the piece is very like the way that Ives himself wrote about his music. To use Ives's term, Lewis alludes to the spiritual "substance" of the work.[37]

11 January 1931, George A. Lewis to Charles Ives

Dear Charlie:

Many, many thanks for the tickets. I enjoyed your compositions very much and was so glad to hear Putnam's Encampment and the Housatonic twice in the same evening. The first time I heard only the water in the latter but was deeply touched to find on second hearing that the hymn about the cross was struggling to rise above the sound of the waters and express itself. Your whole suite was more vigorously applauded on second rendition than on the first. I think everyone caught patriotic themes in Putnam's Encampment. There was genuine enthusiasm and prolonged applause after all of the numbers you had written, but more especially after Putnam's Encampment. I know that I did not catch the full significance of Boston Common, but believe that a second hearing would, perhaps, enable one to get the clue. I thought the even quiet earlier part represented it in the Pre-Revolutionary Period and the later storm and stress part, the struggles for freedom of our country. I saw Mrs.

Myrick and a friend (Miss Edwards, I think it was) at a distance. Ives shone brightly and Mozart was eclipsed. Rah! Rah! Rah! Ives! Ives! Ives! a bas Mozart!

Ever yours,
George A. Lewis

•

Slonimsky's performances of *Three Places in New England* naturally excited Ives as well. In February, he wrote to his daughter Edith at Miss Porter's School in Farmington, Connecticut and described a visit by the conductor and Henry Cowell. The concert mentioned in the letter is probably the 7 February performance at the New School for Social Research; Ives attended the Town Hall concert.

17 February 1931, Charles Ives to Edith Ives

Edith

Mother, I suppose, is just about leaving now.— And I know you all have had a great time and a memorable occasion. I hope the girls didn't throw snow down Tanta May's back. Next time Mother goes to Farmington I'm going too. (I want to give Bobby Porter K. a whirl on the merry go-round.)[38] Yesterday I had quite an exciting time here. Nicolas Slonimsky, the conductor of the Boston Symphony Orchestra, was here with Mr. Cowell.[39] He is a Russian but nobody but he would know it. He is one of those men that act when they talk and talk all the time. But he is always interesting, often amusing and a real kind of a man—you would like him. He came down from Boston to conduct that "New England" Symphony of mine. I didn't go but Mr. Cowell said that "Nick" took all the orchestra by the back of the neck and made them play it right—and so well that Mr. C said the audience all stood up and applauded. He said they liked the "Putnam Park, Redding" movement with all the tunes you know and also the 1st about the "Boston Common statue" with Susanna's great uncle on horse back and the colored soldiers.[40] When they play it in Boston we will all go up and write to Susanna to go to the concert with us. Bob and Brewster were here last week.[41] Bob was too tired to argue, so I got Brewster started and when we got enough of it, I just agreed with him and he stopped.

Love,
Daddy

·

The favorable impression that Slonimsky made on Ives, as reported to Edith, blossomed into a robust friendship that lasted until Ives's death in 1954. Letters to Slonimsky often brought out the playful side of Ives's personality. Ives's humor was not restricted to jokes and wordplay but even manifested itself in his handwriting as the facsimile in Figure 1 of the first page of a letter of 8 May 1931 shows. Ives writes to Slonimsky, who was in Paris to perform *Three Places in New England* and other modernist American works. The Parisian address apparently provokes Ives's opening, mock-French outburst.[42]

8 May 1931, Charles Ives to Nicolas Slonimsky

Mons: Mon Dieú!—Mòn' Lisa, —Bon Ami— (not the mild Sapolio) Bón Soit—Cher—Chez, French is a too violent language for me—no good cuss words: I understand it perfectly (when it's translated).

We hope you had a good trip over and found your mother and all well. I think Mrs. Ives is really more interested in your family reunion than whether the concert (will/won't) (x mark favorite word) go off well (and so am I). Please give her our kindest regards. Perhaps we may see her before another year or so.

I hope attending to so many difficulties etc. at one time won't tire you all out, and that the managers will do their part. A friend of mine who is gradually getting interested in Amer[ican] music—(seeing that article of Henry's started it)— may be of substantial help later—) suggests that programs, notices, etc. be put in "steamers" sailing from N.Y. to France between now and June 1st. Your managers, he says, can get in touch with the "pursers" etc. sailing for Cherbourg.— And also that notices be distributed to the hotels etc. that Americans stop.

However this is not advice.— Do anything you think best and don't worry too much about the situation (that's good advice, which I hate to have anyone give me g— d—.

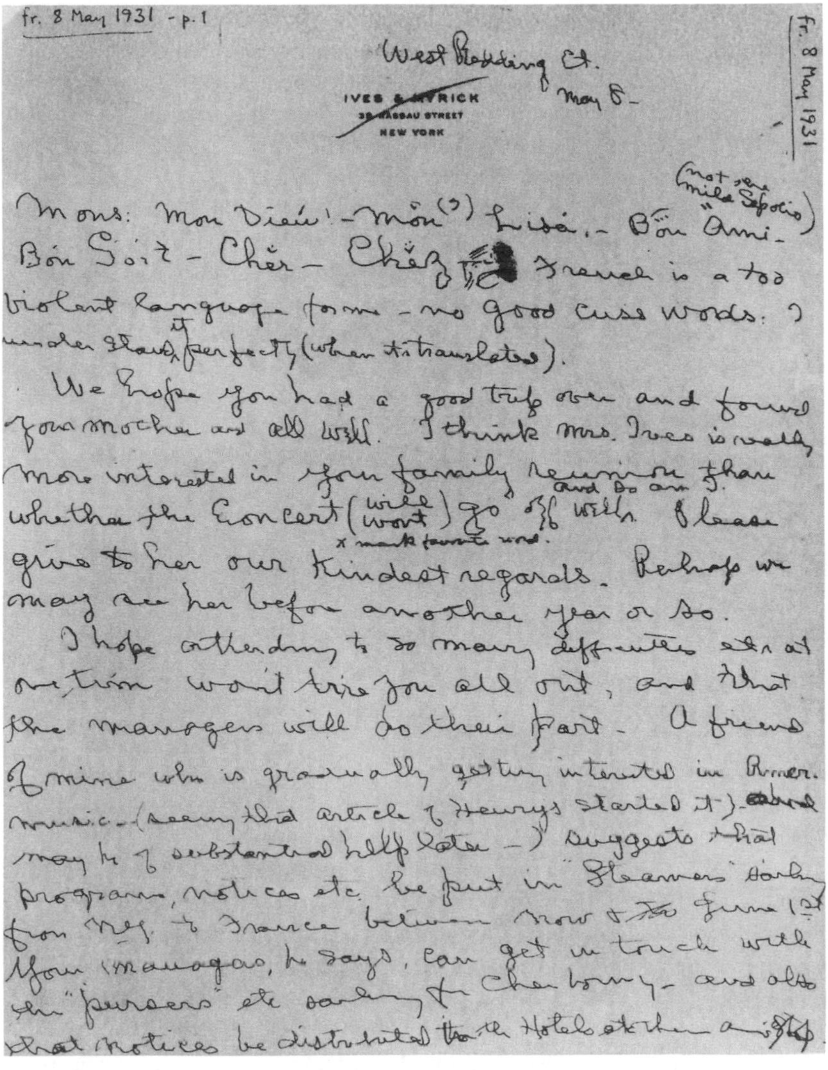

Figure 1: Facsimile of 8 May 1931, Ives to Slonimsky

If not too much trouble please have a dozen or so programs and notices sent to me as soon as possible—as we have heard of a few friends who are going abroad this month. Also if you will, have notices mailed directly to Mr. Thomas Wells, Pres. of Harpers Pub. Co. . . .[43]

Now that you are a reg[ular] Yankee—you will spit through your teeth, talk through your nose, cuss between syllables and let 'em "learn you" in Paris how to compose real Amer stuff.[44] A letter from "Edie" today says "in that in between age" "when one does everything they don't want to do—under protest—& everything they want to—also under protest"—some practical philosophy.[45] Our best wishes to you.

Sincerely,
Chas E. Ives

•

As Ives's reputation grew during the 1930s, he began to receive mail from a wider group of correspondents. In August 1933, folk music scholar John A. Lomax wrote to Ives and asked him to recommend songs for a collection of American folk music. Ives's response is a revealing discussion of the relationship between written pieces such as hymns and folk performance traditions.

29 August 1933, John A. Lomax to Charles Ives

Dear Sir:

In 1922 you did me the honor of printing your new music of one of the cowboy songs I had picked up on the plains of Texas. The effective setting you gave "Charlie Rutlage" has suggested that you might help me on a project which is now engaging my time. I am preparing for publication a volume to be entitled *American Ballads and Folk Songs* wherein I am trying to bring together the most typical of our indigenous Folk songs, the tunes and the words. Recently I have visited many negro convict camps in the South and recorded the music of the black man in confinement (where he always sings). These songs of labor I think will be a slight contribution to American Folk song music. Would you list and send to me any Folk songs that you think should be included in such a collection as I propose?

Sincerely yours,
John A. Lomax

**Undated Sketch for reply to 29 Aug 1933,
Charles Ives to John A. Lomax**

John A. Lomax
Dear Mr. . . .

Let me acknowledge and thank you etc. . . .

What you have already done in the cowboy book has been a fine contribution to American folk art.— And the new book is important work that is needed. But I'm afraid I can't be of much help as in folk music either songs or instrumental tunes etc. which I know are, I'm sure, generally known. I have never been an expert study of folk music, that is I've not tried to find unknown verses. I've only used, often only suggested folk music, that I had known or heard for the most part when I was a boy or young man and would write or use them entirely from "ear"—remembering or getting as near as I could remember the way or ways some of them were sung.

I imagine folk music, like other base musical phenomena may have a rather wider field than would seem to the casual thought. When is folk music not folk music? I remember hearing someone say that anything to be called folk music must be by an unknown composer—that it must come from the people. I'm inclined to think that definition is a little too easy.— Probably the "germ melody" of the tune (at least enough of it to be known as such) came first from some one composer or singer, quite possibly often not written down, changing more or less the more more people sung or played it. But some music by known composers and written down and published, which has been used in communities for a generation or so, has become also local colored.

It seems to me that some of the old hymns and religious tunes, are almost a part of this country's folk music.— Though the names of the composers are in the hymn books. They have grown into the lives of many people in certain sections of the country.

Am enclosing some notes and programs etc. which have some references to this kind of music and also some pages from a "memo" that I jotted down some while ago—trying to describe something of the effect and "ways" of some of the religious hymns.[46]

With best wishes and sorry he cannot be of as much help as he would like to be, he is very truly,[47]

In the mid-1930s Ives began to attract the attention of figures such as Aaron Copland, one of the French-trained American composers satirized in the letter to Slonimsky.[48] Although Ives had been somewhat predisposed to hostility towards Copland, his opinion shifted after the Yaddo performances. It is a measure of Ives's desire for communication with a larger musical audience that he responds to Copland's discussion of his "faults" with an acknowledgement that he too realizes their existence.

24–28 May 1934, Charles Ives to Aaron Copland

Dear Mr. Copland:

I want to thank you for your article about my songs in the "Modern Music" magazine. I saw it only when we came back last month.

You put things well and say what you think—and I appreciate what you say—even as to my faults which you don't want glossed over—you are quite right, I have plenty of them, God knows, and so do I, sometimes—especially when I wake up in the night.

But when you say I glorify the business man, you're wrong. I was paying my respects to the average man (there is one) in the "ordinary business of life," from the Ashman down to the president—among whom, it seemed to me, there was more openmindedness and fair fighting than among musicians.[49]

The songs would have done just as well, without that rear end glossarybo. I was taking a day off from the logic of the mortality tables,—to ride a few whim bolts, and throwing some "over-hand slants" around—some of which have made better truth than logic;—and some of them I could have put much better if I had left them out.[50]

I hope sometime to have the pleasure of meeting you. We were in N.Y. a short while this winter, but I was not well and they kept me on my back most of the time and [I] could do but little as I wanted. Hoping to see you before another year gets by. —With best wishes to you and for your creative work, I am,

Sincerely yours,
Chas E. Ives

•

One of Ives's most extensive epistolary relationships was with avant-garde composer John J. Becker, whose letters record his struggle to survive as an uncompromising musical modernist in the Midwest. Ives supported Becker financially both by paying him to edit pieces, such as *Washington's Birthday* and *General William Booth Enters Into Heaven*, and through loans and gifts. It is easy to understand Ives's attraction to Becker, who chose the path Ives had formally rejected with his "retirement from music" in 1902. Becker became a professional musician devoted to the cause of dissonant music and was willing to accept the consequences for himself and his family.

In the letter of August 1934, Ives evaluates work that Becker had done for him on the *Harvest Home Chorales* and describes another set of pieces he will send to Becker to be "straightened out."

4–5 August 1934, Charles Ives to John Becker

Dear John:

Don't bother to send the "Gen B" score to me.— Any thing that J. J. B. does is good enough for me. I guess from your letter that I didn't tell you that we had decided to sail over to England and stay there for 2 months or so. Mrs. Ives backed up by all the family plus the M.D.s decided that it [is] the best move to make now—an' I hope it is.— The trip over before worked well health-wise.— The tests, counts, etc. have not been satisfactory to the Dr.—etc. and we are sailing next week.— Our address will be as before. . . .

The copies of the Chorals you sent are very well done.— It was a great help.— I filled in some [of] the places in the words and marks.— And will have them copied here by the man in N.Y. who does good work.— You have more important things to do than "copy music." The 2nd choral I straightened out as well as I could and am having it copied.— You couldn't have possibly made it out, the words and the repeats etc. were so mixed up and indistinct.

Am sending under separate cover a couple of photos. of 3 short pieces [in] old manuscript—one a song from which the "Rainbow" p. 35 in Henry's Edition, was arranged from—of this [I] can only find 12 measures (of the score-sketch) 9 measures lost. So any time you feel it convenient piece it out in any way you think best.—

Also—A little "take Off" (as I used to call things like that)— "A Lecture by Pres. Hadley."[51] Hadley was a character, will tell you about him sometime.— He had a drawl of about 10 octaves! I can't make this out, even with my strongest glasses—but maybe you can. The lead pencil marks are so worn. The song "Tolerance" p. 49 in the "34

Songs" was arranged from that. Now please don't bother with these if too much trouble or until you have time.— There's no hurry.

Sunday A.M.

We're glad you feel encouraged about the concert.— And whatever more I can do to help I will if any way possible.[52]

Do any thing you think best with the "Wash Birthday" [*Washington's Birthday*] if you play it.— The bells and the "Jews Harp" parts, could be played on the piano, rather than left out.— I did this once and it sounded quite decently.— If you should play both the "Night" [*In the Night*] and the "Wash Birthday," I think it would be better to separate them on the program.— They both start and end with a kind of night mood—and come to think on it—why on programs do the things of one composer have to be together always.— It's a habit that occasionally might be broken for a reason—Quod quo?

[I] should think some lower brass, might be added as a permanent member of your orchestra—to nourish the bass strata,— even in big orchestras it has always seemed to me that the upper parts override the lower.— I've never heard enough basses. Did I tell you that at the concert you heard in N.Y. that the Horn part "In the Night" on the first 2 pages was played a 5th too low.—[53] It was Nic Slonimsky's fault and partly mine, for not putting it in part—but it is explained in note on back page (which N.S. forgot)— In other words the piece wasn't really played.— The notes in the score are the *actual notes* and the best and most eloquent part of the horn.— That was what was wrong in the rehearsal,—so we see, we can have too much bass—which breaks the above "nice rule."

I do hope things will soon go better and that the strain will be less—but we both have what many don't—the best wives and children in the world. We all send love to you all.

Chas.

We sail Aug. 10. Will write from London.

•

Becker was more active as a musical radical than was Ives, and in his letters to Becker, Ives's ultra-modernist side becomes more pronounced. In the following letter of 23 February 1938, Ives indulges in a characteristic tirade against the music establishment. In it he distinguishes American music from music merely made in America. For Ives, at least in this letter, music derivative of the European tradition, though composed in America, is not American.

23 February 1938, Edith Ives to John Becker

Dear Dr. Becker,

I am acting as secretary for Daddy. I told him I would take down everything except the swear words, and if he feels they are very necessary I will substitute them by exclamation points![54]

He says:

Dear John:—

I will write to the Birchard Company and tell them how I feel about your music. But I'm afraid it won't help much as they lost money on publishing my score. It is my opinion your concerto will be as well printed, and much better distributed, by the New Music Editions.

Birchard means well I think, but he, or they, (whoever runs the shop) are half asleep when it comes to business. They just put their sheets on the shelves and wait for Jack or Rollo to walk in. I haven't yet heard of anyone who knew that Birchard had published anything of mine. I have never met Birchard or any of the firm personally.

But these Philharmonic-nice-lady-bird-afternoon-tea-parties are an insult to music and to "man." I rather think that if I wrote to "Babyrelli" it would do more harm than good.[55] When Carl Ruggles' "Men and Mountains" was going to be played, and even after it was on the Philharmonic program, all the old ladies (male and female, young and old) subscribers, box-sitters etc., signed a round robin letter of protest against this atrocity!!!! Any American Music (~~that is~~ not American but made in America) ~~which~~ the Philharmonic, the Boston Symphony, the Metro-Opera Lilies, or any of these big standardized sellers of entertainment for the candy-box ears,— any new music they play has to be "emasculated" to get the saps' okay. I would get in a row with these g— d—- sissy conductors if I came within cussing distance, even 110 miles off.

I understand there is a strong feeling nowadays among a large number of the younger and middle aged and sturdier musicians, that if the Philharmonic et al orchestras put any new music on their programs, it is a sign of this music's weakness.— That it means nothing more than nice-copy-cat-European-"salon"-pretty little-velvet-sounds to please the pansy ears and help the prima-donna-commercialized-conductors get their money easier—now, I'll shut up.

I'm sorry I don't know as yet exactly what it is best for me to do. As for the Philharmonic, I am out of touch with everybody and everything in this nice lily-pad organization.— Have never subscribed, sent them any scores, and haven't been to their concerts for a long while. However, will try to find out some way I can be of help to you in this matter, and will let you know if anything comes up.

Please thank Mrs. Becker for her letter, and the one she enclosed from young John, which we also enjoyed.

With love from all of us,

> Ever yours,
> Charles Ives
> (Edith)

•

Another composer to whom Ives gave considerable support was Henry Cowell, arguably one of the most important exponents of Ives's music. Cowell's *New Music Edition* and recordings series were vital early means for the distribution of Ives's music. Out of friendship with Cowell and a sense of dedication to "the cause" of contemporary music, Ives provided significant financial support for *New Music,* without which it would not have been viable.[56] In the following letter from February 1935, Ives discusses a proposed list of pieces to be included in a new collection of songs to be printed by *New Music.*[57]

26 February 1935, Charles Ives to Henry Cowell

Dear Henry:

It did us all good to read that fine and *true* tribute to you—it was a decent thing of S.—and it's funny how a man can appreciate an "OX" yet like "jelly cakes" (as Carl R[uggles] says the others are) at one meal,— But that doesn't bother me much, as long as he gets you with his "good eye." I've been going through a kind of a slump for a while or would have written before—as I'm not exactly certain it's best to publish that batch of songs.— The subject matter is too much the same— Politics, war, religion, . . . etc. Should say either have the "Gen B." alone (or with a piece by another composer,) or add a few more to the group to start (or raise) the literary sideboards and take away a

possible appearance of planted propaganda which won't do NM any good—or at least be misunderstood. What do you think? . . .
[shift to Edith's hand]

(Dear Mr. Cowell—I am now acting as stenographer in place of a wobbly pen!—Edith) —"There should be also a short editor's note in the back explaining that certain songs are arrangements from scores. It isn't quite fair to the music or to the pianist not to have this, and some of the scores may be published later. A good part "The Majority" was left out.[58] It couldn't be arranged for piano—about a hundred different lines all going "to once" and it wouldn't make any sense on a nice piano. In the old book [*114 Songs*] I didn't happen to make any remarks to this effect, probably didn't think it important enough to take the trouble—but I do now. An album of ten or twelve songs would cost but very little more. If you think this plan advisable, am suggesting some on the enclosed sheet,—not over a dozen or so more plates.[59]

However the best course may be to let the songs wait 'til July or later on, if you have something to use for the April number.
[shift back to Ives's hand]

I'm sorry to trouble you with all this—just trying to get something off my chest as usual. Do whatever seems best.

> With love from us all,
> Chas E. Ives

Ives continues the discussion about the pieces to be included in *Eighteen Songs* in the following letter from May 1935. This letter touches on one of the major difficulties Ives had in preparing his music for publication and one reason he often relied on the services of editors such as Cowell, Slonimsky, and Becker— his failing eyesight. As early as 1934, Ives began having trouble with cataracts that prevented him from focusing his eyes for more than short periods of time. This eye trouble continued despite a cataract operation in 1937.[60] In view of this and Ives's other health problems, Ives's description of "Requiem," below, is decidedly poignant.

May 1935, Charles Ives to Henry Cowell

Dear Henry:
As usual, I meant to have written before—but some days I can write nice and some days not at all—and so it goes. I think 64—in

three months is good—and the newspaper notice giving both Bach and you as "anniversary." —how about your 250th also?!

It's well you gave me till July for the songs. Am going over as well as I can the ones that were made from old scores, and putting in occasional score parts that shouldn't have been left out in [the] book. But in only a few and but a few measures—and there are quite some mistakes in some songs and others none.— But it all takes me so long as can't work steadily on account of the eyes.— Some days can't do nothin'. So plenty of time is a friend of mine. It has just occurred to me, that as long as we're on this sorry job—it might be well to put in 3 or 4 more, which were not published in the old book [*114 Songs*].— One is to Stevenson's "Requiem" which was not put in [the] book, because there was so much red tape to get the copyright—but now that has expired, I'm told.— There are some others of those in MSS written after the book was out; one is on the dialogue between "Aeschylus and Sophocles" (Landor)—parts of these are very difficult to sing and play.— As I remember one is partly a study in nice inflection in varying pitches and tone divisions etc. The manuscripts are in Redding.— We expect to get up there in a week or ten days, and then I'll look them over, and if they seem alright will have copies sent to you. They will take but few plates, 4 or 5. In this issue I will want [to] take care of the cost of the engraving, printing, etc. and not have it come out of the general [funds].— You need all of that for the other's music. Also if you can, as far as I'm concerned, I'd rather wait till October for the songs if it won't put you out too much. However do whatever you think best. But this might save a possible rush and jamb, at the last minute, if I happen to run into many days I can't use my eyes. Well—good night, keep well and not too busy. Edie and Chester are wondering if you are giving the bears a nice ride these spring days.[61]

Love from the family
Chas E. I.

P.S. Mrs. Ives says she remembers some of these unpublished songs—especially the "Requiem"—as some of the best.— This is a kind of rough one—of a man who wasn't afraid to die—died standin' up and shoutin'—with chords, intervals, etc. that made singers mad in those days—but today not so much cussin'.

•

Ives's description of a "rough man," "standing up and shouting" fits himself well in the following letter to pianist E. Robert
Schmitz.

June 1938, Charles Ives to E. Robert Schmitz

Greetings to you all from London—we came rather unexpectedly.
Everybody including the doctors (who are usually right especially
when they're wrong) seemed to think an Ocean sail would be well for
us—(personally Redding has it on Europe!)—We'll be home before
the end of summer and will hope to see you in the fall.

London is a "nice" place for "nice" music!—Rollo says—(you know
those Rollo lilies who write nice pieces about nice music in the newspapers). 5 columns to say Toscanini played that nice C maj
Sym[phony] "real nice"—but Rollo forgot to say that it was the
587,629th time Tossy had played it—and he knew every note "real
nice"—Believe it—or note![62]

I do hope things are going well with you, and that the summer
classes will be all you deserve them to be. Am very glad to send the
enclosed. Mrs. Ives and Edith send kindest remembrances to Mrs.
Schmitz and Monique.

Sincerely,
Chas E. Ives

Please excuse these snake tracks—I can't see 'em well enough to
see how bad they are—*not* my fault—*Creator's!*[63]

•

By the end of the 1930s, Ives had amassed a significant West
Coast following, especially in San Francisco and Los Angeles.
One of the performers who was instrumental in popularizing
Ives's songs in California was soprano Radiana Pazmor, who
made the first recording of Ives's "General William Booth
Enters Into Heaven." In the following letter, Ives thanks
Pazmor and pianist Frances Mullen Yates for their work on
behalf of his music.

10 June 1939, Harmony T. Ives to Radiana Pazmor

Dear Miss Pazmor,

I am writing for Mr. Ives [who] is not well and it is difficult for him to do so. He wants me to say—he deeply appreciates all you and Mrs. Yates are doing in behalf of his music.— Just the time itself you have to take to say nothing of the work and effort which he is causing you makes it difficult for him to know how to thank you adequately. A man who Mr. Ives used to play baseball with who was also a good singer used to say, "A nine inning game is some hard job and kept us jumping, but it has nothing on getting up and singing a bunch of his songs."[64]

The tempo of "Walking," as Mr. Ives remembers playing it, is about a march or quickstep time—say around 120–130 = a quarter note—except during the funeral. He has no copy here of the song "Majority" but the score (it was originally for chorus and orchestra) is here—at the beginning there is a metronome mark at about 66–72 = a quarter note. When the voices begin, about 52–58 = a half note. 2nd verse, "The masses are thinking," (previous half note = quarter note) and 68–80 = quarter note. "The Masses are singing," 54–60 = dotted quarter note. "The masses are yearning," 52 = quarter note. "The masses are dreaming," 44–48 = quarter note.

Mr. Ives sends his kindest wishes and renewed thanks in which I join,

Sincerely yours
Harmony T. Ives

•

Ives's national acclaim also prompted interest in his work by people much closer to his Connecticut roots. The following letter from a former resident of Ives's boyhood town, Danbury, Connecticut, provides a fascinating remembrance of Ives's childhood. Ironically, awareness of Ives's musical achievements close to home depended on the notice of publications such as *Time* magazine.

27 January 1939, May Benedict Walsh to Charles Ives

Dear Mr. Ives:

The *Herald-Tribune* of January 22nd gave me such an interesting account of your work and position in the musical world that I wish to express my congratulations to a Danbury boy.

Your career has interested me greatly and I have followed your progress for many years.

First: we of the chorus of Gilbert and Sullivan's operas, which your father conducted for several winters, you as a little boy singing, "Jack is every inch a sailor, Five and Twenty Years a Whaler." Next you played the organ in the Baptist church. Here's an incident of that time. You were induced to join the choir in a picnic in Redding Glen. I was selected for your entertainment. In your shy way you enjoyed a walk and were quite pleased to follow me in breaking windows in an abandoned barn. I've been ashamed to have led you in such destruction. By the way, I think I am one of four still living members of that choir.

Later when I was in New York I went to hear you play the organ of the Baptist church there on 57th Street. I think your mother was at church that morning.

More recently, I have been proud to read a long article in *Time*. So when the *Herald-Tribune* gave you a column, I just have to add my word of congratulation.[65] *Time,* which I received yesterday, adds to my pleasure and pride, although the photograph doesn't quite suit me. I can see you are not the little boy this letter started with.

I have lived in Hartford over ten years with my daughter, who teaches math and science in the Bulkeley High School. Much of the pleasure in music has been my good fortune to enjoy even at my age of seventy-four, for the best of everything comes to the Bushnell.

Sincerely,
May Benedict Walsh

The War Years and Last Decade

Another perspective on Ives's music from a person with a similar background comes in a letter from his brother-in-law,
Joseph H. Twichell. This remarkable description of a John
Kirkpatrick performance of movements from the *Concord* and
other Ives works shows both the effects of Ives's music on a
close-to-ideal audience and Ives's position of esteem within his
family. Twichell's assumptions about the gender implications of
the concert setting and of the music itself are particularly fascinating, and his impressions of the music—honesty, integrity,
and familiarity—must have seemed the highest praise to Ives.

26 January 1940, Joseph H. Twichell to the Ives family

Dear Folks:—

. . . As you know, last week Thursday Esther and I, at Minnie's invitation, went to Danbury to hear John Kirkpatrick play the Fugue,
Hawthorne, The Alcotts and some of Charlie's songs. There were
about 50–60 women there and about three men. I had grand luck as
to my seat. I drew a big comfortable chair tucked away back in a corner where, *comfortably*, I could just sit and *listen*. I didn't have to smile
and nod my head and applaud, and I didn't. I just sat and listened.
Of course I went to this affair in a darn uncomfortable frame of mind.
I don't know a d— thing about music. I have heard some really good
music that I really enjoyed. But this was to be a distinctly difficult and
high type of music. I'm particularly fond of the composer, and I
dreaded hearing something of his which would sound to me loony. I
was honestly curious to hear, but not at all happy over what I was
going to hear. Of course what I have to say about it isn't worth a hur-
rah, for I don't know a single thing about music—not a single thing,
except that I like it or don't like it; except how it makes me *feel*. Well,
and I'm trying to speak as thoughtfully and as carefully as I know
how, I enjoyed that afternoon's music more than any other music I
remember ever hearing. It seemed to me the most *honest* music I ever
listened to. I don't know what that means; maybe you do. And it was
so clean and wholesome. I came out of that place a better man than I
want in. Of course it made me homesick as the devil—homesick for
that big room there at 125 Woodland Street.[66] So much of it was to me
so amazingly familiar; something I hadn't at all expected. And I was

sorry, sorry, sorry when it was over. I wanted to sit there and hear a lot more. In all honesty I just can't tell you how much I enjoyed it.— And was I surprised. I had thought it was going to be a tough after-noon. And wasn't it grand: Esther and I just *had* to hustle out right after it was over. No standing around and gassing with people. We hurried out, jumped in our car and drove home to Southport, and all the way home I could just hug the memory of that music to myself. I wouldn't have missed it for a thousand dollars.

As to the *songs* I did really and truly enjoy them all very much. I'd love to hear them again. But one or two of the accompaniments, which Serane played, had me licked. Just what they had to do with the song I couldn't figure. It sounded to me sometimes as if Charlie was trying to put one over on the singer; as if he had said to the good lady, "I'll bet you can't sing 'Nearer My God to Thee' while I play 'Marching Through Georgia'." How in the world she ever sang what she sang while Serane played what she played was more than I could see. If what she sang was what she was supposed to sing, she did darn well.

Anyway, it was for me a never-to-be-forgotten afternoon. It was simply great!

We'll be down to see you before long. Meanwhile good luck, and love to you from both of us.

Joe

•

A second impression from the same household shows Ives's generosity. In his own family and among the families of his friends, Ives was known as a splendid gift giver at Christmas. We see this image of Ives in the following letter, from his nephew, Charles Twichell.

1 January 1941, Charles Twichell to Charles Ives

Dear Uncle Charlie,

On Christmas morning, when I did not find something from you, I was greatly disappointed. I always look forward to your presents, because they are always different and seem just what a fellow can use and like.

The same goes for that swell book. I'm not much of a reader, but anything on a subject like that goes over big. Thank you again.

All going well here and at school. I'm playing football, basketball, and of course baseball. That's the best sport in the world. As a matter of fact, you guessed wrong on that "Charley Shortstop." It should have been "Charley Catcher." Anyone who prefers shortstop to behind the bat, in my mind, is beyond hope. I hope you weren't a shortstop![67]

Give my best to Aunt Harmony,

> Love from us all—
> "Charley Catcher"

•

A third family letter, this one from a distant cousin, shows another response to Ives's music from a person with a background similar to his. Schaefer first wrote to Ives after discovering their kinship, and Ives responded by sending her a volume of songs and a biographical booklet that mentioned a common ancestor. This letter of November 1946 is Schaefer's letter thanking Ives for the music he sent.

19 November 1946, Eugenia Ives Schaefer to Charles Ives

Dear Cousin Charles,

I have been ill, and so have not before this been able to tell you how delighted I am with the music your publishers sent. It is *great* music, sir. It has an earthiness, a vitality which makes it thrilling; and a spirituality which balances it, and makes it really great. I am so proud to have it.

Bless you for "Walking" the *big October morning*, the church bells, the chestnut burrs, the sumac—I can see and taste and feel them all, and your music makes me hear. That song is the essence of our New England. (I have sent one copy on to my Brother in Baltimore.) I am teaching my own little quartet the lovely Christmas carol (did I tell you I had four children— three sons aged 12– 10– and 6, and a little eight year old girl?) I hold up the violin sonata to my ten year old violinist son as something toward which to work (his violin teacher in Norfolk is one of your great admirers, by the way.) I love the *Requiem*. I can hear the hunter's horns and the echoing hills in the close of the song. *Tom Sails Away* makes me cry—*An Election* is stirring, *Paracelsus, Aeschylus and Sophocles* are *big*—the *Innate* and *Resolution* feel of spirituality which makes your music shine out like Portia's candle in this decadent era.

I could go on and on, but I really mustn't. Even tho' I'm "up" again, grippe has left me weak and tottery!

Thank you again for giving me such great and permanent joy.

Eugenia Ives Schaefer

Evening is one of the loveliest lyrical songs I have heard.

•

Many outside his family as well held Ives in high esteem by the 1940s. The work of numerous musicians who had taken up the cause of his music was bearing substantial fruit. In 1941 violinist Sol Babitz and pianist Ingolf Dahl wrote to Ives and offered to prepare an edition of the Third Violin Sonata, which was to include bowings and interpretive marks based on their experiences performing the piece. Their edition was to be put out by *New Music*, which had already contemplated publishing the score. The following sketches for a letter from Ives to Babitz provides considerable information about the piece itself and about Ives's expectations for the edition.

Sketches for 2 September 1941, Harmony T. Ives to Sol Babitz

Dear Mr. Babitz:

We were glad to hear from you again and Mr. Ives greatly appreciates all that you are doing in behalf of his music—and also Mr. Dahl. I am sorry to say that Mr. Ives is not at all well and cannot attend to things as he would like; and so he will be glad of your help, which you kindly offered as to the bowing marks and any other editing which may be necessary. This 3rd violin sonata will probably be published sometime before long and Mr. Ives will have the copy sent to you before the engraver starts—also he would like to have the first proofs sent to you for corrections, as on account of his eye condition the correction takes him quite a long time—but the second proofs can be sent here for him to go over. Whatever business arrangement to compensate you for your services, time etc. you will make Mr. Ives says will be quite alright with him.—[68] And please have the bill for this sent to him personally and not to New Music Edition.

The refrain of the 2nd verse of the 1st movement, about 10 measures (p. 12 of photostat) in the old copy, contains a few optional parts in R.H. piano part and divides the melody between the violin and piano parts, a way he often played it. Mr. Ives thinks it better to put in—it shouldn't have been left out in the ink copy. He will have a photostat copy of this page sent to you as soon as possible—and also there is a measure on the last page which probably had better go in. There is no violin part copy here but Mr. Ives thinks it will be quite all right to play the octaves as you suggest, in the 3rd movement. In the Fourth Sonata, he has 'optional octaves' in a passage.

As to the material requested for the Record album, Mr. Ives remembers that some memoranda were written on or attached to one of the old copies. He thinks it is around somewhere—but if we can't find it, Mr. Ives will have as much as he remembers copied.— We assume there is no great hurry for this. "The 3rd V. Sonata is really more the 1st than the 1st. Part of the 1st movement was played at a service in 1902. The first and third movements are in a way something of a reflection or impression of the old outdoor meetings and services held in many of the country towns in Connecticut in the '70s '80s and '90s, where the spirit of the people elated and unsubjected, played a strong part.

The second movement was played in 1905 (before the 1st v. Sonata was finished) tho' the violin and piano were helped out by friends, a cornet, clarinet, and trombone. It is reminiscent of the old country fairs—the brass band, merry-go-round and drum corps having more of a 'fight' than a 'trio'—with old Farmer John shuffling a back-woods off step."[69]

Under separate cover we are sending some data, biographical, list of compositions and comment references from 1887–1935 in which the music in general is described—something from this might do for the record album—the data from 1935 to date can be sent later if wanted—there are only a few copies here now. Mr. Ives says publishers usually want data like these for their files—if they are not wanted don't bother to send them back. Mr. Ives says he would be glad to have you put them on your shelves with his music 'to remember him by'—

Again we send many thanks and our kindest wishes.

Sincerely yours,
Harmony T. Ives

P.S. As you suggest it will be best to have proofs of any printed matter sent here.

•

The Babitz/Dahl edition of the Third Violin Sonata was beset with difficulties and took considerably longer to produce than had been anticipated.[70] Ives was particularly unhappy with the way that Dahl had regularized the "orthography" of the piano part by altering many of Ives's enharmonic spellings. This case shows that while Ives envisioned performance options in pieces such as the *Concord Sonata,* he was quite certain about the conceptual basis of pieces, such as the "dual-tonality" in this sonata.

Undated Sketches in Charles Ives's hand for reply to 24 June 1944, Harmony T. Ives to Sol Babitz and Ingolf Dahl

Babitz / Dahl

I am . . .

He thanks you for your letter and copy and he much appreciates all you both have done. He is glad to send the enclosed for your services, as suggested in your letter.

On account of the present situation caused by taxes, war funds etc. he has to send 1/2 of the amount now—and a check dated on Aug. 15 for the balance.

The "pencil Remarks" on the title page which you suggest sending for printing are quite illegible but as far as can be seen are just memos and dates as to early performances etc.—and nothing that need be printed. But there were, as Mr. I remembers, some marginal notes written on the back of some of the old Mss pages, which described, in a way, the reason for or some of the things and days which the music tried to reflect. As soon as these pages can be found a copy will be made and sent to you.— though Mr. I feels it may not be worth printing it. However if it is thought best to include he would prefer to have it in small print on the last page.

He is rather sorry that some flats and sharps have been changed into each other. Mr. Ives usually had a reason technically, acoustically or otherwise, for using sharps and flats. If a D-flat is in one part and C-sharp in another on the same time beat, it was mainly due to some acoustical plan—which he had in mind or was working out or trying to in those days.

At the beginning of the 1st verse of this sonata, was a suggestion of a 2 key plan, which he occasionally played on the organ in Church services though mostly as interludes, or short preludes etc.—the lower hand usually in a key a minor 3rd or a major 6th lower than the melody—a sort of hymn of this kind was once played and sung in a service some forty years or so ago—the first ten measures of this sonata is a part of this—and so he would like to have, if not too much trouble the ~~organ~~ piano part put in as to suggest the key of D-flat, not C-sharp and under the melody in E—during the first ten measures just for association's sake. As this is from a kind of chant for organ and voices which he played in organ recitals some 40 years ago: and he remembers that some of the singers (not all) after getting accustomed to this, said that going back to one key, only, they missed something.— It didn't have the strength of the 2 key plan.

But after the first page, whatever changes there are in accidentals (which he hopes are not many, especially in the 3rd movement) do not bother to put them back as in the old copy.— Either way won't "make or break" the listener's ear.

Mr. Ives again wants to thank you both for your interest in his music, for all you have done in its behalf and for your fine performances of this sonata.— Several of those who have heard you play it say it was remarkably well played and beautifully expressed.

We much appreciated Mr. Babitz's remarks and comment in the International Magazine—it was most kind of him.

> With our kindest wishes to you both
> [Harmony T. Ives]

•

While progress on the publication of Ives's works continued with occasional difficulties in the early 1940s, the war in Europe intruded even on the secluded life at Redding and on the lives of those in contact with the Iveses. In this letter of April 1942 from Harmony Ives to John Becker's wife, Evelyn, we see a cross-section of the world surrounding Ives. The description of daily life, the effects of war, and the progress of Ives's music is touching. It is indeed ironic that we have the threat of German bombing to thank for some of Ives's efforts at organizing his manuscripts.

26 April 1942, Harmony T. Ives to Evelyn Becker

Dear Mrs. Becker,

I hope you will forgive me for not having sent you Edie's address—I thought surely I had done so long ago—anyway it is 45 Christopher Street / Apt. 3c . . .

They live in "The Village" as it is called and like it so much. Henry Cowell and his wife live just around the corner from them. I called on her the other day as we learned that she is flat on her back and must be there for four months in order to have an addition to the family. Their apartment is tiny but very light and pleasant.

We are going to Redding tomorrow and very glad to go. Mr. Ives has been spending laborious days going over his mass of papers, sorting and destroying and keeping.— The possibility of an incendiary bomb accomplished what I have been trying to do for years.— His things are all on the top floor and would get it if anything came. He is awfully tired but has a feeling of something done anyway.

His music has been played a good deal this year.— The Szigeti concert where the Children's Day Sonata was played was a beautiful concert and Szigeti played the sonata with real enthusiasm and feeling. *The New Yorker* spoke of it as a "thoroughly ingenious & engaging" piece of music—"engaging" was the word two critics used—and it is that.—[71] We were glad to hear of your doings and Bruce's sayings.

We do not know what is ahead of us these days—my sister's two sons and 1 son-in-law have been drafted—two babies coming. These young couples torn apart are so sad to me.— I hope the war will be over before your boys must go in.

We have seen very few people so I have no news of acquaintances. We have seen Henry once—he is very busy—has put on a good many pounds. We were glad to hear that Carl Ruggles is better than for some time past.

We hope you all will have a pleasant summer.— I remember Mr. Becker said you are a fisherman so I hope you get a chance to cast your line.— I have done some trout fishing myself.

With our best wishes and greetings I am

Sincerely yours,
Harmony T. Ives

•

The war also stimulated a musical response from Ives, although it was not the same eloquent burst of composition elicited by the First World War. Ives's response to World War II was to rework *He Is There!* (1917) by changing the words and working out an orchestration in conjunction with Lou Harrison. The new piece was the choral version of *They Are There!*, which Ives often referred to as the "War Song March." Ives was most anxious to put the new piece to work to boost morale; to him it was an inspiring reminder of the true purpose of fighting the war. Consequently, Ives was much more insistent in promoting this piece than he typically was. He mentions it repeatedly in the correspondence from the war years, especially to those who might perform it. This piece represents Ives's contribution to the war effort, and it is the equivalent to his unsuccessful attempt to join the ambulance corps in World War I. The following sketch for a letter of August 1943 to Lou Harrison involves the creation of the "War Song March." This sketch again demonstrates Ives's memory of his pieces as late as the 1940s.

Sketch in Charles Ives's hand for August 1943, Harmony T. Ives to Lou Harrison

Sorry to give you more trouble and for the delay in sending back the last page, but he cannot attend to things nowadays as he would like to. We hope the enclosed memos as to the last 4 measures will help you more readily clear up this last page of the score—with the exception of the string part in measure #52—the marks in these measures are more matters of detail. We cannot find the last page of the old score, but on the back of one of the old pages—there are a few measure sketches which Mr. I thinks were put mostly in the score. A memo under the 1st violin says that according to the number of players, all the strings will swoop up together each fiddle starting a 1/2 tone under the one before—but Mr. I thinks that will be too much of a job.— And the division of these run ups suggested in the enclosed slip will be enough. It is hard for Mr. I to write clearly nowadays, and I've tried to go over these notes as well as possible and hope you can make them out without much trouble.

In measure #53, there was a fermata over the last trumpet note.— But Mr. Ives thinks it will be better to put the 4th beat of this measure in all instruments except to trumpet and drum a rest.— And then put that which was the 4th beat of this measure as the 1st beat of the last

measure, and that which was the 1st beat 2nd. We have tried to make
this as clear as we can in the score copy which is being sent under
separate cover. On the old sketches of this measure is written in the
margin.— After last Bugle call the march may end if it wants to, the
last 2 beats are but "fisticuffs on the Kaisar's jaw"—and don't always
have to be played—though Mr. I says he for one would vote for them.

He has just noticed that there are no bow marks in the score. But
probably [these] were to be put in when he made the ink copy—but
afterward one was not made.— So perhaps you, Mr. Cowell, or some
violinist, if you would prefer to have one save you that job. Though Mr.
I says that perhaps in a kind of a rough street march step like this, each
fiddler may like to make his own bow marks—down his own street. If
bow marks are made, they may start on the notes which are in common with the chorus time—as in measure 20: B-flat B-flat C etc.

Please excuse this long letter.— But most of it if not all of it is
rather necessary in a hurry up job like this.

Mr. I again wants to thank you for attending to all this.— It is kind
of you to do it.

Sincerely
[Harmony T. Ives]

•

The above sketch demonstrates the close working relationship
Ives had with Henry Cowell's protégé, Lou Harrison. In 1947,
just after Ives had received the Pulitzer Prize for his Third
Symphony, Harrison, who had conducted the premier of the
work, had to be institutionalized for what was termed "a treat-
able case of schizophrenia." Fellow composer John Cage wrote
letters to several of Harrison's friends asking for financial help
for him. Characteristically, Ives provided the money to pay for
his hospitalization. Ives sketched a letter to Harrison and a
reply to Cage on the same sheet of paper.[72]

**Sketch in Harmony Ives's hand for reply to John Cage 13 May 1947,
Harmony T. Ives to John Cage**

I am writing . . .
We are so sorry to hear of Lou Harrison's illness. It happens that
we had this cheque made out to him before your letter came. It

• 253 •

represents one half the amount of the Pulitzer award that Mr. Ives recently received. Mr. Ives feels that Lou had done so much in behalf of the 3rd Symphony that he wants to share this part of the award with him. Will you tell him this is not a present but a recognition of his help? and give him our love.[73]

We hope to hear good news of him and Mr. Ives says he will be glad to help if necessary in further expenses. . . .

[Harmony T. Ives]

•

The award of the Pulitzer Prize to Ives turns on a remarkable story. Curtis Davis, a student at Columbia and an Ives enthusiast, had arranged for the Third Symphony to be recorded from a radio broadcast in 1946. Davis then began to play this recording for interested musicians at Columbia. Eventually the Pulitzer committee used Davis's recording during their deliberations for the 1947 music prize. The following two letters are Davis's letter to Ives, dated one day after the Pulitzer award announcement (5 May 1947), and Ives's letter in response.

6 May 1947, Curtis Davis to Charles Ives

Dear Mr. Ives:

As a long time admirer of your music (if that phrase can be applied both to music which is so rarely heard and to myself, as I am only 19), I wish to congratulate you on the award to you today of the Pulitzer prize for your third symphony.

You may perhaps remember that I wrote to you last spring after the world premiere of that work by the N. Y. Little Symphony. As I believe I mentioned then, I had a recording made from the broadcast, which has since been doing me much good service.

I am happy and proud to be able to report that the Pulitzer committee approached me, through Prof. Douglas Moore, and asked me to loan them my recording of your symphony, since I was the only person they knew of who owned a recording of the work. It is a great source of personal pleasure and a vicarious honor to have been able to contribute what little I could to the furtherance of the recognition of music which is so important as yours.

Every time I open one of your scores, it is a source of never ending wonder to me that such enormous growth and artistic integrity, in addition to tremendous originality, could have developed in what must have been for you a highly personalized musical near-vacuum. This music, of which I have fortunately been able to hear more now, is what the American audiences have been looking for, namely a thoroughly American, yet never commonplace composer. I have heard your 2nd String Quartet twice, and it has completely swept me off my feet, particularly the last movement, in which one can forget completely the avowed program concerning climbing a mountain, and is swept away in the grandeur and sonority of what is really one long climax, with an upgrade and downgrade on either side. I only wish that this work had also been broadcast. A recording of it would be one of the gems of my library.

I fear that I have overdrawn your attention to my words. You must be getting more mail than ever now. In closing, allow me to wish you the greatest luck and as many performances as possible. It is an honor to call you an American, and a countryman.

Sincerely,
Curtis Davis

Sketch for reply to 6 May 1947, Harmony T. Ives to Curtis Davis

Curtis Davis
    I am——
We much appreciated your very kind and interesting letter.— He is glad you are one of those who have a deep penetration into the "spirit sources" of music. Mr. I sends you his sincere thanks for making it possible for the committee to hear your recording from his 3rd Symphony broadcast.

If ever there is a record made of the 2nd String Quartet, you are one of the first, he wants to receive it.

Open minded and thoughtful young men like you will be a great help to the life of music.

With our kindest regards,
[Harmony T. Ives]

P. S. Mr. Ives is going to have a copy of his 3rd Symphony score, sent to you from the publisher and asks you to accept [it] with his compliments and best wishes.

•

As demonstrated above, Ives's generosity extended well beyond giving scores to admiring musicians. Frequently Ives's gifts amounted to substantial patronage for his own music and that of others. An example from the mid 1940s concerns the Los Angeles concert series, Evenings On the Roof, promoted and organized by Peter Yates and his wife Frances Mullen Yates. In October, 1944, the American Music Center informed Ives that Yates wanted the parts for the Second String Quartet. Yates intended to schedule performances of works by Ives and Schoenberg in the upcoming season to mark the seventieth birthdays of both men. Ives's sketch responding to this information shows his philanthropy and also gives insight into his unique world view.

Undated sketch in Charles Ives's Hand for Harmony T. Ives to Peter Yates and Frances Mullen Yates

Dear Mr. and Mrs. Yates

I am writing for Mr. I for, as you know he is not well and cannot. We have heard that you are to have some of Mr. Schoenberg's and Mr. I's chamber music played at your concerts this season, and Mr. I deeply appreciates your kindness and generous thought in including in your programs some of his music. The American Music Center in NY wrote a while ago that the parts for the second S[tring] Q[uartet] were wanted. The old copies were so poorly made when it was "played at" some 30 years ago, add this together with its difficulty, [it] almost ended in a 'row'; so we are having new and cleaner copies made. We asked Mr. Lou Harrison to check over the parts when they came from the copyist, before sending them to you, as on account of Mr. I's bad eye condition (he has cataracts on both eyes) he cannot see well enough to do this. We have not heard from Mr. H. but possibly the parts may have already been corrected and sent to you by this time. This Q[uartet] is very difficult to play—but players nowadays are not quite so afraid of a hard job as they were 30 years ago. However Mr.

I thinks that in days like these it is hardly right to give you both and the players so much trouble and take so much of your time.

Mr. Ives is also afraid that these concerts will put you under quite an expense, and he wants to be, at least, of some help and says you must kindly let him, so please use the enclosed [check] in any way to help, and if there is a deficit later on please let him know and he will be glad to send more.

Also it has occurred to Mr. I that if any of Mr. Schoenberg's music, he may wish to include in your concerts, parts have to be made, he would be glad to take care of these as he feels that in these troubled days, especially for those poor oppressed and forlorn refugees, the expense in copying may be beyond their means, so if that is the situation with Mr. S., Mr. I. would be very glad to take care of this expense, if you will let him know what it is; but he does not want Mr. S or anyone for that matter know that he is doing it, so please just say that it comes from friends of the society—or something to that effect.[74] Mr. I does not want Mr. S to feel under obligation to him in any way— so please let these business matters be just between us. . . .

[Harmony T. Ives]

•

Yates's response thwarted Ives's desire to remain an anonymous supporter of the concert series. One wonders if Ives would have agreed with Yates that silence about his patronage was "no longer necessary."

1 October 1944, Peter Yates to Charles and Harmony Ives

Dear Friends:

For once I cannot obey your order to be silent. Throughout his life Mr. Ives has been doing these great kindnesses to other artists. The stories have come to me, here a little, there a little. Always he has forbidden mention of his generosity. Now the silence is no longer necessary. It is with the greatest pride that I have told our musicians of this gift and of that even more generous provision, that we should spend the money not merely for his own music but also for Schoenberg's. The thought of it is an inspiration and awakens among those who know it a desire to hear the music of a composer who is not only noble in his music but also in his own most private actions.

I know that it is dangerous to seem generous when one has a little more money than one needs to get along on. For this reason I have stated the gift in such a way as to make clear that it is a spontaneous action and has been in no way solicited by us. And I am not pouring out the information to the public. Just those who have worked so long with us to make this music available to the public, those who need such inspiration—they are the ones entitled to know of such an action. They join me in gratitude and also in honor of this kindness. . . .

> Your devoted friend
> Peter Yates

•

During the last four years of his life, Ives continued to correspond with many of his friends and fans, including Peter Yates. In April 1951 Yates, who had been programming twelve concerts of modern and early music per season in Los Angeles since 1939, wrote Ives a letter expressing his amazement at the depth of Ives's talent and his growing fame. The letter is a retrospective and also looks forward to the discovery of even more important works by Ives.

10 April 1951, Peter Yates to Charles Ives

Dear Friends:

Honors begin coming from every side to be laid at your door. Even I, moderately well as I thought I knew a small part of your music, am over and over again astounded by the unbounded variety of ideas in every relationship of thought with music which keeps issuing fresh from your storehouse. Such wonders as *Central Park in the Dark* convince me I have scarcely begun to get acquainted with you. And then there was the Second Symphony, which I insist will be called the Patriotic Symphony simply because it is all about home instead of wars, a whole evolution of a symphony from Bach preluding to *Götterdämmerung* a lot more pleasantly and practically polyphonized together out of Camptown Races and Old Black Joe. What a time I had with it! Of course I got my notion of it into an article. You see only the whole articles, but there are many other references, paragraphs, mentions, because I can't keep your music or my love for it out of my mind.

The more of your Leviathan-length comes out of hiding the more I think of old Bach, whom I love best, and I think there is another who will go on growing at the end of two centuries. Perhaps by that time the last of your music will be getting performed, like the Art of Fugue and Musical Offering in 1928.

Meanwhile we have added another to the performances of *Hallowe'en,* expertly timed straight to the big audience chuckle at the end. And it may be we gave, do you know of another? the first reading of *Aeschylus and Sophocles,* which looks simply impossible on paper and sounds as one awestruck composer put it, *apocryphal*—reaching for something more accurate to lean on he added, *cosmic.* And this is no novice but an oldtimer at turning out effective movie scores. The part was exactly suited to the singer's voice. She was afraid the hyper-dramatic spoken "Accursed etc.," might break the mood, but it also was music; everything belonged.

Frances had to cancel her concert this season because of neuritis in the arm, but now she is much better and, first thing, began playing the *Concord.* She sends her love as always.

So now I've worked off a head of steam by praising you as near to your face as I'm able to get. Now for business. If we can get the First [Piano] Sonata, one of our pianists would like very much to start working on it. And I can place the First [String] Quartet, if a copy turns up. I believe you wrote the Quartet is not available, and I remind you of a performance over CBS by the Roth Quartet a number of years ago. And didn't you say the First Sonata is being printed? I know it has been played. I wish I knew how to get these without bothering you.

When we first corresponded it was hard to believe our little home concerts would ever last so long. Here we are finishing the thirteenth season!

I've had my hand at a version of the statement to accompany an award which is to be made to you this year. Now Henry Cowell has it. They tell me I am perhaps too "dithyrambic." I say you can't put it too strongly in honor of a composer whom one is now convinced will soon be thought the greatest composer of the twentieth century. That means I'm gambling a bit on your other uncovered mss. Why shouldn't I!

> Affectionately,
> Peter Yates

•

We catch a glimpse of Ives's reaction to his spreading popularity in the following letter of March 1951 from Harmony Ives to Leonard Bernstein, who conducted the premiere of Ives's Second Symphony the previous month.[75] This letter also documents one of the few recorded instances on which Ives listened to a radio broadcast of his own work.

11 March 1951, Harmony T. Ives to Leonard Bernstein

Dear Mr. Bernstein:

It was a wonderful and thrilling experience to hear Mr. Ives's 2nd Symphony as you conducted it on February 22nd. I have been familiar with it—in snatches—for forty years and more and to hear the whole performed at last was a big event in my life. People did like it, didn't they? Someone wrote in the New Yorker recently of Mr. Ives's music that its hearers are participators in it.[76]

Mr. Ives has had many letters and he wants me to say to you that "the enthusiasm with which it was received was due so much to your devoted interpretation and wonderful conducting." Mr. Richard Bales, conductor of the orchestra at the National Gallery of Art in Washington, wrote that he "just wanted to yell when he wasn't on the verge of tears."

Mr. Ives heard the broadcast tho' he does not hear well over the radio and it took him back so to his father and his youth that he had tears in his eyes. You will be interested to know that his comment on the allegro movements was "too slow"—otherwise he was satisfied.

He thanks you from the bottom of his heart for getting this symphony played and for your skillful and artistic and masterly conducting.

I am so glad I had the pleasure of meeting you. I hope your sabbatical year will be a happy and fruitful one.

With all our good wishes
Sincerely yours
Harmony T. Ives

P.S. Mr Ives will be glad to send you the data on his music of which he spoke if you will let him know where to send it.

•

Two more letters from fans show the ongoing positive response to Ives's music in the 1950s. These letters are informative both in the things their authors say about Ives's music and in the motivations that prompted their writing. Each describes a feeling of being connected with Ives through his music. Partially patriotic and partially spiritual, this idea of connectedness suffuses many letters throughout the correspondence and partially explains the continuing attractiveness of Ives's music and ideas.

4 March 1951, Harold C. Bailey to Charles Ives

My dear Mr. Ives:

I want to express to you my pleasure at hearing a part of your second symphony over the air today. Since I have no technical knowledge of music whatever, I can only say that I liked it very much, the orchestration seemed to me always fluent and sincere and the theme-development both rich and significant.

Had you not been a Connecticut man, I probably would not have troubled you with this letter. But this honor you have brought to our state can hardly go unnoticed by those of us who value its traditions and its illustrious sons through the centuries whose achievements have magnified its fame. In your case the very rarity of Connecticut composers makes your own accomplishment the more conspicuous.

A place should be reserved in our Capitol for such men as Horatio Parker and yourself along with the generals and other noteworthy figures who now occupy the niches.

But however that may be, your music will become increasingly familiar to succeeding generations and a joy to them all. A host of thoughts press upon me as I write such as the curiosity as to how such work could remain buried for half a century and how it has now come to light, but it would be presumptuous to make such inquiries. One cannot help wondering, too, how much more music like it would have been written if our society were better equipped for the reception of genius than it is. Surely Connecticut would have been the gainer from one less successful insurance agency and one more producer of a long series of symphonic and other music.

So as others write you in a vein of discriminating appreciation because they are equipped to understand fully what you have done, let me just add my word as a fellow-citizen and say, "Thank you," again.

Yours faithfully,
Harold C. Bailey

6 March 1951, Frank V. Burton to Charles Ives

Dear Mr. Ives:

I want you to know what a pleasure it was to hear you[r] symphony over my radio on Sunday afternoon. If the annotator can be credited, I am about four months older than you and apparently we grew up in somewhat similar environment and circumstances. My early church connection was with the State Street Presbyterian in Albany. For the Sunday services, we had "Songs for the Sanctuary" and it was there that I first heard "Holy, holy, holy." But for the Friday night prayer-meeting, we had unadulterated Moody & Sankey. The Annotator said the flute played a bit from "America, the Beautiful." If it did, I did not catch it; but I was sure there were snatches from "Bringing in the Sheaves" and "Buelah Land." Am I correct? . . .[77]

Yours sincerely,
Frank V. Burton

On 19 May 1954, Charles Ives died at age seventy-nine of complications resulting from surgery. The response from his many friends and acquaintances was extensive. Nicolas Slonimsky, who had known the Iveses since 1928, wrote to Harmony Ives the following brief letter of shock and denial at the news.

20 May 1954, Nicolas Slonimsky to Harmony T. Ives

Dear Mrs. Ives: —

I opened the paper today, and I shouted: "No! No! No!"
That's all I can still say—no—it can't be . . .

Nicolas

Carl and Charlotte Ruggles sent Harmony a more extensive response. They were unable to attend the funeral but had received a long description of it from John Kirkpatrick who had been there.[78] Harmony's reply to the Ruggleses, although longer than many of her letters on the occasion of Charles's death, typifies her response to letters of sympathy. In almost every letter she repeats that her life has been "emptied of its contents." Harmony and Charles shared an extremely close relationship that had been transformed into a void at his death. In spite of her loss, Harmony's letter to the Ruggleses shows her sense of Charles's continuing presence in her life. She continues to write for both of them as she so often had: she closes the letter by sending "our love" to the Ruggleses.

22 June 1954, Charlotte Ruggles to Harmony T. Ives

Dearest Harmony:

You have been in our hearts, our prayers and our thoughts these past tragic days. We wish so much that we were near to perhaps assuage in some small measure the grief and loneliness of your great loss. Right after the telegram Carl was ill and has said so many times that a Great White Light had gone out of his life. Charlie and Carl are alike in so many ways that I have always felt spiritually very near you. You have always been a great inspiration to me and a help when the days were long and down. [We received a] very beautiful letter from John telling us of the service and a prayer he said in his heart when he said "good bye." We were with you my dear and I know "we shall meet beyond the River." Carl is out under the trees feeling some better. The Iris, lupine and Day Lilies all swaying in the high wind. Love to Edie and our devotion and dearest love to you.

Always
Charlotte Ruggles

All my love to you dear Harmony.

Carl

13 June 1954, Harmony T. Ives to Carl and Charlotte Ruggles

Dear Charlotte and Carl,

I got your telegram—I need all your love and sympathy— Oh— this desperate loneliness.—

Charlie has been so long my joy and my care that my life seems emptied of its contents and I do not know how I shall fill it. I am staying on here to make some attempt to get things in order to empty this house. Henry is coming in tomorrow to help me to bring some order into the chaos in the top floor—Charlie never threw anything away and the accumulation is awesome.

Charlie had what the surgeon called an intolerable hernia condition that had to be corrected but we expected him to recover—for two days he did remarkably well but his heart weakened and the end came.

A sonnet I read in The Spectator has helped me— "We knew joy/ unchanging and thro' this unchanging joy/ I apprehend the joy unchangeable."

You two devoted souls can sense my sorrow—I cannot believe what has happened to me—that I shall see him no more—

We had a simple service at Redding, my brother officiating—just family and neighbors—John Kirkpatrick was there which gave me comfort—and now he lies near his father in the old Wooster Cemetery in Danbury.

Oh, but these partings are hard even if one has a sustaining faith. With our love—and I mean *our* . . .

As ever,
Harmony

NOTES

1. MSS. 14, series IIIa, boxes 27–33. The collection contains both originals and reproductions of letters held elsewhere and is the principal repository of Ives's manuscripts. Citations from the collection are given at the end of this notes section, in chronological order, in the following form: Yale Ives Collection (YIC): MSS. 14/ box number/ folder number e.g., YIC: 14/32/1.

2. Ives prints in the large block capital letters of a six-year old.

3. To further his son's career, George Ives had submitted the *Variations on "America"* to the Ashmall publishing firm in 1892; it was returned unpublished in 1894. See John Kirkpatrick, *A Temporary Mimeographed Catalogue of the Music Manuscripts and Related Materials of Charles Edward Ives 1874–1954* (New Haven: Library of the Yale School of Music, 1960; reprint, 1973), 106.

4. The *Yale Daily News* of Monday, 29 January provides the following program for the Glee and Banjo Club Promenade concert, held at the Hyperion Theater: Part I: "Valiant march" (Banjo Club); "Alma Mater"—Shepard; "Robin Adair"—arr. by Shepard (whistle by Mr. Solley); "What I Have"—Bohn; "Good Night, Good Night, Beloved"—Fitzhugh; Part II: "Waltz 'Lublino'"—Finrochi (Banjo Club); Society Songs, a. "Rah! Rah! Rah! Psi Upsilon," b. "Jolly D. K. E."—Carmina Yalensis; "Rose Marie"— Malloy (Mr. Solley, with Harp Accompaniment); "Valentine"—Parker; "Tutti Frutti"— (Glee and Banjo Clubs); Part III: "Goblin's Frolic"—O'Neill (Banjo Club); "Rub-a-Dub"—Vincent; College Songs a. "Interger Vitae," b. "We Meet Again"—Carmina Yalensis; "Liebeslied"—Paine (Mr. Arbuthnot and Club); "Bright College Years"— Carmina Yalensis.

5. The illegible word here may be "voluntary," but the appearance is closer to "robustlury." Even in his youth, Ives's handwriting was not a model of clarity.

6. The identity of the "Eagle" is unclear and intriguing. If this is a reference to Ives's song "Where the Eagle Cannot See," then the date assigned the song must be revised from 1900 to no later than 1894.

7. Gayle Sherwood has identified this passage as a reference to Ives's *Nine Experimental Canticle Phrases;* Gayle Sherwood, "The Choral Works of Charles Ives: Chronology, Style, Reception" (Ph.D. diss., Yale University, 1995), 102.

8. The Yale University Chamber Concert Series presented eight string quartet recitals and two song recitals in 1894. According to the *Yale Daily News* of 24 October, that evening's concert included Haydn's *String Quartet in B Flat Major,* Op. 76, No. 4; Jean Marie LeClair's *Saraband and Tambourine;* and Dvořák's *String Quartet in D Minor,* Op. 34. The Symphony concert Ives mentions was given on Tuesday, 30 October, under the baton of Anton Seidl.

9. Carol K. Baron speculates that George Ives wrote his essay on music theory in response to requests by Ives like this one for music theory lessons for his classmate Garrison. See Carol K. Baron, "George Ives's Essay in Music Theory: An Introduction and Annotated Edition," *American Music* 10 (Fall 1992): 240–41.

10. Ives played on a scrub team that scrimmaged the starting freshman squad in practice. He may have played briefly as a substitute left end in a game against Amherst College on 10 October 1895. The *Yale Daily News* of that date includes the name Ives in a list of players who participated in the game. There is no indication of graduating class, however, and as there were several Iveses at Yale in 1895, it is not certain that Charles ever played in an official game.

11. The *Yale Daily News* reports that this recital was on 25 October 1894 and lists the following program: *Sonata in E Flat Minor* by Rheinberger, "Aria" by Stradella, "Walther's Preislied" from *Die Meistersinger* by Wagner, "Caprice" by Guilmant, "Adoratio et Vox Angelica" by Dubois, "Concert Piece" by H. W. Parker, "Three Pieces for Violin and Organ" by Rheinberger, and "Prelude and Fugue in A Minor" by J. S. Bach.

12. Mandeville Mullaly was Ives's roommate for all of their four years at Yale. Apparently Ives's scheme to have his brother Moss ghostwrite an article for him never materialized.

13. Buck lived in Brooklyn, and Ives apparently took the train to take lessons with him in Brooklyn or New York.

14. John Kirkpatrick suggests that Ives may have written his arrangement of the hymn, "Rock of Ages," as early as 1891 and used it in a service at the Danbury Baptist Church on 20 April 1893. See Kirkpatrick, *Temporary Mimeographed Catalogue,* 159.

15. Jan Swafford discusses the courtship letters and excerpts a number of them in "La Vita Nuova: The Courtship of Charles and Harmony Ives," *American Music* 13 (Winter 1996): 470–89.

16. Harmony refers to her letter of 21 September 1907, part of which is quoted in Mark Tucker's chapter in this volume. The camp is Roberts Camp at Saranac Lake in the Adirondack mountains, where Harmony and her brother David Twichell vacationed on at least two occasions.

17. Harmony often closes her sentences with a dash which gives her letters a very conversational air and implies a connection between sentences. This punctuation is rendered here as a period, dash, and space.

18. The article is a brief laudatory obituary of Grieg who had died in the week previous to its publication; *The Outlook* 87, no. 2 (14 September 1907): 47–48.

19. The *Kimiash Hills* project was a plan for an opera based on Sir Gilbert Parker's *The Red Patrol*. For a synopsis of the plot, see Charles E. Ives, *Memos*, ed. John Kirkpatrick (New York: W. W. Norton, 1972), 318.

20. As noted by J. Peter Burkholder in *Charles Ives: The Ideas Behind the Music* (New Haven and London: Yale University Press, 1985), 141n8, circumstantial evidence in the letters suggests that 22 October was the day of the couple's engagement; certainly Ives's comments in his letter of November 22 mark this day as the beginning of their spiritual if not their physical intimacy.

21. Burkholder, ibid., 97 and 141n8, identifies this poem, which is unfortunately not preserved with the letter, as the text Ives set as *Autumn*.

22. Cited in Stuart Feder, *Charles Ives, "My Father's Song": A Psychoanalytic Biography* (New Haven and London: Yale University Press, 1992), 208.

23. This is probably a reference to the Third Symphony, finished in 1911, or it may refer to the Second Symphony, revised and copied in 1909.

24. Ives so characterized the publication of the *Concord Sonata* and *Essays* in a sketch for a letter to Edwin Stringham of 22 June 1921, YIC: 14/32/7. See the reviews of the *Sonata, Essays,* and *114 Songs* in Part III of this volume.

25. This review is reprinted in Part III of this volume.

26. "Vibration-music" is Furness's term for music in the traditional sense. He distinguishes it from "word-music" meaning prose or poetry.

27. 24 July 1923, Clifton J. Furness to Charles Ives, YIC: 14/29/9; 6 April 1924, Clifton J. Furness to Charles Ives, YIC: 14/29/9.

28. Ives cites Sedgwick's *Dante: An Elementary Book for Those Who Seek in the Great Poet the Teacher of Spiritual Life* (New Haven, 1918) in the "Postface," reprinted in Charles Ives, *Essays Before a Sonata, The Majority, and Other Writings,* ed. Howard Boatwright (New York and London: W. W. Norton, 1970), 125.

29. Susanna was Edith's friend, Susanna Minturn. Together they were the subject of Ives's song *Two Little Flowers*.

30. This review is reprinted in Part III of this volume.

31. Whitmer uses this phrase in his review. In his next sentence, Ives may have been thinking of the impression the symphony made on *The Musical Courier's* anonymous reviewer, who remembered the sound of the work in performance as "just simply awful, from beginning to end." See the review, reprinted in Part III.

32. On the basis of a thorough examination of Ives's surviving medical records, Stuart Feder has questioned the description of Ives's 1918 health crisis as an actual coronary occlusion. In Feder's view, Ives's breakdown was probably psychological and may have been aggravated by a number of "profound psychological jolts" he sustained in 1918. See Stuart Feder, *Charles Ives,* 286–87.

33. J. Godfrey Wells was Ives's personal physician.

34. For an interview with a former Ives secretary, see Vivian Perlis, *Charles Ives Remembered: An Oral History* (New Haven: Yale University Press, 1974), 48–50.

35. Frank R. Rossiter briefly describes the sketch process and notes the oddity of Ives's use of the third person in *Charles Ives and His America* (New York: Liveright, 1975), 256–57. Stuart Feder also describes the use of third person in the sketches in *Charles Ives,* 339.

36. Poverty Flat was the name of a succession of New York apartments that Ives shared with other recent Yale graduates.

37. For Ives's discussion of "substance" and its opposite, "manner," see Ives, *Essays Before a Sonata,* 75–77.

38. Tanta May was May van Winkle. Bobby Porter Keep was the nephew of the headmistress of Edith's school.

39. Ives is careless or perhaps exaggerates when he writes that Slonimsky is the director of the Boston Symphony Orchestra. Although members of the group were recruited from the BSO, Slonimsky's ensemble was the Chamber Orchestra of Boston.

40. The great uncle of Edith's friend, Susanna Minturn, was Col. Robert Gould Shaw, the Union Army general memorialized in Augustus Saint-Gaudens's sculpture on the Boston Common, which is the subject of the first movement of *Three Places in New England*. Note the liberty Ives takes with the title of the "Putnam's Camp" movement of the set.

41. Brewster Ives is Ives's nephew; Bob may have been a friend of Brewster.

42. The two underlined dates in the top corners of the page are additions made during cataloguing by John Kirkpatrick.

43. Wells, a former classmate, may be the interested friend Ives mentions above.

44. Ives contrasts Slonimsky, who had just gained American citizenship in 1931, with the many American expatriate composers who had made their reputations in France.

45. This comment along with the remarks about Slonimsky's "family reunion" show Ives's abiding interest in family life. His letters are full of talk about his own daughter, Edie, and the children and families of his correspondents.

46. These notes are not preserved with the letter sketch. Ives lists a number of hymn tunes on his sketch for this letter including: "Tappan"; "Meribah"; "Missionary Chant"; "Ware"; "Federal St."; "Work for the Night"; "Cowper"; "Olive's Branch"; "Nettleton, Here I Raise My Ebenezer"; and "Lebanon."

47. This sketch is very interesting in terms of the voice Ives projects. Until the last sentence of the sketch, Ives writes in the first person. This is atypical usage for Ives by 1933. In most of his sketches by this time, he used the third person in anticipation that Harmony or Edith would write the final draft of the letter. Ives reverts to this third-person usage in the last sentence of this sketch. Perhaps he added the closing at a later time than he wrote the body and, in the meantime, forgot that he had been writing directly to Lomax.

48. Copland took steps to promote Ives's reputation as a composer by performing a group of Ives's songs with baritone Hubert Linscott at the Yaddo Festival in Saratoga Springs, New York on 1 May 1932, and by writing a mixed review of Ives's songs, "One Hundred and Fourteen Songs," *Modern Music* 11 (January–February 1934): 59–64. The latter is reprinted and a review of the former is excerpted in Part III below.

49. It is only when Copland questions the ideas and attitude Ives expresses in the "Postface" of *114 Songs* that Ives assumes a defensive tone. Yet, since Ives consistently bases his evaluation of the worth of his music on his belief in the ultimate judgement of the "average man," it is not surprising that he would defend that concept. In effect, Ives was willing to accept criticism of specific songs but not what seemed an attack on the philosophical basis of his music as a whole.

50. The "rear end glossarybo" is the "Postface" to *114 Songs*. "Over-hand slants" may be a reference to pitching. Ives also refers to the actuarial aspect of life insurance with "mortality tables."

51. Arthur Twining Hadley was an economics professor at Yale, from whom Ives took a class in his junior year. Hadley served as president of Yale from 1899 to 1920.

52. Becker was attempting to organize a concert in Chicago which was to include compositions by himself and Ives.

53. The concert was in Town Hall, 15 April 1934.

54. The sketch for this letter differs from those for the majority of Ives's correspondence after 1930. Ives writes the opening paragraph in Edith's voice and then switches to his own voice in the first person for the rest of the letter. Perhaps Becker was such a familiar and frequent correspondent that Ives did not feel the need to use the third person throughout, and he only used Edith as his "scribe" in order to present Becker with a more legible letter. Ives's outburst was prompted by Becker's request, in an earlier letter, for Ives to write to Birchard Publishing Company in order to interest them in publishing his *Concerto Satirico*.

55. John Barbiroli was the conductor of the New York Philharmonic.

56. *New Music* (1927–1958) was a quarterly periodical, managed for the most part by Henry Cowell; it printed contemporary music and included first publications of works by Ives, Ruggles, Schoenberg, and many others.

57. This collection was published as *Eighteen Songs* (*New Music* 9, no. 1) in October of 1935. Note Ives's concern over the subject matter of the songs and the political impression they might give. This concern reflects Ives's consistent desire not to appropriate *New Music* as a tool for his own agenda.

58. Ives seems to refer to his piece, *Majority*, and to be making a more general, punning, reference to omissions in other pieces.

59. The notes Ives made on the "enclosed sheet" provide an informative glimpse of the spreading popularity of his works. The songs to be included are *Resolution*, *Cradle Song*, *La Fède*, *Paracelsus*, *Canon*, *Tarrant Moss*, *Night of Frost in May*, and *The Old Mother* or *In Summer Fields*. In a note next to the song *Resolution*, Ives writes, "Prokofieff's wife sang this in Paris and [I] have had several requests for copies."

60. Ives, *Memos*, 279.

61. Chester is Ives's nephew; the bear reference is to a western vacation Cowell had taken, after which Ives cast him as a sort of wilderness adventurer. For another reference see 26 July 1935, Charles Ives to Henry Cowell, YIC: 14/28/5.

62. Arturo Toscanini was the target of several such outbursts. For Ives, the Italian conductor symbolized the desire of a commercialized music industry to pander to the brainwashed devotees of "soft" music.

63. One can only guess how much of the rage that Ives directed toward the music business in the person of Toscanini actually stemmed from his own discomfort and ill health.

64. While it is impossible to know whether Ives's recollection of the baseball-playing singer is more parable than memory, the image reflects his ideal of the average man. Ives's sketches for this letter lend credence to the identity of the vignette as fiction. The draft of the first half of the sentence reads: "a ten inning game is a man's job," which Ives revises to, "a ten inning game is some hard job and kept us jumping, but ten songs of his . . . ." Ives finally crosses out the whole of this and decides on the passage above.

65. Both the *Herald Tribune* column (Lawrence Gilman's review of the *Concord Sonata*) and the *Time* article of January 1939 are reprinted below in Part III.

66. The Twichell family home in Hartford, Connecticut.

67. Ives had divided his playing time between pitching and shortstop.

68. Characteristically, Ives offered to pay for the edition, including production costs, on whatever terms the editors thought reasonable. He did not want to drain the funds of *New Music*, even though he also provided much of this money on a yearly basis.

69. The quotation marks may imply that these paragraphs are Ives's attempt to reproduce the memoranda he mentions.

70. It was published as *New Music* vol. 24, no. 2, January 1951.

71. The reference is to Robert A. Simon's review of the week's music in *The New Yorker*, 7 March 1942, p. 47, which includes a paragraph on this performance by Joseph Szigeti and Andor Foldes. The paragraph is reprinted below in Part III and includes the word "engaging" but not the phrase "thoroughly ingenious."

72. Ives's letter of mid-May 1947 to Harrison is reproduced in facsimile in Perlis, *Charles Ives Remembered*, 202.

73. Interestingly, Harrison is not the only person to whom Ives distributed funds from his Pulitzer Prize. In a letter of 14 September 1947 from Edith to John Becker, Ives enclosed a check for Becker, not from Ives but from "that ole' Pulitzer feller." Becker, who was somewhat reluctant to accept Ives's generosity, took the check because it came from the Pulitzer money; see the sketch for Edith Ives Tyler to John Becker, YIC: 14/27/5, and 22 September 1947, John Becker to Charles Ives, YIC: 14/27/5.

74. For another instance of Ives's philanthropy to Schoenberg, see Dorothy I. Crawford, *Evenings On and Off the Roof: Pioneering Concerts in Los Angeles, 1939–1971* (Berkeley, Los Angeles, and London: University of California Press, 1995), 124.

75. For reviews of the event, see Part III below.

76. Article by D. W. in *The New Yorker*, 17 February 1951, 97–99.

77. The answer, of course, is yes, in the second and third movements respectively.

78. This letter is printed in Kirkpatrick, *Temporary Catalogue*, 278–79; 21 May 1954, John Kirkpatrick to Carl and Charlotte Ruggles, YIC: 14/30/14.

LETTER REFERENCES

September 1881, Charles Ives to Lyman Brewster, YIC: 14/33/1
25 May 1886, Charles Ives to Amelia Brewster, YIC: 14/33/1
4 February 1894, Charles Ives to George Ives, YIC: 14/33/1
24 February 1894. Charles Ives to George Ives, YIC: 14/33/1
24 October 1894, Charles Ives to George Ives, YIC: 14/33/1
20 January 1895, Charles Ives to Mollie P. Ives, YIC: 14/33/1
29 September 1907, Harmony Twichell to Charles Ives, YIC: uncat., folder 1
25 October 1907, Harmony Twichell to Charles Ives, YIC: uncat., folder 1
26–27 October 1907, Harmony Twichell to Charles Ives, YIC: uncat., folder 1
27–28 October 1907, Harmony Twichell to Charles Ives, YIC: uncat., folder 1
7 November 1907, Harmony Twichell to Charles Ives, YIC: uncat., folder 1
8 November 1907 A.M., Harmony Twichell to Charles Ives, YIC: uncat., folder 1
8 November 1907 P.M., Harmony Twichell to Charles Ives, YIC: uncat., folder 1
22 November 1907, Charles Ives to Harmony Twichell, YIC: uncat., folder 5
26 November 1907, Charles Ives to Harmony Twichell, YIC: uncat., folder 5
11 December 1907, Harmony Twichell to Charles Ives YIC: uncat., folder 1
12 December 1907 P.M., Harmony Twichell to Charles Ives, YIC: uncat., folder 1
14 December 1911, Charles Ives to Walter Damrosch, YIC: 14/29/1
23 May 1914, Charles Ives to Amelia Brewster, YIC: 14/33/2
15 March 1921, T. Carl Whitmer to Charles Ives, YIC: 14/32/13
10 April 1921, Henry Bellamann to Charles Ives, YIC: 14/27/8
Undated answer to 10 April 1921, Charles Ives to Henry Bellamann, YIC: 14/27/8
20 August 1921, Charles Ives to Anne Collins, YIC: 14/27/12
15 November 1921, Charles Ives to Henry Bellamann, YIC: 14/27/8
11 August 1922, Clifton J. Furness to Charles Ives, YIC: 14/29/9

Undated Sketch for Charles Ives to Clifton Furness, YIC: 14/29/9

Second sketch for 19 May 1923, Charles Ives to Henry Dwight Sedgewick, YIC: 14/31/17

1 June 1923, John Philip Sousa to Charles Ives, YIC: 14/32/6

24 March 1929, Charles Ives to T. Carl Whitmer, YIC: 14/32/14

Early July 1929, Sketch for Charles Ives to Julian (Mike) Myrick, YIC: 14/30/18

11 January 1931, George A. Lewis to Charles Ives, YIC: 14/31/4

17 February 1931, Charles Ives to Edith Ives, YIC: 14/33/2

8 May 1931, Charles Ives to Nicolas Slonimsky, YIC: 14/32/2

29 August 1933, John A. Lomax to Charles Ives, YIC: 14/30/15

Undated Sketch for reply to 29 August 1933, Charles Ives to John A. Lomax, YIC: 14/30/15

24–28 May 1934, Charles Ives to Aaron Copland, YIC: 14/27/13

4–5 August 1934, Charles Ives to John Becker, YIC: 14/27/4

26 February 1935, Charles Ives to Henry Cowell, YIC: 14/28/5

May 1935, Charles Ives to Henry Cowell, YIC: 14/28/5

23 February 1938, Edith Ives to John Becker, YIC: 14/27/5

June 1938, Charles Ives to E. Robert Schmitz, YIC: 14/31/26

27 January 1939, May Benedict Walsh to Charles Ives, YIC: 14/32/12

10 June 1939, Harmony T. Ives to Radiana Pazmor, YIC: 14/31/3

26 January 1940, Joseph H. Twichell to the Ives family, YIC: 14/32/10

1 January 1941, Charles Twichell to Charles Ives, YIC: 14/32/10

Sketches for 2 September 1941, Harmony T. Ives to Sol Babitz, YIC: 14/27/2

26 April 1942, Harmony T. Ives to Evelyn Becker, YIC: 14/27/5

Sketch in Charles Ives's hand for August 1943, Harmony T. Ives to Lou Harrison, YIC: 14/30/2

Undated Sketches in Charles Ives's hand for reply to 24 June 1944, Harmony T. Ives to Sol Babitz and Ingolf Dahl, YIC: 14/27/2

19 November 1946, Eugenia Ives Schaefer to Charles Ives, YIC: 14/31/14

6 May 1947, Curtis Davis to Charles Ives, YIC: 14/29/1

Sketch for reply to 6 May 1947, Harmony T. Ives to Curtis Davis, YIC: 14/29/1

Sketch in Harmony Ives's hand for reply to John Cage 13 May 1947, Harmony T. Ives to John Cage, YIC: 14/30/3

Undated sketch in Charles Ives's hand for Harmony T. Ives to Peter Yates and Frances Mullen Yates, YIC: 14/32/18

1 October 1944, Peter Yates to Charles and Harmony Ives, YIC: 14/32/18

11 March 1951, Harmony T. Ives to Leonard Bernstein, YIC: 14/28/8

4 March 1951, Harold C. Bailey to Charles Ives, YIC: 14/27/3

6 March 1951, Frank V. Burton to Charles Ives, YIC: 14/27/9

10 April 1951, Peter Yates to Charles Ives, YIC: 14/32/18

20 May 1954, Nicolas Slonimsky to Harmony T. Ives, YIC: 14/32/5

13 June 1954, Harmony T. Ives to Carl and Charlotte Ruggles, YIC: 14/31/12

22 June 1954, Charlotte Ruggles to Harmony T. Ives, YIC: 14/31/12

Part III
REVIEWS

Part III

Selected Reviews 1888–1951

COMPILED BY GEOFFREY BLOCK
AND EDITED BY J. PETER BURKHOLDER

These reviews highlight the most important stages in the reception of Charles Ives's music during his lifetime, from the first known public performance of his music through the premiere of his Second Symphony by Leonard Bernstein and the New York Philharmonic, which solidified his reputation as a major figure in American music. Some reviews are laudatory; others are critical, even dismissive. Through them can be traced Ives's progress from a young composer of orthodox works, to an isolated modernist with many critics and a few champions, to an almost mythic figure with a reputation among some critics as America's greatest composer.

The pattern of reviews also reveals the remarkable shape of Ives's career. Shortly after the 1902 premiere of *The Celestial Country,* he resigned from his last position as a church organist and retreated into relative isolation as a musician. Only with the publication of his *Second Pianoforte Sonata, "Concord, Mass., 1840–1860"* in 1920 did he begin again to reach out to the musical public. It was his more recent, more dissonant, and more complex works that were performed or published first: the *Concord Sonata,* published soon after its completion and premiered in full in 1938; the Second Violin Sonata, *Three Quarter-tone Pieces* for two pianos, and Fourth Symphony, all premiered soon after they were completed in the early 1920s; and *Three Places in New England,* completed in the 1920s and performed in the United States and Europe in the early 1930s. His earlier music, closer in style to nineteenth-century Romanticism, did not begin to appear

· 273 ·

until near the end of his life, the Third Symphony (ca. 1907–11) in 1946, the Second Symphony (ca. 1902–9) in 1951, and the First Symphony (ca. 1898–1902) only in 1953, a year before he died. The appearance of his major works in roughly reverse chronological order has resulted in a number of misunderstandings about Ives, some of them apparent in these reviews.

The following reviews are presented in chronological order and grouped by the performances and publications they review. In most cases, the entire review or the entire section devoted to Ives is reproduced here, and details of style have been left as in the original.[1]

• • •

Holiday Quickstep premiere, 16 January 1888

Holiday Quickstep was composed in December 1887, when Ives was thirteen. The comments on the piece in his hometown newspaper constitute the first known review of an Ives composition. The entire review is given here to show the context for the performance.

Amusements: The German Dramatic Association
from *The Danbury Evening News*

The members of this association gave one of their popular entertainments in the Opera House, last evening, and were favored with a large attendance. The comedy, "Raising the Rent," was presented by Paul Wenzel, Max Pauli, Otto Kranz, George Eisenhardt, Gustav Moelmann, Mrs. Hirsch, Mrs. Lied, Mrs. Mangold. All did exceedingly well and the four acts were played without a hitch. Mr. Pauli and Mrs. Mangold had "fat" comedy parts, and the audience was kept in continual laughter when they were on the stage.

After the play, which was finished before 10 o'clock, a German singing society from New Milford delighted those present with some beautifully rendered selections, and were rewarded by hearty applause.

Dancing was commenced shortly after 10 o'clock, and a large number indulged in the pleasant pastime until an early morning hour.

The music was furnished by the popular Standard Orchestra, and it is not necessary to remark that it gave the best of satisfaction. The overtures, as well as every number on the dancing programme, were artistically rendered.

The feature of the evening, in the musical line, was the rendition of the "Holiday Quickstep," composed and arranged for an orchestra by Charlie Ives, a thirteen-year-old son of George E. Ives. Master Ives is certainly a musical genius, being an accomplished performer on several instruments, as well as a composer and arranger. The "Holiday Quickstep" is worthy a place with productions of much older heads, and Master Charlie should be encouraged to further efforts in this line. We shall expect more from this talented youngster in the future.

Danbury Evening News, 17 January 1888, p. 3

• • •

The Celestial Country premiere, 18 April 1902

The following articles about the premiere of his cantata *The Celestial Country* mark the only known occasion that a performance of an Ives work was reviewed between 1888 and 1924. Across his copy of the *Musical Courier* review Ives later wrote "Damn rot and worse."[2] Shortly after these reviews appeared, Ives resigned his position as organist at Central Presbyterian Church in New York, his last professional position in music.

A New Cantata
from *The New York Times*

A concert on Friday evening at the Central Presbyterian Church, in West Fifty-seventh Street, was signalized by the first production of a new cantata, "The Celestial Country," by Mr. Charles E. Ives, the organist of the church, the words being Alford's not particularly felicitous English version of Bernard of Cluny's famous hymn. The work is scored for solo, quartet, octet, chorus, organ, and string orchestra and two horns. As heard on this occasion it obviously suffered from the want of the chorus, the octet being the extent of the vocal force available, the choral climaxes thus failing of their intended effect, and the scale being to that degree lost. This misfortune the conductor attempted to obviate by diminishing his pianos almost to inaudibility and thus preserving the dynamical relations, but this expedient could not be altogether successful.

The composition seems worthy of a more complete hearing. It has the elementary merit of being scholarly and well made. But it is also spirited and melodious, and, with a full chorus, should be as effective in the whole as it was on this occasion in some of the details. The most successful numbers, as it was heard, were the quartet, "Seek the Things Before Us," the baritone aria, (sung by the contralto,) "Naught That Country Needeth," and a pretty intermezzo for strings.

The cantata was preceded by a miscellaneous concert, comprising selections on the organ from Bach, Brahms, and three French composers of the seventeenth century, the "Quis est Homo," and a notably finished performance of three movements of Beethoven's first string quartet by the Kaltenborn Quartet.

The New York Times, 20 April 1902, p. 12

Charles E. Ives' Concert and New Cantata, "The Celestial Country"
from the *Musical Courier*

At the Central Presbyterian Church last Friday night the organist, Charles E. Ives, a Yale graduate and pupil in music of Professor Parker, gave an invitation concert which had for its principal number a new cantata by Ives, "The Celestial Country," words by Henry Alford, for solo, quartet, chorus, organ and string orchestra, augmented by two horns.

The work shows undoubted earnestness in study and talent for composition, and was fairly creditably done, the thirty singers and players entering into the spirit of the thing with enthusiasm.

Beginning with a prelude, trio and chorus, with soft, long-drawn chords of mysterious meaning, picturing the far country, the music swells to a fine climax, various themes being heard, used later on. Indeed, throughout the work there is homogeneity, coming from the interweaving of appropriate themes. Following the opening chorus there is a bass solo, sung on this occasion by the alto, however, Miss Emma Williams; it is lyric and full of grace, in B flat, and the low F's at the close came out finely.

There follows a quartet in D minor, difficult, with chromatic harmonies, and in the trio with alternating $\frac{3}{4}$ and $\frac{4}{4}$ time measures. It comes to a pianissimo close on the words "Until the eve be light" most effectively. The Intermezzo for strings alone, con sordini, is song-like, with the first violin and later the viola singing the melody, and this, too, comes to a close in softest tones. This Intermezzo the Kaltenborn Quartet will find useful for their concerts. It is full of unusual harmonies and pleasing throughout.

The a capella octet which follows has interwoven the principal theme of the quartet, followed by the tenor solo, one of the effective numbers of the cantata. This is in G major, well suited to a lyric tenor voice, with a graceful running figure in the accompaniment, the climax coming on the words "Till our faith be sight" on a high A, which rang out clear and true, sung by Tenor E. Ellsworth Giles.

The finale is composed of a chorus, chorale and fugue. This shows some original ideas, many complex rhythms and effective part writing, the chorale in $\frac{4}{2}$ time, the fugue built on the theme of the chorale. With an obligato soprano on the high C, all voices fortissimo, the work comes to a triumphant close.

Those who shared the first presentation of this work were Miss Anne S. Wilson, soprano; Miss Emma Williams, alto; E. Ellsworth Giles, tenor; and Geo. A. Fleming, baritone, constituting the solo-quartet; the Kaltenborn String Quartet, assisted by two horns (who did not always do their full duty, by the way), and a semi-chorus of a score of voices, members of the Musical Art and Mendelssohn Glee Clubs, Organist-Composer Ives at the organ directing the work. . . .[3]

Preceding the cantata there was a short concert, Mr. Ives playing a Bach fugue and some seventeenth-century marches, the latter by Rameau, Lully and Couperin, also "Selig sind die" from the Brahms Requiem. The Kaltenborn Quartet played three movements from Beethoven's Quartet, op. 18, No. 1, in F with considerable finish, the scherzo going especially well. Miss Wilson and Miss Williams united in the "Stabat Mater" duet, "Quis est homo," singing with beautiful unity of ensemble. Miss Wilson's voice sounded especially beautiful and clear, united with authority and delivery, while the noble alto organ of Miss Williams shone to great advantage. This duet was the pearl of the evening in ensemble and style.

An audience completely filling the church listened with expressions of pleasure, and at the close the composer was overwhelmed with congratulations, which he accepted in modest fashion.

Musical Courier 44, no. 17 (23 April 1902): 34

• • •

Concord Sonata publication, 1920

In 1920, after a long period of isolation as a composer, Ives published privately his *Second Pianoforte Sonata, "Concord, Mass., 1840–1860"* and an accompanying book of *Essays Before a Sonata* and sent them to acquaintances and important figures in the musical world, including several journals. The resulting reviews varied from satirical or uncomprehending to laudatory. What is perhaps most surprising is that the works were reviewed at all, as almost no one in the musical world knew Ives's name. Henry Bellamann's review, which reflected in part his correspondence with the composer, is perhaps the origin of the long-held but now discredited view of Ives as a composer of lofty aspirations who was not entirely in control of his medium.[4]

A Pseudo-Literary Sonata!!!
A. Walter Kramer
from *Musical America*

It is dedicated to us and yet we are not so proud of the dedication. What is it? It is a Second Pianoforte Sonata, "Concord, Mass., 1840–1860" (*Published by the Composer*) by one Charles E. Ives of Redding, Conn. Two volumes, beautifully bound in red cloth, lettered in gold, appear, one containing the music (?), the other, the size of a small book, entitled "Essays before a Sonata." The dedication reads: "These prefatory essays were written by the composer for those who can't stand his music—and the music for those who can't stand his essays; to those who can't stand either, the whole is respectfully dedicated." That is why we say the sonata is dedicated to us. *We can't stand either.*

Mr. Ives has written a sonata—he calls it a sonata—comprising four movements, "Emerson," "Hawthorne," "The Alcotts" and "Thoreau." It is full of literary meaning, assuredly; the composer says so, anyway. And it is without doubt the most startling conglommeration of mean- ingless notes that we have ever seen engraved on white paper, and we say this after having reviewed music for the last ten years, music of all kinds, from Béla Bartok's Second String Quartet to the songs of Lord Berners!

The composer, we hope, has had a good time writing the "sonata" and the essays. It is well that at least one person had a good time in connection with these remarkable productions. In the "sonata" there is a slip of paper, on which these words are printed: "Complimentary—copies are not sold." At last a composer who realizes the unsalable quality of his music. Allah be praised!

Musical America 33, no. 23 (2 April 1921): 36

Concord Unconquered
from the *Musical Courier*

Somebody—we suspect the composer—sent us two nice books, neatly bound in board covers, well printed by the Knickerbocker Press, New York. There was a slip inside that said: "Complimentary: copies are not to be sold." The composer and author need not have worried. We should not have bought either book. One of them is called "Essays Before a Sonata." There is no music in it. The other is the sonata itself. Some would insist that there is no music in that, either, but we reserve our judgment. It is called "Concord, Mass., 1840–60," and sub-titled "Second Pianoforte Sonata," so the composer presumably has written a first one that escaped our notice. His name, by the way, is Charles E. Ives. On the flyleaf of his essays (124 pp. 8vo.) are these words, quoted—very likely from himself: "These prefatory essays were written by the composer for those who can't stand his music—and the music for those who can't stand his essays; to those who can't stand either, the whole is respectfully dedicated." We are sore afraid we shall never know whether or not we can stand his music. Unless Charles drops into our sanctum some time and insists upon playing "Emerson," "Hawthorne," "The Alcotts" and "Thoreau"—so the four divisions of the sonata are named—we know we shall never know, for nobody else will ever be able to play it for us, since the musical nomenclature of Charles is entirely a personal affair. Only occasionally, and as a patronizing concession, does he write a time signature or a bar. (These latter, indeed, are merely dropped in every page or two, apparently to mark the spot where the composer stopped composing while he knocked off for luncheon or dinner.) And the writing is thin, indeed, when he doesn't employ at least three staves for the piano. Looking it through (not at the piano), we are convinced, however, that in the "Alcotts" section, Charles, consciously or unconsciously, lifted for his main theme a goodly section of one perfectly good tune, entitled, in the old Baptist hymn books, "Missionary Chant," and written by one Zeuner, who lived from 1795 to 1857. The late Zeuner, however, would be scandalized could he see his tune all undressed, as Charles has used it, with no proper bars nor time nor anythin'.

And—to resume—until Charles has played all the wisdom of Eastern Massachusetts for us, we shall not read the essays. For us they will not be "Essays Before a Sonata," but "Essays *After* a Sonata"—if ever.

We can think of only one explanation—Charles lives at Redding, Connecticut. Unless our memory deceives us, that, too, was the home of Samuel Clemens. Perhaps Charles aspires to become the Mark Twain of music. We should be glad to propose him a "Jumping Frog" theme. In the first few moments—we cannot say "measures," for Charles scorns such things—the theme would descend far into the depths of the musical pool, dragging the composer along with it, there to remain cool and silent forever.

Musical Courier 82, no. 17 (28 April 1921): 22

Reviews: "Concord, Mass., 1840–1860"
(A Piano Sonata by Charles E. Ives)
Henry Bellamann
in *The Double Dealer*

There is much "tumult and shouting" about the American composer and American music, much calling upon the heavens to witness that the great cause of star-spangled opera and symphony has suffered from neglect at the hands of impresarios and conductors, much dark muttering against sinister foreign influences that prevent our own eaglets from singing their just and due songs from proscenium arch and concert platform. Sometimes the American composer himself joins in the outcry to the decided impairment of his dignity and the dignity of music in general.

Music is always just music, neither *American* music, nor *French* music, nor *Spanish* music, but *music*—the universal voice of thought and feeling on a high plane—taking on sometimes the accidental color and characteristics of immediate surroundings. Its *national* character is but a superficial difference in idiom—rhythm, harmony and melodic contour. No serious musical mind can be interested in the *applique* of Indian or negro characteristics as artificial decorations of compositions which do not spring from an Indian or negro manner of thinking. On the other hand any effort which goes deeper into some mode of thought or manner of living essentially and exclusively American must interest as a movement in the direction of artistic integrity. Again, it would not be the "national" characteristics which would have value, save as they grew flowerlike from bole and branch,—it would be the value of some unique phase of our North American life brought to artistic expression . . .

In the midst of all the furore, critical and uncritical, about contemporary music, one is rather stunned to discover a new composer who has quietly written three symphonies, four violin sonatas, a string quartet, two suites for orchestra, two piano sonatas and two hundred and fifty songs. One is still more interested when one is informed that the composer is a Yale graduate, a pupil of Horatio Parker and that he was "raised on Bach and Beethoven." The interest becomes astonishment when [a] printed score of one of the larger works reveals music unlike anything one has seen before—a broad, strong and original style with no recognizable derivations from Debussy, Strauss or Strawinsky. You will look in vain through publisher's catalogs or concert programs or the anecdotal columns of self-advertising—you will not find the name of Charles Ives, composer of the monumental piano sonata which bears the unusual title, "Concord, Mass., 1840–60."

The sonata appears in a handsome, cloth-bound volume of seventy-two pages. Concerning it and his ideas about it, the composer writes: "The sonata is an experiment which perhaps goes too far. It was not written primarily to be played—certainly not to be played with two hands. This is the first of a series which I propose to have similarly printed and thrown at the music fraternity—chancing that a few may be interested. In this way, you see, no one has to buy the music, sell it, play it, or listen to it—except with both eyes open; there is no audience to throw things at the performer or the composer; the artist does not have to risk his reputation, nor the publisher his capital, and the music public is left in peace to work out its own salvation (whatever that means), and I to do the same without disturbing anyone but the neighbors."

From the Knickerbocker Press comes a volume by Mr. Ives called "Essays Before a Sonata," which is inscribed— "These prefatory essays were written by the composer for those who can't stand his music— and the music for those who can't stand his essays; to those who can't stand either, the whole is respectfully dedicated."

The sonata is divided into four movements entitled in order, *Emerson, Hawthorne, "The Alcotts," Thoreau.* The essays announce that "the whole is an attempt to present one person's impression of the spirit of transcendentalism that is associated in the mind of many with Concord, Mass., of over a half century ago. This is undertaken in impressionistic pictures of Emerson and Thoreau, a sketch of the Alcotts and a Scherzo supposed to reflect a lighter quality which is often found in the fantastic side of Hawthorne. The first and last movements do not aim to give any program of the life, or of any particular work, of either Emerson or Thoreau, but rather composite pictures or impressions. They are, however, so general in outline that from some viewpoints, they may be as far from accepted impressions (from true conceptions, for that matter) as the valuation which they purport to be of the influence of the life, thought, and character of Emerson and Thoreau is inadequate."[5]

Turning to the book we find a score without time or key signature and no measure divisions. Certain rhythmical divisions supply guidance. The music is broad and stately, the rhythmic arches are very wide. No fixed tonality, no rhythmic unity. It sways as freely as a tree top in the wind. Indeed there is no unity of idea in the sense that one part grows out of another. One feels only a psychic kind of connection that might in this case reasonably be called a musical logic. The Emerson movement is as majestic and free as clouds with the certainty of carved bronze. It is enormously difficult to play. It is truly doubtful if the composer meant it to be played—many places require a rearrangement or recasting unless an extra player is utilized.

Themes and chords move against and over each other in the style of chordal counterpoint met with in Casella. Again there are passage complexities offering as much resistance to digital solution as those of Malipiero. The effects resemble those of neither of these composers. The only resemblance the writer finds to any composer is in the Emerson movement when certain contours recall Strauss. Even this is a resemblance that strikes the eye rather than the ear.

This first movement is not pianistic—little of the sonata is—probably no effort was made to make any part of it pianistic. It must have been conceived abstractly. One misses, almost throughout, familiar pianistic outlines. In reading it away from the piano there is almost the feeling of perusing an orchestral score. The hand does not unconsciously grope for the keyboard. Yet many purely pianistic effects are contrived and effectively used. The beauty of this division of the work is severe and difficult. It is a beauty of high and remote things. It is austere. It is informed with the stark and ascetic beauty of lonely and alien reaches of human imagination.

The second movement given to Hawthorne "does not attempt the fundamental part of Hawthorne which has to do with the influence of sin upon the conscience, but tries to suggest some of the wilder, fantastical adventures into the half-child life, half-fairy life fantasmal realms." The entire movement is fantastic in the extreme—light and delicate for the most part—and depends for a fine interpretation on the player's familiarity with and understanding of Hawthorne's place in the world of strange, elfish and supernatural things. Some pages of *Hawthorne,* like some pages of the *Emerson,* are not practical for one player, such as Page 25, which requires [a] combination of notes to be held down with a block of wood for the production of harmonic effects. There are occasional measure divisions in this movement. On pages 40 and 41 is a climax of Ornstein-like fury but used to finer purpose.

"The Alcotts" is the shortest movement, only five pages, and is in every way the simplest. It boasts occasional time signatures and, for a few lines on the first page, a key signature of two flats in the right hand and four in the left.

There is a simple quiet beauty about *"The Alcotts."* It and the *Hawthorne* are more obviously successful, because more *external* than either *Emerson* or *Thoreau.*

The Thoreau movement, closing the sonata, is perhaps even more difficult to understand than the Emerson movement, certainly more difficult to play. But as a portrait of the man, a re-creation of his way of thinking, a meditation upon him and his life and his thought, a resultant philosophical attitude of mind in the reader, it is finer and more successful than *Emerson.* It is close in texture, more pianistically playable, than *Emerson,* and perhaps holds the interest better. For a few lines there is opportunity to use a flute. It seems better to the writer to permit this to remain an abstraction as its introduction breaks the mood. Most of the movement exists in a superb twilight and is, according to the composer's directions, to be played in a lower dynamic ratio.

Is it a great work? Is it successful? Is this a direction music may legitimately take? Each student must answer these questions for himself. There will be as many reactions as there are individuals coming in contact with it—probably all of them different. One asks in turn: What do you demand of music? What do *you* get out of it? *What equipment, literary, philosophical and musical do you bring to it?*

The composer admits that perhaps his experiment has gone too far. Most interestingly, he wishes to have another try at it.

But no serious student, having as a background a knowledge of the amazing achievements of modern music, can help feeling that Mr. Ives' sonata is a piece of work sincerely done, and if a failure, a rather splendid one.

Certainly it must be considered in a class by itself. Conceived independently of any instrumental idiom, it must be regarded as an essay of lofty thought and feeling expressed in musical notation. One arises from a reading of it with much, much more of satisfaction than dissatisfaction. Its loftiness of purpose is evident; its moments of achievement elevating and greatly beautiful.

The Double Dealer 2 (October 1921): 166–69

Ives Puzzles Critics with His Cubistic Sonata and "Essays"
Edwin J. Stringham
in the *Rocky Mountain News*

As the moon's pale splendor
O'er the faint cold starlight of
heaven is thrown,
So thy voice most tender
To the strings without soul has
given its own.
—Shelley

Some time ago I received a copy of a "Concord" sonata for piano and a book of "Essays" to accompany the same written by a Charles E. Ives of New York, and both published by the author. The book of essays is dedicated "to those who do not like the music, the music to those who do not like the essays, and both to those who like neither." The nature of both prose and musical works were of such a different nature from the usual that I was reluctant to write a critical review of them without plenty of time to digest as much of them both as possible.

Altho I have had plenty of time to look them over since I received them, I still am at sea, and present my impressions rather than judgment, hoping that some kind and understanding soul might help me "get underneath the hide," so to speak, especially of the music. So, in the beginning, I admit lack of full understanding, and the reader should be prepared to take what I might say with a grain of salt—perhaps more potent disguise.

The "Essays" are interesting studies of Emerson, Hawthorne, "The Alcotts," and Thoreau, preceded by a "Prologue" and followed by an "Epilogue." They were written "primarily as a preface or reason for the second pianoforte sonata, Concord, Mass., 1845—called a sonata, for want of a more exact name"—as the author states in the preface.

Some of the composer's statements are witty, informative and make unusually fascinating reading. They give personal observations of the characters mentioned that should find a place among the biographical literature. They are well worth reading.

Ives Essentially a Humorist

Mr. Ives essentially is a humorist—there is the rub. When he attempts to describe in musical terms the information contained in the "Essays," I cannot take him seriously and, candidly, I am of the opinion that the composer is having a good time making sport of the "cubistic" type of music. The first sentence of the "Prologue" says: "How far is anyone justified, be he an authority or a layman, in expressing or trying to express in terms of music the value of anything, material, moral, intellectual, or spiritual, which is usually expressed in terms of other than music?" He begins with a question and ends with one—at least as far as the mind and ear of the listener are concerned. Again, he intimates that the music is not to be considered from an aural side. I agree with him and again I say that he is poking fun.

The "Sonata" is terrifically difficult to perform and, I think, not worth the trouble involved to master it. The logic underlying its composition, if there is any, is not at all obvious, visibly or aurally. There are no bar lines, time values are disregarded, melody—as is commonly understood even in modern works—is religiously avoided, and queer instructions to the performer (!) abound thru the work. Fancy this. "To be played with a board about thirteen and one-half inches in length and of sufficient weight to press down the keys." A flute player must be hired for a few bars at the end of the sonata—for what?

True, it is filled with figure invention, splendidly bound and exceptionally well engraved. Best of all, the author insists that the work is not sold and that he is unwilling to make money out of his art. If the music were understandable, he would be a blessing to art: but—. Another reason why I think Mr. Ives is joking is that he has had the advantage of exceptional musical training and that he enjoys the reputation of being a well rounded and talented musician. The jump from Bach to the "Concord" is too great in difference to be true—at least serious.

Sonata is Experiment

In answer to a request I made to him concerning his ideals and training, the composer says, in part, "I graduated from Yale and while there studied under the late Prof. Horatio W. Parker— . . . and was organist and choirmaster of the Central Presbyterian church, New York. . . . I received a groundwork in music from my father who believed that all families should be raised on Bach and Beethoven. . . ."[6]

Concerning his ideals, he says, " . . . An interest in any form of art should not be strapped down and money dug out of it. The sonata is an experiment, which perhaps goes too far. . . . To have a manuscript played or published, usually requires some kind of a compromise." Some truth, indeed, but not all of it. I can fancy a publisher demanding a great deal of compromise in the art (?) Mr. Ives produces.[7] He is fortunate in being able to indulge in his whims; but I regret the style of his music.

We have heard some strange music written by Stravinsky, Schoenberg, Ornstein, Casella and others; but this particular work surpasses them all in cacophony. I did succeed in finding a few orthodox chords in one or two places and venture the guess that they were oversights. The only impression one gets from playing the work is that instead of being interpretations of the material and spiritual realms, they are direct delineations of a boiler-shop or the sounds emanating from a conservatory of music when in full blast.

In due credit to Mr. Ives, I must say that I do not understand his form of art—even tho I have a great sympathy with the "moderns"— and that I consider his motives of a joking nature and that he must not be taken too seriously—not even slightly seriously. I cannot but feel that he is trying to see how far clever jargon (and that in itself is to be considered complimentary) can go if printed. The same amount of talent and cleverness in other channels would go far, I am sure.

Rocky Mountain News (Denver), 31 July 1921, pp. 1, 17
(The newspaper mistakenly identifies Stringham as "Edward.")
Reprinted with permission of the Rocky Mountain News

**Review of *Second Pianoforte Sonata, "Concord, Mass., 1840–1860"*
and *Essays Before a Sonata*, by Charles E. Ives**
Ernest Walker
in *Music & Letters*

"These prefatory essays were written by the composer for those who can't stand his music—and the music for those who can't stand his essays; to those who can't stand either, the whole is respectfully dedicated." These words, with which Mr. Ives introduces himself to his public, show that he possesses a sense of humour: of which there might perhaps otherwise have been some doubt. The essays (120 pp.) and the sonata (63 pp. of music with 8 pp. of letterpress repeated from the essays) form a whole which is "an attempt to present one person's impression of the spirit of transcendentalism that is associated in the minds of many with Concord, Mass., of over a half-century ago": in both essays and sonata there are sections entitled "Emerson," "Hawthorne," "The Alcotts," and "Thoreau," and the essays have also a Prologue and an Epilogue. The somewhat flamboyant culture of the essays is at times distinctly shaky, and Mr. Ives' literary style is not only transcendental but also breathlessly Massachusettsian: but his general drift can be made out fairly well, and some of the few pages that are in any way concerned with music have good sense under their verbiage. The sonata, however, is the thing, and a very unusual thing it is.

A reviewer of modernist piano music has necessarily hardened himself to a great deal and is not easily taken aback: but "Concord, Mass." may be safely recommended as a tonic to anyone bored with the reactionary conservatism of European extremists. Mr. Ives has, indeed, some patents that are perhaps entirely his own—such as the simultaneous pounding of the piano by both clenched fists (an interesting effect best practised on someone else's instrument)—or the employment of "a strip of board 14 3/4 ins. long and heavy enough to press the keys down without striking," twelve black or sixteen white keys according to circumstances, but apparently a magic board, as a book of the proper dimensions fails to produce the proper effects, no sufficient resonance having been previously set up in the lower octaves—or the bewildering notation in virtue of which Mr. Ives (like Humpty Dumpty in *Alice through the Looking-glass*) makes a semibreve or anything else mean just what he chooses it to mean, though what he actually does choose is often far from obvious. No doubt there must be misprints in this music that for pages and pages on end sounds pretty much the same with any other rhythms or clefs or accidentals: but it can hardly be nothing but misprints. And every now and then (the oases, if they can be so called, amount to about 2 per cent. of the whole) we come across passages of the plainest common chords that sound exactly like a beginner's first attempts at harmony exercises. Mr. Ives' style is sadly familiar here: so, indeed, in quite another way, is the style of the 98 per cent., at any rate in households where the baby or the cat has access to the piano.

The copy of the sonata sent for review is marked "Complimentary: copies are not sold." But if Mr. Ives declines to barter his transcendentalism for filthy lucre, he may perhaps be willing to give it away on application to him at Redding, Conn., U.S.A. It is well worth trying.

Music & Letters 2, no. 3 (1921): 287–88

• • •

114 Songs publication, 1922

Ives followed the *Concord Sonata* and *Essays Before a Sonata* with a third privately published work, a collection of *114 Songs*. The *Musical Courier* review was again satirical. A more searching review by Aaron Copland written and published more than ten years after the book of songs itself, in 1934, appears in chronological order below.

Ives
from the *Musical Courier*

Who is Ives?

We have not the least idea. We only know that he sends us music from time to time, and that we have grievously misunderstood him.

Last year he sent us a piano sonata. We did not treat it kindly. When we arrived at a passage to be played by placing a board fourteen inches long on the keys of the piano and gently pressing it down, we felt annoyed. We said so.

The mistake was ours. We apologize. We had no idea that it was intended for a joke. We rather associated it with the efforts of some of the modernists—Cowell, for instance, who strikes the keys with his entire forearm—bass drum effect with the left elbow, tootle-tootle piccolo with the fingers. He goes Ives one better, and certainly does not intend it for humor.

However, Ives has swept away the clouds of misapprehension and has given us a delicious moment by sending in a copy of his latest publication, consisting of 114 songs, privately printed. The book is not sold or put on the market and "will be sent to anyone as long as the supply lasts." It would be highly instructive and significant to record the number of copies sent for.

Ives is the American Satie, joker par excellence. He adds and appends facetious comments upon his own work the which, alone, make the book worth while. The book, he says, is a kind of buffer state, "an opportunity for evading a question, somewhat embarrassing to answer—'why do you write so much ———, which no one ever sees?' There are several good reasons, none of which are worth recording."

That is Satie all over: "Several good reasons, none of which are worth recording." He then goes on to give one of these reasons—if we understand what he says, a thing of which we cannot be by any means sure. Anyhow, he seems to express the idea that music should be composed by everybody, like writing letters, not with any idea of inducing publishers to risk their money in its publication, but merely as a means of communion with congenial minds. Let us quote a paragraph:

"Every normal man . . . has, in some degree, creative insight (an unpopular statement) and an interest, desire and ability to express it (another unpopular statement). . . . There are a few who think (and encourage others to think) that they and they only have this insight, interest, etc., and that (as a kind of collateral security) they and they only know how to give true expression to it, etc. But in every human soul there is a ray of celestial beauty (Plotinus admits that), and a spark of genius (nobody admits that)."

As for the music, it was evidently not sent us for review, and to review it would be an impertinence, as much of an impertinence as to criticize a letter written by one man to another man neither of which is us. But some of Ives' comments and stage directions are amusing: "a weak cheer,"—"men with high liquid notes, and lady sopranos may sing an octave higher than written,"—"bright and doleful,"—"not sung by Caruso, Jenny Lind, John McCormack, Harry Lauder, George Chappell or the Village Nightingale,"—"which is worse? the music or the words?"—"the voice part of this aria may be omitted,"—"we are all sorry for Harpalus, notwithstanding the music,"—"the notes are indicated only approximately; the time, of course, is the main point," etc., etc.

Ives sets everything to music, and comments musically upon everything: politics, philosophy, American music, the opera, the war, everything—and uses many musical quotations, all carefully noted as to their source. Many of the poems he has written himself, and they indicate many influences, chiefly the New England philosophers and Walt Whitman.

Only two pertinent observations occur to us. The first is that to print such a book costs a lot of money and is out of the reach of most of us; the second is that only few people, scarcely any amateurs, possess sufficient piano technic to play these compositions, and so the message must, in many cases, remain unread.

Perhaps old fashioned "practical" methods are best after all.

Musical Courier 85, no. 12 (21 September 1922): 20

• • •

Second Violin Sonata premiere,
18 March 1924

In the 1920s, several Ives works were premiered in concerts devoted to modern music, of which this recital of violin sonatas was the first. The *Herald Tribune* review shows distinctly varying reactions to each of the three sonatas, while Winthrop Tryon in *The Christian Science Monitor* discusses only the Ives sonata in his review of this concert, part of an omnibus review of the week's performances.

Goldstein Completes "Modernist" Recital at Aeolian Hall:
Violinist's Interpretation of Pizzetti's Sonata Pleases
Audience for Its Avoidance of the Bizarre
from the *New York Herald Tribune*

Another demonstration of the ways of the piano and violin sonata was offered yesterday morning at Aeolian Hall by Jerome Goldstein, who, with Rex Tillson co-operating at the piano, concluded his series of "Modernist" recitals from Darius Milhaud, Charles E. Ives and Ildebrando Pizzetti.[8] The laurels of the occasion seemed to belong to Pizzetti.

With the repertoire of the Carnegie, Aeolian or Town Hall violin-recitals not particularly eager to stray beyond a somewhat limited circle of standard works, Mr. Goldstein's three recitals have served a useful purpose in showing what lies outside it, although the prospect of the transfer of Milhaud's second sonata to the superactive list did not seem, judging by yesterday's performance, one to be regarded with enthusiasm. The work seemed uneven, and in the last two movements there were periods of melody parted by others of ultra-modernism for its own sake. In the third movement there was long harping on a few notes of tenuous thinness. The finale, however, had a lively, pleasant tune as its main theme. These latter movements were well described in Mr. Goldstein's prefatory words as "obvious."

An American work followed, the second sonata of Charles E. Ives, which was written about fifteen years ago, but played from manuscript yesterday. With movements entitled "Autumn," "In the Barn" and "Revival" it was, to a considerable extent, program music, of what might be called an advanced French post-romantic type, but with a certain American flavor. It was described by the violinist as embodying the transcendental idea of the Concord group, but "shot through with modern ideas."

The most significant sonata, however, of the three was the Pizzetti sonata, in A, dated 1919, a notable example of modernism in the sonata form. Undeniably of this decade, it avoided the bizarre; there was ample musical material in its thematic ideas, and while it did not aim for sweetness it did not shudder at melody.

New York Herald Tribune, 19 March 1924, p. 15

"Freischütz" at the Metropolitan—
Other Music of a New York Week
Winthrop P. Tryon
from the *Christian Science Monitor*

A Business Man Who Composes

Charles E. Ives was represented on the program of a sonata recital which Jerome Goldstein, violinist, and Rex Tillson, pianist, gave at Æolian Hall on the morning of March 18. Mr. Ives, I should know from his music, is an American. He is, I have more specifically been told since the concert, a New Yorker, and a down-town New Yorker, too. He is a man of business who composes. None of your garret artists, then, who labor in the cold and among the cobwebs. He is one of those who write comfortably in a library, with flowers, if they wish, in a vase on the table.

Music, it is sometimes said, should spring from the soil; but I do not know why the pavement is not as much a part of the soil as the pasture, nor why a person should not meditate sonatas as appropriately in a Wall Street office as in a New Hampshire kitchen. And yet, Mr. Ives, man of the city though he may be, bestows, in the work which Messrs. Goldstein and Tillson performed, his attention upon country scenes. What is more interesting still, being a man of modern business views, he turns his thoughts in the piece in question not only fieldward, but to the past. In fine, he describes rural American 70 years ago. He puts, if I err not in my discernment, some of the ideas into notes that Henry D. Thoreau, in his journals of the fifties, struggled with and would, I believe, have expressed in terms of instrumental scoring, if the technique had been his to do it.

Mr. Ives' work would not, indeed, remind anyone of the out-of-door sounds that Thoreau heard and described in detail, so much as of the social sounds of the village, which he often pretended to ignore, but which he really pondered deeply. The composition is a sonata for violin and piano, the designations of its three movements being "Autumn," "In the Barn" and "The Revival." To attempt to describe it, movement by movement, would necessarily mean to be superficial; and I will only observe that the several divisions seemed to me to be built largely out of New England ballad and sacred tune material, some serious, others trivial, and all characteristic of the period under contemplation.

Christian Science Monitor, 24 March 1924, p. 10
(Excerpt)

• • •

Three Quarter-Tone Pieces premiere, 14 February 1925

Ives's contacts with E. Robert Schmitz, head of the Franco-American Musical Society (later the Pro-Musica Society) led to performances of his experimental *Quarter-Tone Pieces* and two movements from his Fourth Symphony on concerts of modern music. The second movement of the symphony was subsequently published as an installment of *New Music,* a quarterly consisting of new musical scores without commentary. It was easily the most complex score ever printed.

Franco-American Musical Society
Olin Downes
from *The New York Times*

The program given by the Franco-American Musical Society last night in Aeolian Hall was the occasion, as an advance notice put it, of "the world-premiere to the public of quarter-tone compositions for two pianos," by Charles St. Ives [sic] and Hans Barth.[9] These works were played by Hans Barth and Sigmund Klein. The quarter-tone pianos were apparently two pianos tuned a quarter of a tone apart in pitch. Robert Schmitz, mentioning two European composers who had made special studies of the quarter in composition, cited Ferruccio Busoni, "an Italian musician educated in Germany," and Alois Haba, "a German musician educated in Germany." Our impression was that Haba was a Czech and that, while he had studied in Germany with Schrecker, much of his education had been received in Prague. At any rate, he played for us quarter-tone compositions of his own on a piano he had perfected last Summer in Prague, and these compositions had a quality far more native to small divisions of tones than those heard last night.

The music heard last night impressed us in all three cases as having been thought in the customary tonal and semi-tonal medium. The result was simply that the music sounded a good deal out of tune. At a first hearing it had little interest, whereas Haba's music, while remindful somewhat of the music of Ceasar Franck, gave the listener the impression of musical conceptions which sought finer and more flexible tonal divisions than those in use in the Western Hemisphere. And Franck would probably have rejoiced in such subdivisions.

The New York Times, 15 February 1925, p. 26
(First half of review)

• • •

Fourth Symphony,
first and second movements premiere,
29 January 1927

Music: Pro-Musica Society
Olin Downes
from *The New York Times*

The "international referendum concert," given by the Pro-Musica Society yesterday afternoon in Town Hall, offered a program that consisted wholly of works new in America or played for the first time anywhere.[10] To this latter class belonged the "Symphony for Orchestra and Pianos," by Charles Ives; to the former Debussy's incidental music written for an Odéon performance of Shakespeare's "King Lear" in 1904, and Darius Milhaud's "chamber opera," "Les Malheurs d'Orphée." This work was conducted by Mr. Milhaud in person. The other conductor was Eugene Goossens.

At the risk of appearing provincial, chauvinistic, this writer records that his preference among the new works of the afternoon was for the music of Mr. Ives.[11] This music is not nearly as compact, as finished in workmanship, as smart in tone, as that of Mr. Milhaud, but it rings truer, it seems to have something more genuine behind it. There are inepititudes, incongruities. The thing is an extraordinary hodge-podge, but something that lives and that vibrates with conviction is there. It is not possible to laugh this piece out of countenance.

Mr. Ives began his symphony in 1910 and completed it about ten years ago. The symphony has four movements, a prelude, a fugue, a third movement in a comedy vein and a finale, according to the program notes of Henry Bellamann, "of transcendental spiritual content." The prelude and the lively movement were the ones heard yesterday.[12] The esthetic program of the "symphony" is less explicable than the music—"the searching questions of What? and Why? which the spirit asks of life." The prelude, apparently, is supposed to propound these questions and the latter three movements to supply diverse answers. Be all this as it may, the principal characteristic of the prelude is a New England hymn sung in full harmony by mixed voices, with orchestral commentary of a nature rather groping and incongruous with the choral material.

There is the thought of a New England Sabbath—Mr. Ives is a New Englander—when the soul turns in upon itself and questions the infinite. Then, the fugue being omitted, comes the "lively movement," a kind of insane scherzo, in which Mr. Ives thinks of "comedy," but "comedy in the sense that Hawthorne's Celestial Railroad is comedy. Indeed, this work of Hawthorne's may be considered as a sort of incidental program in which an easy, exciting and worldly progress through life is contrasted with the trials of the Pilgrims in their journey through the swamp."

Pilgrim hymns are heard, but are "crowded out" by noisy and restless music.

"The dream, or fantasy, ends with an interruption of reality—the Fourth of July in Concord—brass bands, drum corps, &c. Here are old popular tunes, war songs, and the like." There is a big orchestra in this movement, and a dozen irregular and conflicting rhythms. The program speaks of the blend of cross rhythms, of long and short rhythmic curves, rhythmic clashes, "rhythmic planes"—a basic rhythm marked by gongs and deeper metallic figures; above that drums of various kinds; above these wood and brass used "rather as percussion," and the solo piano in the rôle of leader. There is much more explanation of Mr. Ives's music in the program, but the music is more illuminating.

There is something in this music: real vitality, real naivete and a superb self respect. The lachrymose hymn, reappearing in the fast movement, is jostled out of existence for periods, only to bob up here and there, as homely and persistent as Ned McCobb's daughter. And then Mr. Ives looses his rhythms. There is no apology about this, but a "gumption," as the New Englander would say, not derived from some "Sacre du printemps," or from anything but the conviction of a composer who has not the slightest idea of self-ridicule and who dares to jump with feet and hands and a reckless somersault or two on his way to his destination.

And the picture of the Concord Fourth of July is really amusing, really evocative of the spirit of that time and day. Those were not safe and sane Fourths; they were Fourths that some survived, when patriotism was more than jingoism, and a stirring thought; when the nation was in its childhood and firecrackers took off the ear or put out an eye.

The scrabble of war songs and brass band tunes that all the villages knew, the noise of the circus, the blare of the band, are in this eccentric symphony, with its holier-than-thou hymn tunes, its commotion, its rowdiness, blaze and blare. There is "kick" in the piece, regardless of the composer's philosophic or moral purpose, his scheme of rhythms, and all the rest. It is genuine, if it is not a masterpiece, and that is the important thing.

New York Times, 30 January 1927, sec. 1, p. 28
(First half of review)

Music: A New Opera, a New Symphony, and a New Debussy Fragment
Lawrence Gilman
in the *New York Herald Tribune*

Of the two movements from Mr. Ives's Symphony we must say that we wished we might have heard the two other movements that were omitted. Mr. Bellamann, in his admirable program notes, tells us that Mr. Ives was employing what are now known as typically "modernistic" devices a good many years ago; and this is easy to believe, for his writing in this symphony has a sureness of touch which is not that of a neophyte learning an unfamiliar technique.

Mr. Ives is an American, and his symphony is the musical testament of a New Englander; but in this instance he has no need to ask us (in the biting phrase of Philip Hale) to "cover mediocrity with a cloak of patriotism." This music is as indubitably American in impulse and spiritual texture as the prose of Jonathan Edwards; and, like the writing of that true artist and true mystic, it has at times an irresistible veracity and strength, an uncorrupted sincerity.

This symphony of Mr. Ives is evidently built upon a far-reaching spiritual plan. It has, as Emerson said of Whitman, a long foreground. We repeat that we should like to hear the entire score.

New York Herald Tribune, 31 January 1927, p. 11
(Excerpt)

• • •

Fourth Symphony,
second movement publication, 1929

Recent Publications: New Music, January, 1929
from the *Musical Courier*

New Music, January, 1929—The January edition of New Music, a quarterly of modern composition, published in San Francisco by Henry F. Cowell, has just appeared. This magazine, as has already been recorded in earlier reviews, contains no reading matter, its offering being confined exclusively to musical scores of the ultramodern type. The present issue contains the Fourth Symphony of Charles E. Ives, or at least, although it is so stated on the cover, as a matter of fact it appears that this issue contains only the second movement of this symphony. The symphony actually consists of four movements, of which the prelude and this movement were performed in New York in 1927 by Pro Musica, under the leadership of Eugene Goossens. This movement is scored for full orchestra, solo piano and orchestra piano played by four hands. It is said that Charles E. Ives was born in Danbury, Conn., and comes from old American ancestry. Therefore it might be assumed that his music would, in some slight way, reflect

Americanism, but the present reviewer, who is also of American birth and of very old American ancestry, is unable to perceive any sign in this music of an expression of what he feels to be Americanism. This does not mean that the reviewer is right and that Ives is wrong, or that Ives is right and the reviewer wrong, since at present no one is able to define Americanism, or to suggest what its expression in music might be. The reviewer does not pretend to be able to read this score and to form any mental picture of its sound, but his memory of it from the Pro Musica performance is that it was just simply awful, from beginning to end.

Musical Courier 98, no. 10 (7 March 1929): 46

New Music
T. Carl Whitmer
from *The Musical Forecast*

[Reviewed for The Musical Forecast by one of "the moderns" of Pittsburgh.][13]

The latest product of their musical courage from the Far West is the publication by the quarterly called New Music (San Francisco), of Charles Ives' new work for orchestra, a movement from his Fourth Symphony. Mr. Ives has a home in New York City and another in Redding, Conn., showing that he is a business man; but, with an inextinguishable ardor for creative work. He is a careful, slow worker, never courting fame by quick and sure-fire methods beloved of the superficial. He is exacting to the nth degree in self-criticism.

This score is, in his own words, "not so much a scherzo as a comedy in which the easy and worldly progress through life is contrasted with the trials of the Pilgrims in their journey through swamp and rough country. The occasional slow episodes—Pilgrims' hymns—are constantly crowded out and overshadowed by the former. The fantasy ends with an interruption of reality with the Fourth of July in Concord. So there are brass bands, drum corps, etc." The and-so-forth is likely what the casual hearer will get at first hearing. But, listen intently and you will find one of the most stirring, stunning pieces of rhythmic polyphony in contemporary music. Technically, the involved combination of effects shows a marvel of inner hearing, to say nothing of adroitness of management. Ives has cast aside, as altogether unworthy, all prettiness of effects and gets down to the bottom of elemental man—of you with your social superficial self lifted away. You are now primitive in force and not sophisticated. This innerness plus machinery of the man-from-Mars makes great music. Here and there sophisticated technique elbows the roughest themes and frenetically expressed emotions bump a finesse of taste and silken hair-splitting effects. Glissandos in double basses and cellos slide down, giving you the effect of dropping elevators plunging you down to Gehenna. And all so logically—if this can be said to apply to the sub-emotional depths. Rarely have I seen a modern piece which is so mental and fundamental. Of course, it takes quite all the usual strings and wood wind and brass plus celesta and triangle and high bells and low bells and tympani and Indian drum and snare and bass drums and cymbals and gongs. Add to this a solo piano and then an orchestra piano with two players who need both skill and punch. Indeed, all the players who do Ives' work ought to take a lesson from his way.

The day this symphony was rehearsed for its production two years ago was a strenuous one for the players. Ives took one up to an upper room to clear the atmosphere of its cocktailish rhythms. The score looks as if chickenpox had struck it. The gooseflesh may stick out from your experiences. But, this would soon pass and with an orchestra that knows its work, a conductor that can feel the essential soul of it, the apparently limitless "musical gases" that escape would do their work and you would say with me that if we were to mention six fine new works, this would be one of them.

The Musical Forecast (March 1929): 5–6

• • •

Three Places in New England
Boston premiere, 25 January 1931

In 1929, Nicolas Slonimsky solicited an Ives score for his Chamber Orchestra of Boston, and Ives rescored his orchestral set *Three Places in New England* for that ensemble. It was premiered at Town Hall in New York on 10 January 1931, but was apparently not reviewed. Slonimsky's group gave the first Boston performance two weeks later, which was reviewed in several papers, most generously in the *Boston Herald*.[14] Later that year Slonimsky conducted the piece in Havana and ultimately in Paris as part of a concert of

American modernist music, giving Ives his first performances in Latin America and Europe. The French reviewers
were not entirely convinced by the Americans, tending to
find them derivative of European modernists, but several
singled out Ives and Varèse for praise.[15]

Music: Chamber Orchestra of Boston
Stephen Somervel
in *The Boston Herald*

Charles Ives, whose "Three Places in New England" Mr. Slonimsky's
program notes describe as "transcendental geography by a strange
Yankee genius," is certainly a strange and interesting composer,
though it would be rash to say, with no better foundation than a
single hearing, that he is or is not a genius. This work, sketched in
1903–1908, and written in 1914, is modern in the exact manner of
those painters whose canvases—so redolent of this chaotic age—are a
patchwork of jagged fragments overlapping, dovetailing, with an
added complexity which painting cannot rival, namely that of a
bewilderingly crowded simultaneity, an extraordinary contrapuntal
freedom. This is especially true of the second of the pieces, in which
the American village band is not so much parodied as portrayed in a
jumble of fragments and splinters of popular band tunes, dancing in
an all-pervading cacophony that somehow does not seem meaning-
less. In the first of the pieces, inspired by the Boston Common
memorial to Col. Shaw and his colored regiment, the obscure and
brooding suggestion of Negro tunes is mournfully punctuated by a
muffled drum-beat.

Boston Herald, 26 January 1931, p. 12
(Excerpt)

• • •

Three Places in New England
Paris premiere, 6 June 1931

M. Slonimsky a dirigé tout un programme de musique américaine
[Mr. Slonimsky Conducts an All–American Program]
Paul Le Flem
from *Comoedia* (Paris)

M. Slonimsky, directeur du Chamber Orchestra of Boston, a dirigé, samedi, un premier concert d'orchestre. Il lui eût été aisé de suivre, selon l'usage, la loi du moindre effort et d'offrir un lot d'ouvrages connus, échappant à toute censure et universellement admirés. Rompant avec la routine, il a composé un programme avec des partitions dont nous ne connaissions pas la première note, et s'est imposé un travail ingrat et pénible de répétitions qui n'aura pas de demain. Au succès honnête, assuré à quiconque se tient sur une route tracée, il a préféré se lancer dans l'aventure de la partition inconnue.

Venant d'Amérique, M. Slonimsky a eu l'idée d'emporter avec lui pour nous les présenter, quelques partitions transocéaniques. Chercheur par tempérament, il ne retient de l'école américaine contemporaine que les compositeurs inscrits aux partis avancés, ayant fourni des preuves de leur humeur combative et de leur désir de régénérer un art suspect de passéisme. Les noms qu'il choisit sont ceux de Adolph Weiss, Charles Ives, Car [Carl] Ruggles, Henry Cowell, Amadeo Roldan, ce dernier, Cubain d'origine, se séparant assez nettement par ses tendances de ses co-listiers de soirée.

Les quatre premiers compositeurs se réclament des plus récentes et des plus troublantes acquisitions de la musique d'aujourd'hui. Ils vivent dans cet[te] atmosphère comme dans leur élément naturel. Synthèses d'accords, polyapthmie [polyrythmie], contrepoint se pénétrant les uns les autres, sonorités d'orchestre crues dédaignant, en général, la demi-teinte, tels sont les traits qui leur sont communs. Mais l'un d'eux, Charles Ives, semble s'être créé, avant le Sacre du Printemps, *un style qui par ses audaces, situe leur auteur parmi les précurseurs. Il apparait, auprès de ses compatriotes, comme le musicien le plus spontanément doué dont les hardiesses truculentes, parfois gauches, ne se mettent pas en contradiction avec les aspirations de sa sensibilité. . . .*

Charles Ives présente Trois coins de la nouvelle Angleterre, *d'un tour humoristique dont on aime la franchise parfois un peu lourde. Il est aussi savant que ses voisins et manie la polytonalité sans qu'elle lui explose entre les doigts. Mais il sait ajouter à sa science quelque chose de sensible, de frais et de vivant qui n'est pas un déchet de cornue. Il y a une infinie douceur dans le pre-*

mier morceau dont la détresse calme émerge d'un fond harmonique sans bar-barie. La marche de village, *dont le rythme se décale curieusement au prof-it d'une croche retardataire, s'anime avec vigueur, et ne redoute pas la vulgar-ité canaille d'un tour de valse de circonstance. Quant au dernier morceau dont, au début, les divisions polytonales de violons en sourdine laissent le passage libre à un thème d'une adorable fraicheur, évocateur de larges espaces, il ne tarde pas à enrichir ses sonorités. Puis, une saute d'humeur, et tout ce vacarme plonge brusquement dans un pianissimo final et bref.*

Mr. Slonimsky, director of the Chamber Orchestra of Boston, con-ducted a first orchestral concert on Saturday. It would have been easy for him to follow custom and the law of minimum effort and offer a set of well-known works that are beyond censure and universally admired. Breaking with routine, he assembled a program of scores of which we knew not the first note, and took upon himself the ungrate-ful and exhausting task of endless rehearsals. Instead of the respectable success assured to those who stick to the well trodden path, he preferred to throw himself into the adventure of the unknown score.

Coming from America, Mr. Slonimsky had the idea of bringing with him some trans-Atlantic scores to present to us. An explorer by temperament, he chose from the contemporary American school only the most advanced composers, those who have proved their fighting spirit and their desire to regenerate an art that has been preoccupied with the past. The names he chose were Adolph Weiss, Charles Ives, Carl Ruggles, Henry Cowell, and Amadeo Roldan; the last, of Cuban origin, parted rather distinctly in his stylistic tendencies from the other composers of the evening.

The first four composers make use of the most recent and most disturbing innovations in the music of today. They live in that atmos-phere as in their natural element. Interpenetrating syntheses of chords, polyrhythm, and counterpoint, raw orchestral sonorities that for the most part scorn shading—these are the traits they have in com-mon. But one among them, Charles Ives, seems to have created for himself, before the *Rite of Spring*, a style whose audacities place its author among the pioneers. Compared to his compatriots, he appears to be the most spontaneously gifted musician, whose savage daring, though sometimes awkward, is never in contradiction with the aspira-tions of his feeling. . . .

Charles Ives's *Three Places in New England* is by turns humorous, with an amiable sincerity, and at other times a little heavy. He is as knowledgeable as his colleagues and manipulates polytonality without letting it blow up in his hands. But he knows how to add to his craft something sensitive, fresh, and alive which is not a mere extravagance. There is an infinite sweetness in the first movement, in which a quiet distress emerges from a tranquil harmonic background. *The Village March* [*Putnam's Camp*], whose rhythm is curiously displaced due to a late eighth-note, builds up energy and does not eschew the common vulgarity of a popular waltz. As for the last movement, at the opening the polytonal divisions of the muted violins leave room for a theme of adorable freshness, evoking large spaces, but he does not delay in enriching his sonorities. Then there is a change of mood and all of the cacophony suddenly dives into a final and brief pianissimo.

Comoedia (Paris), 8 June 1931, pp. 1–2
(Excerpts)

Les Concerts
Florent Schmitt
from *Le Temps*

En deux séances, à la salle Gaveau, M. Nicolas Slonimsky, directeur du Chamber orchestra *de Boston, nous donne un aperçu de la production actuelle américaine, cubaine et mexicaine. Il m'est difficile de parler en détail, après une audition rapide et pas absolument au point, de onze oeuvres d'une complexité extrême et qui, si elles ne se ressemblent pas toutes, offrent cependant entre elles plus d'un trait d'analogie. Il est peu vraisemblable d'ailleurs que, si Strawinsky n'eût inventé* Le Sacre du printemps, *ou Schoenberg le* Pierrot lunaire, *la plupart de ces oeuvres aient jamais vu le jour. On retarde un peu au Nouveau-Monde.*

Notons cependant, à travers ces débauches de polytonalité, et d'une polyrythmie à laquelle une percussion luxuriante ajoute l'appoint de sonorités inédites, bizarres et parfois indiscrètes, certaines oeuvres qui relèvent, sinon d'un tempérament essentiellement original, du moins d'une expérience et d'un savoir réels. Ainsi des Trois coins de la Nouvelle-Angleterre, *avec ce sous-titre sans fausse modestie:* Géographie transcendantale par un Yankee *d'un génie étrange et dense, de M.* Charles Ives, *un musicien très érudit doublé d'un philosophe, et que je connaissais déjà par sa* Second pianoforte sonata *où il célèbre à sa manière, qui est la manière forte, les écrivains Emerson, Hawt[h]orne et Thoreau.*

In two performances at the Salle Gaveau, Mr. Nicolas Slonimsky, director of the Chamber Orchestra of Boston, gave us a sampling of current American, Cuban, and Mexican musical composition. It is difficult for me to speak in detail, after a quick and probably imperfect hearing, about eleven works of extreme complexity which, if they are not all alike, nonetheless share a family resemblance. It is unlikely, if Stravinsky had not composed the *Rite of Spring*, or Schoenberg *Pierrot Lunaire*, that most of these works would ever have seen the light of day. The New World is a little behind.

Yet we note, through the debauchery of polytonality and polyrhythm to which a luxuriant percussion adds sounds that are novel, bizarre, and sometimes indiscreet, certain works that offer, if not an essentially original temperament, at least an authentic experience and a true understanding. Thus *Three Places in New England*, with a subtitle that has no false modesty: "Transcendental geography by a Yankee of a strange and complex genius." It was composed by Mr. Charles Ives, a very erudite musician who doubles as a philosopher and whom I know already for his *Second Pianoforte Sonata*, in which he celebrates in his strong style the writers Emerson, Hawthorne, and Thoreau.

Le Temps, 20 June 1931
(Excerpt)

La vie musicale à Paris [Musical life in Paris]
Boris de Schloezer
from *Les Beaux-arts*

*Parmi les Américains du Nord, il y a lieu de mettre à part Charles Ives: celui-là n'est plus jeune: les premières esquisses de la partition que nous avons entendue—*Trois coins de la Nouvelle Angleterre*—datent de 1903, et montrent en Ives un véritable précurseur, un talent audacieux, qui manque de connaissances technique et d'habileté, mais qui en allant tout droit son chemin, en travaillant absolument seul—car on assure que, vivant à la campagne en solitaire, il n'a jamais entendu une note de Stravinsky—a découvert nombre des procédés rythmiques et harmoniques aujourd'hui en vogue. Chez lui cependant, en dépit de ses gaucheries, ou plutôt à cause même de ses gaucheries, ce modernisme acquiert une saveur toute particulière.*

Among the North Americans, it is worth singling out Charles Ives. He is no longer young. The first sketches of the score that we heard—*Three Places in New England*—date from 1903 and show Ives as a true precursor, an audacious talent, who may lack technique

and skill but who, sticking to his way and working absolutely alone—
because we are sure that, living alone in the country, he never heard
a note of Stravinsky—discovered a number of rhythmic and harmonic processes in vogue today. In his music, in spite of his awk-
wardness, or rather because of it, modernism acquired a remarkably
individual flavor.

Les Beaux-arts (Brussels), 26 June 1931, p. 1
(Excerpt)

American Compositions in Paris: Works by Advance Guard of
Native Writers Introduced in French Capital at Season's End
Henry Prunières
from The New York Times

The presentation of American music has been the object of two symphony concerts directed by Nicholas [rightly, Nicolas] Slonimsky,
leader of the Boston Chamber Orchestra.[16] They revealed to Paris the
works of the advance guard of the young American and Antillean
schools, which are wholly unknown here, and, with the exception of
the compositions of Edgar Varese, a naturalized Franco-American,
little known, I believe, even in the United States.

I cannot say that these concerts had a very great success. The first
left a terrible impression of emptiness, which the second succeeded in
effacing only in part. If it be true that Charles Ives composed his
"Three New England Scenes" [Three Places in New England] before
acquaintance with Stravinsky's "Le Sacre du Printemps," he ought to
be recognized as an originator. There is no doubt that he knows his
Schönberg, yet gives the impression that he has not always assimilated the lessons of the Viennese master as well as he might have. The
second part, with its truculent parody of an American march in the
Sousa vein and the unloosing of its percussion achieves a picturesque
effect. The third part presents a typical American theme with pretty
orchestral effects. The composer is manifestly a musician.

New York Times, 12 July 1931, sec. 8, p. 6
(Excerpt)

• • •

Set for Theater or Chamber Orchestra premiere,
16 February 1932

In the 1930s, more of Ives's works were played in public for the first time. Several of them attracted attention in *Modern Music,* the organ of the League of Composers, including brief mention in articles by such prominent younger composers as Marc Blitzstein and Aaron Copland. Copland's long and searching review of *114 Songs* in 1934, a dozen years after its publication, may have been prompted by his participation as pianist in the 1932 Yaddo Festival performance of seven of the songs, which were subsequently reprinted as a group.

Premieres and Experiments—1932
Marc Blitzstein
from *Modern Music*

Charles Ives' *In the Night* [the third movement of the *Set for Theater Orchestra*] has a lovely texture of plangent sound, simply that, recalling the post-Impressionists and particularly Roussel (but considering when it was written, there can be no possibility of imitation or influence). Ives, except in works of this sort, seldom has sufficient craft. I feel a sketched rather than an achieved intention; this may be due to his almost deliberate dependence upon the spirit of minstrelsy. The result is highly theoretical.

Modern Music 9 (March 1932): 121–27
(Excerpt from p. 124)

• • •

Seven Songs premiere,
1 May 1932

Yaddo—A May Festival
Alfred H. Meyer
from *Modern Music*

It is to be hoped that the future may look back upon the First
Festival of Contemporary American Music, held at Yaddo, Saratoga
Springs, New York, April 30 and May 1 [1932], as an event of the
first water in the annals of music and that it may prove to be the first
of a notable series which should take its deserved place along with
the several famed and widely heralded European festivals. . . . .

Wider in scope were the seven songs of Charles Ives, revealing
imaginative power of the first order.[17] The melody is strikingly
unconventional and economical, with marvelously apt certainty of
expressive touch. The accompaniments often contain shrewdly
chosen bits of realistic suggestions,—as the sturdy rhythm of the dissonant chords in *Walking,* the exhilarating accelerando in *The Seer,*
the virtual piano solo during the recited portions of the cowboy
ballad *Charlie Rutlage.* I know of no finer example of a purely
musical humor, almost Rabelaisian in character, than that of the
burlesqued treatment of the "religioso" final verses of this ballad.
And with what touching sincerity and gentlest of impressionistic
accompaniments Ives got to the heart of the genuinely religious in
Whittier's lovely hymn, *Serenity.*

Modern Music 9 (May–June 1932): 172–76
(Excerpts from pp. 172 and 174)

• • •

Washington's Birthday performance, 1932

Experiment and Necessity—New York, 1932
Israel Citkowitz
in *Modern Music*

A similar confusion in its intention vitiated *Washington's Birthday* by Charles Ives. The first part, though over-long, had genuine poetry. The scramble of village bands [in the Barn Dance] achieved something definite in musical appeal. But the slow [final] section, trite and stupidly devotional, what was its function? It was too banal to have been meant as a serious expression; and if it was meant as a photographic specimen of the way some people feel on February 22nd, it certainly had no place in a musical work. I am not proposing a rigid purism as to what is "proper" conduct for the well-bred musical work. The satiric, the grotesque, the exotic, any element at all is free to enter into its composition. But one law stands over the dissociative effects of all these elements: they must be absorbed into and motivated by a continuous, self-sufficient musical fabric.

Modern Music 10 (January–February 1933): 110–14
(Excerpt from p. 112)

• • •

114 Songs
retrospective review, 1934

One Hundred and Fourteen Songs
Aaron Copland
from *Modern Music*

In 1922 Charles Ives issued a privately printed collection of one hundred and fourteen songs which he had composed over a period of thirty years. During the first ten years of its existence this unusual volume aroused little or not comment. But apparently this neglect was of only temporary significance, since it is no longer unusual to find the songs on an occasional program of contemporary music. To make them available to a larger public many have been reprinted; seven by the Cos Cob Press and thirty-five others (including some new ones) by *New Music*.

Besides these one hundred and fourteen songs—an achievement in sheer output of which any man might be proud—the original edition contains an essay, or more exactly a series of loosely connected paragraphs, in Ives' characteristically animated, though diffident, style. Here one comes upon several surprising statements. In the first place, we find Mr. Ives apologizing for having published the volume at all. His excuse is that by doing so "a few clear copies could be sent to friends." But later he gives a different reason; . . . "this volume," he says, "is now thrown, so to speak, at the music fraternity, who for this reason will feel free to dodge it on its way—perhaps to the waste basket." At any rate he assures us that from his own standpoint the publication of this stout book containing "plenty of songs which have not been and will not be asked for," is merely a kind of house-cleaning. "Various authors have various reasons for bringing out a book . . . Some have written a book for money; I have not. Some for fame; I have not. Some for love; I have not. Some for kindlings; I have not. I have not written a book for any of these reasons or for all of them together. In fact, gentle borrower, I have not written a book at all—I have merely cleaned house. All that is left is out on the clothes-line . . ."

Obviously Ives is a modest human being. But he carries modesty to an exaggerated degree, for after having apologized for presenting his fellow citizens with a unique volume of American songs he very nearly manages to apologize for being a composer in the first place— a composer, that is, in the usual sense of the term. While it is true that he did compose these songs, and admits having composed them, he wrote them only "on the side" as it were. Composing to him constitutes only one part of a busy life; as everyone knows, Mr. Ives is a successful man of business. But if we are to believe him, this does not make him different from other business men for, he says, "every normal man . . . has, in some degree, creative insight, and a . . . desire . . . to express it." This leads him to picture for us a time when every man will be encouraged to be his own Beethoven.

But Mr. Ives is not content to pause there. It is generally assumed among us that the composer who can dedicate his life to the single purpose of musical creation without distraction of any kind is a particularly fortunate creature. Ives has little sympathy for this attitude. He holds that to devote oneself to the business of life is serious, and to devote oneself to writing music while in business is serious, but to devote oneself solely to business of writing music is somehow not serious. It tends to impoverish the artist in the man, instead of developing a spiritual sturdiness—a "sturdiness which . . . shows itself in a close union between spiritual life and the ordinary business of life." As one remedy for bringing the merely "professional" composer back into actual contact with reality he suggests that "for every thousand dollar prize a potato field be substituted so that these candidates of Clio can dig a little in real life . . ."

It would serve little purpose to argue this last point with Mr. Ives. But the question which is of interest is this: why did Ives take so timid an attitude in presenting his songs to the public (since he is certainly not a timid soul either in his music or in his prose style) and why did he choose to glorify the businessman composer as opposed to the so-called professional composer? Let us put off attempting an answer for the moment and examine the songs instead, both for their own sake and for whatever light they may bring to bear on these two questions.

The first impression, on turning to the one hundred and fourteen songs themselves, is bound to be one of confusion. For there is no order here—either of chronology, style or quality. Almost every kind of song imaginable can be found—delicate lyrics, dramatic poems, sentimental ballads, German, French and Italian songs, war songs, songs of religious sentiment, street songs, humorous songs, hymn tunes, folk tunes, encore songs; songs adapted from orchestral scores, piano works, and violin sonatas; intimate songs, cowboy songs and mass songs. Songs of every character and description, songs bristling with dissonances, tone clusters and "elbow chords" next to songs of the most elementary harmonic simplicity. All thrown together helter-skelter, displaying an amazing variety and fecundity of imagination, but without the slightest key or guide for the benefit of the unsuspecting recipient of this original edition.

It is self evident then that this publication was not designed to give the musical public a clear conception of Ives' gifts as composer. In fact—and this seems to me to be crucial—Ives apparently not only had no public in mind when printing this book, but he hardly had even the "few friends" of whom he speaks in mind. The truth is he had only *himself* in mind. For after gathering together the fruits of thirty years' work (which, in effect, literally was a kind of "house-cleaning") Ives found himself alone with his songs.

No artist creates for himself alone. To be cut off from the vitalizing contact of an audience, to compose in a vacuum as it were, will of necessity profoundly influence the character of a man's work. Do these songs, then, examined individually show signs of just such an isolation?

To take the least representative group first: how otherwise can we explain the publication of songs which the composer himself says "have little or no value." He specifically names eight of these; at least fifteen more might easily be added to the list. Most of them were composed in the eighteen-nineties and belong to the sentimental, silver-threads-among-the-gold variety. To these may safely be joined about fifteen others, written about the same time, which, if they are not quite worthless are nevertheless hardly better or worse than hundreds of songs in the same genre by other composers. The songs to French and German texts belong in this group, closely patterned as they are, after foreign models. Nevertheless, here in the shadow of Schumann, Massenet and Brahms, one catches a first glimpse of the later Ives. A somewhat daring middle section, an unexpected close or sharply-tinted chord betray the future pioneer.

The first songs of importance date from around 1900. *Where the Eagle* is an excellent example of this group, which includes *Berceuse, I Travelled Among Unknown Men,* and *The Children's Hour.* It is only one page in length, but it is remarkable for its depth of feeling, its concision, its originality. Certainly no other American composer at the turn of the century was capable of producing a song of this worth. It is not that these songs are completely without influence (Hugo Wolf, in particular) but the emotional content is authentic; in the rich harmonies and sensuous line of the *Berceuse,* or in the charming flow and imagination of *The Children's Hour* one knows oneself to be in the presence of a real creator.

The historical significance of Ives as an innovator has been stressed in these pages.[18] Although the above-named songs are "modern" for their time, they are by no means revolutionary. But how else than revolutionary can one describe a song like *Walking* (dated 1902). In imitation of the village church bells heard on a Sunday morning walk, Ives essayed harmonies which are as daring, if not more so, as any Debussy and Strauss of the same period. This song plainly demonstrates the origin of much of Ives' venturesomeness; he is a musical realist, a copier of Nature. It is further illustrated in songs like *Rough Wind* (1902) and *The Cage* (1906). The latter, with its curious melodic line and its omission of bar lines, is obviously meant to suggest the turning about of an animal in its cage. It should be noted, however, that these songs are more successful as experiments than they are as finished artistic productions.

In so brief a summary, one can hardly do more than mention the songs composed around 1908–1910 (comparatively undistinguished), or those adapted by the composer from his orchestral and chamber music.[19] To judge these adaptations as songs would be unfair. However *The Housatonic at Stockbridge* (which originally was a movement in a set of pieces for orchestra) and *At the River* (from the *Fourth Violin Sonata*) are admirable arrangements of what in the first place must have been cherishable music and remains so in their new garb.

Ives, like no other serious American composer before him, was fascinated by the kind of music that any village band plays. The three "war songs" and the five "street songs" are attempts to incorporate popular material into a serious musical style. His method in several of these songs is to evoke the mood of the past at the beginning with the aid of rather complex harmonies and then to give the popular music in unadulterated form. This mixture of styles is not a happy one; it results in making them the least successful of those thus far considered.

But the works on which Ives' reputation as a song composer must eventually rest are the remaining forty or more which are dated 1919–21.[20] Taken as a whole, and despite many and serious shortcomings, these songs are a unique and memorable contribution to the art of song-writing in America, an art that is still in its first youth among us; a contribution which, for richness and depth of emotional content, for broad range and strength of expression, for harmonic and rhythmic originality, will remain a challenge and an inspiration to future generations of American composers.

Where else in American music will you find more sensitiveness or quietude than in a song like *Serenity*, with its subtle syncopations and its instinctive melodic line; where more delicate tone painting than the setting of lines from *Paradise Lost* called *Evening*; where a more rousing or amusing knockout of a song than *Charlie Rutlage* with its exciting cowboy quotations; where songs to compare with *The Indians*, or *Ann Street*, or *Maple Leaves* or *The See'r* or *The New River* (this last contains remarkable Hindemithian premonitions). There are others of course, almost as good, *The Swimmers, Two Little Flowers, Like a Sick Eagle, The Greatest Man* . . . All these are characterized by an essential simplicity—no matter how complex the harmonic or rhythmical materials may be, there is always a directness of emotional appeal and always an unadorned, almost naive, melodic line for the voice.

These qualities are present even in songs which are not successful as a whole. *Walt Whitman,* despite the unforgettably apt setting of the phrase, "How is it I extract strength from the beef I eat," remains an unsatisfying fragment, and the deeply moving last page of *Grantchester* does not compensate for the fact that the song as a whole is not sus tained. One could add other examples of songs which are mere fragments, or over-complicated in harmonic texture, or deficient in consistency of style.

Weaknesses, such as these and others—and it would be foolish to gloss them over—arise from a lack of that kind of self-criticism which only actual performance and public reaction can bring. This indispensable check on the artist Ives never had. A careful examination of these songs will convince the open-minded reader that he lacked neither the talent, nor the ability, nor the métier, nor the integrity of the true artist—but what he most shamefully and tragically lacked was an audience. "Why do you write so much — which no one ever sees?" his friends asked. And we can only echo "Why, indeed," and admire the courage and perseverance of the man and the artist.

Little wonder, then, if we find Ives over-timid in presenting the songs to the public for the first time; and little wonder if we find him rationalizing his position of business-man-composer until he made it appear to be the only natural role for the artist to assume in America. For Ives had every reason to be timid and to rationalize in a world which had no need for him as an artist.

This small drama which I have pictured here is by no means the drama of Ives alone, but in a larger sense is that of every American composer of serious pretensions. The problem of the audience—not a passive audience, but an active one—an audience which *demands* and *rejects* music—which acts as a stimulus and a brake, has never been solved. Not every composer deserves such an audience, of course. But for men of the stature of Ives that audience must be found, or American music will never be born.

Modern Music 11 (January–February 1934): 59–64

• • •

Washington's Birthday publication, 1937

Scores and Records
Aaron Copland
in *Modern Music*

Another score of interest is the first movement from Charles Ives' *Symphony of Holidays* (New Music Orchestra Series)—*Washington's Birthday,* composed in 1913. What unique things Ives was doing during that period! And what a shocking lack of interest to this very day on the part of our major symphonic organizations in this true pioneer musician. A score like his can best be judged from actual performance. What is most striking from a mere "reading" is the contrast between the "homely" program attached to the piece and the incredibly complex means for achieving it.

Modern Music 14 (May–June 1937): 230–33
(Excerpt from p. 232)

• • •

Concord Sonata premiere,
28 November 1938

The *Concord Sonata* is not only one of Ives's major works, it was the work that more than any other made Ives's reputation. The publication in 1920 was largely a failure. Even Henry Bellamann's mostly favorable review contributed to the piece's reputation as unplayable. John Kirkpatrick first saw the sonata in 1927 and gradually learned to play it, beginning with "The Alcotts," the third movement and the least difficult to play. He first performed "Emerson," the first movement, in public in 1935 and in late 1938 premiered the entire sonata in a private concert series at Cos Cob in Greenwich, Connecticut. Paul Rosenfeld was the only major critic in attendance, and his positive review in *Modern Music* helped to launch Ives as a major figure and the *Concord Sonata* as a major work.[21] Even more important was Kirkpatrick's New York premiere of the work on 20 January 1939 and the glowing review in the *New York Herald Tribune* by Lawrence Gilman, who called the work "the greatest music composed by an American." The excitement generated by that premiere and especially by Gilman's review led to a reprise performance of the sonata on 24 February at the first public concert devoted entirely to the music of Ives. In the reviews of that concert can be sensed the beginnings of a backlash, as the critic Oscar Thompson and the composer Elliott Carter expressed misgivings about Ives's craft.

• 313 •

Ives' Concord Sonata
Paul Rosenfeld
in *Modern Music*

The scene was The Old House, an ancient lamp-lit mansion near the post-road at Cos Cob [Connecticut]. There, before an intrigued, tense, somewhat puzzled little audience on November 28th, John Kirkpatrick gave what to all appearances was the first complete public performance of the work containing possibly the most intense and sensitive musical experience achieved by an American. It is *Concord, Mass., 1840–1860,* the second pianoforte sonata of Charles E. Ives.

Sonorities frequently unique in character and finely veiled, penetrating with a curious sensuous spirituality in which the secretive soul of Puritanism would seem again to have materialized itself, constitute much of its medium. The structure is Beethoven-like in breadth of conception and cyclic, oftentimes in the grand style, elevated in mood and pitch, stirring rhythmical, melodious with a subtlety not incomparable to that of Debussy or Schönberg; and one of those in which every note during entire pages is rhapsodically alive, tremulously expressive, fraught with special poetic emphasis and meaning.

The exploitation of a pair of melodic germs, one of them actually the tattoo of Beethoven's *Fifth Symphony,* the other a tender, wooing, chromatic little subject, furnishes the principal material of its four extended and complementary movements. They are a broad andante, a fantastically wild scherzo, a simple intermezzo and a slow quiet finale restrained in point of dynamic scale. Various new material, in instances of a folk-song-like character, including *Hail, Columbia!,* the hymn-tunes *Shall We Gather At The River* and a Scotch folk-melody, is texturally introduced into the three latter movements;[22] and the work, which is tonal in spots, polytonal in others and in still others perfectly atonal, is a subtle, sometimes a trifle coarsely but oftentimes exquisitely drawn web of these thematic and melodic wisps. The style in the opening movement is momentarily Lisztianly grand, frequently flighted and oracular, at times prophetically rapturous and wistful, at others almost paroxysmal with the excitements of the instants which untrammel the spirit. That of the scherzo is humorous in the syncopated passages which Kirkpatrick calls "proto-jazz" but prevalently spookish and dithering to a degree which makes the whole unbridled, extravagantly frolicsome section a supreme bit of spook-romanticism and more than any similar page in Reger the habitation of a *poltergeist.* It is in this scherzo too that Ives, who anticipated European polytonalism and polyrhythmicality in works earlier than this sonata (the date of its publication at least was 1920) surpasses Ornstein and well nigh out-Cowells Cowell in the bold use of tone-clusters, in instances containing as many as sixteen close-lying notes. However he takes pity on the performer and spares the piano incarnadining effusions of manual blood by prescribing the use in the performance of these chords of a strip of wood fourteen and three-quarter inches long and heavy enough to press the keys down without striking them. The ensuing softly blent sonorities are ghostly.

The contrasting diatonic intermezzo is a naive movement, almost sentimental but for the nobility of the style and completeness of the form. Actually it is an opposition and interplay of lofty and majestic and humble, homely sonorities: the *Fifth Symphony* material and the Scotch folk-tune. Then in the stilly mysterious finale with its slow almost monotonously swaying beat, the second cyclic theme, the wooingly chromatic one, attains its fullest development in singularly glamorous music. The subtle melodic invention and veiled elusive quality of tone are at their sublimest here, and the rhythm is profound. Twice the weighted, tremulous volumes surge gropingly upwards and forwards before culminating in the fluting peroration of the sonata. There might that night at Cos Cob have been some question of the perfect beauty, the fully realized intentions of the heroically initial movement. There was, indeed there could, be none of that of this finale. It seemed music as beautiful at the very least as any composed by an American.

It thrilled, it touched, again and again, the entire work; releasing something in the depths, restoring enchantment to them and to things. Some of the "vibrations of the universal lyre," of the earth itself, seemed in the music; and for more than one conscious member of its audience it brought the body to the state where Nature seemed to flow through it once more, and the whole of it was "one sense," and he felt "a strange liberty in Nature and a portion of herself." Thus it could be said that the work had transmitted its composer's experience, the comprehension of the forces and values of the Concord transcendentalist band. It was a nationalistic one, this experience; an American instance of the one vocal in all nationalist music: that of the individual at the stage when, possibly in consequence of some activation of his inmost self, he comprehends his relationship not only to the present life of his group, race or nation, but to its very past. Imaginatively he grasps the forces and the values of the individuals who existed on his soil before him, the forces and values of the group, race or nation incarnate in them; recognizing their survival in the best of himself and comprehending them with love. In the small book of

Essays Before A Sonata with which Ives, Shaw-like, prefaced *Concord, Mass., 1840–1860,* the composer mentions a moment of this mystical fellowship in which "Thoreau—that reassuring and true friend—stood by him one 'low' day when the sun had gone down, long, long before sunset": and *Thoreau* is the title of the sonata's concluding movement, and *Emerson, Hawthorne* and *The Alcotts* those of the other three. For just the frequency of states of sympathy with Nature when "the whole body is one sense," of conditions of "liberty in Nature" when man is a part of her and the self and all which limits it are divinely acceptable, and humblest clay "instinct with celestial fire" smites upon the infinite: precisely the frequency of these states was the essence of Concord an hundred years since, the genius of the prophetic Emerson, the fantastic Hawthorne, the homely earth-fast Alcotts, the deeply-earth-submissive hermit of Walden Pond, and is the source of the American and democratic idea. But in moving us towards the transcendentalists and their fount, the music moved us towards Ives himself. He seemed the "Hesper of their throng," a seer and surely one of the most exquisitely sentient of American artists.

Modern Music 16 (January–February 1939): 109–12

• • •

Concord Sonata
New York premiere, 20 January 1939

**Music: A Masterpiece of American Music
Heard Here for the First Time**
Lawrence Gilman
in *The New York Herald Tribune*

Piano recital by John Kirkpatrick, at Town Hall, Friday Evening, January 20.

PROGRAM
1. Sonata in C major, Op. 53   Beethoven
   I Allegro con brio
   II Introduzione, adagio molto
      Rondo, allegretto moderato—prestissimo
2. "Concord, Mass., 1840–'60"   Charles E. Ives
   (First complete performance in New York City)

Music by an unexampled creative artist of our day, probably the most original and extraordinary of American composers, yielded the outstanding experience of Mr. John Kirkpatrick's piano recital last evening at Town Hall.[23]

The music in question was written by Charles E. Ives, a New Englander, now dwelling in New York, whose name means nothing whatever to most music-lovers and musicians—although that fact is almost certainly of small interest to the individual in question. For Mr. Ives is one of those exceptional artists whose indifference to réclame is as genuine as it is fantastic and unbelievable.

•

Charles Ives is sixty-four years old, and for nearly half a century he has been experimenting with musical sounds, and writing them down on paper, working quietly and obscurely (as revolutionary spirits in the regions of the mind so often work), known only to a few inquisitive students and observers who at first suspected, and were afterward sure, that this astonishing artist is one of the pioneers of modern music, a great adventurer in the spiritual world, a poet, a visionary, a sage, and a seer.

•

The two distinguished composers who are sometimes said to have produced the best music written in America cannot be called Americans at all: they were born in Europe, and their music is about as "American" in quality as the Mediterranean or the Quai d'Orsay. But Charles Ives is as unchallengeably American as the Yale Fence, on which he must often have sat while he was a student at the University, whence he was graduated in 1898. He entered business in New York a little later, and for many years he was active as senior member of an insurance firm.

•

But during most of his six decades Ives has been thinking about music. His father was a musician and an experimentalist. Young Ives, as a child in Danbury, listened to the village band, or to the old village fiddler, or to the decrepit harmoniums that accompanied the singing in the church.

He was fascinated by the magic and mystery of acoustics, by problems involving pitch and quarter-tones,[24] by the native and basic elements of the genuine type of our American folk-music. Before he was twenty-five, he had begun those audacious experiments in the organization of sound and the development of scales and counterpoint and rhythms which, for those who have studied their outcome in his later works, make the typical utterances of Schönberg sound like Haydn sonatas. And we are to bear in mind that when Ives was evolving this incredible ultra-modernism of the American 'nineties, Schönberg, then in his early twenties, had not yet ventured even upon the adolescent Wagnerism of his "Verklärte Nacht"; and the youthful Stravinsky was playing marbles in Oranienbaum.

•

Since then, Ives has written much music—orchestral, choral, and chamber works; music for a quarter-tone piano; many songs. Some of this music has been played here and in Europe; and some of it has been published; but it remains virtually a terra incognita for all save the inquisitive and persistent.

Ives has been engrossed by the task of enriching and developing music as an instrument of expression. His music can speak of Æschylus and the Fourth of July, of Lincoln, and General Booth, and barn dances, and Emerson, and Boston Common, and Putnam's Camp, and the Housatonic at Stockbridge, and night and death and destiny. He is neither an exhibitionist nor a poseur nor a fashionable fakir. He is an artist, working slowly and in retirement, merciless in self-examination, indifferent to that publicity which for many of his slicker younger colleagues is the Earthly Paradise and the breath of life.

•

The unprecedented work that we heard last evening at Town Hall from the intrepid Mr. Kirkpatrick was written a year or two before the War. It is a sonata, entitled "Concord, Mass., 1840–1860." Its four movements bear four names: (1) "Emerson"; (2) "Hawthorne"; (3) "The Alcotts"; (4) "Thoreau."

This is an astonishing program indeed!—a glimpse of The Flowering of New England a quarter century before Van Wyck Brooks produced his celebrated masterpiece.

The composer himself has told us what he aimed to give us. In the "Emerson" movement he shows us "America's invader of the

• 318 •

unknown, an explorer of spiritual immensities. We see him standing on a summit, where many men do not care to climb, peering into the mysteries of life, contemplating the eternities, hurling back whatever he discovers there—now, thunderbolts for us to grasp, if we can; now placing quietly, even tenderly, in our hands things that we may see without effort—asking us to perceive that every ultimate fact is only the first of a new series."

·

The "Hawthorne" movement does not attempt to show us that aspect of Hawthorne's mind which was concerned with the relentlessness of guilt, the influence of sin upon conscience.

Ives has given us here what he calls "an extended fragment," music suggestive of Hawthorne's "wilder, fantastical adventures into the half-childlike, half-fairylike phantasmal realms. It may have something to do with the children's excitement on that 'frosty Berkshire morning, and the frosty imagery on the enchanted hall window,' or something to do with 'Feathertop,' the 'Scarecrow,' and his 'Looking Glass,' and the little demons dancing around his pipe bowl; or something to do with the old hymn tune that haunts the church and sings only to those in the churchyard, to protect them from secular noises, as when the circus parade comes down Main Street: or something to do with the concert at the Stamford camp meeting, or the 'Slave's Shuffle': or something else in the Wonderbook—not something that happens, but the way something happens; or something about the ghost of a man who never lived, or about something that never will happen, or something else that is not."

·

In the movement called "The Alcotts"—the briefest and most access-ible of the sonata—the composer evokes for us Concord Village itself, "which reminds one of that common virtue lying at the height and root of all the Concord divinities."

We walk down the broad-arched street, "passing the white house of Emerson—ascetic guard of a former prophetic beauty—and come presently beneath the old elms overspreading the Alcott house. . . Within the house, on every side, lie remembrances of what imagina-tion can do for the better amusement of fortunate children who have to do for themselves. . . And there sits the little old spinet piano which

Sophia Thoreau gave to the Alcott children, on which Beth played the old Scotch airs, and played at the Fifth Symphony" . . .

But this is not all that Mr. Ives gives us here; for much of this movement consists of a superbly beautiful and moving fantasia on the opening theme of Beethoven's symphony—the so-called "Fate" theme, which Mr. Ives has chosen to view rather as "the soul of humanity knocking at the door of the Mysteries, radiant in the hope that it will be opened."

•

If we must have a program for the Finale of the Sonata, the "Thoreau" movement, Mr. Ives suggests that we follow Thoreau's meditations on an autumn day of Indian summer at Walden—"a shadow of a thought at first, colored by the mist and haze over the pond. . . . He remains in this mood, and while outwardly still, he seems to move with the slow, almost monotonous, swaying beat of the autumnal day. . . . His meditations are interrupted only by the faint sound of the Concord bell—it is prayer-meeting night in the village. . . . 'At a distance over the woods the sound acquires a certain vibratory hum, as if the pine needles in the horizon were the strings of a harp which it swept.'

"It is an evening when the whole body is one sense; . . . and before ending his day, he looks out over the clear, crystalline water of the pond, and catches a glimpse of the shadow-thought that he saw in the morning's mist and haze. He knows that by his final submission, he possesses the 'Freedom of the Night.' He goes up the pleasant hillside of pines, hickories, and moonlight, to his cabin, 'with a strange liberty in Nature, a part of herself.'"

•

This sonata is exceptionally great music—it is, indeed, the greatest music composed by an American, and the most deeply and essentially American in impulse and implication. It is wide-ranging and capacious. It has passion, tenderness, humor, simplicity, homeliness. It has imaginative and spiritual vastness. It has wisdom and beauty and profoundity, and a sense of the encompassing terror and splendor of human life and human destiny—a sense of those mysteries that are both human and divine.

•

Certain pages of the sonata are of enamoring, subduing charm and sweetness—as in the "Alcott" movement. The Hawthorne movement is a Scherzo of unearthly power and intensity, transcending its subject. In the Thoreau movement, there is music of a poetic fervor and exaltation in which the essence of Thoreau's imagination is imagically captured and conveyed.

But it is the thought of Emerson that has drawn from Mr. Ives a quality of musical utterance which is altogether extraordinary and unique. Beginning at the section marked "Allegro—*pp*—quite fast," we have pages in which the expressional power of musical speech is mysteriously extended and released. This is wonderful writing, alembicated and otherworldly; music worthy of the great and mystical saying of Emerson himself: that the essence of all things "is not wisdom, or love, or beauty, . . . but all in one, and each entirely . . . so that a man is nourished by unfailing fountains . . . and when, for an instant, the air clears, and the cloud lifts a little, there are the gods still sitting on their thrones: they alone, with him alone."

•

It remains to be added that to Mr. John Kirkpatrick, who made this music known to us in its entirety, an immeasurable debt of gratitude is due. His own achievement as an artist was something not soon to be forgotten—a prodigious feat of memory and execution. The sonata is almost unplayable. Its difficulties are appalling. Mr. Kirkpatrick conquered them as though they did not exist. His performance was that of a poet and a master, an unobtrusive minister of genius.

New York Herald Tribune, 21 January 1939, p. 9

Pianist Plays Work By Ives:
John Kirkpatrick Gives Town Hall Recital
Irving Kolodin
in the *New York Sun*

It is one among the legends of contemporary American music that great merit reposes in the unplayed, and, for the most part, unpublished works of Charles E. Ives. He is the American born in Danbury some sixty-five years ago who enjoys, among the progressive wing of young American composers, the reputation of being their spiritual godfather, though his activities as a composer have long been subordinated to the insurance business. Thus the opportunity presented by John Kirkpatrick in Town Hall last night to hear Ives's second piano sonata, "Concord, Mass." was not to be passed by lightly.

In his voluminous program notes, Mr. Kirkpatrick acknowledged his inability to discover trace of any complete performance of the work in New York previously. Listening to his discourse of it was sufficient answer to the riddle of its neglect. It is long (not less than an hour in performance), aurally difficult, and textually complex. The work does not follow the conventional progression of piano sonatas, but seeks to portray the personality and works of Emerson, Hawthorne, the Alcotts and Thoreau (the transcendentalists of Concord) in its four movements. When the work was originally published, it was accompanied by a book of six essays, concerned with the music and its subject matter.

This is, in all, a formidable proposition in listening. Simply a page of this music is enough to impress the listener with Ives's musicality, the fervor of his desire to write music, the amazing perception which enabled him to anticipate, by a score of years, some of the most recent developments in writing here and abroad. Yet none of these things, as isolated phenomena, was equivalent to music. It was the reaction of this listener that Ives's single, most serious deficiency was a lack of discipline, an inability to distinguish between the gold and the dross that issued from his imagination. Certainly Mr. Kirkpatrick played the work with unsurpassable enthusiasm, with great facility and, if the external evidence was to be believed, complete comprehension. The other work of the evening was Beethoven's "Waldstein," played simply and energetically, but with some curious tempi.

New York Sun, 21 January 1939

American Music—Swing Drops In—Recitalists
Robert A. Simon
in *The New Yorker*

What was easily the most astonishing achievement of the week was John Kirkpatrick's performance of Charles E. Ives' second piano sonata. . . . Mr. Kirkpatrick handled it with no apparent effort, and lent to it an improvisatory manner that seemed exactly right for this music.

Mr. Ives has been more written about than performed, apparently. Mr. Kirkpatrick's presentation of the sonata was the first hearing that the composition, in its entirety, has had in town—and no wonder, because "Concord, Mass., 1840–60" is a large project for any pianist. If there is such a thing nowadays as original music, this is it, and its originality makes it hard to assimilate at a first hearing. Presumably, Mr. Ives' compositions won't appear so strange when one gets to listen to them frequently, and more performances seem to be in order.

The New Yorker 14, no. 50 (28 January 1939): 44–45
(Excerpt from p. 44)

Insurance Man
from *Time* magazine

Thirty-five years ago, before Stravinsky and the Viennese Atonalists had cut their modernistic teeth, a shy, bearded Yankee named Charles Ives was busy writing his own kind of modernist music. Nobody paid much attention to Composer Ives's strange, complicated scores. But little by little the few music-lovers who did hear them began to realize that Ives was neither a trickster nor a crackpot, but a writer of real, live music. Today Ives is regarded even by conservative critics as one of the most individual and authentically American of all U. S. composers. But performances of his music are still few & far between.

Last week Ives's *Second Pianoforte Sonata*, almost entirely neglected since he completed it in 1915, got its first Manhattan performance at a recital by enterprising U.S. Pianist John Kirkpatrick. Composer Ives's long-unheard work turned out to be a sort of musical equivalent to Author Van Wyck Brooks' *The Flowering of New England*. Subtitled *Concord, Mass., 1840–60*, it attempted to paint in music the surroundings and personalities of such famed New Englanders as Hawthorne, Emerson, Thoreau and the Alcotts. Most listeners found Composer Ives's complicated tone-portraits hard to grasp at one sitting. But respected New York *Herald Tribune* Pundit Lawrence Gilman unwrinkled his critical brow, crowed ecstatically: "Exceptionally great music . . . the greatest music composed by an American."

Many people who have never heard of 64-year-old Composer Ives know him as the crotchety, grizzled, retired partner of the conservative William Street insurance firm, Ives & Myrick. A practical Yankee, bristled-bearded Ives long ago decided that he couldn't make a living writing the kind of music he wanted to write. On his graduation from Yale in 1898 he served as a church organist, playing in Danbury, Conn., Bloomfield, N.J., and finally in Manhattan. Weekdays he plugged as a clerk for Mutual Life Insurance Co. Industrious and daring both as businessman and composer, Ives soon formed his own insurance managing agency, helped build it into one of the largest of its kind in the U.S. But Ives never let his business interfere with his composing. His evenings and holidays were spent, pen-in-hand, over an old desk, piling up a huge heap of manuscripts that were later to bring him fame.

Shrewd Charles Ives refuses to see anything strange about his unusual double life. Says he: "There can be nothing 'exclusive' about a substantial art. It comes directly out of the heart of experience of life and thinking about life and living life. My work in music helped my business and my work in business helped my music."

One reason for Composer Ives's long obscurity is his horror of publicity. Though he has lived and worked in the midst of Manhattan's hubbub, he has never taken any part in the city's musical life. He never goes to concerts, abhors evening dress, is mortally terrified of being photographed. He never reads daily newspapers, and no journalist has ever succeeded in interviewing him.

A philosopher as well as a composer and businessman, Ives often writes lengthy prefaces to his compositions. Each movement of his *Second Pianoforte Sonata* is preceded by a long essay in hard-bitten English. Of them he remarks in his dedication: "These prefatory essays were written by the composer for those who can't stand his music—and the music for those who can't stand his essays; to those who can't stand either, the whole is respectfully dedicated."

Time 33, no. 5 (30 January 1939): 44–45

Charles Ives at Last
Goddard Lieberson
in the *New Masses*

If American music has a Tom Mooney, it is Charles Ives, whose compositions have for many years been imprisoned in an obscurity which amounts to criminal neglect. Part of this obscurity has been due to the apathy of the "top" critics toward his works, which, in the past, they have invariably cast aside as incoherent or obtuse. There has been a total disregard of his music by soloists and orchestras—the fate of much of our American music—and consequently Ives has reached the age of sixty-four with less hearings than Sibelius receives in a single year. To those who know and champion his works (these are chiefly composers), Ives stands for an indigenous American music, virile and inventive. He broke through to paths upon which, many years later, Stravinsky and Schönberg set cautious feet. That the latter two were accepted in concert halls where Ives was not may be explained by the fact that they were more timorous in their excursions into dissonance; of course, too, they were Europeans and thus singularly attractive to the American bourgeois idea of that time that art was capable of flourishing only in Europe.

How, then, could one help but be surprised when John Kirkpatrick, American pianist, bravely programmed Ives' *Concord Sonata* for his Town Hall recital of January 20. His marked the first New York performance of the complete work, and though we are grateful to Mr. Kirkpatrick for his splendid performance, it is a shameful landmark, since this music was written before the World War—written, indeed, at a time when Debussy's whole-tone scales brought forth cries of horror from those who, with difficulty, had only recently adjusted to Wagner. Perhaps it would have been asking too much to expect those same people to recognize in Ives' *Concord Sonata* a new tonal speech, and an American one at that.

The four movements of the sonata are called (1) "Emerson," (2) "Hawthorne," (3) "The Alcotts," and (4) "Thoreau." Despite this titling, the music is not programmatic in the sense of Strauss' musical illustrations of bumptious burghers. Here, rather, is music which is deeply personal. It is filled with musical thought so vital that it can hardly wait to leave the brain, course through the hand, and get on to manuscript paper. Ideas are abundant, not only on each page, but in each measure. These ideas Ives puts into his music with such vigorous devices of harmony and rhythm as to startle and frighten the unimaginative and the decadent. He speaks in many languages, in refinements of tone quality, overtones, polyrhythms, atonality, metrical changes of a surprising nature, and complicated jazz rhythms. These are not mere devices, they are functional to the evolution of a single idea.

The musical expression of Ives began about 1895. It stopped only when ill health made it impossible to continue. Since then, Stravinsky and Schönberg have made reputations on the basis of a "new" and "dissonant" music. Meanwhile, unrecognized, an American composer has steadily and modestly created a standard which refutes the charges of all who persist in denying the existence of an important American music.

New Masses, 7 February 1939, p. 30.
(Lieberson signed this review with his pseudonym, John Sebastian)

• • •

Concord Sonata, Songs, and Fourth Symphony,
third movement, arranged for piano: all-Ives concert,
Town Hall, 24 February 1939

**Concert Devoted to Music by Ives: Performers Are
Minna Hager, Mezzo-Soprano, and John Kirkpatrick, Pianist;
"Concord" Sonata Played; Town Hall Audience Listens
Also to Group of Songs—House Is Crowded**
Olin Downes
from *The New York Times*

A concert of Charles Ives's music was given last night in Town Hall by
John Kirkpatrick, pianist, and Minna [rightly, Mina] Hager, mezzo-
soprano. The hall was packed. Literati and cognoscenti were present
in larger numbers than had been witnessed since the last Town Hall
concert of the League of Composers.

This knowing audience had turned out largely because of the special publicity which had followed Mr. Kirkpatrick's courageous introduction of Mr. Ives's "Concord" sonata in the same concert hall on
Jan. 20.

If snobbism was present it was not the fault of a ruggedly individual composer. Articles acclaiming the sonata itself and other articles recounting the strange and interesting career of the man of business and insurance who had been all his life creating highly modern
scores had prepared the public for a sensation. Therefore many people who would have passed by the "Concord" sonata before it had
received critical approval, without the flicker of an eyelash, were now
present, audibly and visually to be counted among those who really
understood and appreciated the singular music of Mr. Ives.

Written in Four Movements

And it is singular music, music of singular ingredients and a singular
point of view, music of a composer incorrigibly himself in his purpose
and feeling, if not invariably free from other musical influences, or
able fully to express visions which obsess him. Consider the
"Concord" sonata. The titles of this sonata, written between 1911 and

1915, in four movements, are "Emerson," "Hawthorne," "The Alcotts" and "Thoreau." The sonata is described by the composer as "an attempt to present one person's impression of the spirit of transcendentalism that is associated in the minds of many with Concord, Mass., of over half a century ago."

Emerson is here conceived as "America's deepest explorer of the spiritual immensities" and this movement introduces a version of the fate theme of Beethoven's Fifth Symphony—the theme not in minor but major, emblematic of "the Godliness of spiritual courage and helpfulness." The "translation of this motive places the motive above the relentlessness of fate knocking at the door" and "toward the spiritual message of Emerson's revelations." The motive haunts the first movement and reappears in other movements of the sonata, thus binding them together. It appears to gather force with repetitions and with various rhythmic or harmonic alterations.

"Hawthorne" is the Hawthorne of the "half child-like, half fairy-like phantasmal realms." This in fact is a fanciful scherzo of various moods. "Concord" [i.e., "The Alcotts"] is the picture of "spiritual sturdiness" lying at the root of that New England town with its arching elms. "Thoreau" is the Thoreau of the Indian Summers, the days and nights by Walden, the harp of the winds, the end of the day and the return of the "shadow-thought" that he dimly perceived in the morning mist; and Thoreau's "liberty in nature, a part of herself."

New England Hymn Influence

This is mood painting—transcendental moods, and sometimes common, sometimes "transcendental" figures of musical speech. The sonata is lengthy in the treatment and development of ideas, but it is not easy to be brief with so many thoughts, nor is it easy, on a first hearing of the sonata on the writer's part, to come to a definite conclusion about such music.

Some of its characteristics are evident. One very fine one is the influence of New England hymns and the tunes that the band played in the village square. The whole thing a creation spun out of a man's home memories and consciousness—not a fabric of tone to fit a model outside of himself. An American composer thus dares be himself.

The sonata is filled with interesting ideas. Its structural form will be clearer with later hearings. The stuff of a fearless man and artist is in it. Whether the expression is always felicitous, whether the work would gain by elisions and condensation is a question that also must wait. The

PART III: REVIEWS

passages which strike one the quickest are those when the musician's fancy lovingly lingers over the melodies of his childhood, and a homely and tender idea of his own wraps itself about the old tune, varies and transforms it according to the expressive need of the passage.

Two Groups of Songs

Something of the same origin of inspiration is encountered in the songs, of which there were two groups sung by Miss Hager, and of which a number, in response to applause that was enthusiastic throughout the evening, were repeated. The homelier the song, say we, on the average the better. "Autumn": the composer thinks of the Autumn, her work done, the empty fields, the declining sun, the Peace of God, and his melody is very close to a church chant. "Down East" brings irresistibly the memory of "Nearer, My God, to Thee," the Sunday morning, the chores done, the melodeon and the historic song.

Perhaps the best of all the songs is the dramatic, satirical, fanatical, pathetic setting of [Vachel] Lindsay's verse, "General William Booth Enters Heaven." With the songs of a lighter or more humorous character we are not so much struck. The humor is sometimes a little self-conscious and in some cases after patterns of other songs by well-known composers.

Yet none of the songs heard last night is complaisant or merely conventional. They represent a composer who thinks his own way and is not to be stirred from his course. As a consequence of this, he stands forth today an artist in his own rank and one to whom last night the public rendered homage.

New York Times, 25 February 1939, p. 18

Kirkpatrick Plays Program of Ives' Work: Pianist Repeats "Concord" Sonata; Group of Songs Offered by Mina Hager
Francis D. Perkins
in the *New York Herald Tribune*

As a logical sequel to his recital of five weeks ago at Town Hall, when he had played Charles Edward Ives's second piano sonata, "Concord, Mass., 1840–'60" for the first time in full before a New York audience, John Kirkpatrick gave a concert entirely devoted to the music of this unimitative and exceptional but relatively little known New England composer last night in the same auditorium before an audience of very good size and attentive disposition. The program, whose keystone was the "Concord" sonata, repeated in view of the extraordinary interest aroused by its earlier performance, began with Mr. Kirkpatrick's piano arrangement of the third movement of Mr. Ives's fourth symphony, which is a fugue on Lowell Mason's well-remembered hymn, "From Greenland's Icy Mountains." Mina Hager, mezzo-soprano, and Mr. Kirkpatrick performed seven songs in the second part of the concert, and closed the evening with seven more, ending with the setting of Vachel Lindsay's "General William Booth Enters Into Heaven."

Mr. Ives, now in his sixty-fifth year, has been composing for several decades, but, while known to some extent among those interested in American music as a creator of unusual imagination and originality, he has, it is said, concerned himself little about performances of his music in public. It may be questioned whether his works have appeared in as many as a dozen programs here in the last fifteen years. A few songs have had occasional hearings. The prelude and second movement of the fourth symphony were played in a Pro-Musica concert in January, 1927, and the third movement was heard orchestrally in a Federal Music Project concert under Bernard Herrmann last February.

Music Seems Indigenous

Yesterday's program as a whole impressed as the work of a musician who has marked out his own creative paths, developed his own individual style, and both in his choice of texts or inspirational subjects and in their expression in the music itself, written music that seems indigenously, pervasively American. The types of works in this list ranged widely, from the plangent harmonics that arrested the ear in the first and earliest of the songs, "Walking," and seemed of a much later date than 1902, to the simplicity of songs such as "Two Little Flowers," "Down East" or "Berceuse."

Many of the songs might better be styled poems or expressive pictures for voice and piano, owing to the co-ordinate importance of the instrumental part and its contribution to the underlying atmosphere of each work. In some, the vocal style was free lyric declamation, others gave an impression of unsophisticated melody; some were brief but vivid sketches and other[s], such as "General Booth," relatively extensive. Some unevenness of value could be noticed; the strong and characteristic feature of the songs as a whole was not so much the salience of their musical ideas, considered apart, as the remarkable and convincing faithfulness with which they realized the subject, atmosphere, local color and essential emotions of their texts. This vividness of atmosphere also pervaded the treatment of Mason's immortal hymn tune.

Wins Long Applause

The "Concord" sonata has already been discussed after its earlier performance. A first hearing gave a sense of a work which stands apart in instrumental American music, which impresses with its imagination and re-creation of atmosphere, but which calls for no little further acquaintance for complete realization. Not a few of its hearers must have found it baffling, but it was followed by a long and fervent demonstration. Mr. Kirkpatrick, expressing thanks, regretted that the composer could not be present. As before, the highest of praise was due to him for sensitive and admirable performance of the sonata, and Miss Hager was also to be greatly lauded for the expressiveness and sympathetic insight with which she set forth the songs, of which several had to be repeated. Earle Voorhies played the drum in "The Indians" in the last group.

New York Herald Tribune, 25 February 1939, p. 9

Views on an All-Ives Concert: Pianist and Singer Devote Program to Music by American Composer
Oscar Thompson
in the *New York Sun*

An American composer had a rare evening in Town Hall last night. His was the only music heard. The audience was a large one, predisposed to applaud. To the end that his musical purposes might be better understood, printed annotations were at the disposal of all who cared to peruse them. But Charles Ives, true to his reputation of being something of a recluse, was not present to bow.

In his absence the bows were taken by John Kirkpatrick, pianist, and Mina Hager, mezzo soprano, the artists who collaborated in an all-Ives program. Before January 20 Mr. Ives, who is now in his sixty-fifth year, was spoken of as the American composer everybody praised but whose music nobody knew. Prior to that date an all-Ives program might not have attracted a corporal's guard. It was Mr. Kirkpatrick's success with the "Concord" sonata at his January recital, and the opportunity this success afforded for fresh evaluations of both the composition and the composer, which changed all that.

Instead of indifference and neglect, there was manifest at last night's concert not only curiosity but a certain eagerness to find merit and pleasure in the piano works and the songs presented. "By request," the "Concord" sonata was repeated by Mr. Kirkpatrick. The pianist also set before his auditors a fugue on Lowell Mason's missionary hymn, "From Greenland's Icy Mountains"; an arrangement for piano by Mr. Kirkpatrick of the third movement of Mr. Ives's Fourth Symphony. Miss Hager sang two groups of songs, with Mr. Kirkpatrick as accompanist. A small drum, played by Earle Voo[r]hies, was added to the ensemble for a vocal piece called "The Indians."

The sonata having been ably and succinctly dealt with in these columns by Mr. Irving Kolodin in his review of Mr. Kirkpatrick's earlier recital, first attention may be given here to the songs. These, according to Goddard Lieberson in an article on Ives as an innovator, published in Musical America, present the best approach to the musical personality of Ives. The songs in Miss Hager's first group, were composed in 1902 and 1921. Ill health is said to have curtailed the composer's output in recent years.

Qualities of the Songs

The first song presented, "Walking," set something of pace in ingenuity for the others. It also illustrated a curious liking on the part of the composer for mildly dissonant piano parts, in contrast with relatively simple and even naive vocal writing. If little more than cleverness could be attributed to "Walking," the second song, "Autumn," was mood impressionism, not unworthy of Debussy. Though bolder of line, there was a similar effectiveness in the Miltonic "Evening." Cleverness again in "Two Little Flowers" and "The Greatest Man"; quaintness in "Ann Street."

As one of the hallmarks of the independence, the Americanism of Ives, his espousers have pointed admiringly to his bold use of parts of hymn tunes and popular songs of other days as basic or incidental material in his compositions. "Down East" (one of "Five Street Songs") was an example of this device in Miss Hager's first group. Incorporated are phrases from "Nearer My God to Thee," as linked with childhood memories of the little melodeon in the red farmhouse of boyhood days. Whether the appeal of this song is not primarily sentimental rather than musical will bear argument.

Of greater elaboration, but likewise built up about a quotation, is the better known song, "General Booth Enters Into Heaven," with its refrain: "Are you washed in the body [rightly, blood] of the lamb?" This, and the amusing little "Side Show," with its borrowed question about "Mister Reily who keeps the hotel," had a place in the singer's second group, along with "The Indians," "The Seer," "At the River," "Berceuse" and "The Things Our Fathers Loved."

In these songs was melody—now distinctive, now close to the banal. Considered collectively they were of livelier interest than the typical American-English group that fills a place of duty at the end of the orthodox song recital. But they are not profound songs. They lack the emotional and musical substance of the songs of the masters. With their quips, verbal or musical, some of them smack more of the drawing room than of the concert hall.

Miss Hager had the sympathy, the vocal skill and the musicianship to project their moods engagingly, though she was only partly successful in making their words understood, a very important detail it should be said, in dealing with songs so replete with whimsy.

Fugue From a Symphony

Mr. Kirkpatrick's arrangement of the fugue movement from the symphony was expertly made and as expertly played. The results were only moderately imposing as music. Perhaps only a composer of originality and daring would have taken Mason's hymn as his point of departure for an exercise in counterpoint. But was the choice a good one? The voices are clearly articulated; indeed, there is more of transparency than of structure. As an orchestrator, Ives has also his reputation for individuality. It may be that an Ives program without one of his symphonic works in its original estate remains at best a very incomplete representation of his gifts.

The sonata "Concord, Mass., 1840–1860," with its four movements entitled (1) "Emerson," (2) "Hawthorne," (3) "The Alcotts," (4) "Thoreau," is essentially a work of associations, and there may be a need to guard against a tendency to evaluate it on a literary or fanciful basis rather than a musical one. What, one wonders, would be the purely musical reaction of a trained and responsive listener from abroad who had never so much as heard of Concord, Emerson,

Hawthorne, the Alcotts or Thoreau? This question of association, which may be largely extra-musical in its promptings, remains one of the perplexities of music criticism. An earnest effort last night to hear this sonata purely as music left with this reviewer substantial doubts as to whether the work possesses the basic stuff to make a strong and intelligible appeal direct to the ear, without which the most ingenious of program music is unable to maintain itself. Mr. Kirkpatrick's performance was one as masterly as it was courageous.

New York Sun, 25 February 1939, p. 28

The Case of Mr. Ives
Elliott Carter
in *Modern Music*

To tell the full story of the first and second New York performances of Charles E. Ives' *Concord Sonata* at Town Hall, January 20th and February 24th is not my purpose here, for that deserves a whole article. In tabloid form, however, it would read as follows:

> First performance: very small house.
> In the next ten days: enthusiastic reviews cribbed from Ives'
>   prefaces by critics most of whom had not been at the concert.
> Second performance: packed house and disappointment of critics
>   on hearing work, obviously for the first time.

For a good long while now many of us have been puzzled about the musical merits of the *Concord Sonata* and other of Ives' longer pieces. I came to know the sonata in the years when Stravinsky first scandalized America in person and Whiteman gave the Carnegie premiere of the *Rhapsody in Blue*. A keen time with lots of enthusiasm and lots of performances of new music to which I sometimes went with Ives himself. Sunday afternoons, after these concerts, a few of us would go down to Gramercy Park where Ives then lived, or later uptown when he had moved to Seventy-Fourth Street, to discuss the music in the calm atmosphere of his living-room, a Henry James, old New York interior. They were lively talks, new music was new and very "modern" and Ives was much interested. Often he would poke fun, sit down at the piano to play from memory bits of a piece just heard, like *Daphnis and Chloé* or the *Sacre*, taking off the Ravel major seventh chords and obvious rhythms, or the primitive repeated dissonances of Stravinsky, and calling them "too easy." "Anybody can do that" he would exclaim, playing *My Country 'Tis Of Thee*, the right hand in one key and the left in another. His main love, however, was for Bach, Brahms and Franck, for he found in them spiritual elevation and nobility, which, like many a critic of his generation, he felt contemporary music had simplified away. To start the day fresh, he would often play a fugue from the *Well-Tempered Clavichord* before breakfast and long hours at the office. Not that he needed much cheering up, for, being a good sturdy Yankee with plenty of vitality, he poured lots of pep, salty humor and good spirits into everything he did.

During these afternoons we would coax him to try some of his own music, and as he saw we were sincere and not merely polite he would jump to the piano and play. Then the respectable, quiet, Puritan atmosphere was oddly disturbed, a gleam would come into his eyes as fiery excitement seized him, and he would smash out a fragment of *Emerson*, singing loudly and exclaiming with burning enthusiasm. Once the captain of the football team at Yale, he put the same punch into his music. It was a dynamic, staggering experience which is hard even now to think of clearly. He hated composers who played their works objectively "as if they didn't like them." This strong, wiry Yankee vitality, humor, and transcendental seriousness were very much to our taste and we always came away from Ives full of life's glad new wine and a thousand projects for the future.

In those days Ives was practically never played. Once, in 1927 at a Pro-Musica concert, two movements of his *Fourth Symphony* were given under the direction of Goossens who sat up all one night with a towel around his head trying to figure out how to keep the orchestra together in the places where the bar lines do not coincide. Ives had the percussion to his house to teach them the rhythms. It is no wonder the work didn't go any too well, for the score of the "lively movement," later published by *New Music*, has complexities well nigh insurmountable. At the time we asked why he didn't write his work more practically, so that performers could play it more accurately. He would reply that it was written as simply as possible, and then play over precisely what was written indicating that it was not as hard as all that. We remarked that certain very complicated textures would never sound but he countered that he had already tried them out when he conducted a theatre orchestra at Yale. Then we asked why the notation of the *Concord Sonata* was so vague, why every time he played it, he did something different, sometimes changing the harmonies, the dynamic scheme, the degree of dissonance, the pace. He even made a transcription of *Emerson* with many notes changed and the dynamic plan completely altered. He said that he intended to give only a general indication to the pianist who should, in his turn, recreate the work for himself. In a footnote to *Hawthorne,* he writes: "If the score itself, the preface, or an interest in Hawthorne suggest nothing, marks (of tempo, expression, etc.) will only make things worse."

This improvisational attitude toward music, so familiar in swing, affects all of Ives' more mature work. It affects his conception of performance and of composing. Unlike Chopin and Liszt, who wrote out very accurately in note values what they improvised, Ives leaves a great deal to the mercy of the performer. In his composition, the notation of a work is only the basis for further improvisation, and the notation itself, frequently of music first conceived many years before, is a kind of snapshot of the way he played it at a certain period in his life.

The improvisation often consists in adding dissonances, harmonies and complicated rhythms to a fundamentally simple work. This is obvious in many songs, and especially in a comparison of *Hawthorne* with the scherzo of the *Fourth Symphony,* which contain much identical material, greatly overladen with extra harmonies and complicated themes. The fuss that critics make about Ives' innovations is, I think, greatly exaggerated, for he has rewritten his works so many times, adding dissonances and polyrhythms, that it is probably impossible to tell just at what date the works assumed the surprising form we know now. The accepted dates of publication are most likely those of the compositions in their final state. Anyhow the question is not important. Ives himself has said that he prefers people to judge his music not for when it was written but for what it is.

Up to the time Kirkpatrick gave his performances no one had heard the *Concord Sonata* in its entirety in a concert hall. Some of us came wanting to see in the whole work what we saw in fragments. We found ourselves sadly disappointed. Kirkpatrick's extraordinary feat of interpretation did make a great deal of the music assume a shape through clever dynamic planning. But all the ingenious interpreting in the world could not dispel the fact that the sonata is formally weak. Kirkpatrick played the work with more finesse and less breadth and grandeur than Ives does, but this is understandable as Ives rarely ever played the whole work through but stuck to little fragments which he particularly loved; the whole work as a piece seemed to interest him less.

To turn to the music itself. In form and esthetic it is basically conventional, not unlike the Liszt sonata, full of the paraphernalia of the overdressy sonata school, cyclical themes, contrapuntal development sections that lead nowhere, constant harmonic movement which does not clarify the form, and dramatic rather than rhythmical effects. Because of the impressionistic intent of most of the music, the conventional form seems to hamper rather than aid, resulting in unnecessary, redundant repetitions of theme, mechanical transitions uncertain in their direction; unconvincing entrances of material; dynamics which have no relation to the progress of the piece. Behind all this confused texture there is a lack of logic which repeated hearings can never clarify, as they do for instance, in the works of Bartok or Berg. The rhythms are vague and give no relief to the more expressive sections, the much touted dissonant harmonies are helter-skelter, without great musical sense or definite progression. The esthetic is naive, often too naive to express serious thoughts, frequently depending on quotation of well-known American tunes with little comment, possibly charming but certainly trivial. As a whole, the work cannot be said to fill out the broad, elevated design forecast in the composer's prefaces.

However, there is also much good in the sonata. Usually the statement of themes is beautiful: in *Emerson*, the beginning, the first "verse" section, the allegro, and the coda; in *Hawthorne*, pages 27 to 32 which lead up to the "pilgrim's song" and the funny parody of *Hail, Columbia;*[25] though less characteristic of Ives' best, the *Alcotts* maintains a consistent level: and *Thoreau*, with its lovely beginning and its beautiful "walking theme" is in the best Ives manner, though it too has a long redundant section which might be relieved by cutting pages 65 and 66.

While his music is more often original than good, the good is really very personal and beautiful. Unlike that of Charles Griffes, here is a fresh and touching impressionism, different from anyone else's. With Griffes, Ives shares many formal weaknesses as well as a similar sensitivity to curious chord formations, but though he has more scope, he is less able to realize his musical purpose. Despite all the problems about music and American culture which form the interesting context of the Ives case, it is not possible on the basis of the music we know to rank him among the great originals of American art, with, for instance, Ryder and Whitman. Unlike theirs his work, though original, falls short of his intentions. In any case, it is not until we have had a much greater opportunity to examine and hear his music, that

Ives' position as a composer can be determined. The present canonization is a little premature.

Modern Music 16 (March–April 1939): 172–76

• • •

Sonata No. 4 for violin and piano (*Children's Day at the Camp Meeting*) premiere, 14 January 1940

After the premieres of Ives's later and most adventuresome works in the 1920s and 1930s, the 1940s brought performances of two of his most accessible works, the Fourth Violin Sonata and the Third Symphony. Both are based on hymn tunes, and the symphony won the Pulitzer Prize in 1947.[26] By this point, reviewers were uniformly taking Ives and his music seriously. The first review given here, of the premiere of the Fourth Sonata, is of a League of Composers concert, which included this sonata and Walter Piston's violin sonata, both played by Eudice Shapiro, violin, and Irene Jacobi, piano.

Music: Musical Americana
Francis D. Perkins
in the *New York Herald Tribune*

Neither of the two sonatas for violin and piano had been heard here before in public. Mr. Ives's work, which takes about eleven minutes to play, does not offer a detailed program to supplement the suggestions of its title, but some general reflection of the atmosphere which this implies can be found in the melodic character of the musical ideas, whose treatment, while not conventional, is consonant with their prevailing vein. The principal theme of the brief first movement is extensive and articulated rather than pronounced in profile; the peaceful close of the largo presented a tune of a Fosteresque character.

New York Herald Tribune, 15 January 1940, p. 9
(Excerpt)

• • •

Sonata No. 4 for violin and piano New York performance, 25 February 1942

Musical Events: Plenty Going On
Robert A. Simon
from *The New Yorker*

Charles Ives, whose music, as has been said, is more written about than played, was represented at Joseph Szigeti's violin recital by his fourth sonata, subtitled "Children's Day at the Camp Meeting." The sonata, with its reminiscences of hymn tunes, has a genial sturdiness and is set forth in terms of fiddling rather than violinism. Mr. Szigeti, who is noted for the aristocratic art which he brings to his performances, treated Mr. Ives' engaging music to just the kind of fiddling it needs, and his pianistic associate, Andor Foldes, didn't hesitate to sock the keys right smartly when that was in order. The people liked the sonata, and they might have raised even more of a rumpus over it if it hadn't had such an abrupt ending.

The New Yorker 18, no. 3 (7 March 1942): 47
(Excerpt)

• • •

Third Symphony premiere, 5 April 1946

Symphony by Ives in World Premiere: Composer's Third Featured by Little Symphony Here, With Harrison on Podium
Noel Straus
in *The New York Times*

The Third Symphony of Charles Ives received its world première at the concert devoted to works by contemporary American composers given by the New York Little Symphony last night at Carnegie Chamber Music Hall under the sponsorship of the League of Composers. Joseph Barone, the ensemble's regular leader, directed the first half of the program. The rest of the offerings, including the

Ives novelty, was performed by Lou Harrison on the podium as guest conductor.

That the symphony of Ives presented on this occasion had to wait forty years for its initial hearing is a sad commentary on the neglect that has been meted out to one of this country's most gifted composers throughout his long career. The work, though written between the years 1901 and 1904, while Ives was still in his twenties, loomed like a mountain peak above the other compositions played, all but one of which were also creations of youthful aspirants. For, though the symphony represented Ives' methods of procedure before he had reached the maturity of his powers, it possessed a freshness of inspiration, a genuineness of feeling and an intense sincerity that lent it immediate appeal and manifested inborn talents of a high order.

Lessened in Conservativeness

When Ives began the composition he was obviously more conservative in his approach than he became as the content grew. For of the three movements based on hymn tunes, the first, an Andante, moved the most warily along traditional lines. But in the central Allegro the composer showed greater daring in his harmonic texture, and in the final Largo he introduced passages of a boldness far ahead of their time.

The symphony proved striking, too, because of its melodiousness, its natural contrapuntal skill and its raciness. It was music close to the soil and deeply felt. And if it was rather loose in its structural patterning, and too much alike in its scoring throughout, it was blest with a richness of orchestral sonorities that matched the richness of imagination abounding in every page of this youthful opus.

Mr. Harrison conducted this difficult symphony in a manner that made known a real gift for the baton. Here, and in the "Portals" of Carl Ruggles, and his own "Motet for the Day of Ascension," the young director led with an easy sense of authority, a simplicity and directness, a command of orchestral tone, and a fine rhythmic security that spoke well for his future in this field.

New York Times, 6 April 1946, p. 10
(First two-thirds of review)

• • •

The Unanswered Question, Central Park in the Dark, and Second String Quartet premieres, and performances of the Third Symphony and Second Violin Sonata, 11 May 1946

What may have been only the second concert devoted entirely to the music of Ives was given in 1946 as part of Columbia University's second annual festival of modern American music. This concert included the Second Violin Sonata, the recently premiered Third Symphony, and premieres of three other works that were to become among Ives's best known compositions: *The Unanswered Question, Central Park in the Dark,* and the Second String Quartet. The quartet was repeated at the Yaddo Festival in the fall.

Ives Music Played at Columbia Fete: "The Unanswered Question" and "Central Park in the Dark" Heard for First Time
Olin Downes
from *The New York Times*

Those who arranged the programs of the Columbia University's second annual festival of contemporary American music, under the auspices of the Alice M. Ditson Fund, did an admirable thing when they scheduled for performance yesterday evening in McMillan Theatre an entire program of compositions by Charles Ives. The concert was given by ensembles and a chamber orchestra of students from the Juilliard Graduate School.

The program included Ives' [Second] Violin and Piano Sonata, played by Shirley Mesner, violinist, and Alice Shapiro, pianist; seven songs, sung by Mordecai Bauman, with accompaniment by Lucy Brown; the Second String Quartet—by Robert Koff and Walter Levine, violinists; Rena Robbins, violist, and Alla Goldberg, 'cellist, and, finally, an orchestra divided in two halves, one behind the stage and one on the platform, for the first performances of "The Unanswered Question" and "Central Park in the Dark," and Ives' Third Symphony.[27] These works were conducted by Edgar Schenckman, on the stage, and Theodore Bloomfeld, collaborating conductor behind the scenes in the two works that preceded the symphony.

It is not easy to summarize the impressions of this concert of a singularly gifted composer, or even to be sure how trustworthy such impressions may be, in view of some features of the performance which obviously did imperfect justice to the music.

Series of Impressions

The sonata, while certainly to be taken as a piece of "absolute" music, is at the same time a series of impressions and memories of the New England Mr. Ives knows and loves—the New England of the autumn— rhythms that tingle the blood; a Barn Dance which is an extended treatment of dance tunes of ancestral origin, and "The Revival." The score is in three movements. There are melodic fragments that jump out of the context, as the work flies by. Also there are pages when one wants to hear an orchestra; where, as in the finale, the violin exhorts and the piano becomes the voice of the shouting multitude.

The songs had the most immediate—or the most audible— response from the audience which packed the auditorium and hung on every note. Some of them are stirring and indeed captivating by their simplicity and truthfulness of melodic expression. Others are literary songs, or songs really meant for recitation. The text always dictates the music, but in songs like the invocation of the "Housitonic River at Stockbridge" [rightly, "The Housatonic at Stockbridge"] the music fulfills expression of the text as only inspired music can.

The simplicity of "The Child's Prayer" ["The Children's Hour"?] is another case in point. "Charlie Rutledge" ["Charlie Rutlage"] was one of the most enthusiastically greeted of the lot, and a fine vigor and tang of the populace it has. "General William Booth Enters Heaven" needs more wildness than Mr. Bauman gave it. It's an astonishing song of the "shout" kind.

The string quartet amused the audience with its movements called "Discussions," "Arguments," and no doubt useful quotations of "Hail Columbia" and other well-known American tunes, in a kind of a fantastical "quodlibet" of the modern age. And there is a page where, over the ostinato of the 'cello, the tension mounts and the music kindles in beauty and noble passion. No other composer would or could write like this.

Divided Orchestra Music

The music for the divided orchestra failed to go over the footlights, because of bad acoustical arrangements which made the orchestra back of the stage practically inaudible to any but those who sat in the front seats. Therefore undue preponderance was given to the few instruments which answered the strains from back-stage. This work is really an extreme experiment in impressionism, needing a far more sensitive balance and coordination of all elements than it received to bring it off.

But the most completely integrated and effective of all the instrumental music impressed us as being beyond doubt the Third Symphony for chamber orchestra. This symphony as a whole affects the listener by the simplicity of its approach, and the deep feeling with which old hymn tunes are used. The curious coloring and austereness of line result in a broad and noble climax of the whole work.

New York Times, 12 May 1946, p. 42

Hearing Things: Charles Ives
Paul Henry Lang
in *The Saturday Review of Literature*

Charles Ives, scion of an old New England family, is something of a legend in American music. . . . As we listened to the music of this Connecticut Yankee it was apparent why he so simply and honestly decided to embark on a manner of life which would leave him "unhampered." This is music from the bowels of the earth; bewildering music, at times powerful, tender, evocative, witty, at others incomprehensibly clumsy. What makes these pieces the more extraordinary is the date of their composition: they were written before "Elektra," before "Le Sacre du Printemps," before "Pierrot Lunaire," and they exhibit a personality, an inventive talent, as original as those of the protagonists of modern music whom he antedated and anticipated. There are rhythms brisk and American to the core, melodies betraying a lively fantasy, and harmonies that can be found nowhere else. The last movement of the violin sonata ("The Revival") presents an impressionistic musical canvas that rivals similar works of the best French masters; at the same time it has vigor and a curiously haunting affinity with traditional American melodies. Among the songs presented, the emotional range and diversity of which are remarkable, there were masterpieces of the first order. Original, tender, barbaric, refined, and coarse-grained they are, and American as Walt Whitman. Then came two works in large form, a quartet and a symphony (No.3), which are diffuse and curiously inarticulate in their chosen medium. It is very difficult to reconcile the freshness of the songs and of the sonata with the lameness of the symphony, to understand how a man with Ives's innate gifts and thorough musical training can be so helpless in the orchestral medium.

When Ives's compositions were conceived, the stylistic revulsion from post-romanticism had already begun, but most European composers—and all the Americans—were still clinging tenaciously to the plushy grandeur of the music of the end of the century. In this post-romantic world Ives stands as an independent and utterly straightforward musician, an American of the twentieth century. His compositions testify to his honesty of spirit and purpose: to him imitation is not only worthless but dishonest. He dared to be a completely American composer when every other musician pined for the harmonic-erotic nirvana of the "Liebestod," tried to coax Till Eulenspiegel into a few more escapades, or was basking in the autumnal splendor of the Brahmsian symphony, raking over the lawn for forgotten leaves. He looked around him and discovered that Danbury bears no resemblance to Bayreuth, Munich, or Vienna, and he resolved to be himself and to translate the New England countryside into music.

It is incontestable that the output of this genuine creative talent is lacking in focus, and yet, admiring his intentions and his sincerity, one cannot easily suppose this lack of center to be due solely to individual defects. It is hard to believe that because of some shortcoming or other, he was unable to cope with what others, less endowed, were able to see, organize, and shape into something comprehensive. Ives was not an armless Raphael. Of the works heard at the Columbia Festival there were songs the mastery of which is equalled only by Moussorgsky, and the violin sonata represents a convincing solution of the almost insurmountable problem of mixing two heterogeneous instruments, a problem that every composer from Beethoven onward has struggled with. On the other hand there is the almost inept handling of the orchestra, the monochrome of the outer movements of the quartet. Is it perhaps that the song—Whitman in music—can be an eminently American phenomenon without any limiting factors and without inevitably invoking traditional stylistic features as do quartet and symphony? Ives loves the songs, hymns, and "spirituals" of his native New England, and, combining them with the organist's meditative improvisation, he tries to shape them into symphonic fabrics. But this sort of lyricism is anathema to the symphony, it cannot rise to the epic-dramatic intensity demanded by the genre. On the other hand, the old fiddle tunes of the American countryside again provide a link with the composer's hereditary environment, hence the successful blending in the sonata which, of course, is a "sonata" in name only.

During the short span of his really active period Ives developed constantly, but his development did not lead anywhere, for it returned—by long detours—to the original point of departure. What makes it so difficult for the critic to appraise this art is that we do not seem to know either what determined the choice of the point of departure or the direction of the detours. Nor do we know whether the composer's creative forces were exhausted when he largely abandoned composition, or whether ill health or other causes arrested him short of a flourishing of his art, for which everything he had so far done was only a modest preparation. What, then, is Charles Ives? The only answer to this question can be silence filled with wonderment. We do not know anything about him, nor do his works reveal his world. But there is a more important question yet to be asked: what does Ives mean to us? Perhaps some day we shall recognize him as the first musician who realized the futility of Western European gropings for new music which at the same time held on to the post-Wagnerian faith. There is a more than superficial resemblance between Ives and Moussorgsky. Both achieved their greatest in the song, both remained amateurs in the larger forms. But while Moussorgsky stands before us in his letters as completely naked as Rousseau in his confessions, Ives remains an enigma, and one cannot throw off the vague feeling that this inexplicibility is not an accident, and is bound up with the absence of a center in his oeuvre, that the curious primitivism of his symphonies is not due to lack of training and craftsmanship—patently the case with Moussorgsky—but is a symbol of the lack of a center, of a focus, in the life of the young century. There were a few moments of that memorable concert at Columbia University when one could not help feeling that at one time Ives had in his power the solution of the great problems of music at the crossroads. That he did not avail himself of this opportunity constitutes an American tragedy. There was no American musical culture into which he could have integrated his new art, and his predicament called for a revolutionary upheaval, a tabula rasa in form, language, and technique, in which his music could have found fulfillment. But revolution, which for the great Russian novelists was as natural in letters as in politics, is alien to the modern American mind, accustomed to the concept of orderly evolutionary change. Charles Ives's music belongs to a world of revolution divested of its revolutionary reality.

Saturday Review of Literature 29, no. 22 (1 June 1946): 43–44
(First paragraph omitted)

• • •

Second String Quartet performance at Yaddo, September 1946

Yaddo Festival
Lou Harrison
from the *New York Herald Tribune*

The Yaddo Music Group presented during the Music Period at the Yaddo Estate, Saratoga Springs, N. Y., a series of six concerts devoted to American music, Sept. 13, 14 and 15. . . .

The performers made evident both respect for and a pleasure in the music they were presenting. Intensive festivals of this sort are, of course, wearing to both the performers and the audience, but the reward of coming away with a more or less consolidated picture of our creative culture at this time is ample compensation for the labor involved.

. . . The major events of the series were [Wallingford Riegger's "Dichotomy" for orchestra], Carl Ruggles's elevated and striking "Evocations" for piano [played by John Kirkpatrick], which are superb organizations of counterpoint according to the second, and Charles Ives's Second String Quartet [played by the Walden Quartet], which concluded the series. This work is, for this reporter, the finest piece of American chamber music yet. It is difficult going for a while but one becomes increasingly aware of the vast mastery in Ives's composing means, and in the final movement, in which the men, who have been demonstrated as discussing and then arguing things in the two preceding movements, walk up to the hills and "gaze into the firmament," a musical revelation occurs. It is hard to convey in words what every one present felt at this moment. Music of this kind happens only every fifty years or a century, so rich in faith and so full of the sense of completion.

New York Herald Tribune, 22 September 1946, p. 7
(Excerpts)

• • •

Three Harvest Home Chorales New York premiere, 3 March 1948

The *Three Harvest Home Chorales* were premiered on a program with Mozart's Requiem, Hindemith's *Five Songs on Old Texts,* and Ives's *Psalm 67* in a concert by the Collegiate Chorale conducted by Robert Shaw.

Music: Crude but Careful
Virgil Thomson
in the *New York Herald Tribune*

Preceding the [Mozart] Requiem the choir had sung alone Charles Ives's Sixty-seventh Psalm, a dissonant diatonic piece that never quite comes off, and Five Songs on Old Texts by Paul Hindemith, expert madrigal writing in a modern version of fifteenth-century style. New to New York were three Harvest Home chorales by Ives, for chorus, organ, string basses and brass. The second of these has melodic life and by moments rhythmic pattern. All are polytonal and of intrinsic harmonic interest. Whether they are musically interesting all through and genuinely expressive or merely supreme examples of Yankee ingenuity I am not sure, though they were performed twice. It is not important to know that, anyway, since Ives's vast production is a storehouse of many good things, including examples of Yankee ingenuity; and it is always a pleasure to hear any of his work carefully performed.

New York Herald Tribune, 4 March 1948, p. 17
(Final paragraph)

• • •

Concord Sonata recording, 1948

The first recording of the *Concord Sonata,* by John Kirkpatrick, was recorded in 1945 but not released until 1948. Nicolas Slonimsky's review is that of an insider in the Ives circle, for he had become an intimate friend of Ives's and had conducted the premiere and tour of *Three Places in New England*.[28]

Bringing Ives Alive
Nicolas Slonimsky
in *The Saturday Review of Literature*

The Paris publication of *Le Guide du Concert* in its issue of January 30, 1948, printed an extraordinary note: "L'Amérique n'est plus une nation a-musicale: elle compte une cinquantaine de compositeurs de talent; on cite: Ch. Ives, R. Thompson, Virgil Thomson . . . [more names follow]."[29]

Thus, America has been finally admitted to the family of musical nations! But what is more important than the recognition extended by the editors of *Le Guide du Concert* to American composers, is the fact that non-conformists of the American musical scene are now finding recognition in their own country. Particularly gratifying is the now general recognition of the great significance of the music of Charles Ives, the musical transcendentalist among American composers.

Ives has done nothing to hasten this recognition. He accepts honors, distinctions, and prizes with a look of good-natured enmity, as though these honors were children's toys, almost indecent when tendered to a man who has passed the Biblical three-score and ten. And he is caustic about prizes for people who write "nice music." There is no greater invective in the rich vocabulary of Charles Ives than the adjective "nice" applied to art.

There is nothing "nice" about the "Concord Sonata," in the Ivesian sense, but it is now permissible, even for sober-minded non-Ivesians, to call it great music. Lawrence Gilman wrote in his oft-quoted review: "This sonata is exceptionally great music—it is, indeed, the greatest music composed by an American, and the most deeply and essentially American in impulse and implication."

John Kirkpatrick, who gave the first integral performance of the "Concord Sonata" in New York on that memorable occasion January 20, 1938 [rightly, 1939], has now recorded it for Columbia. Kirkpatrick spent two years of devoted study on this work, which is probably the most formidable piano composition ever written, and his recorded performance reflects his profound understanding of Ives's music. This is not just good pianism, but a new pianistic technique, in which the unplayable is achieved through diligence and determination. It is a cause for rejoicing that the "Concord Sonata," in

Kirkpatrick's performance, has been released by a major phonograph company, and made accessible to all music lovers.

The full title of the "Concord Sonata" is "Second Pianoforte Sonata, Concord, Mass., 1840–1860." It was written between 1909 and 1915. The sonata was published privately in 1920, at Ives's own expense, and distributed gratis. The first edition of the "Concord Sonata" is now a collector's item, but fortunately it has been reissued by the Arrow Music Press. Concurrently with the publication of the "Concord Sonata," Ives printed a booklet, "Essays Before a Sonata" with a typically Ivesian dedication: "These prefatory essays were written by the composer for those who can't stand his music—and the music for those who can't stand his essays; to those who can't stand either, the whole is respectfully dedicated."

The "Concord Sonata" is in four movements named after the great writers of the Concord circle, Emerson, Hawthorne, the Alcotts, and Thoreau. The first movement is largely derived from an uncompleted "Emerson Piano Concerto." The "Hawthorne" movement was first conceived "in terms of a piano or a dozen pianos"; the third, "The Alcotts," was for organ, or piano with voice, or with violin. The "Thoreau" movement was planned "in terms of strings, colored possibly with the flute or horn." A reference to the originally intended instrumentation appears in the annotations at the end of the music: "A flute may play throughout this page. If no flute, the brace below the first is for piano alone . . . but Thoreau much prefers to hear the flute over Walden."[30]

This interchangeability of instruments in the music of Ives is the despair of performers who are eager to put Ives on their programs. Thus, a violin sonata may suddenly sprout a line for trumpet solo; the accompaniment for a song may reveal, without preliminary warning, a part for violin obbligato. Ives's works abound in cued-in parts for various instruments unmentioned in formal description of the music. Or else, Ives would put in an extra blue note, with a parenthetical remark: "Use Saturday night."

The "Concord Sonata" is transcendental music in the philosophical conception of the word. It is a new type of impressionism, in which ideas and convictions, and even politics, are used as programmatic content. It is because the music of Ives requires thought and penetration on the part of the performer that Ives is so insistent on giving a wide margin of interpretive freedom. Thus he remarks, "A metronome cannot measure Emerson's mind and oversoul, any more than the old Concord Steeple Bell could." In another place Ives directs the player to strike the notes with the thumb "in as strong and hard a way as possible, almost as though the Mountains of the Universe were shouting as all of Humanity rises to behold the 'Massive Eternities' and the 'Spiritual Immensities.'" And there is a visual thrill in store for those watching a "live" performance of the "Concord Sonata," when, in the "Hawthorne" movement, the pianist picks up a strip of board and applies it to play two-octave groups of notes on the black or on the white keys, to illustrate Hawthorne's "Celestial Railroad."

Here is another Ivesian footnote: "The melodychords in R. H. [the right hand] are but to suggest some of the outdoor sounds over the Concord Hills and the right-foot pedal beginning here can be guided by the phrase marks in the upper clef." There are also such asides as, "A drum corps gets the best of the band—for a moment."

Ives is extremely sensitive to musical symbols, motives and mottoes expressive of inner contents of the music. In the "Concord Sonata," Ives makes repeated use of the initial four notes of Beethoven's "Fifth Symphony." He uses the motive explicitly in "The Alcotts" movement: "And there sits the little old spinet-piano Sophia Thoreau gave to the Alcott children, on which Beth played the old Scotch airs, and played at the 'Fifth Symphony'."

Much has been written about the prophetic use by Ives of the devices of polytonality, atonality and polyrhythmy. But these modern techniques are employed by Ives not as sophisticated enchantment of ultra-modern music, but as a natural soul-extension to reach for the transcendental. Alternating with agonized discords, Ives writes tunes of tender simplicity. Ives's melodies are unmistakably American, church-hymn American, or ballad-like American, or barn-dance American. Perhaps in this combination of homely reminiscence and complex rhythm and harmony, lies the secret of the uniqueness of Ives. This is also the reason why, despite so few performances, the music of Ives has become a source of irresistible attraction to the new generation of American composers.

Saturday Review of Literature 31, no. 35
(28 August 1948): 45 and 49

• • •

First Piano Sonata premiere, 17 February 1949, and performance, 27 March 1949

Ten years after the New York premiere of Ives's Second Piano Sonata (*Concord*), the First Piano Sonata was finally premiered by William Masselos, some three decades after its completion.

William Masselos: Pianist Presents Ives Sonata at Y. M. H. A. Hall
Peggy Glanville-Hicks
from the *New York Herald Tribune*

There was cheering at the Y. M. H. A. Hall last night when William Masselos came to the end of the first complete performance of Charles Ives Piano Sonata No. 1, written 1902–1910. The long, massive work is full of the fabulous Ives talent, and is as turbulent as a storm at sea and as prodigal of ideas as a forest of trees. There's Dada, too, at times, with respect to the blunt or witty juxtaposition of daily scene musical reference within Ives's own tonally anchored chromatic massivity.

The music gets close to atonality, but it is more a dissonant block-polyphony method achieved seemingly from instinct and sheer momentum rather than by deliberate design or theory. Moments of meditative beauty it has too, and Masselos discovered them all.

He brings as an artist strength, insight, grace, and an astonishing technical control, both mechanically and of that region where the devices of technique become fused in interpretive exposition. He possesses pianistic qualities that, in less erudite programs than he chooses, could win him conventional laurels galore. That he places such gifts in the service of discovery of new works, or the rediscovery of temporarily overlooked masterpieces, can evoke nothing but the greatest admiration for his deep musicianship and artistic devotion.

New York Herald Tribune, 18 February 1949, p. 18
(First half)

**Masselos Pleases in Piano Program: Displays His Talents in
Recital Devoted to Brahms, Beethoven, Ives, Weber and Ravel**
Olin Downes
from *The New York Times*

Sonata by Ives

What shall one say of the Ives Sonata? A work of immense length,
very rich in ideas, rising to passages of a rare vision! At the same
time a score which needs some condensation and some artistic discipline. This at least is a first impression. There is enough in it for six
sonatas. There are passages of sheer grandeur and drama, and
memories too.

This sonata is music of great difficulty and frequent complexity. . . .
It was courageous and it was exciting to see a young artist thus challenging his audience with new music, and doing so with the conviction
and the communicativeness of his years.

New York Times, 28 March 1949, p. 17
(Excerpts)

• • •

Second Symphony premiere,
22 February 1951

Ives's major symphonic works were premiered in reverse
chronological order: the Fourth Symphony (in part) in
1927, soon after it was finished; *Three Places in New England*
in 1931, about a decade after completion; the Third
Symphony in 1946, 35 years after it was completed; the
Second Symphony in 1951, more than 40 years after it was
written; and the First Symphony not until 1953, more than
half a century after it was composed. Of all these premieres,
that of the Second Symphony had the biggest impact,
because of the prominence of its performers, Leonard
Bernstein and the New York Philharmonic; because of Ives's
growing reputation over the previous several years; and
because it is an appealing work in late-Romantic style with a

great deal of individual character but almost none of the difficulties of Ives's later music.

Symphony by Ives is Played in Full: Bernstein Leads Philharmonic in Composer's 2d, Heard in Entirety for First Time
Olin Downes
from *The New York Times*

It was reserved for Leonard Bernstein, to his eternal credit, to give the first performance anywhere in its entirety of the Second Symphony of Charles Ives, at the concert of the Philharmonic-Symphony Orchestra last night in Carnegie Hall.

It is not necessary to emphasize the fact that this symphony, an astonishing work today, was completed just fifty years ago, and that it has lain that long awaiting a public hearing, to prove the composer's originality. But it is testimony to Ives' complete conviction in his art, and audacity in expressing himself, to reflect upon the impression that this particular symphony, by no means the most daring of Ives' scores, would have made if it had been heard when it was completed at the beginning of this century.

As a matter of fact, the origins of the symphony date farther back than that. Mr. Ives commenced work upon it in 1897, and the finale is in part the material of an overture called "The American Woods," which he completed in 1889. He was born in 1874. At the turn of the century America was scarcely aware of the mature music of Debussy or Richard Strauss. The Stravinsky of even "The Firebird" was undreamed of.

Mr. Ives did not wait for him, or indeed for any composer other than himself to decide what should go with his scores. He has said of this Second Symphony, in characteristic fashion, that "it expressed the musical feelings of the Connecticut country around Redding and Danbury in the Eighteen Nineties—the music of the country folk. It is full of the tunes they sang and played then, and I thought it would be a sort of bad joke to have some of these tunes in counterpoint with some Bach tunes"—this citation of Bach apparently referring to the more serious melodies of his own creation and to the contrapuntal form of the symphony.[31]

If the symphony were the work merely of a folk-lorist, if the score consisted only of references to old-time American tunes, it would have no particular individual or artistic significance. But these tunes, with their profound meanings to a creative artist, are matters of reference.

The symphony is an immense structure, especially in the first movement. The tonal speech, if you want to put it that way, is by turns, rudely, tenderly, fantastically and cantankerously Yankee. It is unvarnished and unsymmetrical, sometimes dour and ungracious, if sometimes discursive and sometimes for a moment falling into a formula of composition.

It is not a symphony to be easily estimated or put in a category at any time. The first movement alone, in its material and extensiveness and variety of treatment, is an immense symphonic fragment. The slow movement is the one most completely grasped at a first hearing, and it is of unique inspiration and a noble elevation of thought.

Because of poor health the composer could not be present to hear his long-silent symphony.

New York Times, 23 February 1951, p. 33
(Final two paragraphs omitted)

Music: From the Heart
Virgil Thomson
from the *New York Herald Tribune*

Leonard Bernstein, conducting the Philharmonic-Symphony Orchestra last night in Carnegie Hall, made music of a rare loveliness with a program in no way banal. Really there were two programs, a Mozart program and an American one. In the first Mr. Bernstein starred as a piano soloist. In the second a fifty-year-old work by Charles Ives received a rousing first performance. . . .

Charles Ives's Second Symphony, composed in the late 1890s but never before performed in its entirety, is a five-movement rhapsodic meditation on American hymns of the nineteenth century, American dance ditties and football songs. It is essentially a landscape piece with people in it. The first movement gives us the lush Connecticut valley through a musical technique derived from the Bach choral-preludes. It is sustained, songful, organ-like, graciously contrapuntal, predominantly a piece for strings, with at the end a quotation from "Columbia, the Gem of the Ocean" to make the note of faith specific.

From here on, song and dance material dominate. There is a deeply ecstatic slow movement based on the hymns "Bringing in the Sheaves" and "Beulah Land." There are two long animated movements involving dance music and the Yale "Boola Boola" song, with a restatement in the last one of the initial landscape material and an

apotheosis in which "Columbia, the Gem of the Ocean" sails out complete over a jolly and busy texture containing dances and gay songs in
contradictory keys.[32] A Fourth of July picnic might well be the scene
here evoked. Orchestrally, harmonically and melodically the symphony is both noble and plain. It speaks of American life with love and
humor and deep faith. It is unquestionably an authentic work of art,
both as structure and as composition.

New York Herald Tribune, 23 February 1951, p. 16
(Excerpts)

Berstein Conducts Ives Symphony No. 2
Robert Sabin
in *Musical America*

Charles Ives's Second Symphony had to wait half a century for its first
performance, but Ives was at least half a century ahead of his time, so
that his music sounds far more natural and comprehensible to us than
it would have to our grandfathers. Nor is the Second Symphony one
of his most challenging works; it is far less revolutionary than Three
Places in New England and many other of his orchestral pieces. The
symphony was completed in 1901, but the last movement contains
material from an overture written in 1889, called *The American Woods
(Brookfield)*. The whole work is (in the composer's own words) an
expression of "the musical feelings of the Connecticut country around
here (Redding and Danbury) in the 1890s, the music of the country
folk. It is full of the tunes they sang and played then."

   The symphony opens with a flowing, contrapuntally ingenious
Andante, in which "Columbia, the Gem of the Ocean" makes its
appearance near the close. There is a Mahleresque freedom in Ives's
treatment of this movement, but it is long-winded and unnecessarily
repetitious. The following Allegro has dance-like rhythms and raciness of harmonic flavor. The slow movement is a free fantasy on old
hymns with a reference to America the Beautiful at the end that gives
a clue to the tenderness and faith expressed in it. Ives has "the gift to
be simple" in this deeply moving Adagio. The final Lento maestoso
and Allegro molto vivace are even more folkish than the opening
movements, and the symphony ends in a characteristic scramble of
harmonies and rhythms that make wonderful sense. Ives's Second
Symphony is a loose, scattered work with episodes of academic imitation cheek by jowl with superb music. It is utterly sincere, and like

Virgil Thomson's *The Mother Of Us All* (which is anticipated by two generations) a wholesome and natural expression of American life before the world wars and the triumph of the machine age. Mr. Bernstein conducted it with both love and technical mastery.

Musical America 71, no. 4 (March 1951): 32–33
(Final paragraph omitted)

excerpt from Current Chronicle
Henry Cowell
in *The Musical Quarterly*

Charles Ives is always planning to look over the disordered piles of manuscripts he still has in the barn on his farm in Connecticut, but he hardly ever gets around to it. However, in the fall of 1949 he did do some rummaging about and came out looking dusty and with some photostat sheets, of which he remarked to the writer: "This old thing . . . maybe you'd look at it." The "old thing" proved to be his Symphony No. 2, in five movements. He started it in 1897, when he was still at Yale University as a student of Horatio Parker; it was completed in 1901, after he moved to New York. It incorporates, as the second theme of the last movement, a quotation from an earlier piece of his, *The American Woods*, which was completed in 1889. Ives pointed out that this is a "Stephen Foster kind of tune", and that it has, placed in counterpoint against it, the sort of jigs, gallops, and reels that "might be played, and often were" by old farmers on a fiddle. It is full of snatches of simple tunes, some original, some quotations from songs and dances familiarly performed by plain folk in the Danbury region at the turn of the century; there are also some popular college tunes.

The old photostat was duly examined, deciphered, admired, and given to a publisher. It would seem, as so often with works of Ives, that various parts of the work were played with small orchestras while it was being written. But the first complete performance took place in February of this year, with Leonard Bernstein conducting the New York Philharmonic-Symphony Orchestra, in Carnegie Hall. The work was a great success with the audience, and both Ives and Bernstein were eulogized by the press.

This Second Symphony bears rather the relation to Ives's later work that *Verklärte Nacht* does to that of Schoenberg. Both men became famous for quite different and far more startling kinds of music.

Verklärte Nacht is a perfectly respectable piece, with some germs of later, more interesting developments; but it would hardly have been heard as often as it is, were it not for the public interest built up in a kind of music from which this particular work is rather remote. In the same way, one cannot call Ives's Symphony No. 2 entirely unoriginal, but it contains only in the most embryonic state the unique outpouring of dissonances, rhythms, polyharmonies, polymeters, etc., for which Ives has become especially known. Undoubtedly audiences are flattered by the discovery that they are able to enjoy such works as these, often without realizing that what they are listening to is not at all what they have been hearing about. The reception given to Ives's Symphony No. 2 was certainly helped, among slightly more knowing auditors who had braced themselves to hear unbearable dissonance, by the grand bagful of tunes in a familiar idiom that they were offered instead—tunes harmonized with only an occasional unexpected progression.

The work is polyphonic much of the time, the polyphony formed of pieces of familiar tunes set against each other, in easily understandable association. The tunes are rarely sounded all the way through, and there is apt to be some distortion of rhythm. The melodic line often leads to some point not suggested in the original version. So in the fabric of sound familiar bits are frequently tossed to the surface and disappear again before one can recall just what they were. The impression of the work would doubtless be much more nostalgic if we knew the tunes still; but many of these are no longer remembered; even Ives has forgotten the names of most of them.

The effectiveness of the Symphony No. 2 does not, however, rely only on nostalgic association. The tunes are often sprightly and attractive even if one has never heard them before, and they lead smoothly from one to another, with some unexpected key change and occasionally asymmetrical design. The underlying form is always easily discernible.

Ex. 2[33] comes from near the beginning of the first movement; it shows three simple related melodies, in counterpoint that conforms to standard practice, except that the viola and 'cello parts are sometimes in octaves and sometimes separate; and there is a typical even rhythm of two in the last measure of the first violins, against the rhythm of three in the other parts. Ex. 3 shows a version of the first theme of the second movement; it displays the sort of syncopated, minstrel-like, jerky rhythm later to be found in more concentrated form in most of Ives's scherzo movements. Ex. 4 (the first 6 measures of the third movement) is characteristic of Ives's slow movements, so often religious in feeling. The chords are plain, yet there are several surprising, wide-swinging key changes, before the dominant is reached. Between the third and

Ex. 2

Ex. 3

Ex. 4

fourth measures in the first violins there is a subtle rhythmic distinction, the dotted half note being divided equally in one case and unequally in the other. The fourth movement, Lento maestoso, brings back in majestic syncopation some of the elements of the first. The last movement "goes lickety-split", to quote its composer, in the style of a one-step. Ex. 5 shows two familiar tunes in counterpoint, one with the accent thrown off an eighth note. After quotations from at least twelve known tunes, there is a grand crescendo and the melody of *Columbia the Gem of the Ocean* is sounded in trombones *fortissimo*, against fragments of *Love's Old Sweet Song, The Fisherman's Reel, In the Sweet Bye-and Bye,*[34] *Turkey in the*

Ex. 5

Straw, and so on, leading to the declamation of *Reveille* in the trumpets—and to a final terrific discord. Ives says this was the formula for signifying the very end of the very last dance of all: the players played any old note, good and loud, for the last chord. It was the common practice in the days of the Danbury Band conducted by Ives's father. At the end of an otherwise conventional symphony this came as a real shock to the audience; but since no one doubted that it *was* the last chord, the intended effect was certainly obtained.

The Symphony No. 2 is easier to perform than most of Ives's orchestral works. There are no real rhythmic problems, and the instrumental parts are perfectly playable. Since its moving qualities—its exaltation and its humor—are couched in familiar terms, it is not hard to assimilate. Without being as exploratory as his later works, it is nevertheless a finely wrought symphony, full of feeling and vitality, and there is no practical reason why it should not be frequently played and greatly enjoyed.

The Musical Quarterly 37 (July 1951): 399–402

NOTES

1. We have adhered to the following principles in selectively correcting the text of the reviews reprinted here: (1) Differences in italicization and/or capitalization of titles of works of music have been left untouched, as have incorrect titles so long as this would invite no misunderstanding; (2) idiosyncrasies of spelling or punctuation and minor errors have been retained when eliminating them would mean sacrificing some of the particular flavor or character of the author or publication cited; (3) small corrections of spelling or punctuation have been made silently, while larger corrections are noted. These notes were added by the editor, unless otherwise noted.

2. See the facsimile in Vivian Perlis, *Charles Ives Remembered: An Oral History* (New Haven: Yale University Press, 1974; reprint, New York: W. W. Norton, 1976), 33. On p. 32 is a facsimile of the program for this performance.

3. Here, "as showing what a daily paper had to say," the reviewer quotes the second through eighth sentences of the *New York Times* review printed above.

4. For Bellamann's first letter to Ives, see the selected correspondence in Part II, above.

5. The quotation marks in this paragraph were omitted in *The Double Dealer,* but this passage is an almost direct quotation from *Essays Before a Sonata,* differing only in small details.

6. The original uses three asterisks throughout for the ellipses, which are here rendered in the more usual style.

7. The original has "Mrs. Ives."

8. An announcement of the concert is reprinted in Perlis, *Charles Ives Remembered*, 73. Substitutions were made before the concert, for Rex Tillson is not listed, and the announcement lists Louis Gruenberg's Violin Sonata, Op. 9, as the first number instead of the Milhaud Second Sonata.

9. The program for this concert is reprinted in Perlis, *Charles Ives Remembered*, 126. Ives's *Quarter-Tone Pieces* and a sonata by Barth were the only quarter-tone works on the program, which otherwise ran the modern gamut from Bartók to Tailleferre.

10. The program for this concert is reprinted in Perlis, *Charles Ives Remembered*, 126. Of the Ives Fourth Symphony, only the first two movements were played.

11. The original has "Mr. St. Ives" here and at the next reference, the same slip Downes had made in his review of the *Three Quarter-Tone Pieces* two years earlier.

12. The order of the middle movements was later reversed, so that the fugue became the third movement and the lively comedy movement the second. It was this latter movement that was performed on this concert and published by *New Music* in 1929 (see the reviews of the publication, below).

13. Brackets in the original.

14. For quotations from other reviews, see Frank R. Rossiter, *Charles Ives and His America* (New York: Liveright, 1975), 225–26.

15. See also Philip Hale's splenetic reaction in "Mr. Slonimsky in Paris," *The Boston Herald*, 7 July 1931, p. 14, reprinted in Charles E. Ives, *Memos*, ed. John Kirkpatrick (New York: W. W. Norton, 1972), 13–14. This famous editorial is not a review, as Hale did not hear the Paris concerts, and does not mention Ives, but is an attack on the entire enterprise.

16. An announcement of these two concerts is reprinted in Perlis, *Charles Ives Remembered*, 154. Ives's *Three Places in New England* appeared on the program for the first concert.

17. The program for this concert is reprinted in Perlis, *Charles Ives Remembered*, 164. In addition to the four songs named below, the set of seven included *Evening, The Indians,* and *Maple Leaves.* They were performed by Hubert Linscott, baritone, and Aaron Copland, piano, on a concert that also included Copland's *Piano Variations* and Walter Piston's *Sonata for Flute and Piano,* which Meyer singles out as the first and second most enthusiastically received compositions at the festival.

18. Henry Cowell: Charles Ives, Vol. X, No. 2. [Copland's note.]

19. It is regrettable that several of this group, such as *Ich Grolle Nicht*, for some reason not apparent have been included in the recent edition of Ives' songs brought out by *New Music*.—A.C. [Copland's note.]

20. Many of these songs were composed at an earlier period, but were either rewritten or rearranged at the time of publication, which explains the large number bearing the date 1921.—A.C. [Copland's note.]

21. Information on Kirkpatrick's early experiences with the work from his interview with Perlis, *Charles Ives Remembered*, 214–25. Rosenfeld had earlier published an enthusiastic overview of Ives's music in *The New Republic*, reprinted in part IV, below.

22. Rosenfeld may be confusing "Hail! Columbia," which does not appear, with "Columbia, the Gem of the Ocean," which appears in "Hawthorne." *Shall We Gather at the River* does not appear in the sonata. The middle section of "The Alcotts" may evoke the "Scotch songs" Ives mentions in his essay on the movement, and Henry Cowell and Sidney Cowell, *Charles Ives and His Music,* 2nd ed. (New York: Oxford University Press, 1969), 198, find the Scotch song "Loch Lomond" at the first $\frac{9}{4}$ measure in the middle section.

23. A facsimile of the program for this concert appears in Perlis, *Charles Ives Remembered*, 222.

24 . "Quarter-notes" in the original.

25. Actually, the tune used is "Columbia, the Gem of the Ocean"; Carter here repeats the misidentification by Paul Rosenfeld, noted above in note 22.

26. Parts of the story of Ives's Pulitzer are told in the selected correspondence in Part II, above.

27. Although not so identified by Downes, the Second Quartet was also a world premiere, several months before its performance on September 15 at the Yaddo Festival in Saratoga Springs by the Walden Quartet, reviewed below by Lou Harrison.

28. On Slonimsky's relationship with Ives, see the selected correspondence in Part II, above.

29. Ellipsis and brackets in the original.

30. Ellipsis in the original.

31. There are in fact references to Bach's Three-Part Invention in F Minor in the first and fourth movements and passages from the E-minor Fugue from Book 1 of *The Well-Tempered Clavier* in the finale. See J. Peter Burkholder, *All Made of Tunes: Charles Ives and the Uses of Musical Borrowing* (New Haven: Yale University Press, 1995), 126–29.

32. "Bringing in the Sheaves" occurs in the fast second movement, not in the slow third movement as implied in the previous sentence. The only known college song in the symphony is "Where, O Where Are the Verdant Freshmen?" in the second movement; "Boola Boola" does not appear. And the climax of the last movement does not involve polytonality; all the tunes are in F major.

33. The examples from Ives's Symphony No. 2 are printed here by permission of the publishers, Southern Music Publishing Company, Inc. Copyright 1951. [Cowell's note.]

34. The previous three tunes are probably misidentifications. For the borrowings in this piece and particularly at this moment, see Burkholder, *All Made of Tunes*, 102–36, especially 123–24.

Part IV

CONTEMPORARY VIEWS
OF IVES AND HIS MUSIC
PROFILES 1932–1955

·

Charles E. Ives

PAUL ROSENFELD
1932

Last February, the Pan-American Association of Composers gave an important concert at the New School. The program included two momentous first American performances. Besides the fiery, pungent little "Energia" by Carlos Chavez, it presented the "Set for Theatre Orchestra" of the little-known composer Charles E. Ives. Naturally, the "great newspapers" were entirely without representation in the audience. Not even one of the third or fourth musical critics, those who sign grudging little reviews with cryptic initials, was there. For musical news is constituted for the "great newspapers" not by the event of a man going mad and biting a dog, but by a dog going mad and biting a man: by Toscanini's performance of the Ninth Symphony, not by the revelation of the presence of another first-rate talent and great man in the group of living American composers. Yet that was one of the chief effects of the concert. No one present could longer doubt the position of Charles E. Ives in the company of the creative American artists.

It had previously been recognized by the spirited young musicians responsible for the more general acknowledgement now tardily accorded to Mr. Ives, and for the productions given a few of his works. But this recognition had been so esoteric, and the performances so infrequent, and the works presented so very fractionally representative of the mass of Ives's product, that to the public of amateurs both his place and figure perforce remained vague and indeterminable. Even the production of the "Set for Theatre Orchestra" did but press back a little the mist covering the great mass of the composer's pieces.

Four symphonies, the first two of which are in strict conventional form, three orchestral suites, two cantatas, three violin and two pianoforte sonatas, two overtures, a string quartet, three quarter-tone pieces and upwards of two hundred songs form the body of it; and we in New York have so far been given to hear, besides a few of the songs, only two of the orchestra suites and two movements of the Fourth Symphony. And only a relatively few of the other pieces, the cantata in Markham's "Lincoln," the second piano sonata, a collection of songs and a few other works, are accessible to students in print or photostat copies. Still, the impression given by the "Set for Theatre Orchestra" was so strikingly analogous to the impressions left by the compositions of Ives previously performed, that the great place assigned him by the series of experiences may quite reasonably be conceived to be his own.

It is doubly distinguished. For one thing, it is the honorable place of the pioneer in atonality. For Ives, born in 1874,[1] was writing in uncompromising dissonances as early as 1903, the year in which the sketches for certain of his orchestral pieces originated. And the atonal passages in Mahler's symphonies were composed later than that time. And the famous "Three Pieces for Pianoforte" of Schoenberg was published only in 1911. Ives's experiments in polyharmony actually antedate the century. While he was still a Yale undergraduate and pupil of Horatio Parker's, he began a composition for the organ with a chord in D-minor superimposed on one in C-major. The effect is said to have robbed him of the, at their warmest, somewhat frosty sympathies of our Orazio Vecchio. And these innovations were not theoretical but products of necessity. For Ives is an American with an immediate relationship to the medium of music. The freshness of his thematic material proclaims it; and the sureness of his grasp of the expressive power of the melodic interval.

Simultaneously with his occupation of the place of the pioneer atonalist, he fills the even more enviable position of one of the few originally gifted composers of impressionistic or descriptive or imitative music borne by America.

It is possible that acquaintance with the whole of Ives's music may alter one's impression, and show the whole work more conformable to the absolute and classical category. The chance seems slight, since a preponderance of traits in both the symphonic and programmatic works already revealed to us points to the descriptive, the imitative, the literary, bent of his inspirations. One of the chief characteristics of the music of Ives is the inclusion of traditional melodies, with something besides purely musical intention. The composer has not only modeled many of his wonderfully fresh melodies on the peculiar inflections of American hymn tunes and dance tunes, Negro chants and ragtime. He has planted "The British Grenadiers" bodily in the orchestral pieces called "Putnam Camp"; given the horn in "In the

Night" a minstrel-show melody to sing; introduced patriotic tunes into the savagely sardonic song "In Flanders Fields"; quoted a theme from "L'Après-midi d'un Faune" in the setting of Rupert Brooke's "In Grantchester." And these themes and the hymn tunes in the Fourth Symphony and the fiddler music in "In the Inn," are used for their extramusical associations, their representative values. "The British Grenadiers" stands, for example, for revolutionary America, which sang it in superb indifference to its text. The Debussy quotation illustrates Brooke's lines:

And clever modern men have seen a Faun
A-peeping through the green.

The hymn tunes in the symphony represent an other-worldly attitude toward this life.

Again, the three pieces comprised in the "Set for Theatre Orchestra" are definitely descriptive or imitative or, at the very least, atmospheric in intention. The dissonant, dumb, smothered pages of "In the Cage" express the state of a captive animal and, by extension, the state of caged humanity. The wildly modernistic potpourri "In the Inn" conveys an impression of the old countrified song and dance meetings. "In the Night" is a magical mood-painting, in the spirit of impressionism, although couched in a sharply autochthonous idiom. The more ambitious suite, "Three Places in New England," actual cause of the present writer's conversion to the Ivesian faith and his happy conviction of the composer's possession of creative forces, is even more deliberately descriptive, as the very specific titles of its subdivisions may indicate. The first section is called "The Shaw Monument in Boston Common" [rightly, *The "St.-Gaudens" in Boston Common*];[2] and the slow, fuzzy, gentle music, built of what appear to be reminiscences of plaintive Negro chants, is long in getting under way, and straggles and lingers, and after a momentary mobilization, dies off on an interrogatory phrase of the piano. One not only thinks "the Negro," but "the developing American mind." The second section is named "Putnam Camp," and represents conflicting band music. A commonplace waltz is jumbled with a foxtrot; the second band marches up at a tempo 25-percent faster than that of the first band; the piccolos shrill "The British Grenadiers"; and the America of fact and the America of revolutionary legend march away together in horrid polyharmony. The third section, "The Housatonic at Stockbridge," which is the hero of the suite and easily one of the freshest, most eloquent and solid orchestral pieces composed in America, transcribes in polyrhythms the movement of the great river in its vernal expansiveness. The violin solo continuously plays a rhythm independent of the orchestra's. The atonal and polytonal figures of the other violins contrast with the tonic harmonies of brass and woodwind. The cold fresh music develops into a sonorous cataract, and dwindles in the muted violins like water flowing away into distance and futurity.

As for the "scherzo" of the Fourth Symphony, Ives himself prefers to call it a comedy rather than a scherzo; indeed, it appears a sort of musical parallel to Hawthorne's "Celestial Railroad." The music contrasts an exciting worldly progress through life with the toils and tribulations of the Pilgrims in their marshes and rough places. Incidentally, the piece furnishes an excellent example of the combination of folkloreistic American music with a barbaric sonority very frequently found in Ives's orchestral works.

It is even possible that Ives's early espousal of the principles of atonality and polytonality is due to the strongly imitative inclination of his eminent talent; and that the experience in nature of models of dissonant tone was prerequisite to his compositions. True, his father, his first teacher, was a ceaseless experimenter in acoustics, and worked out a quarter-tone instrument; and the composer probably inherited his conviction that only a fraction of the means of musical expression were being utilized. While still an undergraduate, Ives himself experimented with unusual chord structures, exotic scales, harmonic rhythms and other revolutionary effects, and tried out his innovations with the help of the orchestra of the old Hyperion Theatre in New Haven! Still, it appears that it was while listening to the humorous musical distortions of church organists, village bands and itinerant fiddlers, that his imagination was actually touched by dissonant idiom. And it is in the form of imitations of the sounds of life, those produced by clashing bands and Fourth of July celebrations, as well as by "natural" causes, that certain of his happiest atonic and polytonic effects come to us.

One effect of this anticipation of a worldwide movement, and a grisly one at that, is to be read from the postscript contributed by Ives to the privately issued collection of a hundred and fourteen of his songs.[3] The tone bears witness to life driven back upon itself. It is half-apologetic, half-defiant, and altogether self-conscious, like that of a man who has found no support and anticipates an unsympathetic reception, and feels continually forced to explain and to justify an occupation which under normal conditions requires no explanation or justification. The miracle is that Ives persisted in composing. Lucky for him and us he was a business man, the manager of an insurance company! In the nineteen-tens, there was no preparation for him in Europe. What the conditions in America were can be gathered from the fact that only a few weeks ago, long since the Schoenbergs and the Stravinskys and the Hindemiths have demonstrated their particular mastery, Professor Daniel Gregory Mason publicly vented the opinion that those composers who wrote atonically or polytonically did so merely because they were too unendowed to be able to compose in the old dramatic forms!

But Ives had to give an integration of many hitherto disparate layers of American experience, through the medium of tone. And Wagner and Strauss and Debussy had shut behind them the door through which they had passed, once and for all time.

It is precisely for his utter faithfulness to spirit that we rejoice in and honor him today.

—from *The New Republic* 71 (20 July 1932): 262–64

NOTES

See also Rosenfeld's review of the 1938 *Concord Sonata* premiere in part III above. In this and all the profiles that follow, punctuation, spelling, and titles of works have been standardized only minimally, along the lines outlined in the Notes section to part III.

1. Redundant "was" before "born" in original, omitted here.

2. The movement was about Augustus Saint-Gaudens's monument to Col. Robert Gould Shaw and the unit he commanded, the Fifty-fourth Massachusetts Regiment, the first black regiment to fight in the Civil War.

3. Charles E. Ives, *114 Songs* (Redding, Conn.: By the Author, 1922; reprint, New York: Peer International, Associated Music Publishers, and Theodore Presser, 1975), 261–62. Reprinted with annotations as "Postface to *114 Songs*," in Charles Ives, *Essays Before a Sonata, The Majority, and Other Writings,* ed. Howard Boatwright (New York: W. W. Norton, 1970), 123–31.

Charles Ives

HENRY COWELL
1932

What is an American composer? The subject of American composition is now being much agitated; yet the candidates for the position of the great American composer sometimes presents curious credentials. Ernest Bloch is an American citizen, but he lived abroad until fully mature, and his music has no vestige of departure from European standards. Deems Taylor is a real American by blood and birth, but his music is a weak dilution of Wagner and Puccini. Aaron Copland is a step different from these—he is an American born, and he makes use of jazz elements in some of his music; jazz originated in America. Yet his whole technique of composition, as well as his point of view aesthetically, is taken bodily from the teachings of Nadia Boulanger, of Paris. Roy Harris is belligerently American as far as his philosophy goes—but his music is a mixture of conventional Brahms with a tincture of semi-modern French "atmosphere." One can go on indefinitely, showing that most of those who are discussed as great American creative leaders are usually only partially American at the best. This is probably in itself characteristic of us. We have sprung from Europe, for the most part, as a people. It would be folly to expect that we would start here with an entirely new musical foundation, any more than we have changed our race by moving across the water. Thus it is no reflection on the merits of the gentlemen mentioned above to point out that they are not as exclusively of this land in every respect as they would usually like to be considered.

We have, however, one composer—and probably only one composer—who is just as much based on American traditional practices in his music as any European composer's work has ever been based on the traditions of his country. That composer is Charles E. Ives, born in Danbury, Connecticut, and now fifty-seven years old.

Ives has not only developed through concentrated feeling and highly wrought musicianship a new mode of musical expression based on Yankee village music and transmuted into a musical art, but he also created many materials, usually credited to Schönberg and Strawinski, and used them in his early works. Ives employed them many years before these European masters. America has been many years behind Europe in recognizing the value of Schönberg and Strawinski; it is therefore natural that virtually no one in America recognized that Ives' contribution was of worldwide import at the time when he made it. It is only within the last two or three years that Ives' position has begun to be realized by those who are interested in the progress of the world's music.

Now a whole group of important modernists are falling over each other in their eagerness to do him sudden honor—honor for works which have been composed twenty or thirty years, and which were never performed or published until a year or two ago. Perhaps the sudden rush to the Ives banner is due to the fact that when his works were published in *New Music Quarterly* and sent to Europe, and when the indefatigable Nicolas Slonimsky performed his works abroad with leading symphonies, Europeans recognized that here was the most potent and original figure they had been shown in American music, and said so in loud print, under the signature of critics of known significance. Americans who were accustomed to following these European gentlemen continued to do so and now hail Ives, although before the European approbation they would have probably picked out almost anyone else as being the leading American composer!

II

Ives is a fundamentally serious composer. This is now a necessary thing to know of any new composer, as there are many who openly do not aim at seriousness, but who believe that to amuse is the aim of music. Ives has lots of genuine Yankee wit, but underlying breadth of purpose. There is spiritual integrity behind his works, and the best of them contain the ecstasy of angelic choiring—that quintessence of feeling which is religious, but is the religion of music rather than of the church.

Ives was brought up in a small Connecticut town. He was very sensitive to this early environment. He not only became imbued with American traditions in a place where America first took a line of demarcation in feeling from Europe, but he also heard the village music, music which although often utilizing fragments of English or Irish melody as a basis, changes them radically in practice. These changes, which are usually entirely lost in writing down the music, are the very things which make the music American; the only elements that are not like the British or Celtic beginnings.

Ives heard the country fiddler, the town band, the congregational singing. A less sensitive person trying to utilize this music as a foundation for a cultivated symphony would cut out all the really original elements, leaving only that formal husk represented by familiar notation. Ives was not content to do this. He heard distinctly the fascinations of subtle characteristic features of the music which were usually thought to be crudities—notes which were thought by musicians to be out of tune; notes in which the rhythm was off the beat; singing in which a congregation sang a nebulous group of tones surrounding a centre, rather than a single tone in the middle! All such things, and many other similar departures, Ives realized were not crudities nor mistakes, but were repeated over and over, were enjoyed, were in reality the genuine and correct American practices containing the real feeling of the Yankee. Cut out these elements, and the music is denatured.

So Ives has created a whole musical style based on these typical American usages. Although he often uses folk-themes, this is not the main point—the main thing is that all the fundamental materials of his music, emotional content, rhythm, harmony, melody, etc., should have arisen from these Americanisms in music; this happens not because Ives strives for that result, but rather because he *is* a Yankee villager! In order to create his result, which now includes numerous symphonic and other works, he has had to create and initiate in every musical field. He has carried rhythmical harmony, or the combining of different simultaneous rhythms, farther than anyone else in the world ever has—and this is something that can be measured definitely, because rhythm is mathematical as well as musical. He originated polyharmonies and tone clusters and almost every conceivable sort of dissonance when they were essential to his expression; but he has never been afraid to use the simplest concord. To be all-embracing and synthesize almost every possible musical material—that is his accomplishment. No chord is too cheap, and none too refined, to find place in his music, which runs through a very broad human emotional gamut, and makes use of all known materials to do so. The music is always fullsome, containing anything from delicately adjusted acoustical effects to replete tonal swirls which contain almost every musical sound at once. There is often an improvisatory freedom of spirit about the music which is very refreshing after the over-exact mechanistical sort of development which most modern music is undergoing.

III

Ives always considers the performer an integral part of his work. He realizes, as so few composers do, that the performer does part of the creating of a work as heard by auditors; and he leaves room for the performer to create, to add to his work within certain limits. His approach to his works is as though they were living entities which have the power of growth in the hands of great players. Thus he often gives directions to the performers in his scores which suggest their throwing themselves into the playing of his compositions with unusual freedom, regarding the written down form as only a beginning from which to depart; only a hint as to the depths to be plumbed rather than as a Procrustean bed, to conform to which all original ideas must be sacrificed.

It is delightful in an Ives work suddenly to run into a composer's note which informs you that if you have worked yourself into an emotional frenzy you may play the passage *fortissimo*, while if you still feeling quiet, you may play it *piano* instead! Or to find several different versions of a certain measure given, any of which may be played according to the performer's taste. We have seen alternate versions of pieces before, but only when the preferred version might be too difficult to play, and the composer also included an easier version; never before was the choice a matter of musical taste. Characteristic of the curious sort of original ideas with which his works teem is the passage in one of his symphonic works (the Fourth Symphony) which is written for two independent simultaneous orchestras—each one in a different key, playing a different piece. Counterpoint of two compositions at once! Finally one of the orchestras dies away; and Ives informs the conductor that it may die away anywhere within a page or two. Because the second orchestra is independent in rhythm as well as in key and matter! The suggestion for this double orchestra passage came from an early experience of Ives, in which he was marching and playing in one band, and heard another band, playing a different work, marching toward his band from the opposite direction. They both played at once, each trying to drown the other, and finally the second band was lost in the distance.

IV

To sum up, Ives is Yankee American. He comes from a family which has lived in America for many generations. He is steeped in American traditions and American music through native feeling and early environment. His thorough formal musical education at Yale University did not prevent him from developing original and indigenous musical materials in every field of music, and they have proved essential to his musical expression. Many of these materials are based on typical American country village practices of such subtle and un-notable nature that they were lost until Ives explored them, and built up a system of notating some of them. Some of Ives' materials he originated and used during the period from about 1900 to 1910; Strawinski and Schönberg became world-famous because they originated similar materials during the period between 1909 and 1918. Ives used jazz rhythms in some of his serious music during the same period; Gershwin and Copland have become known because they use jazz themes in symphonic works today.

Yet all these things pale before the most significant fact of all—Ives is great, and all his remarkable explorations in musical substance are utilized by him to give expression to emotions and ideas which although containing humor and delicacy are profound, and cover almost the entire range of human experience.

—from *Disques* (November 1932): 374–76

Charles Ives: The Man and His Music

[Excerpt]

HENRY BELLAMANN
1933

Mr. Ives' business success was founded on the same sort of daring
experiment, together with an interest and confidence in human
nature, that characterizes his music. I am told by a reliable authority
that the principles of this business were often radical and daring, but
that they were based really on the fundamentals of hard-headed
common sense. The business of the firm of which he was the senior
member sprang from very small beginnings. But the nature of the
business was such that it brought him in close relation with thousands
of men of all kinds and conditions. This association of over thirty
years, with its opportunity of knowing and working with so many
men, did what it apparently does not to some men—it gave him a
high respect for, a deep interest and confidence in the average man's
mind and character. This confidence was one of the things which were
put into the building of their business and seemed too visionary and
idealistic to many, especially to the older men in the business. The
young men were assured that this, among some of their other plans,
would cause their failure within a year. There were many discour-
aging and trying years; but some of the plans that seemed the most
visionary and idealistic were the ones that worked out the best. When
Mr. Ives gave up active participation on account of ill-health in 1930,
the firm of Ives and Myrick had grown to be the largest of its kind in
the country; an insurance editor, referring to the firm's achievement,
points out that, as the business grew, the firm retained the respect and
good-will of its competitors.

This business history is mentioned because it has a direct bearing
on what shall presently be said about music. Mr. Ives is no wild-eyed
revolutionary inhabiting the regions of Bohemia. He is a normal

citizen and has for more than a quarter of a century pursued his own way, going to business in the down-town New York district where many of his associates did not know of his interest in music, and all the time accumulating an imposing heap of scores, some of which anticipated the means and methods of the most advanced of the contemporary music—anticipating it by twenty years in some cases.

Even while Ives was a student at Yale the little Hyperion orchestra played successfully a score in which simultaneous rhythms and keys were suggested. And the audience, unsuspecting of what was happening, liked some of it. Mr. Ives' years at Yale under Horatio Parker were not as unhappy as some notices have suggested. He entertains a hearty respect for his teacher; and though his occasional tonal adventures did not meet with approval, the young composer followed the wishes of his teacher and laid the foundations of a compositional technique that was complete in all details. The "correct" compositions of this period bear ample witness to this.

• • •

One enters upon any discussion of the man with trepidation. Mr. Ives is excessively retiring. Few people know him outside of business. It is difficult to bring him to attend concerts even when his own music is being performed. He is a thorough-going New Englander with a deep love of the country and his close friends. One of his remote ancestors, towards the end of the eighteenth century, sold his farm in what is now the region of Beekman Street and East River because "New York was becoming too fancy and too crowded." There is much of this ancestor in Charles Ives.

This discussion of the composer's business career is purposed. It seems to show that a creative career may be carried on simultaneously with business—the two supplementing and complementing each other. (Witness the case of John Alden Carpenter.)[1]

It is not easy to interview Charles Ives. But when finally cornered on the question of his parallel system of life he said: "My business experience revealed life to me in many aspects that I might otherwise have missed. In it one sees tragedy, nobility, meanness, high aims, low aims, brave hopes, faint hopes, great ideals, no ideals, and one is able to watch these work inevitable destiny. And it has seemed to me that the finer sides of these traits were not only in the majority but in the ascendancy. I have seen men fight honorably and to a finish, solely for a matter of conviction or of principle—and where expediency, probable loss of business, prestige, or position had no part and threats no effect. It is my impression that there is more open-mindedness and willingness to examine carefully the premises underlying a new or unfamiliar thing, before condemning it, in the world of business than in the world of music. It is not even uncommon in business intercourse to sense a reflection of a philosophy—a depth of something fine—akin to a strong beauty in art. To assume that business is a material process, and only that, is to undervalue the average mind and heart. To an insurance man there *is* an 'average man' and he is humanity. I have experienced a great fullness of life in business. The fabric of existence weaves itself whole. You can not set an art off in the corner and hope for it to have vitality, reality and substance. There can be nothing *'exclusive'* about a substantial art. It comes directly out of the heart of experience of life and thinking about life and living life. My work in music helped my business and my work in business helped my music."

These views should encourage the young artist who considers "giving up music to go into business." In some cases Mr. Ives believes this to be a mistake or at least unnecessary, though he feels it to be a matter which each man must decide for himself. By being independent of the claims of expediency (a word which always moves this out-and-out New Englander to picturesque comment) the creative artist may pursue his own route, and if he is patient, await results with confidence.

This is in line with advice Mr. John Erskine recently gave to young writers when he said: "If you wish to write, get a job and don't depend on your writing for a living."

It is quite certain that, if Charles Ives had chosen to promote his work on sensational grounds, he would have had the world buzzing about him twenty-five years ago. He chose, rather, to await recognition on quite other grounds. A few of the early works were shown to publishers who shied at their strange idiom and their great difficulty. But for many years the composer has manifested a curious indifference both to publication and performance. One anecdote may illustrate his aversion to all personal exploitation. I urged him to have a photograph taken for use with an article. The explosion was terrifying. For days he went about pointing a derisive finger at me, muttering, "That man collects photographs!"

—from *The Musical Quarterly* 19 (January 1933): 45–58,
excerpt from pp. 46–48

NOTES

This passage focuses on Ives's work in the insurance business and what it reveals about his character, including what has become Ives's classic statement on the relation between music and business in his life. The subsequent discussion of the music overlaps with other reviews and profiles in Parts III and IV and is not included here. For more on Ives's work in insurance, see Michael Broyles's essay in Part I of this volume.

1. Carpenter (1876–1951) studied composition at Harvard with John Knowles Paine, graduating a year before Ives graduated from Yale. Carpenter then returned to work in his father's industrial firm and served as vice-president for more than a quarter century, while making a successful career as a composer.

An American Innovator, Charles Ives

GODDARD LIEBERSON
1939

Success in Business as a Parallel for Daring in Music—Anticipations of New Steps Abroad—A Study of the Composer and His Materials

In the year 1894, Debussy heard the first performance of his "L'Après-midi d'un faune"; Richard Strauss had plans for a tone-poem to be called "Till Eulenspiegels lustige Streiche"; the Metropolitan Opera performed "Elaine," an opera by a composer named Bemberg; Arnold Schönberg was twenty years old and had not yet written "Verklärte Nacht"; Igor Stravinsky was twelve years old and was not to begin serious study of music for seven more years; Alban Berg was doing the things that other nine-year-old boys did in Vienna, and listened to his brother Charley take his music lessons; and in England, the Gilbert and Sullivan repertoire, still not quite complete, kept the later Victorians in a constant state of amusement. In the same year, a twenty-year-old American composed a song called "Song for Harvest Season," the words being a stanza from an old hymn, and the music written for voice, cornet, trombone and organ pedal simultaneously in the keys of E♭, B♭, F, and C:

Song for Harvest Season. ©1933 by Merion Music, Inc. Used by Permission.

This experiment in polytonality may or may not have amused Charles Ives's teacher, Horatio Parker. But whether it did or not, it was inevitable that young Ives should have been doing such experimenting. It was inherent to his spirit, and his intellect; an expression of the early training which he had received from his father, who was a bandmaster and music teacher in Danbury, Conn., where Charles Ives was born.

The elder Ives provided his son with an early musical education and doubtlessly communicated to him some of his own feelings about tonal experimentation. For the senior Ives was a courageous assayer of new musical speech, delving into the possibilities of tone divisions, quarter-tones, polytonality, atonality, and acoustics. It was his wont to place sections of his band on balconies of different levels in order to test the result of sound coming from different planes or distances. He also experimented with chords built of fourths and fifths and exhibited a constant curiosity about the possibilities of new sounds through new orchestral combinations. At the same time, he trained his son in harmony, counterpoint, and instrumentation, and acquainted him with the best in musical literature.

When Ives entered Yale University in 1894, he was already a well-equipped musician, but he continued his music studies with Dudley Buck (organ) and Horatio W. Parker (composition). During his four years in college, he was the organist at St. Thomas's Church in New Haven, and for a number of years following was an organist in several different cities. Indeed, a few editions of *Who's Who* reveal Charles E. Ives as an organist in Albany.[1] Upon graduation from Yale in 1898, he went into business as a clerk for the Mutual Life Insurance Company. He held this position until 1906 and then assisted in forming the firm of Ives & Myrick, and remained a senior partner of this firm until 1930 when ill health caused him to give up active work. From 1898 to 1930, you might have come across the name of Charles Ives in a published collection of "114 Songs," or, if you happened to read the *Eastern Underwriter,* as the signature on an article called "The Amount to Carry—Measuring the Prospect"!

The fact that Ives was a successful business man and, at the same time, a daring innovator in music, has been a source of wonderment to nearly everyone but the person in question. Ives's reason for entering business was a simple one: it merely meant a financial security which would leave him free to compose music as he chose, a real necessity to a person of his character. He may also have felt that the "business" of music was far more odious than the business of insurance. Nicolas Slonimsky in an article for the Boston *Evening Transcript* even suggested that Ives's business experience had a good effect on his music. On this point, he wrote: "It is probable that his (Ives's) business activity created a sense of potential reality in him that made him try unusual methods in musical composition; for if new prospects are found in business, why not new ears in music?" But whatever the reason, one thing is certain, that Ives, long before anyone else, wrote music which defied certain conventions no less than it broke through to paths which for others were unperceived until years after he had walked them.

• • •

A Personal Style

However, it is ridiculous to think of Ives only as a chronological phenomenon, for his music manifests a style which is unmistakably new and individual whether he is writing so-called tone clusters or the simplest harmonic progression. It is merely incidental that Ives preceded Schönberg and Stravinsky in new musical devices which won a certain amount of glory for the two Europeans; the significant point is that Ives was not even considered in America until the breakdown of conventions was imported from other shores! In fact, no better example of the mouldy proverb "a prophet without honor, etc." could be found; for when Charles Ives was finally played in Europe, some of the most sedate critics found in his music the justification for calling America a musical country. In Paris, Paul Le Flem wrote the following for the *Comoedia*: ". . . Charles Ives seems to have created, before the 'Sacre du Printemps,' a style which by its audacities, places its author among the pioneers. He appears among his compatriots as the one most spontaneously gifted, whose daring, sometimes awkward, is never in contradiction with the aspiration of his feeling."[2] A reviewer for *Les Dernières Nouvelles* wrote: "Ives is not imitative; he has something to say. He is a musical artist painter, if such an expression can be used, an impressionist not without a mixture of naive realism; his art is at times awkward and raw, but in him there is real power and true invention . . . which does not follow either the fashion or authorities. Ives is, perhaps, the only one among the American composers whose art is truly national." Alfred Einstein, in writing about American music, said: "Charles Ives is, in my estimation, the most original and national." The *Sovietskaya Musika* in Moscow: "After MacDowell, Ives is undoubtedly the brightest figure on the American musical horizon." From the *Hamburger Freudblatt*: "In Ives . . . one finds a strong, high-moving sentiment, free from the banalities of better known works. This concert is the first indication that America has anything to offer in music." Willi Reich, in connection with a concert in Vienna: "Ives has kept himself apart from European influence, and has worked out his own peculiar style in advance of the development of others. Ives . . . stands as the leader and inspiration of the younger generation of American composers. . . ." In fairness, it must be said that certain critics in America, once given a chance to hear the music of Ives, waxed just as enthusiastic as their European confrères, if with less willingness to place Ives's status in the world scene of music.

Yet Ives has never attempted to obtain critical appraisal of his work. On the contrary, he is probably the most aloof of all composers on this score. It has even been reported that he allows no newspapers or magazines of any kind in his home save the London *Spectator*. Ives has always resisted any infringement on his privacy, as a person or as a composer. Had he wished to cut the capers of the typical salon composer, Ives could have years ago found recognition for himself on the grounds of being "unique" or on some other equally sensational count. But he is even indifferent to performances of his own work and seems to be satisfied solely with the writing of his music. Any notices of his works in newspapers or magazines usually come to his attention only through the action of thoughtful friends. Henry Bellamann tells, in an article for *The Musical Quarterly*, of an incident occasioned by his asking Ives to have a photograph made to accompany an article: "The explosion was terrifying. For days he went about pointing a derisive finger at me, muttering, 'That man collects photographs'."

• • •

What the Songs Reveal

Perhaps the best way to approach the music of Charles Ives is through his songs. In them, he has expressed the many facets of his character; his tenderness, his humor, his rough disapproval of hypocrisy and sham, and the fervid Americanism of a New England Yankee. Too, the songs give a chronological view of Ives's works and reveal the growth of his musical ideas. These ideas range from the simplicity of a Franzian series of chords to a passage of the most dissonant counterpoint. Nor is Ives unwilling to mix two such diverse elements. More often than not, that is the case, and after a few measures of nearly banal harmony there will be an abrupt crash of a harsh chord, or it may be introduced gently as in the following example taken from the song "Resolution," which opens with this charmingly simple harmony:

and then, just as we begin to wonder if perhaps this isn't too sweet, Ives introduces a subtle dissonance:

the ending is superbly simple again, and rhythmically fluid with no marked accents:

Resolution. ©1935 by Merion Music, Inc. Used by Permission.

This song (written in 1921, long after Ives had written scores of such complexity as might turn conductors grey over-night) demonstrates his disdain for a set musical theory (such as Schönberg's twelve-tone dogma) which excludes the use of material other than that dictated by the theory. He is extraordinarily sensitive to the words which he is setting and is equally sensitive to the fact that music bears a relationship to life; obviously, then, it is impossible for him to use materials which do not "fit" his mood, no matter whether anyone agrees with him as to the materials or not.

One of the earliest experiments of Ives in song is called "Soliloquy—or a Study in 7ths and Other Things" written in 1907. It preludes much of what is to come, not only in his own music but in the music of others, particularly Schönberg and Alban Berg. The voice part, in its jumps and intervals and in its juxtaposition to the piano part, is not unlike many passages in Alban Berg's "Wozzeck" (though Ives reached this in an attempt to set down in music a "Yankee's drawl"):

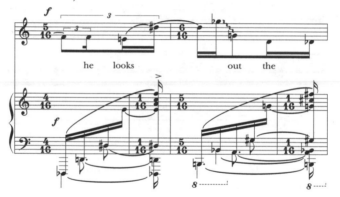

In one part of the song, the accompaniment opens into a long fan-like design of chords which grows smaller and smaller to end in a cluster at the close of the measure:

and the voice part ends in a baffling melodic and rhythmic design:

so eas - i -ly dis - posed of!

Like all of Ives's music, these songs call for a performer's participation to an extent scarcely demanded by the music of any other composer. Ives constantly takes the potential performer into his confidence—leaving whole sections of his music to their discretion and musical taste. It is this trait which is apt to make his music appear terrifying to the average person; music which seems to demand poly-handed players from some other planet! Yet Ives puts it squarely up to the performer—if four hands are needed, well get them! There is no rule which says that a bass part cannot be played by two hands while the treble part is played by two, or maybe four. Ives will sometimes indicate that a chord is to be played one way if by one player alone, or another way if four hands are available at the time.

It is impossible, within the confines of an article, to demonstrate the variety within Ives's songs. He has written nearly 130, and they range from the beer parlor type of harmony (which Ives delights in writing for fun) to an expressionism which brings every aspect of tone and rhythm into play. In the first category, there is the song "In the Alley," under the title of which is written, "Not sung by Caruso, Jenny Lind, John McCormack, Harry Lauder, George Chappell or the Village Nightingale." The piano introduction will suffice to show its mood:

The song "Down East" (1919) further illustrates Ives's willingness to mix the complex with the simple. It is not easy to believe that the few following measures are within the framework of the same song:

The lilting second melody, by the way, is a fine example of Ives's devotion to the type of tunes which are the experience of every American who has gone to church, been at a ball game, or heard a band concert.

All of the songs are worth looking at. Only mention can be made here of "Charlie Rutlage," "The Cage," or the remarkable songs "September" and "December." These last are probably the best-known of Ives's songs, and represent the full flower of his genius. Others like "Majority" and "An Election" make striking use of tone-clusters.

It is also within the songs that one begins to feel the loosening of rhythms from the measured beat. Shifting of main beats to weaker ones, a constant change of time from measure to measure, elided beats, and time signatures of $\frac{4}{16}$, $\frac{1}{16}$, $\frac{5}{16}$, or no time signatures at all, are characteristic of Ives.

Some of the songs are hardly singable, and few of them can be picked up and "sung right off"; nor is it the composer's intention that that should be the case. They represent, rather, the workshop of Ives: repositories for ideas, fragmentary or extended. Yet, "The White Gulls" would repay any singer with its atmosphere and subtlety. Perhaps, the day that Ives's songs make their appearance in the programs of some of our better known singers, the phrase "American group" will come to have more significance.

• • •

The "Concord" Sonata

The recent performance in New York of Ives's Second Piano Sonata, "Concord, Mass., 1840–60," again brought to the attention of the public a work which had been written from 1911 to 1915.[3] Of it, Ives says: "This Sonata is an attempt to present one person's impression of the spirit of the literature, the philosophy, and the men of Concord, Mass., of over a half century ago. This is undertaken in four movements: 1. 'Emerson'; 2. 'Hawthorne'; 3. 'The Alcotts'; and 4. 'Thoreau'." However, that is not all Ives had to say about this work, for, in 1920, he published a small book, "Essays Before A Sonata," which discussed at some length the whole understanding on the part of Ives of the spirit of transcendentalism. The book itself is interesting, and reveals Ives to be a person of sincere and profound thought; one who makes no careless utterances. In this book, Ives rightfully discusses music and the composer in relationship to literature, but makes no attempt to explain or excuse or project or impose his own music with words. There is no need to. The "Concord" Sonata speaks for itself, most eloquently. It is in no sense program music—that is, in no accepted sense. It does not attempt to paint portraits; but if it approaches any style of painting, it is abstraction. For Ives has expressed in his own terms with his own means the values of other philosophers—others, for certainly Ives is himself philosophizing about them. The very opening of the "Emerson" section reveals that thinker to us as a noble person:

with a somewhat dissonant brooding spirit.

In Hawthorne, Ives chooses to show the more fantastic side of that writer, and throughout there are few indications of tempo or expression. Ives has only this to say about playing this movement: "For the most part, this movement is supposed to be played as fast as possible, lightly and not literally, and not always in the same way each time. Marks of tempo, expression, etc., are used as little as possible. If the score itself, the preface or an interest in Hawthorne suggests nothing, marks will only make things worse." Also called into play here is a strip of board with which to play the tone-clusters which are "to sound as distant bells." In this writer's copy of the music, Mr. Ives has written in his own hand: "It is better if another piano—off stage—can play these bell chords." But even if played "on-stage," the result is a most stunning effect. These clusters are notated in the following manner:

* played with a board

There is a great charm in "The Alcotts" movement—a gentle sympathy with the warm home life and genial relationships of that typical New England home. In the living room, there stood a small spinet-piano which Sophia Thoreau gave to the Alcott children and on which Beth played the old Scotch airs and the "Fifth" Symphony. This is suggested in the music:

The section on Thoreau presents all the spaciousness of nature. It is music of breadth and is profoundly moving in its intensity and nobility of expression.

As a whole, the "Concord Sonata" is certainly the most formidable piano composition to have come out of America. It is exceedingly difficult to perform, but its value rises far above any physical problems which it poses.

• • •

Large Orchestral Works

Charles Ives's symphonies, orchestral sets, quarter-tone music, and chamber pieces reveal an even more complex aspect of his music. This is particularly true of the orchestral music which sometimes defies all the rules and regulations with one clean sweep. Conductors who pick up a score in which bar lines do not meet, in which some instruments have time indications while others have a long involved rhapsodic solo on a staff with no bar lines, while overlapping bar-lines are groups of threes, sevens, and fives—well, most conductors gulp and then look around for the nearest Haydn score, and but a few have the temerity to attempt a performance. When one does (as have Nicolas Slonimsky, Eugene Goossens, and Leon Barzin), the results are astonishing. Much more is clear to the ear than to the eye. And music which seemed completely impossible when viewed as ink on paper, turned out to be a combination of sounds which were startlingly beautiful. Ives's orchestral talent is one derived from his early listening experiences coupled with later training. For the most part, the early listening has the upper hand, and there are reminiscences of two bands passing each other while going in opposite directions and playing the while, remembrances of tardy trumpeters who come in too late or too often and always manage to overlap the measures, and recollections of lagging violins, persistent drums, and struggling flutes. All these things appeal to Ives. They appeal to his sense of improvised "go" in which talent for an instrument takes precedence over the written note. Still, that is only one side of Ives's orchestrative mind. The other has to do with his expressionistic nature. His ability to suggest atmosphere, reality and unreality, in tone, represents a true gift. Such works as "Hallowe'en," "Three Places in New England," "The Fourth of July," "Theatre Set" [*Set for Theater or Chamber Orchestra*] and "Lincoln, the Great Commoner" are vivid characterizations of places and people. His power of suggesting a mood, as manifest by the orchestral piece "In the Night," is also extraordinarily effective.

It is in the large orchestral pieces that Ives brings into full play his astounding ability to fluctuate, combine, and invent rhythms. Ives is not one who feels rhythm as a constant number of beats within set squares. His music moves forward to a swiftly changing pattern of rhythmic impulses which derive from a vast counterpoint of separate rhythms. It takes a discerning ear to recognize this counterpoint; but even undiscerned it has an emotional effect. Ives's rhythmic ideas are particularly effective in expressing various aspects of nature, as in the orchestral piece "From The Housatonic at Stockbridge"—here, the overpowering sense of undulation and swirl is due entirely to constant overlapping of rhythm patterns.

In an age when anyone dares anything, Charles Ives stands almost alone in his rhythmic explorations. A glance at one of his orchestral scores shows him to have advanced (with remarkable self-confidence) far beyond the still restrictive ideas of what rhythm should be. Compared to his Fourth Symphony, Stravinsky's "Sacre" is no more than child's play. With the exception of the works of other American composers, Ives's works contain the only music which calls for a fundamental difference in the approach to rhythm. In this, he has carried over into his orchestral works the already stated faith in the performer to carry out "ideas" which are sometimes merely indicated rather than clearly noted. Much of the orchestral music of Ives is yet to be tested in performance—and the day of its test will mean recognition for an astounding creative mind.

• • •

His Musical Personality

The personality of Charles Ives as found in his music is not easily perceptible. One must first break down his own barriers to an art which may seem strange and relentlessly uncompromising. But once the approach has succeeded, a very large figure looms out of the melange of consonance and dissonance and rhythmical complexity. There is perceived a person of high ideals, one who will sacrifice everything for human rights; a person who denies sensuousness for the beauties of nature; and a philosopher with a simple philosophy of common-sense and altruism. Furthermore, a typical New England American, proud of his heritage of freedom and justice, proud of Thoreau, and ashamed of the witch-burning. One wonders how long it will take for this personality to reach a larger audience. That audience will have to come to Ives; for his music is conclusive enough proof that he will not go to them. Ives knows that it is possible to reach a larger public with a lesser product and for the artists who indulge themselves in that luxury, he has these words: ". . . his business is good—for it is easy to sell the future in terms of the past—and there are always some who will buy anything." If the buyers of Ives are but few now, he at least has the satisfaction of knowing that they are steady customers.

—from *Musical America* 59, no. 3 (10 February 1939): 22, 322–23

NOTES

1. Ives was organist at St. Thomas Episcopal Church in New Haven from May 1893 through April 1894, while he was a student at Hopkins Grammar School, then at Center Church on the New Haven Green from September 1994 through June 1898, while he was at Yale. He never had a position at Albany, but served at churches in Bloomfield, New Jersey and then in New York until 1902.

2. See the extract from Le Flem's review in Part III, above.

3. See the reviews in Part III, above. Lieberson's essay appeared in the immediate aftermath of the Ives boomlet that followed Lawrence Gilman's laudatory review.

Ives Today: His Vision and Challenge

ELLIOTT CARTER
1944

"No matter how sincere and confidential men are in trying to know or assuming that they do not know each other's mood and habits of thought, the net result leaves a feeling that all is left unsaid; for the reason of their incapacity to know each other, though they use the same words. They go on from one explanation to another but things seem to stand about as they did in the beginning because of that vicious assumption. But we would rather believe that music is beyond any analogy to word language and that the time is coming, but not in our life-time, when it will develop possibilities unconceivable now,—a language, so transcendent, that its heights and depths will be common to all mankind."

Few composers in our time have come to grips with the basic problems of musical expression, and certainly few have taken so definite a stand as does Charles Ives in his interesting *Essays Before a Sonata* (1920, now out of print).[1] Reading them, one cannot help feeling that such a man with such ideas *must* be capable of writing exceptional music. The tone is elevated, the wit brilliant. Here, as in his music, Ives reveals himself a devout believer in transcendental philosophy, in the immanence of God in nature, in the glorious mission of music which is to be achieved only when freed from the pedestrian ideas of professional musicians, in the ability of man to grasp the divinity behind nature through feeling and not through artificialities of logic. Of American music he says that a composer who believes in the American ideal cannot fail to be American whether he uses folklore or not. Of performing musicians he says that the composer must lead the way, the performer must figure out how to play the music. The book is a little masterpiece; it should be known to all musicians.

The difference between Ives and other mystical composers, Scriabin for instance, is that he believes neither in ritual nor in the methodical training of the intuition which raises man from one level of consciousness to another, leading to a denial of the physical world. Ives follows Emerson. For him the natural world reflects the spiritual, and so is of great concern. Hence the divergence between the patterned music of the Russian and the free, almost random music of Ives.

Ives' dissonance differs from that of most other composers who use it to express physical excitement, sensations of pleasure and pain or effects of distortion in the manner of the modern painters, or to reflect spiritual conflict, as in the works of Baudelaire. Ives is always in quest of the transcendental. On the surface of his work, the infinite complexity of nature, the rapidly changing moods of forest and plain, the web of counterbalancing forces appear confused and dissociated. But Ives' involved texture, while mirroring this superficial confusion, at the same time attempts to show the larger harmony of rhythm behind the natural process. Faith in the purpose and goodness of nature rather than concern over its savage conflicts and hostility determines his choice of moods. In his essays he says that Debussy, in works like *La Mer,* appears interested only in the physical aspects and never sees beyond them.

Ives, with his exalted goal for musical expression, believes that composers should be free always to follow their highest instincts. Difficulty of performance is the performer's problem, not his. The quest for performances, for payment for music, for success, are beside the point. Ives himself makes his money in business and so has been as free in his pursuit of music as one of his instrumental parts, whose bar-lines, rhythms, notes and speed do not tally with the rest of the orchestra. He is as difficult to assimilate into the pattern of the organized musical world as such a part is into an orchestral texture. He has persistently refused royalties, prefers not to have his music copyrighted so that performers may feel free to take liberties and usually insists on paying for publication. Thus he strictly preserves his amateur status, while his reputation—based rather on what has been written about him that on the few performances of his music—constitutes a threat to the professional world.

All who have written about his music, and their number is legion, are convinced that if performed it would meet the expectations aroused by his famous ideals. It probably would—provided the listener made several allowances. He must be ready to grant that the quotation of familiar tunes, with which the music is studded, is a device sufficiently powerful to evoke the particular feelings apostrophized. Then there is also the amount of detail left to the interpreter's discretion. The polyrhythms, which appear to be precisely written, obviously call for an improvisatory technic hard to achieve in ordinary rehearsals. Bernard Herrmann and Nicolas Slonimsky have faced this problem most squarely. Herrmann claims that with the proper rehearsal, everything in Ives is playable. A few years ago he boldly gave an Ives series over C.B.S. and brought to the air several highly effective pieces, among them the *Largo for Strings* and the very affecting first and third movements of the *Fourth Symphony*. Taking advantage of Ives' suggestion that performers should "interpret" the works to suit themselves, Herrmann re-orchestrated part of the first movement and ironed-out some of its rhythmic complexities. But such a procedure followed without great understanding of the music could easily rob it of characteristic qualities.

Another artist, John Kirkpatrick, whose performance of the *Concord Sonata* is well-known, also following Ives' expressed intentions, takes certain liberties with the polyrhythms. With great care and devotion he molds the music into a very moving auditory experience. That Kirkpatrick's conception can be found in the notes is unquestionably true, but it is also true that a good but unsympathetic musician might give a chaotic and unintelligible account of the same score. It is all a question of whether one can enter into the spirit of this music and then recreate it. Such a challenge is good for the profession, it demands a vision that goes beyond the notes.

A quick glance at Ives' total output—which can now be studied in print or in photostat (eleven volumes of chamber music and six orchestral scores) in the Library of Congress, the Fleisher Collection and the American Music Center—reveals many interesting facts. The music shows a rather spasmodic development, from the production of youthful organist with a classical background playing in a Presbyterian church, to the elaborate works most of us are familiar with. There has been, from the start, a preoccupation with hymns, marches, and other native American music. The *First Symphony,* written in the '90's, has a fetching, naive quality; it shows influences of Mozart, Bach and Beethoven and at the same time some strange harmonic progressions that resemble early Shostakovitch. The *Second Symphony,* following almost immediately, reveals chromatic influences, Franck, Brahms and Dvorak. It is made up of arrangements of earlier organ works and an older overture. The *Third,* for a small orchestra, although written only a little later, is a new departure. It has a slow first and last movement and a folksy middle one that is gentle and full of charm. The first is made up of unusual progressions and the last is quite Franckian. Then comes a complete break. The *Fourth Symphony*, written about the time of the last war, is full of the surprising effects most musicians associate with Ives, which were not noticable in his earlier works.

There are two other symphonies, *Holidays in a Connecticut Country Town* [*Holidays Symphony*] (Washington's Birthday, a very solemn and beautiful Decoration Day, an extremely elaborate and wild Fourth of July and a dithyrambic Forefathers' and Thanksgiving Day) and a *Universal [Universe] Symphony* which has remained a rough sketch for the last ten years. *Holidays*, like the *Fourth Symphony*, is in his most advanced style and shows all the facets of Ives' music, as do also the *Second Orchestral Set*, the *Theatre Set [Set for Theater or Chamber Orchestra]*, *Three Places in New England* and a few works in the chamber music volumes. In these latter there are, besides, what at least to this writer appear to be parodies of modern music like his satirical songs about modern life.

The orchestral scores of his later period make use of several devices which deserve more comment than they have received so far. Ives is fond of using a separate instrumental group, playing some kind of ostinato figure and maintaining its own tempo behind a fast movement and even behind a slow one but in different rhythm. This seems designed to give the natural setting of trees and sky against which he places human events. The transcendental background of faint sounds usually starts and ends a movement which may depict, in rather literal fashion, by quotation of themes and in other ways, the noisy or religious or patriotic episodes of everyday life. This latter music is often naively pictorial, while his style verges on impressionism and takes on the most advanced dissonance when it represents the transcendental.

Ives' range is remarkably broad. He offers us the rural, homely qualities of Whittier, the severity of Emerson, the fancy of Hawthorne and the meditation of Thoreau. These moods return again and again in all his later works. The contrast between the transcendental polyrhythm and polytonality, and the human music of hymns, dance and march, is always present.

This year, on October 20th, Ives will celebrate his seventieth birthday. Yet real consideration of his music still lies in the future. However fascinating it may be to speculate about, its actual sound will be more enthralling. Let us hope, for our sake, as well as for his, that performances will not be too long in coming. He has waited now for many years. The musical public has known all about him for more than ten. It is about time for a real demonstration.

—from *Modern Music* 21 (May–June 1944): 199–202

NOTE

1. Since reprinted in Ives, *Essays Before a Sonata, The Majority, and Other Writings*, ed. Howard Boatwright (New York: W. W. Norton, 1970).

Four Symphonies by Charles Ives

BERNARD HERRMANN
1945

The strange neglect of Charles Ives at this time can be ascribed only to our musical apathy. The literary figures of New England's golden age, with whom Ives ranks in spirit, are coming alive again through the efforts of writers like Van Wyck Brooks and F. O. Matthiessen. But out of Ives's great body of works few pieces have been performed, and these only by adventurous singers and pianists. Our orchestras have almost entirely overlooked him. Even on the occasion of his seventieth birthday this year, not one conductor of a major symphonic group felt the need to present a work in his honor.

In solitude, Ives's original mind and soaring imagination developed a technic of expression which owes nothing to Europe but is as daring as the innovations of Schönberg or Stravinsky. When Europe still considered Debussy a modernist, Ives was writing polytonal and atonal music, experimenting with multiple rhythms, acoustical juxtapositions and quarter-tones.

Because all his orchestral music, except the Scherzo from the *Fourth Symphony* and the *Three Places in New England,* is still unpublished, it has seemed inaccessible. And so the misconception has grown that it is difficult. Yet it presents no more problems than works by Stravinsky, Bartok, or Milhaud. Much of this manuscript music is simple and beautiful and could easily be performed.

The idea that all the symphonies except the fourth are dull and conventional is another illusion not based on fact. Each represents an important stage not only in Ives's development, but in the whole of American music. When we leaf through these scrawled and much annotated pages we sense the real restlessness and boldness of a pioneering spirit.

At twenty-four Ives, who was still at Yale studying with Horatio Parker, composed his first symphony (1897–98). Surrounded by the current symphonic successes, he took Mendelssohn, Raff, and

Tchaikovsky as his external models. The brilliant orchestration, clear architecture and pleasing melodies must have made his teacher proud—with some misgivings.

The symphony has a key designation of D minor—the only one by Ives to follow that convention. But the development section of its first movement, an allegro in strict sonata-form, is surprisingly modern. In a ninety-bar treatment of an harmonic sequence through all the choirs of the orchestra, Ives solves his musical problem in a way Vaughan Williams might today.

The principal melodies grope their way above. Here even the scoring is unusual. The recapitulation, with its brilliant Beethovenesque coda, brings us back to the nineteenth century.

The slow movement is indebted to Mendelssohn's organ sonatas, but is elusively American, like a country organist's revery. The Scherzo, a gossamer bit of scoring, has a delicate woodwind theme.

Later violins enter in imitation, followed by 'celli and basses, and the whole rises to an aerial whirl. Strangely out of its time, the canonic weaving of the Trio's second subject suggests an Edmund Rubbra symphony.

The standard finale uses all the Tchaikovsky tricks of sequence and swirling orchestration, yet the brashness and vitality are Ives's own. What the impact of Ives's personality on his time might have been, we can only guess. The symphony was not performed then, nor has it ever been played since.

• • •

Two years of creative groping preceded the second symphony, in which an entirely new influence on idiom and form appears. But it is really an old influence, for Ives, the son of a country organist and bandmaster, had been exposed since childhood to the music of New England. In this symphony he repudiates the European models. Unconventionally, a slow prelude, somber and introspective in mood, forms the first movement. An organ-like melody

is followed immediately by a theme whose startling harmonies suggest Prokofiev.

It is at the end of this movement that Ives makes his first symphonic use of American material. A quotation from *O Columbia the Gem of the Ocean* appears as a counter-theme in the horns. A brief oboe recitative links the Andante to the gay and rollicking Allegro, whose simple tunes and galloping rhythms recall the village band.

Ives has described the third movement as a "take-off, a reflection of the organ and choir music of the Long Green Organ Book of the sixties, seventies, and eighties." To close this restful piece, of such deep feeling, the flute plays a quotation from *America the Beautiful*.

The Finale's maestoso introduction is based on a proud horn motive. It builds to a full sonority which introduces the Allegro, originally part of a previously composed *American Overture*. Against an exhilarating barn-dance tune, fragments of *De Camptown Races* are heard. Ives calls the second subject, a variant *of Old Black Joe*, "a kind of reflection of Stephen Foster and the old barn-dance fiddling over it."

The first theme returns to overwhelm everything. Then the whole pattern is repeated with subtle variations in color and harmony. Now it is decorated by fragmentary quotations from folk and patriotic themes. Some are not easy to identify, since only a few notes of the original melody are preserved, and they are quickly caught up in the rushing speed of the dance. Then at the coda the trombones proclaim the entire *Columbia* song with a loud thumping hooray on the bass drums. It is as though Ives were telling the whole world of his proud heritage. This movement might be called a musical Currier and Ives. The symphony orchestra has been swept aside to make way for country fiddlers and the firemen's band, for a Fourth of July jubilation, the shouting of children, a politician's speech, and Old Glory.

But the conductors of the time shied away from these "Salvation Army tunes." Brahms, who used *Gaudeamus Igitur,* appeared on their programs, while Ives's second symphony, except for a reading by the Hyperion Theatre Orchestra of New Haven, remained unperformed.

• • •

Far from being discouraged by this neglect, Ives immediately began a third symphony. This quiet work, in three movements, is lightly scored for an orchestra of single woodwinds, two horns, trombone and strings. It was composed between 1901 and 1904 while Ives was active in the insurance business in New York. The spirit of the great camp meetings, once so popular in Danbury, runs through this symphony. It is based on old hymn-tunes, and its fervent longing is expressed without show or bombast. Ives, in the role of preacher, speaks words of comfort, tenderness and hope.

A serene opening moves on to a passage whose harmonies might have been imagined by Gesualdo.

Then *O for a Thousand Tongues* is treated in free fugal fashion

and the first mood returns. In the second movement there is less intensity. Ives told me that he wished to represent the games which little children played at the camp-meeting while their elders listened to the Lord's word. He creates the effect in a kind of clapping phrase.

The final Largo treats, in free rhapsodic form, the gospel hymn *Just as I Am.*

In its deep sincerity this symphony is like the great Bach chorales. Its religion has none of the mystic elements of Franck, Elgar, or Wagner, but is pure New England. Gustav Mahler was so impressed when he saw the score that he took it back to Austria. But Ives's fate still pursued him. Mahler died that year, and this noble work has never been performed.

• • •

The fourth symphony, written between 1910 and 1920, is the most elaborate and ambitious of Ives's works. It is scored for an immense orchestra, large percussion section and chorus. And it contains the simplest music and the most complex ever written.

Ives refers to the Prelude as the "What and Why which the spirit of man asks of life." Its strong opening is based on the hymn *Watchman, Tell us of the Night.* Immediately after this, a second orchestra, composed of harps and a few violins placed at some distance from the main orchestra, sets up a kind of musical backdrop. It attempts no melodic counterpoint but establishes an harmonic haze of sound in an entirely different key. The effect is indescribably beautiful; it is like nothing else in music. Against this, solo 'cello and piano express the searching and questioning of the soul.

The hymn returns, now sung by the chorus, and is dominant to the end. The entire movement is only eight pages in score, but its simple dignity is unforgettable.

The succeeding movements are "the diverse answers in which existence replies." The first of these is "not a Scherzo in the accepted sense of the word, but rather a comedy, in which exciting, easy and worldly progress through life is contrasted with the trials of the Pilgrims in their journey through the swamps and rough country. The occasional slow episodes—Pilgrims' hymns—are constantly crowded out and overwhelmed by the former. The dream or fantasy ends with an interruption of reality—the Fourth of July in Concord." This amazing Scherzo uses all the devices of modern music. Its percussion effects alone are as daring as anything by a Varese. A great extroverted physical piece, it hurls the listener into an intoxicating complexity of hymn-tunes, jazz, ragtime, fiddle music and folk-like fragments.

The third movement is a magnificent Fugue. Its simple diatonic harmonies seem especially serene after the Scherzo. Ives calls it "an expression of the reaction of life into formalism and ritualism," but these words convey little of its quality. *From Greenland's Icy Mountain* is the principal theme, *Coronation* the counter-subject. After an impassioned climax, there is a coda of extraordinary poignancy. Over a string pianissimo the clarinet's lovely, questioning melody

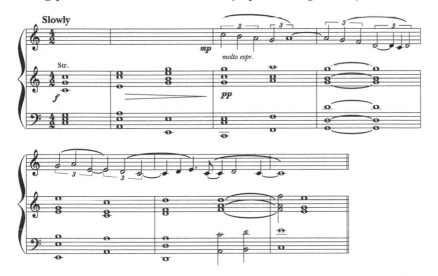

is answered by the reassuring strains on the solo trombone of *Joy to the World*.

The Scherzo of the fourth symphony is modern music liberated, but the Finale belongs to some distant future. After the opening bars, which recall the Prelude, it uses no themes, quotations or motives, no harmonic or rhythmic patterns. Each instrument pursues its own path in ever-changing rhythms, breaking into its own themes. The chorus sings a wordless vocalization. The effect is of a great *sound,* an enormous tutti which swells and recedes. An Oriental would describe such music as the "pure state" which exists in space, chaotic, all-embracing. Whether it can give us musical pleasure in the sense we conceive it today, only a performance can show. But, although the first three movements of the fourth symphony have been presented separately, the great Finale still awaits performance.

This symphony is grand in conception, but Ives planned a fifth on an even larger scale. The *Universe Symphony* was to be played outdoors, with five or six orchestras, bands and a chorus of hundreds. Ill-health has forced him to leave this project in sketches. But his dream reveals the adventurous and transcendent hope of an indomitable spirit. Neither bitterness nor compromise has weakened his strength of purpose. Some day, perhaps, the path he has trod as pioneer will be familiar to everyone.

—from *Modern Music* 22 (May–June 1945): 215–22

Tardy Recognition:

Emergence of Charles Ives as Strongly

Individual Figure In American Music

OLIN DOWNES
1946

When a nation is settling its land, breaking its earth, absorbing constant immigration and the turbulent forces that come with it, it is not surprising if single personalities of exceptional capacities are unrecognized or ridden over roughshod in the scramble by contemporaries too busy themselves to pause and recognize a particular individual's value to the new civilization.

It is just the same in music. In America we are only now establishing our boundaries, only now beginning to assess the achievements of our pioneers, and only now, where our creative artists are concerned, getting really rooted in our soil.

On this soil there start up all sorts of different growths, some of them delicate and some of them hardy, some indigenous but most of them seeds wafted from afar, all mingling together in fantastic combinations, and gradually, in the terms of our spring gardeners, accumulating a mulch from which always stronger growths will develop. And in America, today, we find one of the deepest rooted of these growths—the one which is the most sturdy, luxurious, savorous and thorny, too, in the music of Charles Ives.

Premiere of Third Symphony

The singularly individual quality of his art is attested by recent events which have emphasized the nature of his product and certain co-related facts of his career. In the first place, Charles Ives is seventy-one years old. But last week at the concert of American music by living composers which the New York Little Symphony gave in Carnegie Chamber Music Hall, it was his Third Symphony, then given its world première, which far surpassed everything else on the program for virility, originality, and essential modernity. The reviewers were unanimous upon this point as they were upon that of the racy and national quality of the music.[1] And the symphony, then heard for the first time anywhere, had lain around in a Connecticut barn and adjacent places for forty years!

That sort of thing has happened before when Ives' music was played. One afternoon in 1927, grumbling at the number of concerts that had to be covered, this reviewer lurched into Town Hall, and as quickly as he sat down sat up, electrified. For the orchestra, under Eugene Goossens, at a Pro Musica concert, was playing music of a vigor, raciness and audacity as unheralded as they were astounding. The score was concerned with the composer's recollection of a New England village before the turn of the century on the Fourth of July, with the commotion, the brass bands, the hymns to Old Glory and the rest of it; things he had known as a boy, and which memory had transmuted into astonishingly imaginative vigor. It was a movement—two of them were played—from the Fourth Symphony of Charles Ives, then unknown to us by so much as his name, though he already had passed his fiftieth year.

An Outstanding Figure

It is well to say here that having heard such original music only once—a performance never since repeated in this city—we may have overestimated its unmistakable vitality and novelty of expression. But the impression was so strong, and has been so indelible, that, coupled with other fragmentary manifestations of Mr. Ives' quality as musician, one believes in the presence of a significant creative spirit.

A third episode may now be recounted, which has its regrettable connotations.

Some six years ago certain leading members of the Monte Carlo Ballet, Russian dancers and musicians, were seeking new American music as a subject for choreographic interpretation. They asked the writer for some suggestions in this direction. He gathered together a few American scores that he thought might interest them, one of them by Ives. It was the only score that the group took seriously. They clustered around the piano, where Nicholas Slonimsky, one of the two musicians that we knew in the entire nation who could play from an Ives score, was officiating. Whether Charles Ives would have been disappointed by their conclusions is not here to be conjectured. Choreographic "interpretations" visited upon helpless symphonies are legion and more often than not sheer misrepresentation of the music. The Russians concluded that, in view of the difficulty of the score, it could not be readily converted into a ballet. But the aside of one of them while the discussion was going on was striking. He said to us in a whisper, "Too bad: Stravinsky."

"Still Too Bad; Too Late"

For answer we simply pointed to the date on the music page. It was 1901, in which year Stravinsky was still wet behind the ears, having composed not a single one of his important works. Schoenberg had written "Verklaerte Nacht" by that time, a work which Ives could not possibly have heard. Hindemith had yet to gain a public. The voices, in a word, of the leading modernists of that decade were unknown in America. (And certainly no one in this country, at the time, would have taken Ives' audacities seriously.) When we indicated the date on the score to our Russian friend he said "Still too bad; too late."

Advanced Musical Thinking

That is to say, that although Charles Ives had anticipated in the work under examination the poly rhythms and the poly harmonies of the author of "Sacre du printemps" by a round dozen of years— indeed by almost two dozen years before American audiences heard that very controversial work—musical progress apparently had passed him by. As a matter of fact, this is not so. For the resemblances to Stravinsky were superficial, consisting principally in certain technical formulas in which the American had preceded him, and all his fellows. This was not true of the substance of his music, which is as American, as personal and racial as Stravinsky never was since the "Sacre." What was true was the very advanced musical thinking of Charles Ives, so closely shown in a composition that had been penned more than thirty-five years previous. That is what happened to a man who, whatever the comparative merits of various of his works may prove to be, is by all signs and tokens one of the most independent and progressive of American composers of this epoch.

True, a few of Ives' songs have been sung, a little of his chamber music played. And last season John Kirkpatrick played his "Concord" piano sonata, a work to which much and favorable attention was given in the reviews next morning. The writer did not fully assimilate this sonata at first hearing, and is not as sure of its ultimate value as some of his colleagues were at the time. There were pages that he found loose in structure, sometimes redundant, and a space, as it seemed to him in places, between the conception of the composer and the sometimes naive expression.

Conductors' Complaints

Conductors, shown Ives' scores, almost to a man turn from them, first of all with the complaint that the music is not only extremely difficult but in places impracticable. It may be so, but in these days of super-abundant virtuosity it seems strange that all of them have stopped there; that apparently none has attempted to consult Ives about problems of performance of his works—even in the years when he was not partly invalided, as he is today, and when he, an excellent musician himself, could surely have done much to elucidate difficulties, or even to aid the conductor by some appropriate simplification.

And, furthermore: the Third symphony did not offer such insuperable difficulties, even to a minor orchestra whose director had the courage to play it. Had any conductor but Lou Harrison, who appeared as guest leader with Joseph Barone, the enterprising director of the Little Symphony, even seen, or tried to read, that score? Suppose Stravinsky, Schoenberg, et al, had offered such scores for examination? Would they have remained unexamined, unperformed? It is very unlikely.

It would be a pleasure here to speak at length of the man and artist himself; of the singular idealism and independence of his thinking and his attitude toward the fundamental questions of human existence. It is to be hoped that it will not be necessary for Charles Ives to die for his representative music—included in some eleven volumes of chamber music and six of orchestral scores in the

Library of Congress, the Fleisher Collection and the American Music Center—to gain a hearing.

—from the *New York Times,* 14 April 1946, sec. 2, p. 5

NOTE

1. See the *New York Times* review by Noel Straus in Part III of this volume.

On Horseback to Heaven: Charles Ives

PAUL MOOR

1948

When pianist Paul Moor wrote about Tennessee Williams for us in July, he reported that he was then learning to play Ives' "Concord" Sonata. Here he pays his respects to its composer.

When Charles Ives' Third Symphony won last year's Pulitzer Prize for music, most people, never having heard of him, set down his choice as merely another of the baffling selections the Pulitzer judges are famous for. The public's ignorance was understandable, for Ives' music, when noticed at all, was much more often talked about than played; the rare performances of his works were almost always on programs arranged by experimental groups, usually with small audiences. Practically none of the country's orchestras had played Ives' music, or has since. The performance of his Third Symphony which made him eligible for the Pulitzer was the first time one of his four symphonies had ever been performed intact. This event took place in the composer's seventy-second year. The winning symphony had had to wait thirty-nine years before receiving its first performance; by the time it was finally played, Ives had nineteen years since stopped composing altogether.

Charles Ives was not on hand at the Carnegie Chamber Music Hall the night of the première, which Lou Harrison conducted with the New York Little Symphony. Even in New York, where composers are highly clannish, few of them would know Ives if they saw him. For almost twenty years, his health has forced him to live in seclusion. Every spring he and his wife move to their farm on Umpawaug Hill near Redding, Connecticut; around Thanksgiving they move into their house on East 74th Street in New York. Aside from heart trouble, which forced his retirement in 1930, Ives is troubled by diabetes and has cataracts on both eyes. He is impatient of such annoyances, for at seventy-three he is a vigorous, youthful, even agile man, although his cardiac condition requires him to stay quiet. His temper, though, is no quieter than during his salad days at Yale and tends to get the better of him when he gets into discussions with friends, for he has a lively interest in politics and a withering estimation of politicians; when he gets onto these subjects he soon finds himself shaking his fist and flaying the air with his cane.

To keep life from being too exciting to be healthy, Ives sees few people, and them only rarely and for brief visits. His telephone, which he abhors and will not talk over, has an unlisted number. When in New York he never leaves the house except for an occasional turn round the block; he carries a cane, he explains, not because he has any real use for it but to keep himself from going too fast. He does not own a radio or phonograph. His main contact with music today consists of checking some of his scores which are finally being published. His proofs are blown up to twice normal size to spare his eyes, and even then he must follow a few minutes' work with a few minutes' rest. He has written an overwhelming amount of music—all of it before 1927, and most of it is still awaiting first performance. All of it he wrote without an audience, for it was too "advanced" to have wide appeal. When a visitor arrived at the Ives farm to offer congratulations for the Pulitzer award, Ives didn't even bother to shake hands, saying he had little interest in such prizes and terming them "the badge of mediocrity."

Among progressive American musicians and critics, the neglect of Charles Ives has for years been the cause of a kind of group guilt-complex, for there is not the slightest doubt among authorities both here and in Europe that Ives is one of the richest and most remarkable talents this country has ever produced. The unadventurous audience is usually the excuse for not performing radical new works, but, paradoxically, the salient reason for Ives' neglect is that much of his music, while not too hard to listen to, presents the performer with such horrendous difficulties that few will take the time to master them. His critics, when his music first started being noticed during the early twenties, dismissed him as a crackpot; this lofty opinion prevailed, for few people took the trouble of seeing for themselves. His harmonies and rhythms, written around the turn of the century, were frequently more complicated than those in much of the music being written today. Ives' case is a pure and simple example of genius born in advance of its time and into a culture not ready for it, for even his early work was so far ahead of his contemporaries that performers and publishers were scared off.

II

Although Ives grew up at a time when this country was groveling in its devotion to everything European in the matters of music and musical training, his career from the beginning has been one hundred per cent native. He was born Charles Edward Ives on October 20, 1874, in Danbury, Connecticut. His first American ancestor, Captain William Ives, came from England on the *Truelove* and helped settle New Haven in 1638, when it was still called Quinnipiak. The Ives clan since then has produced several parsons, lawyers, and bankers who have figured with distinction in the building of New England. Charles Ives comes by his retiring nature legitimately; in the late seventeen nineties an ancestor moved from his farm on lower Manhattan Island, noting in disgust that New York had already begun to be "too fancy and too crowded."

Ives' father was the bandmaster and general musical arbiter in Danbury, and a rather remarkable character himself, forming at the age of sixteen the brigade band of the First Connecticut Heavy Artillery, which he led through the Civil War. Later, besides leading the Danbury town band and several local choruses, he gave lessons to the town children in piano, violin, cornet, harmony, sightsinging, and whatever else he might be called on for. He started his son Charlie at music lessons at the age of five.

Bandmaster Ives himself was something of an innovator. One of his hobbies was the science of acoustics; when the Danbury band would assemble in full strength for a holiday or celebration, Ives would divide the sections up and place them at various points and elevations around the town square, having them play different variations on something like "Jerusalem the Golden" while he studied from different locations the confluence of their sounds. Another interest of his was the breaking down of tones, beyond the half-tones customary in conventional music, into quarters and other fractions. Charles Ives recalls that before his tenth birthday his father rigged up twenty-four violin strings to a kind of saw-horse frame and tuned them with weights to almost imperceptible nuances of pitch.

With such activity commonplace in his boyhood, it was logical that Charles Ives should grow up with few inhibitions about musical expression, and no regard at all for the sacred cows of conventional musical training. Even then he showed signs of intransigence, playing things that would start in one key and wind up in another. When his father told him it was customary to start and finish in the same key,

Ives said that was as silly as having to die in the same house you were born in.

Charles Ives started composing at ten, his first work being a funeral march inspired by the demise of a pet cat. This opus was a *succès fou*, and by popular acclamation he followed it with kindred elegies to mark the passing of other neighborhood animals. From the local barber he received instruction on the snare drum, and soon became so proficient that his father added him to the band's personnel. He was also prodigious at the organ; by the time he was thirteen he was playing regularly for services at the Congregational Church. Ives was always a vociferous and energetic performer, and the organ allowed him almost as much room to spread himself as did the drum. "It was fun to open up the swell-pedal and get your feet going *fast*," he says, giving a nimble demonstration. Ives has always esteemed spirit in performances, and has little use for the polite renditions customary with most musicians. Most composers label their loudest passages to be played double fortissimo, indicated by *fff*; a few, in their more abandoned moments, have employed *ffff* to express their feelings; but Ives' manuscripts are liberally salted with such unequivocal directions as *ffffff*. The energetic tootling of his father's band was right up his alley.

It was for the band that Charles Ives wrote his first larger work, which he entitled "Holiday Quick Step." His father conducted it on Decoration Day; the Danbury *News* said simply: "A genius."[1] The young composer did not receive this attention with equanimity; he was seized with anxiety at having his music put on display like that, and the time of the performance found him not at his usual station behind the snare drum but at home, bouncing a ball against the house.

Ives got his academic training in the Danbury Public Schools, the Hopkins Preparatory School in New Haven, and at Yale. His main interest was always music, but he found time for active participation in athletics. At Hopkins he was captain and pitcher of the baseball team which trounced the Yale freshmen in a ten-inning game, and later at Yale, he was on the senior football team. Mike Murphy, one of Yale's most famous coaches, said it was a crying shame Charlie Ives spent so much time at music, for he felt that, by applying himself a little more sensibly, he could have become a champion sprinter.

Ives studied composition at Yale with Horatio Parker; he also studied organ with Dudley Buck and Harry Rowe Shelley. He helped put himself through school by serving as organist at St. Thomas' in New Haven. He was also a DKE, and was not averse to tying one on down at Mory's before moving on to Poli's Theater, where it was the custom of the sons of Eli to swap witticisms from the audience with the amiable vaudevillians on stage. He was gregarious and popular with his schoolmates, and was sometimes called upon for songs for special occasions. One undergraduate opus had lyrics, also by him, which ally him with the most depressing punsters of all time:

> Why did Murphy steal that fish?
> Why did Murphy steal that fish?
> Because he runs a fish shop
>   And he isn't effishent.

III

When Ives finished at Yale in 1894 [rightly, 1898], he considered all things and decided against a professional career in music. Suggestions that his musical education would not be complete without study in Europe were, in his opinion, just silly. By the age of twenty, he had already written music which caused his conservative teacher to purse his lips and tap his foot impatiently. Among those works was a "Song for Harvest Season," written in four simultaneous keys, antedating by many years Europe's development of polytonality, a dissonant device now used by most of the world's composers. Some of his music he had tentatively shown around, but performers and publishers returned it, usually with a stifled giggle. Ives said the hell with them, and determined to continue composing as he pleased, for "if you wanted your music played you had to write something you wouldn't want played."

This conviction, in 1894, was not nearly so evocative of the ivory tower as it would be today. Music then was "pretty" and "nice"— epithets Ives uses frequently when he becomes sarcastic. The lions of the day in London were Gilbert and Sullivan; Debussy had begun to be known in France; but neither Arnold Schönberg nor Igor Stravinsky, the two most acclaimed influences in the field of composition today, had begun writing the music which later created riots in Europe's concert halls. With the exception of Edward MacDowell, who was European by training, America had no composers of any stature, let alone an American "school" such as exists today.

Breaking rules had already become second nature to Ives; since this country was slow to endorse such pioneering even when undertaken by a European, and absolutely refused to countenance such effrontery on the part of an upstart native son, Ives decided to cherish music as an avocation and began looking for another field as a career. He settled on life insurance. If this seems an antic choice to some people, it does not seem so to Ives. It dealt directly with people, which appealed to him. Today he says steadfastly that his business helped his music, and vice versa.

Shortly after Ivy Day in 1894 Ives moved to New York and got a job in the actuarial department of the Mutual Life Insurance Company, at a salary of five dollars a week. In 1899 he became friends with a fellow employee, Julian Myrick, and in 1907 the two were associated in Ives & Company, serving as general agents for the Washington Life Insurance Company of New York. Two years later, when a sale of stock left them out of a job, a vice president of Mutual Life opened a new agency for them under the name of Ives & Myrick, which is still doing business. In the succeeding twenty-one years the two partners put into force some $450,000,000 worth of new business for Mutual of New York alone.

Ives roomed co-operatively with a shifting group of hell-raising young bachelors who had a large apartment off Central Park West and a long-suffering servant to take care of the place. Ives would frequently come direct from the office to his piano, composing until dinner and then on into the evening. He was no drudge, however, for he would just as often go on a double date with one of the men in the apartment, or accompany the group as a whole whenever they decided to paint the town.

He also took a night course in law at New York University. Even so, he found time to write an enormous amount of music. His childhood furnished most of his material, and his compositions were full of Civil War tunes, hymns, and the popular music of that time.

Some of Ives' most iconoclastic music sprang from the most everyday roots. From his memories of church choirs singing a little out of tune came some of his complicated explorations of polytonality; from his father's band, with its amateur members' enthusiastic but not always accurate interpretations, and from the cacophonous results as two bands would approach and then pass each other, came some of his involutions of rhythm. These devices lend a sort of rough, bardic quality to many of Ives' works. Hardly anyone saw this music; Ives was not secretive about it, but neither did he attempt to promote himself. He received far more acclaim for his article on estate planning, which the *Eastern Underwriter* printed under the title "Measuring the Prospect—the Amount to Carry" and which lined up on the side of insurance several quotations from Emerson and Thoreau, two particular mentors of Ives' personal philosophy. Whenever anyone did see his music, the results were invariably disheartening. During the first world war Myrick suggested Ives set to music the poem "In Flanders' Fields," which had been written by a Mutual medical referee in Montreal; Myrick said he would get a professional artist to sing it at a forthcoming banquet. When Ives heard the singer and his accompanist flounder disconsolately through the song he wrote, he listened for a while and then judiciously suggested to Myrick that they drop the whole damn project, which in fact they did.

Before moving from New Haven to New York, Ives had become interested in a young lady with the beautiful New England name of Harmony Twichell, one of the prettiest girls in New Haven, whose brother Dave had been Ives' classmate at Yale. Even after moving to the city, Ives would return to Connecticut for weekends, for he still had a church job there, and he would see Harmony whenever it could be arranged. A few years later she came to New York to study nursing, and Ives' attentions, with enervation of travel removed became more ardent.[2] They were married in 1908 and have one child, Edith, who is married to a New York attorney.

Ives and his wife led a quiet but not a retiring life. They entertained and went out only rarely. Ives followed happenings in the musical world, and would frequently attend concerts where new music was played. He was very fond of Scriabine when he first heard the Russian mystic's music, but his main interest since then has been in Carl Ruggles, a seldom-played Vermonter whose career in many ways parallels that of Ives.

In 1920, at his own expense, Ives published five hundred copies of his second piano sonata, subtitled "Concord, Mass., 1840–1860," a long, complex work of satanic difficulty. He called the sonata "one person's impressions of the spirit of transcendentalism that is associated in the minds of many with Concord, Massachusetts, of over half a century ago." The four movements bear the names of Emerson, Hawthorne, the Alcotts, and Thoreau. Ives wrote an accompanying slim volume called "Essays Before a Sonata"; the dedication read: "These prefatory essays were written by the composer for those who can't stand his music, and the music for those who can't stand his essays; to those who can't stand either, the whole is respectfully dedicated." This defiant sally reveals the rebuffs Ives' music had suffered. He had long since ceased trying to interest commercial publishers in his music. He decided that, since it seemed impossible to be a professional composer without being compromised by professional considerations, he would give his music to whoever wanted it, and would under no circumstances make any money from it; he has never abandoned this decision.

He sent copies of the Sonata to libraries and performers that he thought might possibly be interested. Ernest Hutcheson's reaction to it was fairly representative; some twelve years later, Jerome Moross, an early promoter of Ives and at that time a pupil of Hutcheson's at Juilliard, asked Hutcheson whether he were acquainted with the "Concord" Sonata. "Ives?" Hutcheson said. "Ives? . . . Oh yes—he sent me that piece. I find it useful now and again when the piano bench is too low for one of my pupils." In the "Hawthorne" movement Ives called for a piece of wood 14 $^3/_4$ inches long, heavy enough to depress the keys, producing a soft, ghostly sonority; one critic glanced at the score and hee-hawed that Mr. Ives played the piano with a club. The movements were without tempo indications or time signatures, and frequently without bar-lines; Ives made it clear that the performer was to have all the latitude he wanted, playing various sections fast or slow, loud or soft, as his emotions dictated. Almost no one took the work seriously till nineteen years later, in 1939, when John Kirkpatrick, after studying it for twelve years, played the first complete performance in Town Hall in New York. Lawrence Gilman, the *Herald Tribune's* calm, conservative critic, called it "exceptionally great music, the greatest music composed by an American. . . . It has wisdom, and beauty, and profundity, and a sense of the encompassing terror and splendor of human life and human destiny—a sense of those mysteries that are both human and divine." The other critics were in accord. The effect was in fact so electric that Kirkpatrick repeated it a few weeks later, this time to an eager and sold-out house.

Henry Cowell, the composer and indefatigable champion of modern music, had sought Ives out shortly after the "Concord" Sonata was printed; some friends of Cowell's at the Bohemians, which was then New York's leading musical club, had passed ribald remarks about the work, arousing his interest. Cowell, an extraordinary man whose role in the fostering of American music eclipses any man's of his time, had just established *New Music*, a quarterly for the publication of uncommercial new works, and he wanted some things by Ives to print; he got them, on the condition (stipulated by Ives) that the composer was to receive no royalties. *New Music* is a non-profit organization, so there was little left over in the way of royalties, but some years after that Ives was accidentally sent his share of the spoils, which came to something less than ten dollars. Ives promptly sent it back, with a testy reminder of his original provision.

Undaunted by the supercilious reception given his printed sonata, Ives in 1922 published an edition of five hundred handsome volumes headed "114 Songs by Charles E. Ives," one of the most remarkable musical collections which has ever appeared. They range in merit from first-rate to downright awful: by Ives' own admission, eight specifically are "of no musical value." Others he says in the notes accompanying them, cannot be sung; he originally had followed this statement with the phrase "by nice opera singers," but a friend persuaded him against such cheek. Ives and his wife wrote the texts of many; others come from Aeschylus, Browning, Heine, Landor; one, probably the best known, "Charlie Rutlage," is Ives' rousing version of a cowboy song sent him by John A. Lomax; another, "The Greatest Man," uses a really extraordinary text by Anne Collins which he took from a 1921 newspaper:

> My teacher said us boys should write about some great man.
> . . . I got to thinkin' 'bout my pa; he ain't a hero 'r anything
> but pshaw! Say! He can ride the wildest hoss 'n find minners
> near the moss down by the creek. . . . Dad's some hunter
> too—oh my! Miss Dolly Cottontail sure does fly when he
> tromps through the fields 'n brush! . . .

At the end of "An Election" (which Ives had originally called "Down with the Politicians, Up with the People"), there is a lengthy note describing a proposal of Ives' for a twentieth Constitutional Amendment, to take the government away from the politicians and give it back to the people; friends have tried to tell Ives that songs and concerts are not the field for political agitation, but he is not convinced. "I have had some fights about this," he says tersely. "These things are a lot more important than any damn song or symphony." In spite of the great inconsistency of the songs' value, no less an authority then Aaron Copland says that about forty are a contribution to the art of song-writing that "will remain a challenge and an inspiration to future generations of American composers."

IV

With his music in print, Ives began to be known at last among people who followed the goings-on among *avant-garde* musical circles. *New Music* printed two movements of Ives' Fourth Symphony; it came to the attention of the pianist, E. Robert Schmitz, who took it to the conductor of the Rochester Philharmonic, Eugene Goossens; these movements were performed in 1927 by the Pro Musica Orchestra of New York under Goossen's direction.[3] Goossens, now director of the Melbourne Conservatorium and Symphony, had conducted Diaghilev's Ballet Russe for seven years, introduced Stravinsky's *Sacre du printemps* with the New York Symphony, and was in general thoroughly at home with the modern idiom, but the Ives score gave him quite a turn; the most formidable problem was that there were long sections where the bar-lines in various instrumental parts didn't jibe. "I remember," Goossens says, "I wound up beating two with my stick, three with my left hand, something else with my head, and something else again with my coat tails." Olin Downes, today the first-string music critic on the *New York Times,* was then second-string man on that paper; he wrote a glowing review of the Ives work, but, after correctly listing the composers at the beginning of the review, absent-mindedly referred to Ives thereafter as "Mr. St. Ives"; despite the fact that Ives was fifty-three years old, his name was so unfamiliar, and, in fact, he was only then having the first sizable performance of his music.

In 1925 Ives suffered his first heart attack.[4] For the next few years his health was so tentative that he was absent from his office about half the time. In 1927 he completed some songs, the last of his works to be finished, and in 1930 he retired from business altogether.

The Ives cult and legend had begun. Jerome Moross and Bernard Herrmann, who had both come to know Ives' music through Henry Cowell, were members of an informal Young Composers' Group whose mentor was the only slightly less young composer Aaron Copland. Ives' volume of songs created a sensation at one of the Group's gatherings; Copland was to be in charge of the music period that year at Yaddo, the beautiful Saratoga estate which every year plays host to artists, writers, and composers, and he determined to include Ives in the festival programs. Seven of the songs were sung that summer by Hubert Linscott with Copland at the piano. They were clamorously received, and the cowboy song, "Charlie Rutlage," was the popular hit of the festival. The summer guests at Yaddo returned to their homes around the country bearing word of the exciting "new" composer, Charles Ives; the Ives legend had begun to spread. Soon afterward, when Nicolas Slonimsky conducted Ives' music all over Europe, critics there hailed it, usually adding that it was the first evidence they had seen that America had a real, indigenous musical culture of its own.

The practice of "quoting" musical material, as Ives has done in many of his works, has good precedent. Beethoven used the sounds of country bands in his Pastoral Symphony; many composers have interpolated the folk music of their various countries into their works; Arnold Schönberg, in his Second String Quarter, even found use for "*Ach, du lieber Augustin!*" In Ives, a thoroughly American composer if there ever was one, nothing could seem more logical than his use of such autochthonous material as "Bringing in the Sheaves" and "Whoopie Ti-yi-yo, Git Along Little Dogies." At the time his works were composed, this country's artistic inferiority complex was still as chronic as when Thoreau wrote about it in his journal: "Natural objects and phenomena are the original symbols or types which express our thoughts and feelings. Yet American scholars, having little or no root in the soil, commonly strive with all their might to confine themselves to the imported symbols alone. All the true outgrowth and experience, the lively speech, they would fain reject as 'Americanisms.'"

"I remember something father told me," Ives says. "He said that if a man knows more about a horse than he does about heaven, he should concentrate on the horse and maybe it would wind up carrying him to heaven."

Reading the complete list of Ives' music leaves you appalled by its profusion—symphonies, sonatas, quartets, suites, songs, uncompleted sketches, most of them unpublished and unperformed. When someone once, deploring such an amount of unplayed music, asked Ives why he wrote so much that no one ever saw, he paused and said, "There are several good reasons, none of them worth recording." Whatever the reasons, he continued to compose till his fifty-fourth year with all the helpless intensity of a quest for love. When asked why he found it necessary to fortify his music against facile performance by using bizarre harmonies and rhythms instead of the conventional ones, he said, "Because I heard something else."

Ives' manuscripts today are kept in his barn studio in Connecticut in fireproof steel filing cases. Many of them are in pencil; Ives' notation at its best was never clear, and with the accumulated smears of many years much of it is incomprehensible except to its composer, and he cannot now decipher it because of his cataracts, which cannot be removed because of his heart condition; here the matter rests. His entire output, in bound, photostatted volumes prepared at his own expense, is available for reference at the Library of Congress and at the New York Public Library; it comprises six thick volumes for orchestra and eleven for smaller combinations. This is also available at the American Music Center at 250 West 57th Street in New York, the agent for Ives' published work, which, in spite of being small by comparison with his entire output, is still considerable. *New Music* sponsored recordings of six of Ives' songs, sung by Mordecai Bauman, and of his Fourth Sonata for violin and piano, played by Joseph Szigeti and Andor Foldes. The Werner Janssen Symphony has recorded "The Housatonic at Stockbridge" from Ives' "Three Places in New England," and this summer Columbia released John Kirkpatrick's masterly performance of the "Concord" Sonata.

Commercial publishers began noticing Ives with sudden interest after the sensation created when the "Concord" Sonata was first performed. One firm asked him for permission to publish it commercially (the edition which Ives had had printed is now a collectors' item); Ives reminded them that they had rejected his music thirty years or so before, and refused their offer; the work is available now in the imprint of the co-operative Arrow Music Press. When overtures from publishers began to be no longer a novelty, Ives formulated a little joke he would play. His letter of reply would be two pages long, and he would announce that permission to publish the work in question would be given on two conditions; the letter was so arranged that the first condition—that the composer receive no royalty—ended just at the bottom of the first page. Publishers would read this with high regard and then turn the page to read the second condition, which was that likewise no profit should be made by the publishers; they invariably found this unduly capricious. The firm G. Schirmer, an unashamedly commercial house, is now preparing Ives' First Sonata for violin and piano for publication, but Ives has changed his position only slightly: he has designated other musicians to receive the royalties, on the principle that it's all right for his music to make money, as long as it doesn't go to him. He has never willingly copyrighted anything.

Ives has always been exceptionally generous in helping the cause of modern music, a cause which perennially seems to be dying on the vine for want of funds. Ives has set aside thirty thousand dollars whose income is used to help such projects as the publication of a promising composer's music, or the underwriting of a program of new works. He is in frequent touch with Lehman Engel, the composer-conductor who acts as treasurer of the American Music Center, on such matters. When Henry Cowell (who is now at work on a biography of Ives) founded *New Music,* Ives took twenty-five subscriptions. Money from this fund is sedulously distinguished from any money Ives spends on making his own music available.

V

In spite of his bald, high-domed head, his gray full beard, and the infirmities which bother him today, Ives' clear, unwrinkled skin, flashing eyes, quick wit, and powerful handclasp are not those of an old man. He is as candid and vehement a Yankee as ever, expressing himself as explicitly as eighteen years ago, when he stood up and told a member of the audience who was laughing at some new music being played, "Don't be such a God-damn sissy. When you hear strong music like this, use your ears like a man." When Ives feels the occasion warrants cussing he cusses, and when he feels like spitting he spits. He prefers un-citified clothing: woolen shirts, a wide-wale corduroy vest, tweed jacket and trousers. He has not been in close contact with the musical world since his retirement eighteen years back, but he talks vividly and sometimes waspishly of such luminaries of the twenties as Walter Damrosch, who borrowed a score of Ives' Second Symphony and neither played nor returned it, and Gustav Mahler, the composer-conductor who took Ives' Third Symphony to Europe with him one summer with the intention of conducting it that fall with the New York Philharmonic, but who died before he could make good his promise. Ives works as much as his eyesight will allow at getting his scores into presentable form. During the summers in Connecticut he enjoys being in the open air. In the past two years his health has improved more than friends ever thought possible.

Mrs. Ives, still a beautiful woman, handles his correspondence for him when he feels like answering letters. Sometimes she reads to him. Whenever she can, she attends performances of his music. The devotion of their relationship is as profound as it is unassuming. Their life today is as typically New England as their forbears' was. Even their city house, located in one of New York's most fashionable sections, is furnished in good, solid, unadorned, almost puritan fashion. In Connecticut during the summer Ives enjoys puttering round the place and occasionally swapping yarns with neighbors he has known for years.

In a letter of reminiscence to a friend a few years ago, Ives said, "One thing I am certain of is that if I have done anything good in music, it was first, because of my father, and second, because of my wife. What she has done for me I will not put down, for she will not let me. But I am going to put this down. After any musical friends of mine and others left she never said, or suggested, or looked, or thought that there must be something wrong with me—a thing implied, if not expressed, by most everybody else, including members of the family. She never said, 'Now why don't you be good and write something *nice* the way they like it!'—never. She urged me on my way to be myself and gave me confidence that no one else since Father had given me."[5]

Today, slowly, more and more, Charles Ives' music is becoming known; the vogue of Stravinsky and Schönberg, with the concomitant necessity for performers to realign their musical senses if they want to get on the bandwagon, has mitigated some of the difficulties of performing an Ives work. Today he is listed in *Who's Who*, and in 1945 he was elected to the National Institute of Arts and Letters. Two years ago a group of Juilliard students gave an all-Ives program during Columbia University's Contemporary Music Festival; the audience filled McMillin Theater and had no apparent difficulty assimilating even a full evening of Ives' music. It was hopefully noted that both Dimitri Mitropoulos and Serge Koussevitzky were applauding from the audience, but to date neither conductor has led an Ives performance with his orchestra. The New York Philharmonic-Symphony, the oldest orchestra in the country, has yet to play a work of Ives. Conductors are a queer crew, willing at times to play a contemporary work if they are allowed the defloration of first performance, but once this *droit du seigneur* is fulfilled, the work is almost always cast aside. In the case of Ives, their usual excuse is the lack of rehearsal time. This would be valid in connection with some of Ives' most difficult music, but far from all of it. As for audiences, there is none more stately than that attending the Boston Symphony's series of concerts in New York, but their reception last season of Ives' "Three Places in New England," conducted by Richard Burgin, bordered on an ovation.

The greatest deprivation of Ives' musical life, from every standpoint, was his lack of an audience while he was still composing. Without the reactions, both good and bad, of selective listeners, a composer's battle is immeasurably harder. The ultimate worth of a composer is established only long after his death; but of Ives' potential, with the help of a discriminating audience, of having developed into an even more fully realized musician, there can be no doubt. Even so, it is still altogether possible, with more widespread knowledge of his music, that Ives may turn out to be the decisive influence on a whole generation of American composers yet to come. They could do far worse.

When Ives printed his "114 Songs," he wrote, "Some have written a book for money: I have not. Some for fame: I have not. Some for love: I have not. . . . In fact, gentle borrower, I have not written a book at all—I have merely cleaned house. All that is left is out on the clothes line." These songs, he said, he was now throwing, so to speak, at the heads of the musical fraternity, who were free to dodge them on their way, perhaps, to the waste basket. He also went to some length rationalizing his position as a professional business man and an amateur composer. As his ardent champion Copland has observed, Ives had every reason for timidity and rationalization in a world that had no need for him as an artist. "If I were advising a young composer today," Ives says, "I'd tell him to write one chord, *do mi so,* at the age of ten, and then not do any more composing till he's seventy-five. This is based on experience."

Eight or nine years ago, the musical and artistic directors of the Monte Carlo Ballet asked Olin Downes for some American scores.[6] Of the five or six he gave them, the only one to interest them was one by Ives. Downes got Nicholas Slonimsky to play it for them at the piano. The directors were enthusiastic but regretful. One of them turned to Downes during the music, shrugged, and whispered, "Too bad: Stravinsky." Downes pointed to the date on the score, which showed it had been written before Stravinsky had even begun serious musical study. The ballet director summed up fifty years of neglect in his answer. "Still too bad," he said. "Too late."

—from *Harper's* 197 (September 1948): 65–73

NOTES

1. See the review in Part III.

2. This account of their courtship is incorrect in several details; see the letters from their courtship in Part II, above.

3. The sequence of events is reversed here; in fact, the concert was in 1927, and the second movement of the symphony appeared in *New Music* in 1929. See the reviews of both in Part III.

4. In a copy of this article in the Ives Collection, John Herrick Jackson Music Library, Yale University, Ives wrote "First heart attack was 1917." Elsewhere, Ives gave the date as October 1918 and called it only "a serious illness"; see Ives, *Memos,* ed. John Kirkpatrick (New York: W. W. Norton, 1972), 112. Stuart Feder, *Charles Ives, "My Father's Song": A Psychoanalytic Biography* (New Haven: Yale University Press, 1992), 286–87, doubts that it was coronary occlusion.

5. For the memo from which this was extracted, see Ives, *Memos,* 114.

6. For Downes's account of this incident, see his essay just above.

Posterity Catches Up with Charles Ives

HOWARD TAUBMAN
1949

Charles E. Ives, who was 75 last Thursday, has lived to see posterity catch up with him. It has taken America a long time to recognize that he is the most audacious pioneer in music this country has produced and that in his vast output of symphonies, choruses, songs and chamber music we have a living portrait of the land worthy to stand beside the literature of New England's flowering.

It was only two years ago that Mr. Ives won the accolade of the Pulitzer Prize for a symphony that had its first performance thirty-five years after it was written. It was only four years ago that he was elected a member of the National Institute of Arts and Letters. It was only ten years ago that his monumental "Concord" sonata for piano, which epitomizes in music the world of Emerson, Hawthorne, the Alcotts and Thoreau, had its first complete public performance.

Recognition has come slowly and piecemeal, and it has not yet matched Mr. Ives' accomplishments. Some of his music has been published, mostly at his own expense. Some of it has been performed, but mostly in small halls in out-of-the-way places by little-known musicians. Our major orchestras have not played his symphonies, and the world-famous virtuosos, with one or two honorable exceptions, have ignored his music.

The story of Charles E. Ives' life-long, lonely and fierce devotion to art as he saw it and of his creation of a towering and neglected musical heritage for America reads like fiction. He would hate you for putting it this way, but he could not deny the truth. And the truth has one odd twist: Mr. Ives wrote this music not while starving in a garret but while working full time at being one of the country's ablest and most successful insurance men.

How did he get that way? What forces molded the man and musician? How was it possible, in an age of growing musical consciousness, of swift, mass communication, of eagerness to discover new, authentically American voices in the arts, for him to escape the attention he deserved? What have the long years of indifference done to him?

The music itself answered some of the questions in part. It told you that more than fifty years ago he was writing pieces in several keys or without any keys at all before the international renowned Igor Stravinsky and Arnold Schoenberg had opened up new fields of poly-tonality and atonality. It told you that he pioneered in original rhythms, harmonies and blending of instrumental and vocal timbres long before these developments were adopted by the most advanced composers. It told you, too, that in his use of hymn tunes, country dances, marches, folksongs he wrote out of a memory filled with the minutiae of an older and simpler America and out of a heart filled with affection for this America.

His music served as a further stimulus to encounter the man, as did reading the little that had been written about and talking to some of this old friends. But Mr. Ives lives in drastic retirement. Because of ill health he gave up his business career in 1930. A weak heart and cataracts of the eyes have made it impossible for him to have visits by friends and admirers except on the rarest occasions. An extended interview seemed out of the question.

By a stroke of good fortune it was arranged. Mrs. Ives telephoned early one morning to say that her husband was having a good day. You drove up to the gracious and simple house high on a hill in Connecticut, and Mrs. Ives, gray-haired, gentle and quietly hos-pitable, was on the porch to greet you. She exchanged comments about the brilliance of the sun in late September and the beauty of the hills beyond, with the first yellows and reds flecking the dark green. From inside the house there came a pounding of a cane. Mrs. Ives smiled and nodded and led you in.

Charles E. Ives was standing in a large room which had a high ceil-ing with the bare beams showing their graceful strength. At first glance he looked like a Yankee patriarch you had met in the white hills of New Hampshire. He was gaunt and wiry, and with the help of his cane he stood up straight so that there was only the faintest sug-gestion of stooping shoulders. The gray, scraggly beard gave his lean face an appearance of roundness, reminding you of the portraits of Giuseppe Verdi. He wore rough, country clothes—sturdy shoes, blue denim trousers, a faded blue shirt without a tie, an old, darned sweater and a gray tweed jacket. He took off his dark glasses and looked at you, and the eyes were bright and alert.

He spoke first. "It's good of you," he said, "to come and see this old broom."

He moved toward a couple of straight-backed armchairs near a large window facing west. Though he used the cane, there was something springy in his walk and an air of volatility in his gestures. He pointed his stick toward the window and said, "That's Danbury on the other side of that mountain. That's where I was born and grew up and learned a little about music. Pa taught me what I know."

Pa was George E. Ives, a bandmaster, who at 16 organized a Civil War band that won personal commendation from Lincoln and Grant, and who later taught not only his son but several generations of Danbury youngsters to know good music. Pa, his son once wrote a friend, "started all the children of the family—and, most of the children of the town for that matter—on Bach and Stephen Foster." Pa was open-minded about new possibilities in music. He studied the science of acoustics and invented a quarter-tone instrument. He gave the boy his first lesson at 5. When Charles was 10, his father had him sing "Swanee River" in the key of E flat and play the accompaniment in the key of C. The purpose was, the composer said, "to stretch our ears."

At this point Mrs. Ives brought from the mantel over the fireplace a faded old tintype showing Pa and ten bandsmen in their uniforms. "Can't tell anything from that," Mr. Ives said. "He was a real musician."

The elder Ives saw to it that the boy's development was many-sided. At 13 Charles became the organist of Danbury's West Street Congregational Church, but he also found time to play baseball and football. At Hopkins Grammar School in New Haven later he made the baseball team, and at Yale he was on his class football team. In his cluttered study there hangs a photograph of the football team of the class of '98, with a sturdy young Ives looking out ferociously.

At Yale young Ives studied music with Horatio W. Parker, a leading American composer, whose opera, "Mona," was done at the Metropolitan almost forty years ago. Even before he came to Yale the young composer had begun what all but his father considered his outlandish experiments. At 20 he wrote "Song for Harvest Season," using a stanza from an old hymn and setting it for voice, cornet, trombone and organ pedal, each in a different key.

Ives soon learned not to show Parker his latest compositions. "Ives," the teacher had chided him, "must you hog all the keys?"

Mr. Ives' eyes danced as he recalled his teacher's phrase. Beating time with his cane, he began to sing one of the four-square tunes of Haydn, improvising words for it as he went along. His song went further like this:

"First you write in C. Then you go to G. Then back to C again, and no one calls you wrong."

Throughout the visit he would burst suddenly into song, making up words to comment on the staid music world, with its "old ladies, male and female," in the audiences; the conductors, musicians, managers who want things always exactly as they were. He would brandish his stick vehemently in one hand and beat time neatly with the other. Occasionally he would stop short suddenly, panting for breath. You would look in alarm at Mrs. Ives; she would glance at him out of the corner of an eye and smile at you reassuringly.

When he would catch his breath, he would say, "Don't know why I get excited." And then chanting again, with a gleam in the eye, "No one gives a damn, what a fool I am!"

While at college young Ives held down a job as organist at the Centre Church in New Haven, and after graduation he had similar posts in Bloomfield, N.J., and in New York City at the Central Presbyterian Church. But these were part-time affairs. After he got out of college, he went to work as a clerk for the Mutual Life Insurance Company. In 1906 he formed his own firm, Ives & Co., general agents for the Washington Life Insurance Company, and in 1909 he and Julian S. Myrick organized the firm of Ives & Myrick, managers for the Mutual Life Insurance Company.

His associates have recalled that Mr. Ives showed as much initiative in business as in music; he was a pioneer in such insurance ideas as family protection, coverage for key executives in corporations and provisions to meet inheritance taxes. In twenty-one years, associates assert, Ives & Myrick put about $450,000,000 of new business into Mutual.

Since his business career was a full one, where did Mr. Ives find the time to compose? When you put the question to him, he shrugged his shoulders as though to say, "I composed." Mrs. Ives provided the explanation. "He composed evenings, week-ends, vacations," she said. "He could hardly wait for dinner to be over, and he was at the piano. Often he went to bed at 2 or 3 A.M."

Mr. Ives smiled at her in grateful recollection. "We never went anywhere," he said, "and she didn't mind."

On another occasion Mr. Ives had told a friend that his debt to his wife—who was born Harmony Twichell, daughter of a Hartford clergyman—was as great as that to his father, for she never told him "to be good and write something nice that people would like." She supported him in his conviction that he must write as he felt.

Charles Ives, then, was clearly a man who had to write music. The pressures of business and limited time could not stay his ideas. And he had to write as he saw fit. That meant drawing on the experiences and memories of his boyhood and youth. It meant recalling in tone barn dances, revival meetings, Indians, Halloween, the Housatonic at Stockbridge, a football game, a left-handed pitcher, a Decoration Day parade, the village volunteer firemen, town meetings, harvest time, politics and the country store, minstrel airs played by country fiddlers. He could not resist jesting in his music; he would have his country fiddler playing out of tune. Nor was it always jest. He tried to convey the truth of natural sounds: the echoes made by old instruments, the clashing harmonies of two bands passing each other on a holiday and playing different tunes, the shrillness of children's voices on a picnic by the river.

But his music went beyond literalness. It transmuted the memories and the natural sounds into patterns of orderliness. It commented affectionately on what he had seen and heard, and often, as in his Third Symphony, there were an austerity and nobleness that seemed to speak not only for America but for humanity.

When someone once remarked on his large output of music, he said simply, "I have merely cleaned house. All that is left is on the clothesline."

He has a tendency to wear lightly what laurels have come his way of late. When you said that some of his musical ideas presaged those of Stravinsky and Schoenberg, he observed, "It's not my fault."

Actually he has never heard a single composition by Schoenberg, and the only piece by Stravinsky that he ever heard was "The Firebird Suite," which belongs to the composer's earliest and least experimental period.

It is easy to see how he could not find time to hear the music of others. But except for his earliest days as a composer he seldom heard his own music played. He said he had never heard a full symphony orchestra do any of his symphonies. His music was not played when he was free to hear it; now that it is played a bit he cannot go out to concerts.

One of the myths about Mr. Ives is that he has been indifferent to his career as a composer, that he left manuscripts lying around in barns, that he himself did not know what he had written and when. All of these tales are untrue. He has kept a record not only of each work but of every performance it has received. His study is filled with magazines, newspaper clippings, programs, photostated sheets of music. There is no apparent system in the room. But Mrs. Ives knows that nothing must be tampered with, for he has a dependable filing system in his head.

Why was he neglected for so long? The music offers one explanation. Most of it is difficult. In years gone by the problems he posed were insoluble to interpreters. Mr. Ives mimicked for you the gestures of an eminent conductor four decades ago trying to work out the complex rhythmic scheme of one of his works and giving it up in despair. Nowadays interpreters have learned to handle these problems; two generations of composers have conditioned them to all manner of difficulties that were once regarded as insuperable.

But the difficulties do not comprise the sole explanation. The personality of the man would seem to fill out the gaps in the problem. Charles Ives did not choose to go out and make friends for his music. He was willing, perhaps eager, to have it played and sung, but he did not wish to cozen or bludgeon musicians into performing it.

His attitude may be summed up in a notation he wrote for a volume of 114 songs which he published in 1922, at his own expense:

"As far as the music is concerned, anyone (if he be so inclined) is free to use it, copy it, transpose or arrange it for other instruments. This book is privately printed and is not to be sold or put on the market. Complimentary copies will be sent to anyone as long as the supply lasts."

In recent years music publishers have issued his music at their expense. Mr. Ives took the royalties and turned them over to composers in need. On principle he objected to his publishers copyrighting his music; he believed that any one who wanted it should have free access to it. In the end he agreed only on condition that the profits his music earned should be employed in publishing the music of young composers.

In his active days Mr. Ives' interests were not confined to insurance and music. He kept a close eye on the affairs of the world. He was furious when the United States Senate rejected our joining the League of Nations and went so far as to draw up a constitutional amendment, which would then have been the twentieth, and which set out a scheme for "the broader development of popular expression." He had the amendment printed in circular form, and when you visited him he had a copy ready for you.

As you chatted with him you noticed that there were current papers, periodicals and books on a table near his chair. He manages to find time to work a little, chiefly correcting old scores and proofs of pieces to be published. He labors at these chores painstakingly. He spent four years correcting and annotating the "Concord" sonata before it went to press. In the winters he stays close to his city house; in the summers he is fond of taking walks in the woods behind his hilltop house, and often he sits on a favorite stone for long periods of contemplation. The family circle is small—a daughter, a son-in-law and a young grandson, but most often Mr. and Mrs. Ives are together alone.

He is spared excitement because he is so easily aroused to enthusiasm or indignation. And just talking can be exciting. You realize this as you sit with him, and you hastily arise to go. The visit has been longer than planned. He urges you to stay and have a potato with him, but you know you must not remain for lunch.

As you leave he goes out on the porch, putting on a battered felt hat. As you go down the walk he stands there waving at you. You look back at this proud and humble man, knowing that time is working steadily to raise him to his deserved place among the great creative figures of American musical history.

—from the *New York Times Magazine* (23 October 1949): 15, 34–36

Charles Ives—America's Musical Prophet

[Excerpt]

NICOLAS SLONIMSKY
1954

The above signed belongs to a select group of people who may claim the distinction of being the earliest friends of the music of Ives. It was twenty-five years ago that I met Ives. I will never forget the gradual revelation of his music that came to me when I studied the score of his orchestral set Three Places in New England. The poetic invocation of old America, the turbulence of rhythms and massive harmonies, the stirring motion of waves of musical matter supporting the melodies in a unique contrapuntal design, all this was absorbing to me. The music was unlike any "modern" music of the day. It could not be fitted into any category. It was a transcendental dream, but a dream filled with concrete images that assumed an objective reality.

There was a challenge: could this music be communicated to an audience, even though it was so personal, so difficult to perform, so improvisatory in character?

The rhythmic problems alone were staggering. The second movement, a musical souvenir of Putnam's Camp in Redding, Connecticut, with its Revolutionary memories, contained an episode in which two village bands marching towards the meeting place from two different directions, played tunes at different speeds, so that three bars of one metrical period corresponded to four bars of the other. I met this "polymetrical" problem by beating three bars in $\frac{4}{4}$ time with my right hand against four bars in $\frac{2}{2}$ time with my left. The left hand had to move 33 1/3 percent faster than the right. Downbeats of both hands coincided at the end of a period of three bars in the right hand and a period of four bars in the left hand. Visually, it must have been amusing, but the orchestra seemed to have no difficulty in following my twofold beat.

I conducted Three Places in New England in Boston, New York, Los Angeles, Havana and Paris. The reaction varied from spellbound enthusiasm to speculation as to what the chambers of commerce in New England would say of this dissonant portrayal of its natural attractions. But the most significant reaction came nearly twenty years after my first presentation of the score, from a New York critic who reviewed a second performance of the work given by the Boston Symphony. The critic quoted his own newspaper at the time of the premiere and expressed amazement that a work so intense, so effective and so direct could have been then judged as discordant, confused and noisy. This candid avowal was an apt illustration of something that we, the early Ivesites, knew long ago: namely, that Ives was many years ahead of his time, and that the times would finally catch up with his prophetic visions.

The paradox of Ives's genius (this word has been used without qualification by several otherwise sober critics when writing about Ives) is that his music is at once fantastically complex and appealingly simple. His subject matter is American with hardly an exception; the titles alone show the national source of his inspiration: The Fourth of July; Lincoln, the Great Commoner; Washington's Birthday. His enormously difficult Concord Sonata for piano is in four movements named after the great American writers of the Concord group: Emerson, Hawthorne, the Alcotts, and Thoreau. To describe Hawthorne's "celestial railroad," Ives instructs the pianist to use a strip of wood to produce two full octaves of white or black keys. There are passages of great rhythmic intricacy; but then, as Ives says, "a metronome cannot measure Emerson's mind and oversoul, any more than the old Concord Steeple Bell could."

No matter how complicated the rhythmic and contrapuntal patterns, the fundamental musical thought in the Concord Sonata is melodically simple, evocative of hymn-like American tunes and nostalgic ballads, in a native—one might say a Currier and Ives—manner.

When one listens to the music of Ives without prejudice, as a layman would, the impression received is that of a bright American landscape, grandly designed and touched with sweeping brush strokes that suddenly illumine the scene.

When one examines this musical panorama with regard to the special devices used, as a professional musician would, the analysis uncovers an astonishing abundance of technical virtuosity in writing.

When one considers Ives's achievement in the context of the period during which he wrote most of his music, as a historian would, the conclusion is inescapable that Ives has anticipated every known musical innovation of the twentieth century.

A mere tabulation of new technical devices applied by Ives long before other composers began to experiment with modernistic structures, reveals the extraordinary scope of his music:

(1) Polytonality
(2) Atonality
(3) Dissonant Counterpoint
(4) Tone-Clusters
(5) Polymeters
(6) Polyrhythms
(7) Quarter-tones

In addition, Ives employs a method of free counterpoint that may be described as "controlled improvisation". The essence of this technique consists in giving a rhythmic phrase to an instrument, or a group of instruments, with instructions to keep playing it at varying speeds and varying dynamics for a certain number of bars.

These revolutionary advances in composition were made by Ives before 1920. He has written little music since then on account of a diabetic condition which makes it difficult for him to handle a pen. But his fighting spirit remains undiminished. His fierce loyalty to friends is as remarkable as his intransigence towards those whom he blames for social and musical ills. When he talks, he assumes a fighting stance, his right hand raised and a finger of scorn pointed at the imaginary antagonist. In music, and in life, Ives is fired by passionate convictions. He does not compromise. His beliefs in the goodness of the good and his abhorrence of the badness of the bad are absolute.

—from *Musical America* 74, no. 4 (15 February 1954): 18–19

Charles E. Ives: 1874–1954

LEO SCHRADE
1955

Although Charles E. Ives had brought his work to completion long before his death in the spring of 1954, it is still largely unknown to the American musical public. Some do not even know his name; others have heard of him as a composer remote from professional musicianship; still others have gained a fleeting impression on those rare occasions when one work or another has had a public performance. Even those who make contemporary music an active concern have but a limited knowledge of Ives' accomplishment. For all of this obscurity and neglect, however, it is the present conclusion that Charles E. Ives is the most remarkable, the boldest, and the most original composer this country has ever had.

Admittedly Ives is also an enigmatic composer, difficult to understand or at least difficult to explain. For more than one reason it is hard to comprehend what brought about his uncommon kind of musicianship, what prompted his radical novelties at a time when modern music in Europe was as yet scarcely in ferment. Without a prelude of accumulative revolutionary developments, without the slightest forewarning in the past, Ives' novelties came with the suddenness of an explosion. Many influences inherent in time and tradition pushed a Schoenberg, a Bartók, a Stravinsky along the road they traveled, but there does not seem to be any reason inherent in earlier American music that can be taken to account for Ives' novelty. It may well be that the explosive suddenness of his appearance added to the bewilderment of the public. At all events, in Europe modern music grew as a new branch, or, as some would say, as a symptom of morbidness, of an organism that had steadily been shaped throughout the centuries. With Ives it burst forth as though it had never been a part of any organism.

For several decades Ives' music was never played publicly. Except for a few intimate friends, nobody really knew that there was such a thing as a composition by a man named Charles E. Ives, and he did nothing on his part to dispel this ignorance. Though some works have now been performed in public concerts and a few recorded, even yet the position of his music in our musical life is extremely precarious. A small selection of his work has been published since the 'twenties, yet performances remain exceptional. We hear of excuses, chiefly that Ives' music is excessively difficult to perform. Since most of his works do tax technical facility, the excuse has some validity; but such difficulty holds for all significant works. The real reason they are not more often performed is that in the past we did not care at all for Ives' music, in the present we care only a little.

Yet today a good many modern American composers point, even with a good deal of pride, to Ives as their ancestor, the father of modernism in their music. The claim is false. When they embarked upon their adventures, they knew nothing about the work of Ives; in fact it was so little known that it might as well not have been written at all so far as its exercising any influence on other composers is concerned. Ives' bold and often shocking novelties did not show our modern composers the road to modernism; nor did these musicians seek out the paternal guidance of the "father." They all got the modern idiom in music from other sources, mainly from the European *avant-garde*. Contemporary music as an historical development in this country does not begin with Charles E. Ives. It may have begun with Edgar Varèse, that spirited Frenchman who upon arrival on these shores introduced himself by saying that he refused to recognize only those tones that have been heard before, and who remained quite faithful to his introductory announcement. Charles E. Ives, no doubt, is a remarkable phenomenon of modern music, but by no means the father of modernism in this country.

Born in 1874, this strange and rare man belongs to a generation that in the formative years of youth experienced the nineteenth century for a good stretch of time. Some members of that generation never freed themselves from the heritage of the past even though they have spent the better part of their lives in this century; Sibelius is most prominent among them. There are others whose experience forced the nineteenth century upon them as a serious problem which they solved step by step; by proceeding at last to relentless opposition to the past, they established the new style. Schoenberg is such a composer. There are composers who, born with a vision of the new, at once built up the modern style systematically and with a fascinating logic; the more novelties they created, the more the immediate past receded into the background. Stravinsky is such a composer. There are musicians who began selectively with one of the nineteenth-century idioms, but carried a determined opposition in themselves; gleefully and deliberately they destroyed the old only to strike a balance again after years of struggle and extremes. Hindemith is such a composer. And there are musicians to whom, because of their birthdate, the nineteenth century bears neither artistic significance nor creative obligation; from the very start they have lived wholly in their own age. These are, of course, the youngest, the composers of today. All of them, however, have a logical, reasonable relation to the past; they exhibit a development that can be comprehended and explained. Ives does not fit in any of these groups.

If we look into his works, instrumental or vocal, our eyes are caught by compositions entirely in the style of the nineteenth century, largely in its simpler forms; the appearance of this idiom is no surprise. But in other compositions our eyes are attracted by fantastic novelties. A reasonable explanation will offer itself: like all other composers, Ives must have developed from the old to the new. But when we see the old and new side by side, or on adjoining pages, in a single composition, we are startled. The assumption that the composer advanced with the passage of time from the old to the new simply does not hold good. Because of the way they are associated with each other, both styles must have come into being simultaneously. If we finally inquire into the dates of the compositions and discover that some of the most modern works with their adventurous novelties preceded those in the older style, we must admit that our conclusion has been not only all wrong, but that we are face to face with a most puzzling situation for which we know of no precedent. For it is normal for a composer to begin in his youth with the familiar and in maturity to create the new which he hopes will supersede the old in the end. It is also normal for a musician to set out as revolutionary and then to return to tradition after a sufficient number of youthful misdeeds. But if a composer at any moment of his creative activity speaks two languages simultaneously, it becomes obvious that his work must stand apart from the normal process of evolution. The relations of the nineteenth century and of modernism in Ives' music have nothing to do with development. His styles and forms do not depend on gradual evolution. But if they are not linked to development, what are they related to? There lies the puzzle of Ives' music; its solution must be expected to illuminate the simultaneous use of old and new.

First a word about the composer's musical education. After having shared enthusiastically in the musical adventures of his father, Charles E. Ives studied in Yale College, from which he graduated at the age of twenty-four (1898). His first known compositions date from the years around 1900. While in Yale College he also studied at the Yale School of Music, which, like all academic conservatories all over the world, was a handsomely conservative institution. Its director was Horatio Parker, who, together with his colleagues at Harvard, has often been associated with the so-called "school of academians." Opinions of the audacious tones and ideas of Ives appears to have been unanimous: "mad, hopelessly mad."

After his years of study and a brief episode as organist, Ives resolutely made a decision, both significant and final, that bore upon the whole future of his work. Once and for all he renounced all participation in any form of public musical life, a most unusual decision for a young musician, for any composer. Despite what must have been at times a temptation, he resisted any attempt to bring his work before the public. It may well be that the damning opinion of those who had heard his early music influenced his decision; if so, it can have had but minor importance. The decision emerged from deeper and more forceful reasons. Ives must have learned in his youth that his philosophy of art—and behind it all there was his firm belief in such a philosophy—would irreconcilably conflict with the materialism of his time. He was unwilling to make the least sacrifice of his art for the sake of popularity, for he could only have earned the sweetness of public acclaim by the acidity of compromise. His philosophy was largely ethical by nature; hence he recognized the integrity of his music and musical ideal as the supreme law with which one must not tamper. In view of his extraordinary gift and technical facility he should have had no trouble in coming to terms with popularity. But he never surrendered; nor did he ever waver in the decision he made in his youth. Perhaps some critics will hold that he did not feel strong enough to take upon himself the fight against his environment and for his work, as other modern musicians have done, above all Schoenberg, with whom Ives has in common at least the unerring belief in the integrity of an artistic philosophy. Perhaps he was prudent enough to foresee the outcome of opposition in a country in which convention has unlimited power. It is fitting to quote what he thought of the composer who, craving public applause, creates his works for success, popular success to be sure. His "business is good; for it is always easy to sell the future in terms of the past; moreover, there are always some who will buy anything."

Ives decided he would leave business where it belongs. Instead of exposing his art to risks the consequences of which could not fully be anticipated, he made business his profession, while his artistic work came into being with absolute freedom, but also in complete isolation. His isolated work did not issue from disappointment and bitterness, however; serenity was its basis. None of his statements has the ring of hatred, but many have the bite of sarcasm when aimed at the "trade" called the art of music. Ives did not believe that, in order to live, the musical work must by necessity share the customs of the trade. This belief is part of his philosophy of art. "Living for society may not always be best accomplished by living *with* society"—surely one of the wisest thoughts he ever expressed.

Secluded from the bustling trade of music as well as from all confounding musical influence, Ives kept his work to himself, uncontaminated by materialistic considerations that might have forced him into straits where infringement upon integrity could no longer have been avoided. Even if published, the artistic work (he thought) should not be an article traded for the sake of profit. But he was far from being an unrealistic dreamer in an ivory tower; for as a businessman he had a remarkable success, and as an artist he simply lived what he believed. From youth to death he remained faithful to his belief. Though his work originated in complete isolation, remote from any musical organization, it is comprehensive; it includes symphonies, orchestral suites, overtures, cantatas, and a good many compositions for various groups of chamber music such as quartets for strings, sonatas for violin and for piano, and a large set of songs.

The whole of his art rests solidly upon a philosophy which gives his music its life. This by itself may have made him out of step with his time. Many of his own contemporaries among composers, even the best of them, scorned the belief in the "meaning" or "significance" of a musical composition. Their contempt for an "idea" conveyed through tones was part of their opposition to the nineteenth century; proudly they announced that they were nothing but musicians and that their artistic work was sheer sound, never anything more or anything else. Contemporary composers appear no longer so sure of an anti-intellectual attitude, and the best among them seem to be convinced that the artistic work of music is considerably more than the product of mere "fiddling."

The nineteenth-century style in Ives' work is quite as basic to his conception of musical art as is the modernism. When he took up the simpler forms of the older style, Ives usually left them unchanged. Occasionally he injected slight nuances, hardly perceptible, but sufficiently characteristic to mark a deviation from nineteenth-century techniques. These nuances are frequently associated with dissonances not quite customary in the vocabulary of the past; at times they have an ironic intention. Modern composers often distort the nineteenth-century idiom for reasons of irony. Obviously such irony does not enlist the composer as an adherent of the past. Whenever Ives drew upon the nineteenth-century vocabulary, he always implied a "meaning," a "significance." The old style was intentionally chosen for the sake of an "impression" which the spiritual or physical world makes upon the composer. It served exactly the same idea as the opposite style, that of modernism.

The extreme characteristics of sound in Ives' modern style were fully developed between 1900 and 1906, at a time when no European, not even Schoenberg, had achieved any comparable radicalism. Yet within this style Ives presented tones or tonal combinations with which the mature Schoenberg, Stravinsky, and Hindemith in the 'twenties upset European audiences. With Ives, however, modernism was complete by 1906; and it had grown in an environment much less prepared than any part of Europe.

Today we take for granted that a certain abundance of dissonances is an essential of the modern style. Ives' music is no exception. At the very beginning of the century Ives discovered the need of a new listening approach, of a new aural perception necessary for an understanding of the new sounds, which could not be interpreted by means of traditional theory. He naturally turned against the old and petrified rules of the theory of harmony. Ives' dissonances are in part harmonic, but stand outside the traditional system of harmony. They appear as independent nuances or coloristic effects; they flow from "impressions" which justify their appearance, but provide neither rule nor system. On the other hand, like Stravinsky and many other modern composers, Ives rendered dissonances for the sake of rhythmic accentuation, in such a way that dissonance ceased to be a problem of harmony. Rhythmic accents are pointed up by hammering on a dissonant group of tones. Then, of course, the friction of melodic lines tightly bound together, i.e., the friction of so-called contrapuntal lines, supplies the composition with dissonant areas. Numerous works or sections are governed by a clashing counterpoint of melodies that violates every imaginable rule of traditional harmony. But by attempting to free melody from purely harmonic conceptions, Ives arrived at combinations that strikingly resemble the style of Schoenberg before Schoenberg himself had created his own modernism.

The renewal of counterpoint is united to the renewal of harmony; one cannot be separated from the other. The customary system of keys disappears from Ives' composition; he no longer composes in major-minor harmonies. The traditional chordal structure is not rec-ognized as the constituent of harmonies. Ives combined conflicting harmonies in new entities which Darius Milhaud was later to call "polytonality." He worked with what the severe critics of modern music were to label inappropriately "atonality," and he even experi-mented with quarter-tones.

Most remarkable is Ives' wealth of rhythmic varieties. He became aware of the narrow restrictions, even deficiencies, of our system of rhythmic notation. He consequently did not hesitate to throw out all bar-lines so that rhythms might take an unfettered course. That free-dom allowed the most complicated combinations of rhythms and accents, which Ives put to brilliant use whenever he attempted to capture iridescent nature in a tonal form. He also made artistic use of ragtime before any other composer even dreamed of exploiting the fascinating modern dance rhythms for artistic purposes.

All these transformations effected a complete renovation of the ele-ments with which the composer worked. In this, Ives reached a cer-tain goal. But did he also renew the form, the structure of composi-tion? Did he invent new forms? He used old names; for instance he called one of his outstanding compositions for piano, his "Concord, Massachusetts, 1845," a sonata. He nonetheless was aware that the structure he gave his composition had nothing to do with the tradi-tional sonata. He tackled the whole complex of formal schemes so readily available in music; and he poured out on them all the sarcasm his critical mind could muster. In school he had learned that it is the scheme alone that yields clarity, unity, continuity of structure; that the composer must restrict himself to the fixed scheme (of a classical sonata, for instance) if he wants to achieve artistic unity. With the end-less repetition of schemes as a standard, Ives thought that Tchaikovsky must certainly be the clearest of all. But Ives gravely doubted that repetition of schemes was really essential to unity and clarity, and he was quick in poking fun at those who composed for the sake of pro-longing the life of skeletons. "We know that butter comes from cream—but how long must we watch the 'churning arm!'"

Instead, he turned away from a dull spectacle. In fact, fixed schemes that had been allowed to live for their own sake were contra-dictory to his basic concept of art. But all those who understand musi-cal structures only if they discover the skeleton of a scheme inevitably fail to see in Ives' composition what they call the "inner continuity." And here we are at last confronted with our decisive problem.

Why did Ives break away from tradition all on his own? Why did he create radical novelties unique in his time and environment? What did he mean by placing the most modern and adventurous style directly at the side of the most traditional, old-fashioned idiom? Strangely enough, the answer brings us close to the artistic philosophy of Claude Debussy. Debussy once gave a brief definition of his artistic principles which may well be regarded as the beginning and foundation of all modern music. Musical form should never be anything stable; it should be neither fixed nor schematic. On the contrary, artistic form must always be the issue of continually new invention. Specific conditions—subject matter, idea, text, purpose, or whatever the composer's intentions implies—bear upon the nature of artistic form which thus is subject to incessant change. Instead of following established schemes or ready-made devices, form must always be created anew. Hence musical form must continually renew itself by reference to the artistic intention. Consequently, Debussy thought very little of those who tried to imitate him; for he wanted to free music from all schemes once and for all. But by handling his form as though it were a scheme, the Debussyites violated the very substance of the art they admired.

Debussy's conception of form harmonizes with the basic principles upon which Ives built his philosophy of art. He could hardly have known the statement of Debussy, which was not published until long after Ives had begun his work. It is true, he came to be a thoroughly cultivated and widely-read man; and in the course of time he acquainted himself with Debussy's compositions. But Ives laid the foundation of his art in his youth, and nothing occurred that altered his ideal. In the years of wise maturity he epitomized his artistic convictions in his "Essays before a Sonata," one of the best philosophic discourses on contemporary music, and wide enough in range to include a brilliant exposition of Emerson. Since from the very outset Ives worked to render his ideal a musical reality, it matters little, if at all, whether he got acquainted with Debussy's conception. Early or late, all works of Ives are manifestations of one and the same ideal. Form and style continually change in accordance with the artistic intention, the idea that takes musical shape. Artistic form can, therefore, never be anything preëstablished; neither device nor scheme should ever tie it down. Ives would not avail himself of traditional, schematic forms for their own sake, even though he might name his composition a sonata.

Ives' belief in the ever-changing nature of artistic form explains why he would place old-fashioned harmonies, simple hymns, and old tunes beside the most shocking modernisms. If his idea or vision was akin to the intellectual world of the nineteenth century, he would at times draw upon the musical vocabulary of the period, since he believed that form grows immediately out of the idea. If he intended to conquer new tonal regions, he became the inventor, the creator of unheard-of novelties, and almost with an overflow of imagination, the explorer of new lands. Without speaking the musical language of Debussy, Ives realized the same artistic ideal as Debussy. In terms of his basic principles, though not in his manner of composing, Ives is the American Debussy. A philosophy of art made Ives the most original American composer.

There are other associations between Ives and Debussy. They have in common an intimate relation to nature, which appears in Ives a good deal stronger—or "healthier" as he himself probably would have preferred to say. Ives is essentially an impressionist; he transforms an impression immediately into orderly combinations of tones. The impression might emanate from a landscape, from nature, poetry, literature, philosophy, or from purely imaginative visions. But he thought it entirely improper for the composer to aim at defining the impression in words, since he must give it a tonal version.

Of course not all impressions seem to lend themselves appropriately to musical forms; and in translating impressions into music, Ives at times became the victim of his self-chosen isolation. He lost the chance of keeping the artistic vision controlled by the realities of sound and thus eliminated an essential factor of self-criticism which the actual sound alone can grant. In another respect also his isolation, no matter how noble and idealistic his integrity, has a tragic connotation. The day when Ives' influence should have given guidance to a whole generation of musicians no doubt has passed, and because of these missed opportunities his complete isolation can be considered to have done irreparable harm.

Whatever their origin, all impressions are at any rate intellectual or spiritual in their nature. The spiritual is what Ives continually defined as the substance of the artistic work; and substances so defined were for him the only values that are lasting. Ives did not find them in his own time; he felt himself closest to those men of the past who in their own ways taught the belief in the immortality of spiritual values. Being in many ways out of step with his time, he allied himself to Emerson, Hawthorne, Thoreau, Alcott, to old New England. Like his true kinfolk at Concord in 1845, he believed in progress, and like Debussy he musically proved it by his conquest of entirely new tonal regions. But the belief of his own contemporaries in a material progress he did not share. To him there is no such thing; there is only an intellectual, moral progress. Hence by definition Ives' work unites the two aspirations: the orderly combination of tones in an artistic composition reaches out toward the discovery of a new land, while ethically it achieves a revelation of ancient and eternal values.

—from *The Yale Review* n.s. 44 (June 1955): 535–45

Index

INDEX

List of Contributors

Geoffrey Block is Professor of Music at the University of Puget Sound. He is the author of *Charles Ives: A Bio-Bibliography* (Greenwood, 1988) and the Cambridge Music Handbook on Ives's *Concord Sonata* (Cambridge, 1996) and co-editor of *Charles Ives and the Classical Tradition* (Yale, 1996). He is also the author of a forthcoming study of the Broadway musical from *Show Boat* to Sondheim.

Leon Botstein is President of Bard College, where he is also Professor of History and Music History. He is the author of *Judentum und Modernität* (Vienna, 1991) and *Music and Its Public: Habits of Listening and the Crisis of Modernism in Vienna, 1870–1914* as well as Music Director of the American Symphony Orchestra and Editor of *Musical Quarterly*.

Michael Broyles is Distinguished Professor of Music, Professor of American History, and Fellow of the Institute for Arts and Humanistic Studies at Pennsylvania State University. He is the author of *Beethoven: The Emergence and Evolution of Beethoven's Heroic Style* (New York, 1987), *A Yankee Musician in Europe: The 1837 Journals of Lowell Mason* (Ann Arbor, 1990), and *"Music of the Highest Class": Elitism and Populism in Antebellum Boston* (Yale, 1992).

J. Peter Burkholder is Professor of Music and Associate Dean of the Faculties at Indiana University and president of the Charles Ives Society. He is the author of *Charles Ives: The Ideas Behind the Music* (Yale, 1985) and *All Made of Tunes: Charles Ives and the Uses of Musical Borrowing* (Yale, 1995) and co-editor of *Charles Ives and the Classical Tradition* (Yale, 1996).

David Michael Hertz is a pianist and composer and Professor of Comparative Literature at Indiana University. He is the author of *The Tuning of the Word: The Musico-Literary Poetics of the Symbolist Movement* (Southern Illinois, 1987), *Angels of Reality: Emersonian Unfoldings in Wright, Stevens, and Ives* (Southern Illinois, 1993), and *Frank Lloyd Wright in Word and Form* (New York, 1995).

Tom C. Owens is a graduate student at Yale University. He is currently completing his dissertation on Charles Ives and Americanness in the arts.

Mark Tucker is Associate Professor of Music at Columbia University. His books include *Ellington: The Early Years* (University of Illinois Press, 1991) and *The Duke Ellington Reader* (Oxford, 1993). He spends summers in the Adirondacks near Elizabethtown, New York.